Fundamentals of Journalism

Fundamentals of Journalism

Spencer Crump

Chairman, Journalism Department
Orange Coast College

McGraw-Hill Book Company

New York
St. Louis
San Francisco
Düsseldorf
Johannesburg

Kuala Lumpur
London
Mexico
Montreal
New Delhi

Panama
Rio de Janeiro
Singapore
Sydney
Toronto

Library of Congress Cataloging in Publication Data

Crump, Spencer.
  Fundamentals of journalism.

  1. Journalism. 1. Title.
PN 4731.C7   070.4   73-10042
ISBN 0-07-014835-X

082439

FUNDAMENTALS OF JOURNALISM

  67890 EBEB 79

The editors for this book were Ardelle Cleverdon
and Alice V. Manning, the designers were Michael
Mauceri and Marsha Cohen, and its production was
supervised by Patricia Ollague. It was set in Vogue
by Monotype Composition Company, Inc.
It was printed and bound by Edwards Brothers Incorporated.
World News cover picture taken by Louis S. Gomolak.

Contents

Preface

Competent books for first-year college journalism classes are difficult to find. Many texts emphasize the high school approach, which is usually geared to the consumer rather than the *producer* of news. Other books neglect the preliminaries and are concerned with the technical and abstract questions of communication that are primarily of interest to the graduate student or the professional. This book serves both purposes. It will assist those who hope to earn their livelihood through some form of journalism as well as those who wish to become perceptive consumers with a clear understanding of the rights and obligations incumbent with freedom of the press.

Courses in journalism are as significant for rounding out a student's educational experience as courses in science, art, history, or philosophy. Everyone has an interest in the commodity we call "news." Some make it, some report it, and others provide a market for it. This book emphasizes the "how-to-do-it" techniques of professional journalism. The word "journalism" was specifically included in the title to underline the attention given to the discipline of gathering, organizing, and presenting news as opposed to the study of "communication." The field of communication is concerned with the abstract analysis of principles of, and reasons for, making facts and ideas known. These studies are important, but journalism is the key to communicating.

The world is in the midst of an information explosion. As recently as World War II, most people relied almost exclusively on newspapers for information relating to current events. Today the dimensions of communication have expanded to include radio, television, news magazines, cablevision, news letters, public relations, some forms of advertising, microfilm applications, and spectacular developments in photography.

But newspapers remain the primary subject of this book. Despite the multiplication of the ways to communicate, they are still the core of consumer interest and the training ground for the other news media. Good journalism techniques are the same for television, radio, and newspapers, whether large or small, daily or weekly. All the systems of communication, no matter where the news develops, have the same basic methods of gathering and organizing the facts. They also share a common standard of ethical practice and of journalistic rights and duties.

Along with the information explosion, the literacy and educational levels of our population have risen. Today we have a larger—and more demanding—audience for news writers, or "communicators," to use the modern term, and a need for higher academic standards for journalists. This book has been written specifically for the two-year journalism student in community and junior colleges. The author has sought to provide the foundations for further studies in the specialities of the media at advanced levels. Many cultural aspects have also been included to supplement the practical techniques.

Modern youth, particularly those interested in the field of journalism, ask questions, and they deserve answers. This text seeks to tell not just *how* things are done, but *why* they are done as they are. The queries that a student has might never occur to a seasoned editor, and a teacher may not be aware of some of the problems of the journalist. There is much to be gained in learning the viewpoints of both. The author's background as a college professor and as a working journalist proved helpful in bridging the gap between the newsroom and the classroom. When there are several schools of thought or approaches to journalistic techniques, an effort has been made to present these differences for consideration.

This book, accompanied by supporting class exercises and lectures, should be covered in one or two semesters. It includes chapters on news gathering, writing, editing, stylebook usage, libel, ethics, picture-editing, and make-up, as well as appendixes defining journalistic terms and presenting a typical stylebook.

Examples used within the text are taken from a variety of locations and range from campus to metropolitan news. The use of real names or events has been avoided, but fictitious examples make the same essential point: the competent journalist must be able to handle all kinds of news skillfully, according to the needs and interests of the audience.

Since newspapers are usually the starting point for careers in journalism, campus papers present an excellent opportunity for gaining necessary experience. A chapter has been included on the techniques of producing a newspaper for those colleges that have no student publication and those that wish to augment an existing one. There is also material on vocational possibilities and ways to seek positions in the communications field. Many journalism students will develop skills leading to entry positions in some form of the media. They may want to take advantage of these opportunities while completing their education.

Spencer Crump

Fundamentals of Journalism

1

Journalism's Dimensions: The Past and Future

Journalism is a fascinating field that takes its practitioners to the places where things are happening and to the people who are making history. Diversified, in that it covers virtually all mankind's activities, and challenging to the intellect, "journalism" encompasses fields ranging from reporting with words and photographs to editing, and from newspapers to television. Journalists are the eyes, ears, and curiosity of the public and must be so broad in their outlook that they can translate events in many fields. Society thus accords high esteem to journalists, who through their varied backgrounds help people to understand one another, aiding those at different interest and intellectual levels to communicate.

"Journalism," to follow the definition of most dictionaries, would be confined to writing for newspapers and magazines, and so it was until the 1920s. Prior to that decade, many cities boasted two or more competing daily newspapers, and several large cities had four or more prospering dailies. The average person today interprets "journalism" to include not only newspapers and magazines, but also radio, television, cassette TV, public relations,

advertising, book publishing, and education directed to those fields.

Other fields of communication will develop to carry news. The suggestion that news writers some day may prepare material for thought transmission is no more impossible than television was a century ago.

Because of the lap-over in news-gathering skills, many writers move back and forth between the allied journalistic fields. Newspapers, however, offer the widest range in writing experiences, and more journalists start in this field and transfer to radio, television, advertising, or public relations than begin in those areas and move to newspapers.

This book, therefore, is concerned with newspaper methods, since these techniques form a basic training for many fields of journalism.

Table 3–1 (p. 33) shows that, in a typical year, more graduates of four-year college journalism programs went to work in the newspaper field than in any other of the media. After obtaining on-the-job journalistic experience, many professionals move to different jobs within the news-gathering field.

A GROWING FIELD

The much broader fields of journalism came with the concurrent arrival of (1) a communications "explosion" detonated by the advent of commercial radio in 1920, and (2) an educational boom that is spreading literacy and making people demand more information regarding their world. Radio, only the start of new media for presenting news, spurred the modern technology that is still developing more ways to communicate broader horizons of knowledge to the consumer, who today may be a reader, listener, or viewer.

There are in the United States approximately 1,800 daily newspapers, nearly 10,000 weekly or bimonthly newspapers, 4,500 AM radio stations, 2,500 FM radio stations, 700 television stations, and a growing number of cablevision and cassette TV outlets. Despite the well-known radio-newspaper-television competition for the consumer's attention and the advertiser's dollar, all media are healthier financially than ever before. They employ a record number of men and women who gather news, and the pay scales have constantly risen above the national average.

Education, associated with the technical advances in ways to communicate, once was regarded as the privilege of the few but now is accepted as a basic right and the key to elevating the economically depressed. Economic and educational progress produces an increase in the audiences for newspapers, books, magazines, television, and other purveyors of news and knowledge. The history of journalism in America has paralleled the nation's economic and social progress.

MILESTONES IN JOURNALISM

The history of news gathering dates back to ancient Egypt, when slaves raced to the pharaohs with oral reports. In early modern history, town criers sang important news in the village streets. The printed newspaper started in seventeenth-century Great Britain, where news letters advised businessmen of ship arrivals. While the history of journalism in America provides the basis for entire courses

in the junior and senior years of college, a survey is in order as a preliminary to modern journalism techniques.

THE COLONIAL PERIOD: 1620–1776

America's first newspaper, *Publick Occurrences Both Foreign and Domestick*, started September 25, 1660, in Boston, under publisher Benjamin Harrison. It soon was forced to cease publication for offending colonial authorities. The era's most important figure was John Peter Zenger, editor of the New York *Weekly Journal*, who was arrested in November, 1734, on a charge of seditious libel for criticizing the colony's governor. His lawyer, Andrew Hamilton, won Zenger's exoneration by convincing the jury that its prerogatives included deciding not only if the paper printed the story but, most important, if the material actually was true. Arguing that only false material should be subject to restraint, Hamilton and Zenger set a milestone for journalistic freedom in both America and Great Britain.

Newspapers encouraged colonial unity. Benjamin Franklin's famed cartoon of a snake in eight parts with the legend "join or Die" was widely reprinted. The Stamp Act of 1765, requiring payment of a half penny or penny for each newspaper and two shillings for an advertisement, infuriated publishers and helped unite colonists against British rule. By the time independence was won, America boasted a total of nearly 40 newspapers.

THE EARLY REPUBLIC: 1783–1833

While numerous newspapers began publication during the early days of the United States, most were little more than organs of the Federalist or Republican political parties, and few attempted to appeal to the average person. The first daily, *The Pennsylvania Evening Post*, started in May, 1783, and while it lasted only a month, others followed: *The Pennsylvania Packet and Daily Advertiser* also started in 1783, and The New York *Morning Post* began in February, 1785; the New York *Daily Advertiser* was founded in March, 1785. By 1800, America had 200 newspapers, most of them weeklies. The two most notable publications were the *Gazette of the United States*, founded in 1799 at New York City with the backing of the Federalists, and the rival *National Gazette*, started in Philadelphia by the Republicans.

Events of this era laid the basis for America's cherished freedom of the press. In 1791 the Bill of Rights was adopted, guaranteeing freedom of speech and of the press. Nevertheless, the Alien and Sedition Act, passed in 1798, not only increased the residency requirement for United States citizenship to fourteen years from five but also provided fines up to $2,000 and two years in prison "if any person shall write, print, utter or publish ... any false, scandalous, and malicious writing ... against the government of the United States, or either house of the Congress ... or the president...." When officials used the act to silence criticism, newspapers attacked the law for its dangers to democracy; the public, aroused over what was in effect press censorship, joined in branding the legislation unjust. The law's leading opponent, Thomas Jefferson, became president, and his supporters were elected to control Congress; all convicted under the act were pardoned.

By 1830, there were nearly 1,200 newspapers, including 75 dailies, in America. Most appealed to businessmen or political partisans and carried few stories of interest to working people. The price as well as the contents had little appeal for the average person, who made $6 to $8 weekly, while newspapers cost 4 to 6 cents a copy or $10 a year.

GROWTH OF THE POPULAR PRESS: 1833–1880

The first American newspaper priced for the average person's pocketbook and edited for popular enjoyment appeared on September 3, 1833, with the founding of the New York *Sun*. Its publisher, a young printer named Benjamin H. Day, set the one cent per copy price and its emphasis on police news for appeal to the thousands of store and factory workers who were becoming important in America. A success, within three years the *Sun* sold 30,000 copies daily and inspired many imitators.

The two achieving the greatest success with newspapers of popular appeal were James Gordon Bennett, a Scottish immigrant who founded the New York *Herald* in 1835, and Horace Greeley, a printer who established the New York *Tribune* in 1841. Bennett, experienced as a writer for American newspapers, introduced features which became staples: financial, society, theater, and sports pages. Emphasizing foreign news, he was the publisher who assigned Henry Stanley to find Dr. Livingstone in Africa. Horace Greeley, who perceived American growth patterns and gave the famous advice to "go west," lifted journalism to higher planes by abandoning sensational news for reports of national and international importance. He was a pioneer in opposing slavery and capital punishment, and championed the 10-hour day—an innovation for the time.

INDUSTRIALIZATION OF THE PRESS: 1880–1920

The factors of growing cities, improved printing technology, widespread public education, a growing awareness of America's role in the world, and the tendency for concentration of wealth combined for the development of major newspapers in cities throughout the United States during this important era. Joseph Pulitzer laid the foundation with his New York *World*, which featured illustrations and make-up similar to newspapers of the 1970s. Pulitzer's formula was a mixture of gossip, crime news, and crusading for working people's rights. The *World* did not wait for news: it made news. Through small donations from subscribers, it dramatically provided the $100,000 required for the pedestal for the Statue of Liberty; a woman reporter, Elizabeth (Nellie Bly) Cochran, feigned insanity to get committed to Blackwell's Island so she could write exposé stories, and public officials who took bribes were unveiled by enterprising reporters. Pulitzer also supplemented news with a host of entertainment features, including the pioneering of comic strips.

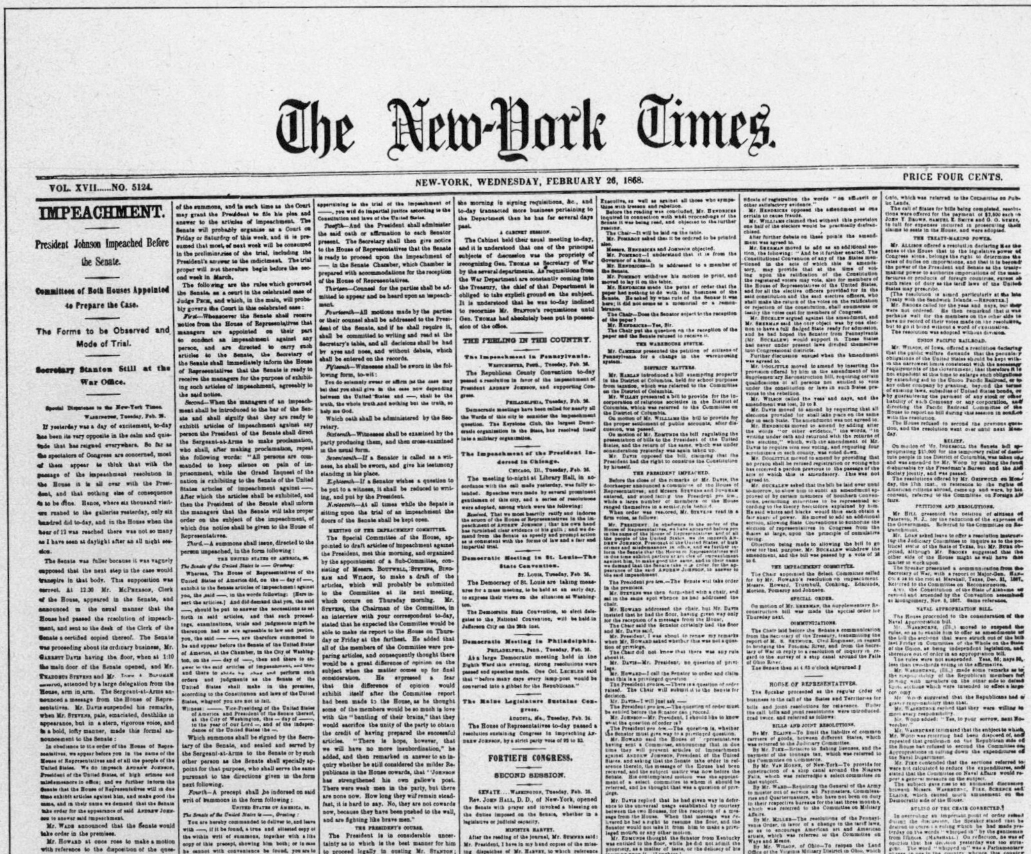
The New-York Times.

VOL. XVII......NO. 5124. NEW-YORK, WEDNESDAY, FEBRUARY 26, 1868. PRICE FOUR CENTS.

IMPEACHMENT.

President Johnson Impeached Before the Senate.

Committees of Both Houses Appointed to Prepare the Case.

The Forms to be Observed and Mode of Trial.

Secretary Stanton Still at the War Office.

Figure 1–1 The *New York Times* has long been recognized as a paper of record because of its faithful coverage of major events. This 1868 issue reported the impeachment proceedings brought against President Johnson.

Figure 1–2 The first issue of the *Los Angeles Times*, which began publishing in 1881. Note the advertisements on the front page, a custom for many newspapers at the time.

Pulitzer pushed the *World* from a financially ailing paper with 20,000 circulation in 1883 to a morning-evening combination in 1892 with a circulation of 375,000—or double that of the nearest New York City competitor.

Among Pulitzer's admirers was William Randolph Hearst, a young Harvard student and scion of a wealthy California mine and ranch tycoon. After successfully imitating "crusade" tactics on his father's newspaper, the San Francisco *Examiner*, he purchased the New York *Journal* to compete with Pulitzer

VOL. XXXVIII. NO. 13,410.   PRICE FIVE CENTS.   NEW YORK, SUNDAY, MAY 8, 1898.   PRICE FIVE CENTS.

DEWEY'S MARVELLOUS NAVAL ACHIEVEMENT---
Spanish killed and disabled, 618—one-third their fighting force. Americans killed, none.

American Flag now flying over Spain's two greatest forts in the Philippines.

THE WORLD'S SPLENDID NEWS VICTORY.

Eleven Spanish Ships Destroyed, 300 Spaniards Killed Outright; No American Ships Disabled, No American Sailors Killed; Only Six Injured---Capt. Mahan, the Pre-Eminent Strategist, to The World: "Commodore Dewey Has Fought the Greatest Naval Battle on Record"---All Spanish Forts Destroyed; Dewey Now Has Manila at His Mercy.

AMERICAN SHIPS, CONSTANTLY IN MOTION, FOUGHT AT RANGE OF ABOUT ONE MILE; THE SPANISH TORPEDO BOATS WERE SUNK AS THEY ADVANCED TO STRIKE.

By The World's War Correspondent, E. W. Harden, who was on the United States Gunboat McCulloch throughout the Battle.

(Copyright, 1898, by the Press Publishing Company, New York.)   (Special Cable Despatch to The World.)

HONG KONG, May 7.—At daybreak on Sunday morning, May 1, Commodore Dewey's Asiatic squadron, six fighting ships, the Olympia, Baltimore, Boston, Concord, Raleigh and Petrel, annihilated the Spanish fleet of the Philippines.

Dewey captured the naval arsenal and the forts at Cavite, Manila Bay.

ELEVEN SPANISH WARSHIPS DESTROYED.

Dewey's fleet sunk seven cruisers, four gunboats and two transports, and captured one transport, several tugs and a small steamer.   Among the cruisers and gunboats sunk were the flagship Reina Maria Cristina, Castilla, Velasco, Don Juan de Austria, the Isla de Cuba, General Lezo, Marquez del Duero, Mindanao and Ulloa.

The Spaniards lost three hundred killed.   Four hundred of them were wounded.

The Governor-General of the Philippines officially reported that the Spanish squadron lost in killed and disabled six hundred and eighteen—about one-third of their fighting force.

Not one American was killed, although the battle was hard fought and lasted three and a half hours.

The American gunners and American guns were infinitely better than the Spanish.

BATTLE LASTED SEVEN HOURS, TWENTY MINUTES.

As a result of the battle the control of the Philippines was wrested from the Spaniards.   Manila is now under American guns and absolutely at Dewey's mercy.   The forts at the entrance of Manila Bay have surrendered and the American flag is flying over them.

The Spanish flag still flies over Manila proper.   But the American fleet is powerful enough to reduce the city whenever Commodore Dewey so desires. The fortifications still standing cannot repel our fleet.

Manila is ours whenever Dewey claims it.

ENTERING THE HARBOR AT MIDNIGHT.

Dewey's fleet of nine vessels—the six fighters, the revenue cutter Hugh McCulloch and the two transports—ran the blockade past the forts of Corregidor Island at midnight Saturday.

Each vessel showed lights only directly astern, so the ships were almost invisible, for they had been painted gray.

The fighting ships passed Corregidor unseen.   But the McCulloch, Capt. Hodgson, on which was The World correspondent, was discovered, and the forts on Corregidor opened fire on her.

The Boston answered with her 8-inch guns and the McCulloch with her 3-inch guns.

The forts fired but four shots and then were silent.

FLEET STEAMED AT FOUR-KNOT SPEED.

Then the fleet kept on up the bay at four-knot speed.   Day was breaking as the ships arrived off Manila.

For the first time, it seemed, the Spanish discovered their presence.   Immediately the Manila forts opened fire.   But Dewey did not answer lest he hit

(Continued on Second Page.)

PRESIDENT'S ENTHUSIASTIC COMMENDATION OF THE WORLD'S GREAT BEAT.

"The New York World apparently had the only information to be had on the subject, and it would be wise for the Navy Department to depend upon it for its information."—*President McKinley, after reading The World's exclusive account of Dewey's Report.*

Figure 1-3   Joseph Pulitzer's *New York World*, in a circulation battle with William Randolph Hearst's *New York Journal*, ran this front page entirely devoted to Commodore Dewey's victory over the Spanish in 1898. It was typical of the era's flamboyant front pages designed to sell on the streets of big cities.

in the nation's biggest market. Drawing on his family's fortune, Hearst paid high wages to draw many talented staff members from the *World*. Both newspapers shamelessly at-

Figure 1–4 This 1904 front page was devoted entirely to the election in an era when newspapers provided virtually all of the news.

tempted to outdo the other by overplaying sex, crime, crusades, and the Spanish-American War.

Pulitzer's comics included "The Yellow Kid," a strip that relied heavily on yellow ink and was drawn by R. F. Outcault. Hearst hired the artist to do a strip for the *Journal*, and Pulitzer obtained a replacement. Both newspapers boasted cartoons emphasizing the color yellow, and thus was inspired the nickname for the sensational, half-truth brand of reporting associated with the *World* and *Journal*: "yellow journalism."

Hearst subsequently spread his newspaper chain throughout America, at one time controlling 28 daily newspapers plus magazines, syndicates, wire news services, and a motion picture company.

America's largest city, New York, boasted a variety of newspapers. The New York *Times* began to grow to greatness following its purchase in 1896 by Adolph S. Ochs, who opposed the "yellow journalism" of the day. Reflecting a variety of tastes and competing furiously, the New York City newspapers through the years helped set reporting and make-up standards for smaller cities throughout America.

Weekly newspapers became dailies as towns grew into cities, and communities with as few as 50,000 residents had up to three competing newspapers during this era. Despite the competition, many thrived in this pre-radio time, but patterns were proving that costly equipment and payrolls made journalism a field for the business entrepreneur. No longer could those without ample capital enter the newspaper field.

Coincident with the development of large daily newspapers, the wire news services grew. The Associated Press, owned by member newspapers and tracing its beginnings to regional collective news gathering that started in the 1840s, relies on publications exchanging news as well as on the agency's staff correspondents. United Press Associations was founded in 1907 by chain publisher E. W. Scripps to serve his afternoon newspapers along with publishers unable to obtain AP membership and consequently its service. Hearst estab-

lished International News Service in 1909 to serve his own and other newspapers. The latter organization and UP merged in 1958 to form United Press International.

ECONOMIC AND ELECTRONIC CHANGES: 1920–1950

While competing newspapers managed to survive during the booming 1920s, the arrival of electronic communication actually would help doom many of them. The first licensed commercial radio station, KDKA, took to the air November 2, 1920, in Pittsburgh. While music and other entertainment predominated, news became part of programming for KDKA and the hundreds of stations that soon were licensed. The gathering clouds of World War II made news broadcasts regular network features during the 1930s, and the minute-to-minute changes of the war itself entrenched broadcast news as an accepted part of daily life. Newspapers found themselves more and more in the position of competing with radio as well as mazagines for advertising and audiences. Added to the difficulties was the Depression of the 1930s, with millions of people unemployed and unwilling or unable to buy newspapers or the goods advertised. In cities where newspapers competed, one or more of the dailies was forced to merge with a rival journal or close its doors. World War II spurred the economy and renewed interest in news, thus giving the salvation necessary for many newspapers to continue publishing.

THE CHANGING ERA: 1951 TO THE PRESENT

By the time America emerged from World War II, television was virtually upon the nation. TV, in experimental stages since the 1920s, became commercially available in 1948 and by the mid-1950s most homes boasted a set. While newspaper consolidations occurred in some cities, most dailies were not damaged greatly by the new medium. Although newscasts soon became important, TV in general gave only news "headlines" and made no attempt to present details or to offer treatment of society, financial, neighborhood, or sub-

Figure 1–5 This issue of the *Los Angeles Times* is typical of home-delivered newspapers during the 1920s. Papers competing for street sales in this pre-radio news era would make front pages with more photos and larger headlines to attract buyers.

sidiary stories. The public continued to rely on newspapers for the bulk of the news. Theaters and radio stations, instead, suffered declines blamed on television.

Figure 1–6 This 1951 view shows the wirephoto room in the Associated Press building in London. Note the cylinders which revolve while a light impulse measures tones for transmission by radio. The operator uses a phone to advise an overseas operator that a particular photo will be sent. (Wide World Photos)

Newspapers began to flourish again. The pre-radio peak of daily newspapers in the 1910s has been estimated at between 1,800 and 2,500 publications (accurate statistics were not kept). Today there are approximately 1,800 dailies. While there are fewer newspapers in metropolitan cities, dailies are thriving in the growing suburban areas. For instance, New York City had 14 daily newspapers during the peak of the 1920s and is now down to only three dailies, but strong newspapers are flourishing in nearby communities which a few years ago had no dailies of their own. For example, *Newsday*, established in 1940 at Garden City, has grown into one of America's largest evening newspapers, and the Jamaica *Long Island Press* also has enjoyed immense gains in circulation. Los Angeles had six competing dailies as late as the mid-1930s and now has but two, but newspapers have been founded and are prospering in nearby communities such as Costa Mesa, Torrance, West Covina, and Thousand Oaks, which once were farmlands.

TECHNICAL DEVELOPMENTS

The ways for communicating news have been improved through the years by develop-ments pertaining to the "print" or newspaper and magazine fields, and to the electronic or radio-television media. Both areas are in continuing stages of development.

Printing Techniques. The early American newspapers were produced by type set one letter at a time by hand and printed, one sheet at a time, on hand-operated presses. Steam power was applied to presses in the early 1800s, and Richard Hoe (1812–1886) pioneered construction of rotary presses producing several pages at a time. William A. Bullock (1813–1867) invented a press in 1850 using a continuous roll of paper and printing it on both sides at once. The era for setting type by hand ended in 1883 when Ottmar Mergenthaler (1854–1899) perfected the keyboard-operated Linotype. Robert Hoe (1839–1909), son of Richard Hoe, developed the high-speed presses in the 1890s which permitted mass circulation. Few improvements in printing came until 1951, when punched tape produced by wire service machines was introduced to operate typesetting equipment. Offset printing, while used for fine printing for nearly a century, was economically feasible for newspapers starting in the 1950s with development of new chemicals, sensitized plates, special inks, and computerized phototypesetting. Benefits of offset printing include lower cost for equipment as well as lower labor costs. "Scanners" and other electronic equipment which can convert stories to type without intermediary keyboards also are innovations for reducing costs and speeding production during the 1970s and 1980s.

Electronic Developments. The development of commercial radio in 1920 and of television in 1948 opened increased vistas for news. Microwaves in the mid-1950s launched regular national news broadcasts, and Telstar in the mid-1960s permitted worldwide TV broadcasts. Cablevision, developed in the

early days of television to bring signals to areas distant from stations, in the 1960s became an industry that also would originate programs. A major development during the 1970s would be cassette television, using magnetic tapes or discs to carry news and enter-

Figure 1-8 Reporters and photographers are with the action. This Associated Press photo shows Dr. Henry Kissinger with Chou En-lai, premier of the People's Republic of China, during a visit in Peking. (Wide World Photos)

Figure 1-7 News photographers and reporters are in the midst of history as it happens. An Associated Press photographer took this picture of a British army sharpshooter on the doorstep of an elderly woman, a rosary dangling from her neck, during violence in Northern Ireland. (Wide World Photos)

Figure 1-9 Television news has grown increasingly important since 1950. Here is Walter Cronkite presenting the CBS evening news.

tainment to the screens of TV sets. All indications are that cablevision and cassette TV will require most of the 1970s for development of their potentials, which promise to be as immense as conventional television.

EXERCISES

1. Visit your library and in the card file under "journalism" note the books pertaining to the history of newspapers; select one book to read leisurely as collateral to the brief history of journalism in this chapter.

2. While at the library, consult the earliest editions of the telephone directory, and in the classified business section under "newspapers" note the names of the publications serving the community. Compare the names to the newspapers now serving the area to ascertain which are still in business.

3. Using a current classified telephone directory, make a list of the newspapers and radio, television, and cablevision stations serving the community. Note the diversity of ways to communicate news.

4. Visit the local newspaper office, and ask permission to inspect copies of its early editions, which are usually kept in bound volumes or on microfilm. Look at editions from representative years and note the changes in the number of pages each day, illustrations, types of stories, and make-up.

2

Problems Facing Journalism Today

Changing times will always bring changing problems for the media through which people communicate and obtain their news. While one person on the newspaper of a little more than a century ago could serve as reporter, editor, advertising manager, printer, and circulator, today's field of news communication requires specialists in areas ranging from art to finance. News reaches the audience through the use of sophisticated electronic and mechanical equipment.

Newspapers during the coming years will face such problems as freedom of information, competition with one another as well as with other media, the challenge of advancing production technology, and survival on the financial front.

VITALITY OF THE NEWSPAPERS

The newspapers which survived the pressures of the 1930s and 1940s are prosperous in most cities and for most families are a vital utility for news of local and world affairs. To serve the public, newspapers should be financially strong to be independent. Despite reverses of the past, newspapers appear able to control costs and to be attractive to investors.

For example, even during the 1970–1971 business recession, the stocks of companies publishing newspapers or with heavy investments in the field surged ahead although prices declined for firms in other areas.

	1970	1971
Booth Newspapers	19	26
Boston Herald Traveler	26	26
Cincinnati Enquirer	30	39
Dow Jones	25½	41½
Gannett Company	21½	56
Knight Newspapers	32½	67
New York Times Co.	16½	22½
Post Corp. (Wisconsin)	9	14½
Ridder Publications	12½	23½
Southam Company	50	62
Thomson Newspapers Ltd.	16	27½
Times Mirror Co.	29½	46

Coincidentally, an investment officer of the First Pennsylvania Banking and Trust Co. of Philadelphia said that newspapers "have dawned as a new growth industry."[1]

---

[1] "Bullish on Newspaper Stocks," *Editor & Publisher*, Sept. 4, 1971, p. 7.

Figure 2–1 While more newspapers than ever are sold daily, many newspapers have consolidated with others because of economic problems. This is the last edition of the morning *Los Angeles Examiner* before it merged with the evening *Los Angeles Herald-Express* to form the evening *Herald-Examiner*.

The officer, Daniel V. Cashman, explained that he based his optimism on these factors:

1. Superior earnings growth, with newspaper companies showing an average growth of 15 per cent annually for the preceding five years, putting them ahead of other fields.
2. Difficulty of market entry, with such a large investment required to start a newspaper that it is virtually impossible to do so, giving many newspapers a "legal" monopoly.
3. An item of necessity, making the relatively low-cost newspaper indispensable to most Americans.
4. Little regulation: compared to other industries, newspapers are uncommonly free from government interference and are likely to remain so in a free society.
5. Stimulus of local advertising: the medium of newspaper advertising is necessary for the average local merchant, and the national trend in advertising is in the direction of local rather than national coverage.
6. A revolution in newspaper production technology is helping to offset tremendous price and wage costs.
7. Excellent earnings results: the balance sheet condition of most newspapers is basically unrivaled by any industry, with newspaper after-tax profits averaging 8.4 percent during the past five years as compared to 5.6 percent for all corporations in the United States.

PROBLEMS AHEAD

Social and technical areas do present problems for newspapers. These concerns will affect the quality and integrity of news coverage in the decades ahead.

FREEDOM OF INFORMATION

Attempts by public officials to pressure newspapers into publishing exclusively "favorable" news are reminiscent of John Peter Zenger's confrontation with the British crown. The 1960s brought intensified efforts continuing into the 1970s by local, state, and federal

Figure 2–2 This famous 1972 Associated Press photo shows Vietnamese children after being burned by napalm dropped accidentally by their own planes. Dissent over how newspapers should play and cover wars has divided journalists as it has other Americans. This photo won the 1972 Pulitzer Prize for "spot" news photography. (Wide World Photos)

officials seeking to "manage" the news, either by reluctance to release information or issuance of subpoenas in efforts to intimidate reporters handling controversial subjects. Freedom of the press, or the privilege to publish facts that a reporter obtains, is one right. A closely allied principle is one giving journalists the access to information held by governmental or quasi-governmental organizations. When authorities ignore or try to circumvent this principle, journalists and the public will lose. Working to obtain Freedom of Information laws on the local and national levels are such organizations as the American Society of Newspaper Editors, the American Newspaper Publishers Association, Sigma Delta Chi Professional Journalism Society, Theta Sigma professional journalism society for women, the American Newspaper Guild, and local press clubs and related groups throughout the nation.

FOI "battles" usually find public officials charging journalists with social irresponsibility in seeking information that should be "restricted," while the press retorts that officials endeavor to cloak their own mistakes and incompetency with a veil of secrecy. The question is simple: Do Mr. and Mrs. Public have the right to know what public servants are doing?

Channel 44: its license was illegal
Studs Terkel: "Agnew is right..."
The Trib: a pitiful, helpless giant

Chicago Journalism Review

MAY 1972   VOLUME 5, NUMBER 5   PRICE 75¢

Pulling ourselves together in New York

Figure 2–3 Journalists are beginning to look at themselves with critical eyes on an increasing basis. *Chicago Journalism Review*, launched by working press members after the 1968 Democratic presidental convention in Chicago, was a pioneer among regional journals critical of the press, TV, radio, and magazine coverage. (Copyright Kimmel: used by permission)

IN CAMBODIA—American soldiers try to spot enemy through rubber trees in the Fishhook region.

IN KENT, OHIO—National guardsmen advance during clash in which four students were killed.
AP Wirephotos

Los Angeles Times

LARGEST CIRCULATION IN THE WEST, 982,075 DAILY, 1,317,220 SUNDAY.

VOL. LXXXIX 2† SEVEN PARTS—PART ONE CC 3 F TUESDAY MORNING, MAY 5, 1970 110 PAGES Copyright © 1970 Los Angeles Times DAILY 10c

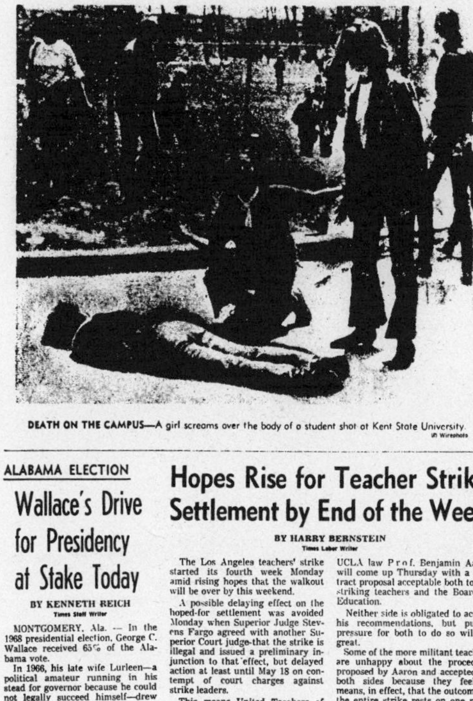

DEATH ON THE CAMPUS—A girl screams over the body of a student shot at Kent State University.
AP Wirephoto

Troops Kill Four Students in Antiwar Riot at Ohio College

Large S. Viet-U.S. Force Opens Third Cambodia Offensive

SAIGON (AP)—Thousands of American and South Vietnamese troops launched a third offensive into northeast Cambodia today, seeking to smash more North Vietnamese base camps and sanctuaries, the U.S. command announced.

The American command said the operation was kicked off early this afternoon in the Se San base area, about 50 miles west of Pleiku, in the Central Highlands.

A spokesman said troops of the U.S. 4th Infantry Division and the South Vietnamese 22nd Infantry Division were participating in the operation.

(Their target is a highlands bivouac area that long has served as an entry point for the Ho Chi Minh Trail into Vietnam, United Press International said. It lies just south of the point where the borders of Laos, Cambodia and South Vietnam meet.

(Communist troops operating from this area have besieged several border Green Beret camps in the course of the war.

Defense Secretary Melvin R. Laird said in Washington Saturday that all North Vietnamese and Viet Cong sanctuaries along the full length of the border would be attacked by the allies.

There are numerous enemy base camp areas in Cambodia from the western Mekong Delta to the area north of Saigon which are outside the areas attacked last week by allied troops.

The two earlier allied drives, one into an area known as the Parrot's Beak and the other into an area called the Fishhook, have accounted for 2,171 North Vietnamese and Viet Cong killed. U.S. losses were given as 16 killed and South Vietnamese deaths were put at 151.

WAR SITUATION AT A GLANCE

The stock market took a heavy beating Monday, reacting to concern over U.S. action in Cambodia. The Dow Jones industrial average dropped 19.07. Part 3, Page 9.

The Vietnam peace talks in Paris hung in the balance as the result of the U.S. Cambodia action. Page 18.

The Senate Foreign Relations Committee said the Cambodian invasion was "constitutionally unauthorized." Page 11.

U.S. troops swept through Cambodia's Fishhook toward what was believed to be a major Communist headquarters base. Page 22.

Soviet Premier Alexei N. Kosygin called for "vigorous measures" to get the U.S. out of Indochina. Page 19.

Official Washington, however, noted that Kosygin gave no indication of any Russian action to counter the United States. Page 19.

For Red China, U.S. action was "frantic provocation." Page 16.

Guards' Gunfire Wounds 11 at Kent University

KENT, Ohio (UPI)—Four students were shot to death on the Kent State University campus Monday when national guardsmen, believing a sniper had attacked them, fired into a crowd of rioting antiwar protesters.

At least 11 persons were wounded, three critically, before order was restored. The university was shut down for at least a week.

The town of 18,000 was sealed off and a judge ordered the university's

California student protesters disrupt campuses. See Page 3, Part 1.

20,000 students to leave the campus by noon Tuesday.

By late Monday night only 300 students, most of them foreign students, remained as 800 guardsmen patrolled in convoys of jeeps and personnel carriers armed with .50-caliber machine guns.

Students and National Guard officials gave different versions of what triggered the gunfire, but the guard admitted no warning was given that the troops would begin firing their M-1 semiautomatic rifles.

The battle was the most violent campus confrontation since the antiwar movement began. The trouble started when about 1,000 demonstrators, defying an order not to assemble, rallied on the commons at the center of the tree-lined campus. Guardsmen moved in and fired tear gas grenades at the mob, which broke and ran.

The protesters then regrouped and confronted about 300 guardsmen on a practice football field. The students, now numbering 1,500, charged down a hill and pelted the troops with rocks. Guardsmen exhausted their supply of tear gas. Students, who tossed back the canisters, surrounded the troops on three sides.

Believes Sniper Fired

Then, according to S. T. Del Corso, state adjutant general, "a sniper opened fire against the guardsmen from a nearby rooftop."

Del Corso, who was in Columbus, the state capital, maintained contact with the troops through Brig. Gen. Robert Canterbury, who commanded the guard force on campus. Canterbury said the students were given no warning before the shooting started.

Student eyewitnesses said they did not hear any gunfire before the guardsmen began shooting.

"All of a sudden," said one male student," some of them turned

Please Turn to Page 6, Col. 1

THE WEATHER

U.S. Weather Bureau forecast: Night and morning low clouds with local drizzles but hazy afternoon sunshine today and Wednesday. High today, 70. High Monday, 80; low, 55.

Smog report and complete weather information in Part 2, Page 4.

ALABAMA ELECTION

Wallace's Drive for Presidency at Stake Today

BY KENNETH REICH
Times Staff Writer

MONTGOMERY, Ala. — In the 1968 presidential election, George C. Wallace received 65% of the Alabama vote.

In 1966, his late wife Lurleen—a political amateur running in his stead for governor because he could not legally succeed himself—drew 54% of the vote in the Democratic primary and became the nominee without a runoff.

In today's primary election, if there is agreement on anything among the political factions in this state, it is that Wallace won't do as well as his wife did in 1966.

Wallace may still win this election. If he does, victory will likely come after a runoff against his long-time protege, incumbent Gov. Albert P. Brewer. (There are five minor candidates in today's race.)

But Wallace's basic strength in the state he claimed to personify so long has seemingly eroded.

A charismatic man whose political fortune was bred on crisis, he may be in trouble in today's election because Alabama is not in the midst of crisis.

He may be in trouble because at least the state's mind, if not its heart, has changed on the vital racial issue.

He has certainly found trouble, because his tactics in challenging Brewer left a bad taste in many people's mouths and some of them had previously been strong supporters.

"Albert doesn't deserve Wallace opposition," was the way one man put it in Birmingham. And in Mont-

Please Turn to Page 12, Col. 1

Hopes Rise for Teacher Strike Settlement by End of the Week

BY HARRY BERNSTEIN
Times Labor Writer

The Los Angeles teachers' strike started its fourth week Monday amid rising hopes that the walkout will be over by this weekend.

A possible delaying effect on the hoped-for settlement was avoided Monday when Superior Judge Stevens Fargo agreed with another Superior Court judge that the strike is illegal and issued a preliminary injunction to that effect, but delayed action at least until May 18 on contempt of court charges against strike leaders.

This means United Teachers of Los Angeles President Robert Ransom, Vice President Larry Sibelman, Executive Secretary Don Baer and Assistant Executive Secretary Roger Segure can devote full time to seeking a settlement instead of to the court proceedings.

A UTLA spokesman said the preliminary injunction issued Monday against the strike will be appealed on constitutional grounds.

The hopes for a quick end to the strike are based on the belief that UCLA law Prof. Benjamin Aaron will come up Thursday with a contract proposal acceptable both to the striking teachers and the Board of Education.

Neither side is obligated to accept his recommendations, but public pressure for both to do so will be great.

Some of the more militant teachers are unhappy about the procedure proposed by Aaron and accepted by both sides because they feel it means, in effect, that the outcome of the entire strike rests on one man.

If Aaron recommends any significant concessions to the teachers, it will be difficult for the strike to continue because the already divided teachers will be further divided on their next move.

Equally heavy pressure will be felt by the Board of Education to accept the recommendations even if Aaron makes concessions to the teachers that the board majority would not have approved before the strike.

Please Turn to Page 26, Col. 1

Index to The Times

BOOK REVIEW. Part 4, Page 11.
BRIDGE. Part 4, Page 4.
CLASSIFIED. Part 5, Pages 1-18.
COMICS. Part 4, Page 19.
CROSSWORD. Part 5, Page 18.
EDITORIALS, COLUMNS. Part 2, Pages 10, 11.
ENTERTAINMENT, SOCIETY. Part 4.
FINANCIAL. Part 3, Pages 9-16.
METROPOLITAN NEWS. Part 2.
MOTION PICTURES. Part 4, Pages 13-16.
MUSIC. Part 4, Pages 15, 16.
SPORTS. Part 3, Pages 1-8.
TV-RADIO. Part 4, Pages 17, 18.
VITALS, WEATHER. Part 2, Page 1.

TV Academy Announces Nominations for Emmys
Part 4, Page 1.

Supreme Court Upholds Church Tax Exemptions
Page 3, Part 1.

Witchcraft Bubbles Again —and Finds New Followers
Part 2, Page 1.

My Lai Disclosure Wins Pulitzer Prize

BY RICHARD DOUGHERTY
Times Staff Writer

NEW YORK—Seymour M. Hersh, the reporter who broke the story of the alleged My Lai massacre in Vietnam, won the 1970 Pulitzer Prize for international reporting Monday.

President Andrew W. Cordier of Columbia University announced the award on behalf of Columbia's trustees who make the annual selections for excellence in journalism and letters under terms of the will of the late Publisher Joseph Pulitzer.

Recognition of the 33-year-old Hersh's expose of the alleged killing of nearly all the residents of a Vietnamese hamlet—including women and children—was not unexpected. The story was written by Hersh for Dispatch News Service. It was syndicated in 36 papers in this country

Please Turn to Page 10, Col. 1

New U.S. Air Raids Halted Over North, but Option Remains

BY TED SELL
Times Staff Writer

WASHINGTON—A new bombing campaign against North Vietnam was publicly declared ended Monday but defense sources said privately that a new policy giving field commanders increased authority on launching air strikes remained in effect.

The formal announcement, by Daniel Z. Henkin, assistant secretary of defense for public affairs, was that three heavy strikes against Communist supply areas just north of the border with South Vietnam were "all that were planned." Henkin said that with the strong attacks, the operation had "terminated."

Henkin, chief spokesman for the Defense Department, said there had been no change in the U.S. policy of protecting American reconnaissance flights.

But on Sunday, equally well-informed Pentagon officials said the policy had in fact been changed, permitting far more massive retaliatory bombing of North Vietnam.

Under the old policy, fighter escorts could attack only whatever single antiaircraft positions fired on reconnaissance planes.

It was made clear over the weekend, in connection with the expansion of the raids, that that policy no longer held. If antiaircraft positions in any military base area fired, escorts could attack both that position and any military targets associated with it.

That expansion of authority, Pentagon sources said Monday, has not been revoked. White House officials,

Please Turn to Page 15, Col. 1

Figure 2–4 Press critics rate the *Los Angeles Times* among the "prestige" or "quality" papers of America.

Weather: *Details on page 67*
Tonight: Hazy, low in 60s
Tomorrow: Sunny, hot

Chicago today

THURSDAY, AUGUST 13, 1970   10 cents

I   Vol. 2, No. 106   2 Sections

7 Star final
Markets

Hospital workers ask 50% pay hike

Fear $15-a-day room cost increase. Page 3

Coed safe, kidnaper seized

Dale·Regina Leach, 20, hugs her boy friend, Steven Ketcham, 21, near Ochopee, Fla. She was kidnaped at gunpoint as she and Ketcham sat on a lonely beach. Police said they found her with James Wesley Ross (below) on the edge of the Everglades. He was held for kidnaping. Ketcham was locked in trunk of his own car, took two hours to batter his way out with tire tools.

AP Wirephoto

Inside the courtroom with Elrod

Story on page 5, sketches on pages 18-19

Exclusive interview — Saudi's King Faisal

Page 2

Figure 2–5 The front page of *Chicago Today* is typical of big city tabloids, which appeal to street sales with photos and a smaller number of front-page stories than home-delivered newspapers.

The State and National Levels. Federal and state officials have "managed" or attempted to create favorable news in several ways. A frequent method is "leaking" or secretly giving "good" news to friendly reporters, who play the information to the advantage of the source in exchange for exclusive stories. Subsequent stories unfavorable to the source handled by more objective reporters may lose impact because newspapers or stations play them down as "old" news.

Another popular method of "managing" news is through providing publicity releases on important or controversial matters only minutes before deadlines. The reporter lacks the time to do substantiating research or careful writing, and therefore is forced to rely on the facts in the release because of the time element.

The press "briefing," usually involving the President of the United States or other high-level officials, is a technique that generates controversy among journalists. Those attending "briefing" sessions agree that stories written regarding the conference will be attributed only to "a high official" and will not identify the source. Defenders of the technique maintain that it allows officials to comment on sensitive issues that they otherwise would not discuss, thus presenting important matters to the public. The opponents of "briefings" argue that the anonymity of the stories gives officials the opportunity to launch "trial balloons" and to withdraw without exposing themselves if the reaction is unfavorable.

The Local Level. City, county, and other local activities involve different pressures to withhold information or focus journalistic attention on favorable news. Some public officials conduct "secret" meetings, excluding representatives of the press, for discussions of matters they wish to shield from the public. While there may be bitter debates or discussions of expenditures of public funds for controversial purposes at these closed meetings, the officials cloak their feelings at open sessions and vote unanimously for or against a project. Such secrecy undermines democracy and deprives the public of its right to know. While numerous states ban "secret" sessions except for personnel matters, few provide penalties for the offending officials, and such bans therefore lack meaning. Another technique local officials use in efforts to "manage" news is forbidding

rank-and-file employees to talk with journalists regarding their work.

Law enforcement agencies, including city, county, and state police and sheriff officers, frequently attempt news management by making information readily available only to the reporters who write stories "friendly" to their viewpoints, while at the same time making it difficult for the writer who attempts fairness by supplementing police reports with information acquired from those who have been accused. One favorite police method is to delay or temporarily "lose" controversial documents until their news value is gone.

A highly questionable technique used by some police departments has been to refuse press credentials, often needed for prompt access to reports, to representatives of "underground" or other newspapers critical of police methods. Police have defended their refusal to issue credentials on the basis that dissident reporters can obstruct justice at the scene of a crime. Journalists condemn withholding credentials, contending the action violates the Bill of Rights by permitting police to judge the contents of newspapers.

Pros and Cons of News Management. Public officials defend their lack of cooperation with journalists by arguing that security may be compromised or important plans damaged if publicized. They maintain that they should be entitled to withold information which, they believe, it may not be in the public interest to divulge.

Journalists retort that restraints on their deciding what public affairs should be covered would be similar to the tactics of a dictatorship, and that in a democracy public officials are the servants of the voters. They also argue that the press, not those involved in government, should decide what issues should be aired in public.

Other Forms of News Management. Although the press scornfully rejects attempts by outsiders to withhold or manipulate information, the media themselves frequently are offenders in "managing" what news the reader can receive. Such news control is potentially the most dangerous, since it is the least likely to be aired publicly.

"Blackouts" by the media. When the management of a newspaper or other medium of communication is closely allied with a political faction or community project, there is a temptation to use only favorable news and not to "dig" for information that might embarrass the sources. Such news bias is particularly dangerous in communities with a newspaper monopoly. When the publication's bias is eventually documented by a magazine, television station, or other source, a news credibility gap develops.

The problem of reporter "guidance." Professional journalists are well trained and know how to handle the construction of a news story with skills as developed as those in other fields. Yet some subjects of stories attempt to persuade reporters to submit copies of articles for approval prior to printing. While writers dealing with technical matters concerning medicine, science, and similar fields may welcome checks for accuracy, the seasoned journalist resents attempts to decide the flavor or direction of conventional stories. Such "reviews" would be time-consuming and therefore a great block to producing a newspaper. Moreover, they would serve the vanities of the story subject instead of the interests of the readers.

COMPETITION

As previously indicated, despite the consolidation of many newspapers and the discontinuance of others, competition among the media remains today in various forms. While competition is economically weakening, it strengthens freedom of the press and of information by providing a diversity of views which, taken together, hopefully approach fairness. Newspapers face competition, potentially draining reader and advertiser support, from the electronic media, magazines, the "underground" press, and, of course, other newspapers.

The Electronic Media. Substantial amounts of money which could have gone into newspaper advertising have gone into radio and television. Most national advertisers, however, alternate in using newspapers, magazines, and radio or television in varying campaigns. The widely held view that the biggest losers to television are the national "general" magazines is borne out with the closing of such leaders as *Collier's*, *Liberty*, *The Saturday Evening Post*, *Look*, and *Life*. Classified ads and local display advertising, which are major sources of revenue for most newspapers, have been relatively unaffected by television. The years ahead will measure the eventual impact on local advertising that may be demonstrated by cassette TV and cablevision.

In considering news competition between television and newspapers, several factors must be considered. TV news can be quicker: in fact, it can be instantaneous. Printed news may be slower, but it can present the added information and more depth that the public apparently expects.

For example, a TV or radio newscaster would require approximately one hour to read aloud the news from a single page in a standard-size newspaper such as the New York *Times* or Los Angeles *Times*. Broadcast news necessarily can only be a comparatively small collection of the first one to three paragraphs of longer news stories.

The Local Magazines. While many national mass magazines have ceased publication because of financial losses blamed variously on TV ad competition and increases in production and mailing costs, a major development of the 1960s was the "city" magazine. These periodicals, usually produced under independent ownership, ostensibly present analytical articles that newspapers would not or did not use. Many such magazines have presented unpopular or unexplored viewpoints, or have treated subjects ignored because they involved people or things protected by local newspapers with special interests. Among the more successful of the magazines have been *Los Angeles*, *Philadelphia*, *New York*, *San Diego*, *San Francisco*, and *Atlanta*. While these publications do not present an imminent threat to daily newspapers, they do provide an alternative for readers and advertisers—as well as for journalists.

The Underground Press. Dogmatically antiestablishment, underground newspapers frequently are more overground, both financially and by availability, than the label implies. These newspapers, usually published weekly or monthly, have a growth pattern closely paralleling the "hippie," antiestablishment, anti–Vietnam war movement, and other alternate-society movements which started concurrently in approximately 1965. The publications fill a need in publishing subject material which conventional newspapers ignored because of alleged advertiser or community pressures, or because editors felt there was no reader interest. These newspapers are excellent examples of the "advocate" journalism providing articles with ample facts substantiating the writer's theories, to the detriment of arguments to contrary views. The more successful "underground" newspapers include the Berkeley *Barb* and the Los Angeles *Free Press*.

Other Newspapers. While relatively few cities contain two competing newspapers, such competition exists, but it uses different techniques. Dailies, of course, are competing with weeklies for news and advertising. Competition among dailies can develop and does when cities expand to the point where their boundaries meet and some residents are unsure which municipality they reside in. Excellent examples of "megapolis" journalism can be found in or near New York City, Chicago, Philadelphia, Detroit, and Los Angeles. The boom in suburban living also triggered a boom in suburban journalism. Southern California is a mass of cities with zigzagging boundaries, with newspapers moving into rival territories to fight for circulation supremacy. In Orange County, 40 miles south of Los Angeles, the Santa Ana *Register* dropped the city name from its flag in the mid-1950s and began circulating throughout the area, including Los Angeles County. Within 15 years its circulation soared past 200,000 from 30,000. One of its competitors, the *Orange Coast Daily Pilot*, produced seven editions "zoned" for various communities and even opened regional offices to increase its local identity. The Los Angeles *Times* and Chicago *Tribune* were pioneers in producing entire sections "zoned" to provide both local news and advertising for communities already served by other dailies or weeklies. Many other newspapers, particularly in big cities, have "zoned" news and advertising to compete with suburban rivals.

THE TECHNICAL FRONT

Advances in newspaper printing technology, as noted, came slowly in the twentieth century, and the greatest changes came following World War II with computerized typesetting and improvements in offset printing. The alternates of retaining conventional letterpress printing or switching to the more flexible offset will face publishers who during the coming decade will be building new plants or expanding existing ones.

CREDIBILITY

When there were two or more competing newspapers in a city, there was a greater opportunity to present varying sides. Mergers and charges that the remaining publishers frequently represent special interests have caused many readers to question the fairness of some newspaper coverage. Newspaper credibility hit the lowest point in the 1930s, when voters overwhelmingly supported President Franklin Roosevelt despite his condemnation in the press by a 3–1 ratio. Newspapers in the 1960s and 1970s, possibly influenced by television competition, appeared more fair in presenting controversial issues. Despite improvements, responsible groups have frequently charged bias or "blackouts" in news coverage. Among the suggested remedies have been more reliance on constructive criticism from journalists and the proposed news councils that would consider charges of unfairness.

News Councils. One public complaint has been that "unfair" stories in newspapers may go unanswered if an editor chooses to be arbitrary. Great Britain's Press Council has been a model in hearing complaints against newspapers and handing down binding decisions holding that a correction or amplification must be published, or that the newspaper indeed was fair and the complaint was without grounds. In the United States, the freedom of

THE CHRISTIAN SCIENCE MONITOR

BOSTON, WEDNESDAY, JULY 1, 1970 — *An International Daily Newspaper* — VOL. 62, NO. 183 TWO SECTIONS — WESTERN EDITION 10c

FOCUS on labor

Hard to fence in

Canada's incomes policy is in trouble.

By means of voluntary restraints, the government had hoped to hold down the wage increases of those earning more than $2 an hour to 6 percent during 1970.

But the Council of Postal Unions, representing 27,000 workers, is militant in demands for 15 to 19 percent in raises over two years.

Its members, who have the right to strike, have been conducting "rotating" strikes—one at a time in selected cities—to press their demands.

Meanwhile, the Canadian Union of Public Employees, 140,000 strong, says flatly it won't settle for just a 6 percent increase.

And in industry, first forest and paper workers and then other major unions have warned of "big strikes" if employers try to hold gains to the government-set guideline.

Foreign parts

During the United Automobile Workers' convention in April, union officials had good news for delegates.

They announced that UAW had "at last convinced Detroit automakers of the need to produce a really small car to compete with foreign compacts, particularly those from Japan and West Germany."

Now the auto union is no longer wreathed in smiles. It is protesting Ford's plan to produce engines and gear boxes for its subcompact, the Pinto, in Great Britain and Germany.

The union is also annoyed by similar plans of other U.S. companies to get major components from abroad.

Detroit's manufacturers say they've got to do it—to compete with the low manufacturing costs of foreign-made small cars.

Girding for battle

Bargaining over wages in most of the telephone industry is still about a year off.

But the Communications Workers of America already is toning up its muscles for a Donnybrook.

Joseph A. Beirne, the union's president, has advised his membership that "CWA will bargain in 1971 for a wage and benefit increase that will make the largest package we've ever won before look like small potatoes.

"A wage adjustment of 20 to 25 cents an hour will not be enough," he said.

He warned the telephone industry that the union "never again will accept a three-year contract on wages" without openings to make possible upward revisions in periods of runaway inflation.

It makes sense

Unionized workers at Wear-Ever Aluminum's plant in Chillicothe, Ohio, are taking a different tack.

They've voted to give up a 6.5 percent wage-fringe increase due this year, including 13 cents an hour in pay, for the best of reasons: to hold onto their jobs.

Most housewives know that Wear-Ever, a subsidiary of the Aluminum Company of America, makes aluminum pots and pans.

Its management complained that labor costs under National ALCOA contracts negotiated in 1968 exceeded those of competitors by at least $1 an hour, making it almost impossible for the company to make a profit at that plant.

When Wear-Ever laid off 200 workers, the Chillicothe local of the Aluminum Workers International Union interpreted the move as the start of a phase-out of that plant's operation and acted quickly to save jobs.

Not now, but later?

The AFL-CIO would like to welcome the UAW — and 1.5 million members — back into the federation.

George Meany extended an olive branch in behalf of AFL-CIO within hours of the election of Leonard Woodcock to succeed the late Walter P. Reuther in the UAW presidency.

But Mr. Woodcock isn't willing — yet — to talk to Mr. Meany about a reconciliation.

UAW will be glad to work closely with any and all AFL-CIO unions, says Mr. Woodcock. But the auto union's 1968 withdrawal from the federation was "on fundamental grounds" that have not yet been resolved.

Where to look

American folklife 'turns it on'

Barbecued buffalo meat, Indian fried bread, and Ozark-style blackberry cobbler are being dished up along with heavy servings of country and folk music on the National Mall in Washington this week. It's all part of the Smithsonian Institution's fourth annual Festival of American Folklife. Among exhibits are a mule-drawn sorghum mill and cornshuck and apple-head dolls.

South Viets dig in

Going it alone in Cambodia

By Daniel Southerland
Special correspondent of The Christian Science Monitor

Neak Leung, Cambodia

Here at the most important South Vietnamese base in Cambodia, the withdrawal of United States forces from Cambodia has meant the loss of U.S. advisers and helicopter support.

The South Vietnamese Marines in charge here say it was good having the American support but that they can get along quite well without it.

"The U.S. air assets helped us a lot," said Col. Ton That Soan, the youthful commander of the South Vietnamese Marine brigade based here. "But it will be no big problem working without them."

The South Vietnamese have established several other small bases in Cambodia, but none as important as the one at Neak Leung. Strategically located, Neak Leung straddles the Mekong River 36 miles southeast of the Cambodian capital of Phnom Penh at the point where the Phnom Penh-Saigon highway meets the river.

The future South Vietnamese performance here could prove crucial to the defense both of Phnom Penh and of the vital portion of the Mekong River lifeline flowing from Phnom Penh into South Vietnam.

The South Vietnamese Marines seem pretty sure of themselves. The June 30 withdrawal date for the U.S. forces in Cambodia holds no special significance for them. After all, they already have had considerable experience operating in Cambodia without American help in areas beyond the 21.7-mile limit President Nixon set for the U.S. forces while they were in Cambodia.

Neak Leung happens to be just inside the 21.7-mile limit. So American advisers and helicopters were permitted to come this far, but no farther.

What the Americans provided were 13 U.S. Marine advisers for the Vietnamese Marines as well as the firepower of Cobra helicopters, the swift reaction of U.S. medical-evacuation helicopters, and the muscle of the huge Chinook choppers with their ability to lift artillery pieces and other heavy loads. Also available were some observation helicopters and some U.S. Navy advisers. The Marine advisers coordinated the use of U.S. air support.

The departure of the Americans, however, does not bring things to a halt. The South Vietnamese have their own helicopters, although none are as powerfully armed as the Cobras. They can still move their artillery — by truck and by boat — although it will not be as mobile as it was when the Chinooks were around. They also have their own "Medevac" helicopters.

The South Vietnamese expect to get some continuing support from American fighter-bombers beyond the withdrawal date and, of course, from their own Air Force.

★Please turn to Page 11

By Joan Forbes, staff cartographer

U.S. holds breath

Courting Nasser runs Red risk

By Saville R. Davis
Staff correspondent of The Christian Science Monitor

Washington

The American peace initative in the Middle East is a trembler, because it could confirm or disrupt the improving trend in Soviet-American relations.

Washington is holding its breath.

The essence of the "new initiative" by President Nixon is for the United States to deal directly with Egyptian President Nasser instead of through Moscow. The Soviet Union could decide, as Washington hopes it will, that this is not an unreasonable move by one of the superpowers at a time of crisis.

Or the Soviet leaders could conclude this was an American effort to undercut Soviet influence in the chief capital of the Arab world.

The latter conclusion by the men of the Kremlin could be a disaster. It not only would doom the present round of peacemaking, it could have consequences far more serious than a continuing conflict between Israel and the Arabs. It could precipitate a direct confrontation between the United States and the Soviet Union—a struggle for predominance in the Middle East which is only latent at the present time and has not passed the point of no return.

There is evidence that President Nixon has gone to very considerable lengths to explain what he was doing, privately, to the Soviet leaders and to express his hope that they would cooperate or at least not take offense. There is no indication whether he has been given any secret reassurance by Moscow. Nor has there been any dependable sign in public, as this is written, of Moscow's considered reaction to the Nixon initiative.

Pressure on Israel

But last week an important forward step in East-West relations was taken by the Communist side in Europe. The Warsaw Pact countries appeared to agree to discuss mutual troop reductions on both sides of the East-West dividing line. This suggests there has been no serious turn for the worse in Soviet-American relations.

From the Soviet point of view, the key to a Mideastern agreement lies in the amount of pressure the United States is prepared to apply to Israel, and on the degree of American willingness not to use Israel as the spearhead for a billigerently anti-Soviet military strategy in that part of the world.

The issue is extremely sensitive. In the nature of things, President Nixon cannot satisfy Moscow fully on these matters and does not intend to. He has warned the Soviet Union that he would not accept Soviet military and naval dominance in the area.

But the Nixon administration has already put pressure on Israel to implement the 1967 Security Council resolution for an even-handed settlement based on the minimum requirements of each side. This may have impressed the Soviet leaders and gained time for Washington to attempt to proceed further.

The chief hope for avoiding Soviet annoyance with Mr. Nixon's direct approach to the Arabs comes in the argument that the American President is keeping his diplomacy within the framework of the UN Security Council resolution and aims to reestablish UN Ambassador Gunnar V. Jarring as the presiding officer over direct Arab-Israeli negotiations. With the Soviet veto in the Security Council and with UN Secretary General U Thant respected by Moscow, the interests of Moscow would seem to be protected, especially as Washington is keeping Moscow informed.

The outcome of President Nasser's visit to Moscow is therefore being watched with the sharpest interest in Washington.

2nd Cl Post Pd at Boston, Mass. and add'l offices

July 1, 1970

Campus warning for Nixon

By Godfrey Sperling Jr.
National political correspondent of The Christian Science Monitor

Washington

The President has received the bleakest kind of assessment from his temporary adviser on campus unrest, Dr. Alexander Heard of Vanderbilt University.

Dr. Heard has reported to Mr. Nixon:

- The end of the Vietnam war will not end campus protest. This unrest will continue to find rallying points around such issues as the environment, civil rights, and urban problems.
- The dissent is broad, going far beyond the actions of the small segment of active militants, and it is based upon a wide and growing feeling that the government simply does not understand, or respond, to the demands of the individual. The dissent, he reports, is aimed at what students feel is a system that is unresponsive—and a President that is unresponsive.

No end seen

Thus, even in advance of a presidential commission probe of campus dissent, chaired by William Scranton, the President is being told in no uncertain terms that he must be prepared to deal with a continuing problem on the college campuses.

Dr. Heard, brought in by Mr. Nixon as a counselor after the campus uproar that followed the U.S. move into Cambodia, is telling the President that as for the student outlook, dark days lie ahead for him.

He says that the radicalism — and the tendency toward violent activity — is even greater among the freshmen and sophomores than among the college upperclassmen.

And he warns of signs of even greater militancy among those youngsters coming along in the high schools.

'Generation gaps' cited

He says there is, indeed, a generation gap between college upperclassmen and lowerclassmen and another generation gap between college and high-school students today.

More and more students today, he is telling the President, feel they can't get into the "system" and that they can't make their voices heard in our society.

At this point all that can be said about the report — and the President's response — is that he is listening to Dr. Heard.

Also, top Nixon aides are hearing the report. Of the latter at least one is known to have regarded the information as overly pessimistic.

But it was from this information from Dr. Heard that Mr. Nixon was influenced, in large part, to set up the commission that will now be taking a long, evaluatory look at the college campuses.

Obviously the President wants detailed observation of the college scene from coast to coast before he is ready to take action on Dr. Heard's report.

Inside today

French vote surprise: Gaullist tide ebbing?

Jean-Jacques Servan-Schreiber's election victory in Nancy may hint that Gaullist strength in France is lessening. It is thought by many to mark a chapter in post-de Gaulle political development. Story: Page 2

Massachusetts challenger takes on a Kennedy

The first hurdle was easy. Josiah A. Spaulding walked away from the Massachusetts state GOP convention with his party's senatorial endorsement in his pocket. But now comes the big challenge. His opponent is Sen. Edward M. Kennedy, and most observers say his prospects of unseating the sole surviving Kennedy brother are slim.

"Nobody is unbeatable," says Mr. Spaulding, "and I don't intend to lose." Story: Page 3

Figure 2–6 The *Christian Science Monitor* rates among America's prestige newspapers, covering national and international affairs methodically.

LOS ANGELES FREE PRESS

25¢ | 35¢ OUTSIDE LA COUNTY

50¢ OUTSIDE THE COUNTRY

Music, Theatre, Film, Books

Growing up in a convent college

Another Century City protest planned

Places to go in Vegas, San Diego & L.A.

CHILDREN OF GOD

Who cares about dead and wounded hippies anyway?
SEE PAGE 14

Volume 9, Number 38 (Issue 427)   In Two Parts   Published Every Friday   September 22-October 2, 1972

LIFE INSIDE SYNANON

Dope & Sex & Business & Privacy & Chuck &...
SEE PAGE 4

Authorities cover up Los Angeles jailbreak

RON RIDENOUR

There was an amazing jail break from New County Jail in Los Angeles in the middle of August which has thus far been entirely unreported by any establishment reporter of press, radio or TV. A three-time loser about to be sentenced to fifteen years to life for multiple counts of armed robbery just walked out of jail and no one among the embarrassed police authorities seems to have told anyone of the prisoner's fantastic disappearing act. *(Editor's note: Since we have observed in the past that establishment police beat reporters rely primarily on information that they are spoon-fed by the police and court clerks, the lack of information about the escape of Jeronimo Ortega is understandable.)*

Jeronimo Ortega, 30 year-old Chicano father of three children, was found guilty on July 8 of six counts of armed robbery and illegal possession of a weapon in an incident the previous year in East Los Angeles. He was confined to jail due to an earlier conviction of illegal possession of a weapon and was serving one year when a teletyped message came to the custodians. The August 11 message from Norwalk's Sheriff sub-station said that Judge William McGinley had granted Ortega's attorney's request for his release on $2,000 bail. The jailers found that hard to believe, according to our sources, and requested confirmation.

The following day, two more teletype messages were received verifying the decision. McGinley's clerk, S.S. Rogers, supposedly gave the sheriff's sub-station a court order to that effect. Someone came to the jail and bailed Ortega out.

When Judge McGinley and his clerk returned from vacation on Sept. 1, they discovered the prisoner was freed. Confused and angry, McGinley asked Mel Albaum, Ortega's attorney, what had happened.

"I told him I had no idea. He had never contacted me and I knew nothing about it until the Judge told me," Albaum said. "But," he told the Judge, "I doubt that he calls me. However, if he does, I'll advise him to surrender." The courtroom broke up in laughter.

Sentencing had been set for Sept. 8 but Ortega did not appear. A warrant was issued for his arrest with a definite stipulation that no bail was to be granted. After having served the maximum ten years for possession of two marijuana cigarettes, a one year term for being a felon with a weapon, and now facing a life in prison, no one really expected the man to walk into court.

As Ortega's first prison experience dragged on, he began to read and listen to others explain causes for discrimination, racism, and other social problems which beset this society. He became conscious of his heritage and gradually organized history classes and cultural groups. He soon headed a new prisoners' group in Soledad called COPA (Chicanos Organizados Pintos de Atzlan — Organized Chicano Prisoners of Atzlan. Atzlan refers to land which first belonged to native Americans).

Upon his release two years ago Ortega continued the rehabilitation program for Chicanos. He became known as a militant and a radical, which brought him and COPA into conflict with the government backed LUCHA (League of United Citizens to Help Addicts). LUCHA is run by Moe Aguirre and is considered by critics to be run for money and power seeking gangsters.

LUCHA and the cops, according to Ortega's defense supporters, wanted the uncompromising leader off the streets. Ortega had refused to help LUCHA get Model City's financing. They claim he was framed in the Sept. 24, 1971, robbery incident.

(please turn to page 3)

"Those who have had a chance for four years and could not produce peace should not be given another chance."
Richard M. Nixon, October 9, 1968

Another Century City protest

Century City June 23, 1967, revisited is the theme of a hastily organized ad hoc group of 30 anti-war organizations who met Tuesday night as the *Free Press* went to the press, in order to show Richard Nixon and the world that he is not welcome in Los Angeles.

Five years ago, when Lyndon Johnson was heavily bombing all of Vietnam, he was met by 20,000 anti-war demonstrators at Los Angeles' newly opened Century City Plaza Hotel. Although police rushed the demonstrators in panic and many were injured, this was undoubtedly one of the events that convinced Johnson to withdraw from the Presidential race.

On September 27, Wednesday, Nixon is launching his reelection campaign in the Southern California area at the same Century City Hotel while he is bombing *all* of Southeast Asia in an even more devastating manner than did Johnson.

With only eight days notice, 75 Los Angelinos met at the Westwood Methodist Church to plan for the broadest united action possible. All conceivable points of view were represented and for the first time in a long time among the peace organizations there was a genuine spirit of unity. Don Kalish, UCLA philosophy professor who has the distinction of having first hired Angela Davis, conducted the

(please turn to page 3)

Figure 2–7 The 1960s brought the development of the "underground" press, also known as the "alternate" or "antiestablishment" press. The *Los Angeles Free Press* proved to be one of the more successful in the field.

Figure 2–8 The expansion of newspaper "groups" or chains helped bring more methodical business management. Panax Corporation, with newspapers in Michigan, uses its own vessel (above) to bring paper from mills in Canada. (Panax Corporation Photo)

the press guaranteed by the Bill of Rights precludes the state or federal governments establishing such councils. Newspapers in some American cities, however, are experimenting with news councils on a voluntary basis.

Introspection. Journalist-edited publications seeking to provide constructive criticism of newspapers serve to show where credibility gaps are developing, hopefully persuading writers and editors to know their shortcomings. *The Columbia Journalism Review,* founded in 1961 at the Columbia University Graduate School of Journalism, has been a pioneer at analyzing perspectives in news coverage. *The Chicago Journalism Review,* launched after the stormy Democratic National Convention of 1968 in Chicago, was the forerunner of

other regional magazines offering critiques of newspaper shortcomings.

Similar publications include (*More*), published in New York City; *Philadelphia Journalism Review, Review of Southern California Journalism, St. Louis Journalism Review,* and *The Unsatisfied Man,* based in Denver. Using working editors and reporters, such publications have dissected faults and helped develop an increasing sensitivity for fairness.

THE "PRESTIGE" DAILIES OF AMERICA

Journalists, sociologists, political scientists, educators, and others often make lists of what they regard as America's most prestigious and influential daily newspapers, as measured by such factors as fairness, the scope and depth of coverage, qualities of leadership, and impact or influence on the mainstream of society. Such factors make "great" newspapers.

Most lists include the St. Louis *Post-Dispatch,* owned by the heirs of journalism pioneer Joseph Pulitzer, the New York *Times, Christian Science Monitor,* Baltimore *Sun,* Los Angeles *Times,* and Washington *Post.*

Others frequently placed on the lists are the Miami *Herald,* Minneapolis *Tribune,* Des Moines *Register,* Kansas City *Star,* Denver *Post,* Dallas *Morning News,* Houston *Post,* Seattle *Times,* Atlanta *Constitution,* and the New Orleans *Times-Picayune.*

It is not a coincidence that most of these newspapers are morning ones; only the *Post-Dispatch, Christian Science Monitor, Star,* and Denver *Post* are published in the afternoon. Morning newspapers throughout the nation are generally the most prosperous. They enjoy lower distribution costs because there is less traffic on the streets during their delivery hours, and their readers are more affluent. The morning newspapers therefore are more attractive to advertisers, and the increased revenue provides more pages and more news.

WAGES AND NEWSPAPER PRICES

Pay scales for reporters and editors hit a low during the Depression, and in 1933 the

Figure 2-9 This is a section of the newsroom at the *Rochester* (N.Y.) *Times-Union and Democrat and Chronicle,* part of the Gannett Co. newspaper chain. Gannett, publicly traded on the New York Stock Exchange, is typical of the trend toward newspaper groups replacing individual or family ownership.

Figure 2-10 Computers and other means of automation are used increasingly to produce newspapers. These computers at the Associated Press facility in Rockefeller Center, New York, can send financial news almost instantaneously to newspapers and radio-TV stations.

American Newspaper Guild was organized. This union covers newspaper employees outside of the mechanical departments, which have their own unions, and its approximately 30,000 members work primarily for the wire services and metropolitan dailies. News department pay scales have increased far faster than the cost of living since World War II. While most news department employees are not covered by Guild contracts, union pay scales affect their salaries positively. Many newspapers, even though not unionized, operate on Guild standards. Beginners usually start at approximately half the salary paid experienced reporters, and advance to the journeyman pay in five or six years.

Weeklies are converted into dailies, but few newspapers have started as dailies since World War II because of immense capital requirements and a high fatality rate for new publications. The price tag for successful dailies, therefore, has risen almost annually since the late 1950s. In the 1970s, for example, a daily with 150,000 circulation can sell for $20 million. Prices vary according to geographical areas, population growth patterns, competition, and plant condition.

"All the News
That's Fit to Print"

The New York Times

CITY EDITION

Weather: Cloudy, mild, rain likely
today, tonight. Very mild tomorrow.
Temp. range: today 34-45; Sunday
23-42. Full U.S. report on Page 49.

VOL. CXXII....No. 42,002   © 1973 The New York Times Company   — NEW YORK, MONDAY, JANUARY 22, 1973 —   Higher newsstand price in air delivery cities   M   15 CENTS

M'GOVERN WARNS OF ONE-MAN RULE; EXHORTS LIBERALS

Says Congress Must Take the Initiative to Place Limits on Presidency

BATTLE IS TAKING SHAPE

Oxford Speech Follows Move in Senate Against Nixon's Withholding of Funds

By JAMES M. NAUGHTON
Special to The New York Times

WASHINGTON, Jan. 21—Senator George McGovern said today that liberals must help to resurrect Congress if the United States is to escape "one-man rule."

Jersey Investigates Alleged Conspiracy Against Legislator

By RONALD SULLIVAN
Special to The New York Times

TRENTON, Jan. 21 — State law-enforcement authorities reported today that they were investigating an alleged conspiracy to plant narcotics in the home of a Democratic New Jersey legislator and had identified aides of a Republican State Senator as prime suspects.

NIXON IS PRAISED AT CAPITAL RITES

300 Inauguration Workers Hear 3 Preach at White House Worship Service

By EDWARD B. FISKE

WASHINGTON, Jan. 21 — President Nixon marked the first full day of his second term by serving as host today for 300 inauguration workers and members of his new Administration at a White House worship service.

9 Hostages Escape and 4 Gunmen Surrender To End 47-Hour Siege of Brooklyn Sports Store

Three of the four suspects being brought into the 90th Precinct stationhouse on Union Avenue. The fourth, wounded on Friday, was taken to Kings County Hospital.

Hostages being helped down from the roof of a furniture store adjoining the sporting goods building onto the roof of a Spanish grocery. From there they went to the street.

Robbers Give Up Vow to Die For 'Victory and Paradise'

By ROBERT D. McFADDEN

A two-day ordeal of blazing gunfights, death and terror at a Brooklyn sporting-goods store ended dramatically yesterday afternoon with a daring roof escape by nine remaining hostages and, several hours later, the peaceful surrender of four trapped gunmen.

Captives Called Themselves 'Servants of Allah' in Letter

By RONALD SMOTHERS

The four gunmen who surrendered yesterday described themselves in a letter as "servants of Allah," and there was other evidence that they were militant adherents of a form of Islam.

Air Force Doctors Said to Take Part In Indochina Raids

By SEYMOUR M. HERSH
Special to The New York Times

WASHINGTON, Jan. 21—Two military physicians have charged that some of their medical colleagues have actively participated in dozens of bombing raids over Southeast Asia, in violation of international law, military regulations and the Hippocratic oath.

U.S.-CHINESE TIES IMPROVE SLOWLY

But Many Obstacles Remain After a Year—Taiwan Issue Is Fading

By ROBERT ALDEN
Special to The New York Times

UNITED NATIONS, N.Y., Jan. 21—In a year of gradually improving relations, the United States and China have come a long way toward the normalization of trade as well as diplomatic and other contacts.

NIXON IS BRIEFED BY GENERAL HAIG ON INDOCHINA TRIP

Aide Talks to Kissinger on Return From Saigon, Then Both Talk to President

WASHINGTON OPTIMISTIC

2d White House Session Due Before Chief Negotiator's Trip to Paris Tomorrow

Special to The New York Times

WASHINGTON, Jan. 21 — Gen. Alexander M. Haig Jr. conferred with President Nixon and Henry A. Kissinger today shortly after returning from Saigon, where he sought approval of the agreement being drawn up by the United States and North Vietnam to end the Vietnam war.

Haig Briefs Leaders

Pennsy Case Is Lawyers' Dream

By ISRAEL SHENKER

The Penn Central may not be the greatest railroad in the world, but it is a gravy train for lawyers.

NEWS INDEX

Key Anti-Portuguese Leader In West Africa Is Assassinated

By The Associated Press

DAKAR, Senegal, Jan. 21—Amilcar Cabral, one of the most prominent leaders of the African struggle against white supremacy, was assassinated last night in front of his home in Conakry, the capital of Guinea.

Amilcar Cabral at his home in Conakry.

President and Mrs. Nixon saluting members of the Mormon Tabernacle Choir after White House worship service yesterday. Portrait of Franklin D. Roosevelt is on the wall.

Figure 2–11   The *New York Times* is one of the "prestige" or "quality" newspapers of America.

Los Angeles Times
Southern Communities Section

SUNDAY MORNING, JUNE 7, 1959

Office and Phone Numbers
720 E. Artesia Blvd., N. Long Beach
Times Office: 202 West First Street, Los Angeles 53, Calif. MAdison 5-2345

INGLORIOUS ENDING—Stacked in junk heap at Terminal Island yards of National Steel & Metal Corp., these old PE red cars will be salvaged for steel, closing to many Southlanders a nostalgic era.
Times photos by Maxine Reams

MILEAGE CHECK—Electrician Garland Scott stands in front of automatic coupler which he has just checked for "mileage inspection chart" certificate.

Dovey Seen as Target of Vickers Foes
Ouster Move Off if Chief Is Fired, Spokesman Says

LONG BEACH—A move to oust Sam E. Vickers as city manager probably will be dropped at Tuesday's City Council session if he will agree to the dismissal of Police Chief William H. Dovey.

A spokesman for councilmen favoring the ousting of Vickers said the conflict over Chief Dovey has been one of the major disagreements with the city manager.

The spokesman, who declined use of his name, said the move against Vickers "probably will be dropped" if he removes Dovey from office.

'Face Saving'

A councilman who wants to retain the city manager said the move against Dovey is being inaugurated as a "face saving" attempt by the anti-Vickers faction because the group is losing the votes required for an ouster. He pointed out that Dovey has said he will retire in the fall.

At least five of the nine councilmen originally were reported ready to vote for Vickers' dismissal but the forces now are believed to have dwindled to three. Proponents of the ouster are not openly still active, however.

Dovey, a veteran of nearly 40 years on the force and police chief for the last 10 years, has been subject to criticism from Councilman D. Pat Ahern, who says certain conditions in the city are "deplorable" and wants better enforcement.

Chief Is Appointed

Under the city charter, the police chief is appointed by the city manager and councilmen cannot remove an individual from the office.

Vickers declines to comment on the dismissal move.

A rift was reported also between Mayor Ray Kealer and Mrs. Vi Dovey, wife of the police chief and secretary in the mayor's office. The rift was reported over operation of the mayor's office.

Action on the move to dismiss Vickers was postponed at the city fathers' last meeting because Councilman Charles Dooley was absent. Consensus among councilmen is that a dismissal motion will be made only when all nine Council members are present.

Three Support Vickers

Councilman William Dalmeast, meanwhile, said he will oppose any move to oust Vickers. Vice-Mayor Virgil Spongberg and Councilman Lewis Reese also said they will fight to keep the city manager. The other six councilmen declined to give their opinions on the impending move.

Vickers also was backed in a resolution adopted by the directors of the Long Beach Apartment House Assn. which commended his efficiency.

50% Turnout Expected for Recall Vote

BY JACK McCURDY

BELL—A record municipal vote of 50% is forecast by City Clerk W. H. Poole in the recall election Tuesday aimed at Mayor Percy A. Yerian, whose conduct in office is being attacked by the Bell Citizens Committee for Good Government.

Poole says 7,533 persons are eligible to vote at 34 polling places from 7 a.m. to 8 p.m. in this city's first recall election since W. C. Stewart and John Anderson defeated a move to unseat them in 1940.

2,200 Petitioners

Approximately 2,200 signed petitions for the recall election, which will cost the city about $4,000, Poole says.

If a simple majority votes for Yerian's recall, then either Mrs. Dorothy E. Griffith or James P. Clark, whichever receives the most votes, will serve out Yerian's unexpired term.

Candidates Independent

Mrs. Griffith, a housewife, and Clark, a manufacturing cost analyst, say they are independents and not affiliated with the citizens committee.

Mrs. Griffith is campaigning for greater beautification of the city and off-street parking to boost growth of the retail center.

Clark says he will vote for the recall on the basis of Yerian's voting record in the Council. "If the recall is successful, the best man to replace Yerian is one who is not committed on one side or the other on the Council," he said.

Yerian Sees Win

Yerian, a retired telephone technician who was elected to the Council in April, 1958, and became mayor last April, says he will definitely win if there is a large turnout at the polls.

"This thing has got to stop," he says. "We cannot stand for a group recalling an honest man just because its members do not like him."

H. M. Johnson, president of the citizens committee and secretary-treasurer and business agent for the American Federation of Grain Millers, AFL-CIO, predicts Yerian will be recalled and that "either of the candidates will make a better councilman than Yerian."

Five Charges

There are five charges against Yerian in the recall petitions:

1—That he "attempted to interfere and thwart the will of the City Council in a proposed investigation of the street department."

2—That he "has shown
Please Turn to Pg. 6, Col. 3

Old Red Cars Up for Last Run Down Line
Study Will Decide if Turn-of-Century Trains Continue L.A.-Compton-L.B. Trips

BY SPENCER CRUMP

LONG BEACH—A study will be completed early next year to determine if the big red interurbans—remnants of the world's biggest trolley system, the Pacific Electric—will continue to run from Los Angeles to Compton and Long Beach.

And if the survey justifies keeping the trains, the trolleys which became familiar as the Big Red Cars no longer will keep their famous color. They'll be painted light green to match other equipment of the Metropolitan Transit Authority.

Coincidentally the study Please Turn to Pg. 2, Col. 4

is being launched as the Long Beach line celebrates its 54th birthday. When the Big Red Cars first arrived on July 4, 1904, they brought so many people that hotels were overcrowded and via...

SERVICING TRAINS—Above Aurelio Castro scrubs down one of 53 electric cars remaining of original 900 in use during line's heyday. Below from left Lewis Fordyng, Henry Hammond and Henry T. Richardson repair truck assembly.

DEPARTURE—Commuters board big red car bound for home, job, shopping or visiting. PE trolleys have been part of Southland scene for 54 years.

L.B. Budget Lists 3.5% Tax Boost

LONG BEACH—Property owners will face an increase of approximately 3.5% in their tax bills under an all-time high city budget of $28,848,506 submitted by City Manager Sam E. Vickers, which will be considered Tuesday by the City Council.

The 1959-60 budget is $1,532,747 higher than the current year's budget, which previously was a record for expenditures.

Pay Increases

Approximately $1.1 million in the budget is earmarked to give a blanket 5.5% pay increase to all city employees and various special increases for certain categories.

The current tax rate is $1.3224 per $100 assessed valuation and would rise to $1.37057 if the Council adopts the budget as submitted. The rate would be $1.35485 or slightly more than 1.5 cents less if the pay raises are not given.

Council Split

Councilmen differ in their opinions as to the granting of pay raises if property tax rates are to increase and indicate they will thrash the matter out at the Tuesday session.

Various property owner groups are opposing increases in the city's budget and are urging the Council to hold the line on tax boosts. City employee representatives say raises are necessary because of higher costs of living.

Under Vickers' proposal, the special pay increases in addition to the 5.5% increments would go to several hundred employees whose salaries, he reports, are low compared to those in nearby cities.

WILL OF L.B. WOMAN CONTESTED
$500,000 Bequest to State for Medical Research Challenged

LONG BEACH—Bequeathing of a half-million-dollar estate to the state of California for "research of hypertension and cancer" by a Belmont Shore investor will be challenged in court by a group of her relatives residing in West Germany.

Relatives of Mrs. Irma Hoefly, who died March 20, 1958, also will seek to set aside a jury award of $88,000 in cash from the estate to the woman's former companion, Mrs. Marie Spille of Glendora Ave.

The will is being challenged because the money was left to the state without indicating that it was to be used for charity, according to Atty. Donald C. Kimber, who represents the Hoefly relatives in Germany.

Bequests to Kin

Meanwhile, the state also is appealing the jury award to Mrs. Spille on the contention that the panel misinterpreted a clause it maintains gave her only furniture.

The relatives received small bequests in her will, which was handwritten in German.

Kimber said bequests to the state should be set aside because the will can be interpreted to permit the money to be distributed to profit-making organizations rather than charitable groups.

A hearing on the matter is scheduled for Oct. 8 in Long Beach Superior Court.

Mrs. Hoefly was the widow of Julius Hoefly, restaurant owner and a Belmont Shore property owner who died in 1941.

Budget Hearing Set for Downey Tuesday

DOWNEY—A public hearing on Downey's preliminary 1959-60 budget of $3,966,400 will be held Tuesday at 8 a.m. in the City Hall.

The budget calls for $2,338,045 in operating funds, a $745,000 reserve and $883,000 for capital improvements.

Reserve Urged

The city's finance advisory committee recommends a $750,000 reserve and feels a 10-cent tax increase is necessary to accomplish this.

City Manager Oren L. King says the city will be able to maintain the recommended reserve without boosting the 29-cent tax rate. He says revenue and carry...

Council Split

Differences between King and the finance committee over whether or not tax increase is needed may trigger debate in the Council, where Mayor Edwin Giddings and Councilman Scott Temple are publicly in favor of boosting taxes "to meet our needs now." The other three Council members, however, are reportedly against any tax hike.

The budget, King says, calls for additional fire, police, public works, engineering and library personnel.

Figure 2–12 Newspapers serving megapolis areas find it a problem to provide community news. Regional or community sections pioneered by the *Los Angeles Times* help "local" coverage of events.

EXERCISES

1. Arrange for a class visit to a printing plant using the offset method of production for a first-hand view of this technique which is growing in popularity.

2. Visit the public library and determine whether a "city" magazine is published in the community. If so, compare its contents with those of daily and weekly newspapers.

3. Using the financial section of the local newspaper, compare the current prices of the newspaper company stocks listed in this chapter.

4. Check the newsstands in your community, and note the daily, weekly, "underground," and other newspapers that compete for reader interest.

The Journalist: Personal Attributes and Educational Requirements

The role of the journalist has broadened with the years, just as the scope of newspapers and the electronic media has expanded to fill the public's changing interests. Even so, the personal attributes that help make a good journalist remain basically unchanged. There have been, however, considerable changes in the educational requirements.

PERSONAL ATTRIBUTES

The personal attributes usually associated with journalists can be likened to aptitudes, since they are indicators of abilities that can be developed and refined through classroom studies and at work in the journalistic field.

CURIOSITY

A prime requirement for the reporter or editor is native or inborn curiosity, for without it there would be no asking of questions or delving into backgrounds to find "submerged" or hidden information that might lift a story situation from one paragraph into a prize-winning series revealing significant facts. The person who instinctively asks questions and

wonders why things are happening has an attribute that is vital for daily use in journalism.

Closely allied to this quality is skepticism, or the inquiring mind that seeks to verify the truthfulness and logic of information. Skepticism, positively questioning things, should never be mistaken for cynicism, or negative distrust and disbelief even in realities. The good journalist, unearthing facts, will answer the questions or doubts raised by the reader's subconscious curiosity.

The reporter who lacks curiosity will find little to write about.

A SENSE OF FAIRNESS AND RESPONSIBILITY

The journalist is a person who can view the various sides of a question and present the facts with fairness and responsibility. The news writer and editor want to offer not only *both* sides, but *all* of the sides involved in a situation so that the reader can weigh the facts and reach an intelligent judgment. Reporters and editors are entitled, as are all human beings, to the right to hold prejudices and opinions. As journalists, however, they must lay aside their biases and be fair while on the job.

A TEAM PLAYER

Journalists must work together on a newspaper or in any other news medium. Serving with pride as a team, they give the audience news of many dimensions and perspectives. Team-playing means that each staff member diligently performs his own assignments with skill and also does his utmost to help fellow workers. There are moments near deadlines when a reporter may face, at one time, writing tasks, an interview, and phone calls; the unwritten rule at most newspaper offices is for those who have completed assignments to pitch in to help without being asked. Journalists respect deadlines, knowing that their stories, photographs, or other assignments must be submitted on time—not a half-hour late, when the presses for the day may be rolling. The news room "team" must have the copy on or before deadline if it is to produce the edition for which the public is waiting.

Team-playing on a news staff does not prevent the writer or editor from exercising his own creativity, nor does it mean that they must adopt "group" ethics. It simply means performing assignments and keeping other staff members, particularly the editors directing activities, informed as to what is transpiring. The reporter or editor who feels he can "do it all" is wrong and eventually will let the rest of the team down. Journalism is not the field for the "loner."

A PERSON WHO ENJOYS NEWSPAPERS

The person who probably will succeed in journalism is one whose interests include reading newspapers and who reads one regularly. Reading a newspaper helps the prospective journalist learn what the field is all about and develop a "feeling" regarding such matters as writing styles, make-up, headlines, and picture usage. It is true that these areas can be treated in books, college classes, and discussions with professionals, and during on-the-job training. Yet, only the regular reading—and enjoyment—of a newspaper can provide the

background essential to make these learning activities meaningful.

The regular reading of a newspaper helps develop the "feel" for what is and is not news, just as the aspiring professional artist would handle art materials for years before enrolling in a specialized college class in an art technique. Similarly, the person with the journalistic aptitude demonstrates that ability by perusal of a newspaper. Moreover, he probably has been enjoying newspapers for years.

NUMEROUS FIELDS OF INTEREST

Another important attribute for the successful journalist is holding interests that are considerably wider and more diversified than those of the person who is content to enter a less challenging field. The prospective journalist is hardly expected to be an expert in all of the arts and sciences, but his native curiosity will motivate the probing of many areas of knowledge. Journalism offers no refuge for the person who frequently remarks, "I'm not interested in that."

A SENSE OF EMPATHY

Everyone is interested in things that affect or revolve around their own personal world. Journalists must be able to go, almost instinctively, much further and have understanding of other people's aspirations, fears, hopes, needs, feelings, and interest fields. By developing empathy, or an understanding of people, the writer and editor will be able to extend the subject field and depth of stories to a much greater audience.

THE ABILITY TO EXPLAIN IDEAS

The journalist, whose curious mind seeks more information, also must be able to explain concepts clearly and concisely to his audience. The reporter in a large sense is a "translator" who takes difficult and sometimes even abstract ideas and uses understandable words to explain them to readers. Presenting facts without explaining them is not acceptable in modern journalism.

The good reporter talks with scientists, physicians, city officials, lawyers, judges, janitors, repairmen, secretaries, ranchers, bankers, salesmen, and other people who work in worlds filled with technical phrases and then "translates" this information, using understandable words for the technicalities, into stories that the public will understand.

AN APTITUDE FOR SPELLING AND PUNCTUATION

Just as a carpenter must have an affection for and skill in using tools before erecting a building, the journalist must enjoy and understand handling the English language in order to write a news story. The successful reporter will have an interest in his tools—words and sentences—so that he can handle them easily and effectively.

A knowledge of basic punctuation and the wisdom to consult a dictionary when in doubt over spelling are essentials for the journalist. The person who finds writing a drudgery instead of a pleasure should seek a career in another field, since words and sentences are necessary to translate reports to the audience whether it is reached via print or electronics.

CHANGING EDUCATIONAL REQUIREMENTS

Aptitudes form the basis for the formal education which is so important for the journalist. Early American writers and editors "found" their way into the field because of their interest in politics, a subject emphasized in the first newspapers almost to the exclusion of other news. Even when newspapers turned to more diversified reporting to attract general readers, starting in the 1830s, the average reporter required little formal training. The years have produced more sophisticated newspapers appealing to more intelligent audiences and written by increasingly better-educated reporters.

JOURNALISM TRAINING

Journalists of 50 to 100 years ago usually were men who started as copy (or errand) boys and learned newspaper techniques by watch-

ing editors and reporters at work. Completion of high school normally sufficed for the average reporter through the late 1920s, although for the previous 10 years those with college backgrounds were favored for the best jobs on the larger newspapers.

The early twentieth century marked the start of college programs specifically designed to train journalists. Pioneering were the Graduate School of Journalism at Columbia University, opened in 1912 after an initial endowment by Joseph Pulitzer, and the University of Missouri, which has a large program regarded as one of the best in the world. Other institutions leading the way with journalism education programs include the University of Iowa, Kent State University, University of Minnesota, Northwestern University, University of Southern California, University of Syracuse, and Stanford University.

Today, there are few universities, four-year colleges, or community colleges in America that lack journalism programs. Recognizing the importance of good communications, colleges have programs of varying sizes and specialties leading to degrees in such fields as news reporting, advertising, radio-television, public relations, and photography.

College journalism courses are oriented to the producer, as contrasted to the consumer of news emphasized at the high school level. Depending on the institution, college journalism classes range from methods and ethics of gathering news to analyzing the trends and effects of the news media. One yardstick of quality in selecting a journalism program at a four-year college or university is provided by the American Council for Education in Journalism (ACEJ), directed by practicing journalists and journalism educators. The ACEJ accredits programs that meet its high standards. While colleges with excellent journalism programs may not have applied for council accreditation, those listed by the ACEJ are ones selected on the basis of rigid standards.

While virtually all journalists agree that today a college education is vital, they dissent, as do educators, about what its contents should include. The groups are divided into those advocating a *journalism* major and those endorsing a major in a *liberal arts* or *other* specialized field of study.

The "Journalism Major" View. Those advocating that a student major in journalism believe aspiring journalists should enroll in courses surveying and analyzing various forms of communication as well as in classes pertaining to the techniques of reporting and editing. While journalism and related courses constitute the student's major, they are supplemented by a minor or electives in fields of interest chosen by individual students.

The "Non-Journalism Major" View. The other side recommends that a student minor in journalism, and thus develop writing skills, but select a major in an academic field suitable for use as a writing specialty. Proponents argue that the non-journalism major can develop journalistic skills when employed by a newspaper or radio-TV station, and that job opportunities will be improved because of the academic background.

The student following the "journalism" program would receive a bachelor's degree with a major in that subject, while the one following the "non-journalism" major course of studies would receive a degree in the academic field that he selects for a major.

Both views have strong advocates among the editors who hire journalists. Even these editors frequently change back and forth in their advocacies in accordance with the performances of the people they hire. Prospective journalists would do well to discuss educational requirements with several editors and reporters, as well as with college instructors and counselors.

STARTING THE CAREER IN JOURNALISM

Journalism classes and practical experience on a college newspaper help prepare the student for a career. Few colleges, however, can hope to duplicate a week-long schedule filled with the pressures and deadlines to which working journalists become accustomed. To supplement campus training, many journalists and educators encourage students to obtain practical experience by working on a newspaper or in the electronic media while in col-

lege. These duties preferably should be on a part-time basis that would not interfere with studies leading to a degree which eventually will enhance the journalist's value. Practical experience provides a salary to help pay expenses and, highly important, gives the aspiring journalist the opportunity to develop a camaraderie with working members of the press. The student not only earns esteem, but also develops professional work habits and earns a reference which may be invaluable in future job-seeking.

When to Begin a Career. A start in the journalistic field at a comparatively young age also is desirable. Those who begin working part-time while in school find the best positions opening to them because they acquire an education and practical experience concurrently. Some editors express reluctance to hire inexperienced people over the age of 26 because those in the higher age brackets usually require higher starting salaries and are more difficult to train.

Most newspapers and radio-TV stations are constantly busy and always on deadlines. Staff members, therefore, lack the time to participate in organized training programs, and the managements usually prefer to pay higher wages to a person with experience than a lower salary to a person who must be trained. The person desiring a job in journalism should think soon of where to start, even though that place may seem humble. By acquiring experience, the aspirant may climb the ladder to the position he seeks. Those who work near editors and reporters, even though in part-time or seemingly "low" positions, will be able to learn journalistic techniques and advance as they prove their abilities.

Help from the News Staff. Most experienced reporters, photographers, and editors started at the bottom of the ladder and worked upward, usually with helping hands from older staff members. Newsrooms traditionally are friendly places, with friendships, humor, pride in good work, and a "team" atmosphere. Journalists enjoy working with newcomers and helping them develop their aptitudes.

How Much Education Is Needed? While a high school education no longer is sufficient for most jobs with above average interest and pay, the amount of college training required to enter the journalistic field can vary by year, locale, individual newspapers, and each aspirant. With ability and luck, a young man or woman may obtain a reporting position on the basis of training in a community, or two-year, college. Others may find the job competition so keen that they must obtain bachelor's or master's degrees to enter journalism at the level they desire. The best positions as reporters and editors normally will go to applicants who can offer experience and education, with the maximum of both obviously being the most desirable.

Growing Opportunities for Women. Writing and editing the social pages of newspapers for years were the major opportunities offered women journalists. Without downgrading this popular feature, it can be said that many talented women writers wanted to handle subjects with deeper meaning. Although the general news area was not closed to women and some made their way to executive news positions, the doors did not open for larger numbers of women news staff members until the late 1950s and the 1960s.

The "Women's Lib" movement helped to make editors more aware that they had discriminated in hiring. Aspiring women journalists made it clear that they were not embarrassed in covering crime news or frightened of riots, and when given the opportunity frequently could out-write their male counterparts. The decades ahead will see more women assume positions as reporters, photographers, and editors as job discrimination ends.

More Opportunities for Minorities. Members of racial and ethnic minorities are finding increased opportunities in journalism as newspapers and radio-TV stations recognize that ability should be the only determinant in selecting reporters and editors. Members of minorities who prepare themselves academically and by seeking part-time practical experience will be finding positions as the media seek to achieve the ethnic balance in staff members that society increasingly expects.

PROFILE OF THE JOURNALIST

The personal characteristics of editors and reporters vary greatly. Newspaper publishers are usually conservative, as are the owners or officers of many large corporations. Reporters, on the other hand, tend to be more

Table 3–1. The Destinations of Four-Year-College Journalism Graduates*

HOW THE MEDIA SHARED THEM:			WHERE THE OTHERS WENT:		
	%	No. reported		%	No. reported
Daily newspapers	15.2	816	College j-teaching	1.5	79
Weekly newspapers	3.3	178	High school j-teaching	2.2	119
Wire services	0.9	50			
Television news	2.4	129	Other teaching	1.6	87
Radio news	1.5	81	Graduate school	8.0	433
Public relations	8.1	434	Military service	4.9	262
Advertising	5.0	268	Miscellaneous jobs	9.5	510
Magazines	1.9	100	No job, unreported	34.1	1,835
TOTAL MEDIA	38.2	2,056	TOTAL NON-MEDIA	61.8	3,325

* Information provided by The Newspaper Fund, Inc., a foundation to encourage careers in journalism supported by Dow Jones & Company, Inc. This table is based on a survey of June, 1971, graduates; the foundation makes an annual report on journalism graduates.

Figure 3-1 Informal discussions with working journalists help students learn about the field—and help journalists learn about students. This discussion at Orange Coast College in Costa Mesa, Calif., featured (from left) Spider MacLean of Radio KWIZ, Santa Ana; Glenn White, sports editor of the *Orange Coast Daily Pilot*; and Carl Sawyer, assistant sports editor of the *Orange County Register*. The session was taped for other students to view. (Photo by Joan Milcarek)

liberal. There is debate over the reasons for this trend: one group of psychologists argues that people who are sympathetic to social problems are attracted to the journalistic field, while another group contends that exposure to life's problems in covering stories causes journalists to adopt liberal views. While there may be a tendency toward liberalism in reporters, there are many who hold conservative views.

Regardless of liberal or conservative persuasion, of course, good reporters, editors, and publishers strive to present news fairly and without bias. This dedication to fairness is a by-product of the tradition that journalists will present all sides.

Most reporters are not "joiners" to the degree found in many salesmen, who by the nature of the pressures of their work associate with luncheon clubs and fraternal organizations. Journalists frequently are sought as members, but cite two reasons for declining: (1) they may lose their objectivity if they belong to an organization that seeks publicity, and (2) their frequent assignments to cover meetings of such groups give them sufficient contact, so that they prefer to spend free time in other pursuits.

Journalists do enjoy meeting and talking with each other, and press clubs encompassing people from newspapers, radio, television, and public relations flourish in many cities, as do chapters of Sigma Delta Chi Professional Journalism Fraternity, an organization open to both men and women.

EXERCISES

1. Visit your library and inspect the college and university catalogs, noting the scope of the journalism courses and programs opened.

2. Request your local newspaper to arrange for a reporter or editor to attend a class question-and-answer session; ask his or her recommendations regarding journalism education.

3. Contact a former student now working in the journalistic field, and ask for comments regarding the first weeks on the job.

4. Prepare a brief questionnaire pertaining to recommended educational backgrounds, and arrange to have it distributed to news staff members at local radio-TV stations and newspapers.

4

The Organization of a Newspaper

The subscriber receives a neat little package, a newspaper, on his doorstep. Wrapped in it are many things: news of the world, the nation, and of neighbors; crossword puzzles and comics; the latest on sports and fashions; where to buy a car, shop for groceries, or sell a used desk; there is pathos, humor, information, and excitement. Few readers realize the number of highly skilled craftsmen who helped bring the newspaper to the door. There are printers, circulation supervisors, carriers, telephone operators, advertising solicitors, artists, office machine operators, editors, photographers, and reporters.

Many people, overlooking these varied skills, make the mistake of assuming that the reporter, so graphically characterized on television and in old movies, performs many of these duties. Except on the smallest of weekly newspapers, duties are highly structured and specialized.

Newspapers typically operate with three departments. They are the (1) business, (2) mechanical, and (3) news departments.

Figure 4–1 depicts a newspaper's organization, with emphasis on the news department.

A NEWSPAPER'S OPERATION

Heading the newspaper organization is the editor and publisher, who is the newspaper's owner or the representative of its owners. With the value of newspapers increasing, few individuals own publications outright as they did a century ago, when lower capital requirements permitted more personalized ownership. Today, the larger newspapers are owned by corporations pooling the wealth of individuals. The "editor" portion of the publisher's title correctly indicates "editing" prerogatives, but the many executive duties prevent him from being a "working" editor.

Reporting directly to the editor and publisher is the general manager, who coordinates operations of the three basic departments. This executive's duties usually do not include decisions regarding how news will be covered, although the general manager may determine the amount of space which will be devoted to news as opposed to advertising.

THE BUSINESS DEPARTMENT

Two important parts of the business divi-

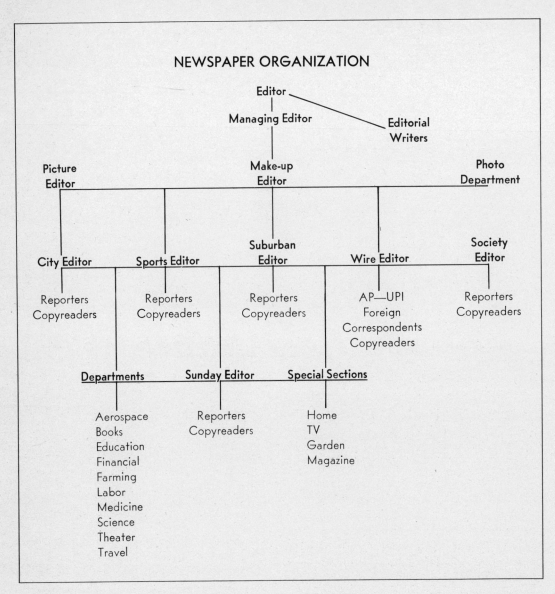

NEWSPAPER ORGANIZATION

Editor

Managing Editor

Editorial Writers

Picture Editor

Make-up Editor

Photo Department

City Editor

Sports Editor

Suburban Editor

Wire Editor

Society Editor

Reporters
Copyreaders

Reporters
Copyreaders

Reporters
Copyreaders

AP—UPI
Foreign
Correspondents
Copyreaders

Reporters
Copyreaders

Departments

Sunday Editor

Special Sections

Aerospace
Books
Education
Financial
Farming
Labor
Medicine
Science
Theater
Travel

Reporters
Copyreaders

Home
TV
Garden
Magazine

Figure 4—1 Organization of the news department of the typical medium to large newspaper. Typesetters, press operators, and other production personnel work in the mechanical department, while those associated with advertising and circulation are in the business department.

sion are the circulation department, which directs distribution of the newspapers to street stands and homes, and the advertising department. The latter department is divided into divisions for display and classified advertising, each of which is usually solicited by different salesmen. The business department also includes bookkeepers, janitors, and telephone operators.

THE MECHANICAL DEPARTMENT

The function of printing the newspaper is performed by the mechanical department. Its divisions include (1) the typesetters who operate the hot metal or photographic (for offset) typesetting machines, (2) the craftsmen who make the plates for the press, and (3) the technicians who make offset negatives or engravings to reproduce photographs.

THE NEWS DEPARTMENT

The news or editorial department is the one whose operation is covered by this book. While the publisher, holding the dual title of editor, technically heads this department, he does not deal with day-to-day operations in the news department. This task is performed by the managing editor.

Figure 4–1, showing the organization of a daily newspaper, depicts the operations of a medium to large publication (75,000 to 200,000 circulation). On larger newspapers, there would be a larger division of duties, with numerous assistant editors assisting in directing the staff. On a small newspaper (5,000 or less circulation), all duties on the chart could be supervised by a city editor, a society editor, and a wire editor, who together would share only one reporter.

Principal Editors. On larger newspapers, the key news executives are (1) the city editor, directing reporters covering activities in the newspaper's primary circulation area; (2) the wire editor, coordinating news received over the wires of Associated Press, United Press International, or other news services; (3) the sports editor, directing local sports coverage and selecting sports news received from wire services; (4) the editorial page editors, direct-ing editorial writing and the selection of letters to the editor and political cartoons; (5) the state or regional editor, supervising correspondents working for the newspaper in areas more distant from the plant; and (6) the society or women's editor, handling social or family-oriented news.

In regard to "women's" sections, it should be noted that this field of reporting and editing has changed immensely in the past few years. Traditional social events are becoming secondary in importance to news of greater interest to liberated and better-educated women, and many newspapers, particularly the larger ones, are changing the names of these sections to reflect the deeper appeal. Smaller newspapers tend to follow suit, but make the changes more slowly. These trends are discussed in Chapter 21.

Other Editors. Those also occupying important positions in producing a newspaper include (1) the chief copy editor, directing the copyreaders who edit stories and write headlines; (2) the make-up editor, coordinating the newsroom with the mechanical department; (3) special section editors producing Sunday supplements, television guides, home magazines, and special sections; and (4) department editors, who direct coverage of fields such as aerospace, finance, gardening, theater, automobiles, book reviews, and real estate.

Reporters. The newsroom staff member with whom the public is the most familiar is the reporter, who indeed is the backbone of editorial operations. Several types of reporters, or writers, serve on a typical staff. They include (1) the beat reporter, assigned to cover a particular "beat" or place such as a police station, school board, theater row, court house, city council, or other regular source of news; (2) the general assignment reporter, who waits in the newspaper office for news breaks such as speeches, interviews with visiting celebrities, a development relayed by a beat reporter, or other activities that may occur; (3) the special assignment reporter, who may be given a specific assignment to conduct an investigation or develop a series of articles; and (4) the rewrite reporter, whose duties include

Figure 4–2 News wire services provide newspapers with regional, state, national, and international news. This 1952 photo shows the Paris bureau of Associated Press. Reporters, copyreaders, and an editor confer while operators transmit news via teletypes. (Wide World Photos)

Figure 4–3 Here is the newsroom of the *Chicago Tribune*, one of America's major newspapers. Walking in the aisle at the right is Tom Jones, staff member who won a 1971 Pulitzer Prize. (*Chicago Tribune* Photo)

(*a*) taking notes from another reporter over the phone and writing a story, (*b*) rewriting another reporter's poorly written story, or (*c*) writing news stories based on material brought or sent to the office by a public relations counsel or club publicity officers.

Reporters frequently interchange jobs because of vacancies, promotions, illnesses, or other factors. Many journalists—particularly the most skilled and successful—are qualified to do several types of reporting, although on the larger newspapers writers are more apt to be specialized than on smaller ones where a reporter performs overlapping tasks.

Developments in Reporting. Changing times bring exciting new things to write about. More emphasis is being placed on the "investigative" reporter, who painstakingly probes neglected records and forgotten witnesses to produce stories which often are of national or international consequence. The reporter, trained in the natural and social sciences, who handles stories dealing with ecology finds himself in one of the newest and most important fields of journalism. More and more newspapers are adding ecology reporters as readers continue to express concern over ways to protect the environment.

Two other rapidly developing areas of specialized reporting are those of urban affairs and minority relations, two closely allied inter-est fields. Reporters can achieve a great deal of personal satisfaction and feelings of accomplishment by translating, to the public, efforts for urban renewal and programs for alleviating community tensions. Newspapers, particularly those serving large cities where problems are the greatest, find that reporters specializing in such coverage make story situations more viable.

Consumerism is another growing field of specialization for the reporter interested in in-

Figure 4–4 A technician examines a paper printed by offset, which utilizes a photographic process. Note the lightweight aluminum printing plate on the machine; below it is the rubber plate which transfers the image to paper. (Harris-Seybold Co. Photo)

Figure 4–5   Most sections of a newspaper occupy one large room, where staff members work as a team, as shown in this view of the newsroom of the *Des Moines* (Iowa) *Tribune*. The news editor is in the foreground, with the city editor to the right and the wire editor in the slot behind the news editor. In rear of the picture is the women's department and to its left are the farm and sports departments. Reporters' desks are out of view. (*Des Moines Register and Tribune* Photo)

Figure 4–6   This scene of the newsroom of the *Des Moines* (Iowa) *Tribune* shows the wire editor in the "slot," while around the "rim" are the copyreaders who write headlines and edit copy. Left, a reporter and copyreader discuss a story with a city editor. (*Des Moines Register and Tribune* Photo)

terpreting the battles of consumers. This field of reporting has developed greatly since Ralph Nader made consumers aware of their power.

Other Positions. Miscellaneous jobs in the news department include (1) photographers; (2) artists who draw cartoons and retouch photos; (3) copy boys or girls, who usually are men or women in their early twenties who run errands and sometimes progress to reportorial positions; (4) columnists, who on a full-time or part-time basis may write daily or weekly columns; and (5) darkroom technicians, who process photographs and frequently are training to be photographers.

"Combination men" is the term used to identify men and women who double as reporters and photographers on the smaller newspapers. They are usually people who basically are reporters, but have learned to take pictures. The larger newspapers use reporter-photographer combinations in fringe areas where the news volume does not justify assigning a reporter and a photographer.

Climbing the Ladder. Many reporters are content to remain reporters and have no aspirations to be editors because of the many challenges found in reporting and writing. The normal routine for those who wish to advance is to become a copyreader, a job frequently available to a reporter who has shown the ability to follow the stylebook, check facts, organize stories well, use imagination, and achieve fairness. Copyreaders may move on to become assistant city editors or full editors. Old movies frequently depict reporters as drinking heavily and changing newspaper jobs often. This, *if* possibly true at one time, is no longer accurate. Journalism is a career calling, and most newspaper men are sober individuals who remain for years at one newspaper.

The question arises regarding which positions in a news department are the best. No one can give a single answer to this question, because there are so many types of people. The best position is the one that gives the journalist the most pleasure.

Figure 4–7 Newspaper production requires increasingly sophisticated mechanical equipment. This row of presses not only prints the newspaper but folds it in sections. (*Rochester Times-Union and Democrat and Chronicle* Photo)

Figure 4–8 A craftsman composing a newspaper page with photographic negatives, which take the place of lead in offset printing. (Panax Corporation Photo)

Figure 4–10 Mattie Greene, a general assignment reporter for the *Detroit News*, discusses a story with John Gill, a copyreader. Unlike the "beat" reporter responsible for a single area, general assignment reporters cover a variety of happenings.

Figure 4–9 The newsroom at the *Los Angeles Times*, with clocks reporting the time in various parts of the world to help accuracy in stories. Note that each desk has a bottle of glue, used to paste stories together.

Figure 4–11 The newspaper "morgue" or library is a valuable resource for journalists and contains clippings and photographs. Here is librarian Carole Doby of the *Fort Worth Star-Telegram*.

Figure 4–12 Leon Dash, reporter for the *Washington Post*, completes a story. Note his telephone with buttons to make calls quickly over various lines or transfer calls to other staff members. (Photo by Ken Feil)

Figure 4–14 Jim Jones, reporter for the *Minneapolis Star*, checks a story he has just written. In the background are the rows of desks typical of newsrooms.

Figure 4–13 Staff members with various skills work together in newsrooms. Dorothy Jurney, assistant managing editor of the *Detroit Free Press*, confers with Jon Buechel, a staff artist. (*Free Press* Photo by chief photographer Tony Spina)

Figure 4–15 An innovation for newspapers during recent years has been the ombudsman, who serves as a liaison between the publication and its readers. This is Robert Maynard, former associate editor of the *Washington Post*, who became its ombudsman.

SMALLER NEWSPAPERS

Newspapers with smaller circulations are organized along the same basic lines as the larger ones. Many positions are combined, however, because the newspaper's smaller revenue and fewer pages will not warrant a large work force. Many beginning journalists prefer to start on small newspapers because of the diversity of experience offered, while on large publications each job may be so departmentalized that one will not have the opportunity to develop a wide range of skills.

Even though a newspaper is small, its reporters, editors, and photographers want to show pride and skill in their work. The journalist who fills a position well at a small paper will be able to apply those skills in doing good work at a larger newspaper.

EXERCISES

1. Most newspapers conduct plant tours. Contact your local newspaper to arrange a tour for an on-the-spot view of how a paper is produced.

2. Examine a current copy of *Editor &* *Publisher Yearbook*, available at a newspaper office or your public library. In the section listing editors, note the lengths of the entries for the newspapers with which you are familiar.

3. Invite an editor from a local newspaper to give a brief talk on the organization of his news staff.

4. Develop a news staff organization chart designed to make your campus newspaper operate with more efficiency.

5

The Contents of a Newspaper

The early American newspapers offered information pertaining to births, weddings, deaths, ship arrivals, crime, prices for crops, politics, taxes, and related items. Today's newspapers continue to provide such news, but in competing for audience attention against television, cablevision, motion pictures, and magazines, they entered another field: entertainment.

The news contents of a newspaper, of course, remains the vital part that persuades the reader to become a regular subscriber. The fringe offering of entertainment becomes larger in the newspapers with bigger circulations and consequently more pages.

THE INGREDIENTS OF A NEWSPAPER

Aside from advertising, the contents of a newspaper can be broken down into (1) entertainment features and (2) news stories. The latter cover a wide range of writing techniques and approaches.

ENTERTAINMENT FEATURES

Mixed with news items throughout a newspaper's pages are the entertainment features, which are a bonus to readers. These non-news features include comics, crosswords and other puzzles, cartoons, dress patterns, and columns on such specialized interests as chess, pets, astrology, child care, geriatrics, and photography.

Large newspapers can afford to have many such features produced by their staffs, but most dailies buy the material from syndicates that profit by selling to publications throughout the nation.

THE NEWS CONTENTS

The remaining and basic part of the newspaper, of course, is news. It can be characterized, categorized, divided, and described in a number of ways. One hears a great deal about "objectivity" pertaining to newspaper stories, but only a machine could truly be objective regarding news. The better phrasing would be that newspaper writers should endeavor to be "fair" in stories. Every news situation has several dimensions or sides, and the good reporter seeks to cover as many as possible.

THE THIRD PERSON IN NEWS

In writing news stories or feature articles, the third person reigns supreme. This means that the reporter *cannot* use such personal designations as "I" or "we," "my" or "our," "me" or "us," or similar references. This paramount rule comes from the journalist's traditional endeavor to be neutral; the insertion of "I" or other personal identifications into a story violates this effort. The use of personal designations also presumes that the reporter's name will be atop the story, and by-lines are the prerogatives of the editor and reserved for the articles he regards as best.

Exceptions to this rule are made in the rare cases of reporters who may be eye-witnesses or otherwise involved in important stories. Reporters, particularly those new to journalism, should not anticipate by-lines by inserting personal references in stories. Editors will advise when they feel a reporter should involve himself in a story by using "I."

Columns, which of course are not news stories but personal commentaries, are another exception to the rule of not using "I" or "we."

Although stories are written in the third person, this does not mean they should be devoid of feeling. The reporter can—and should—add drama, humor, pathos, and excitement to stories by quoting the source and citing relevant facts gathered while obtaining the story. The writer, in giving the facts fairly in an article, avoids making a value judgment as to whether the situation is good, bad, or indifferent. The skillful reporter will gather facts and assemble them in a story enabling the reader to evaluate and reach a decision.

"TIMELY" AND "TIMELESS" STORIES

News is a perishable commodity that must be given to the public while it is fresh, or it will be as useless as ice cream one forgets to put back in the refrigerator. This type of news is "timely," meaning the reader must consume it while still usable. For example, news of a play scheduled for 8:30 tonight must appear not later than in today's newspaper or it will be useless for those wishing to attend the performance. News of vital legislation passed by Congress or a city council is "timely" or ur-

Figure 5–1 "Tarzan," based on the books by Edgar Rice Burroughs, has been a comic strip favorite for decades. Here is writer-illustrator Russ Manning at work on the feature. (United Features Syndicate Photo)

Figure 5–2 William S. White writes his syndicated column on national and world affairs. Many newspapers use columnists presenting varying viewpoints to help readers shape perspectives. (United Features Syndicate Photo)

Figure 5–3 Syndicated comic strips are another phase of journalism. Vince Hamlin (left), creator of "Alley Oop," works with his assistant, Dave Graue. (Newspaper Enterprise Association Photo)

Figure 5–4 Stella Wilder is an example of a writer who provides a syndicated column to diversify a newspaper's contents. "Your Birthday" is a daily column on astrology. (United Features Syndicate Photo)

gent because readers want this information promptly.

Some news has a longer life and is therefore "timeless," or relatively so. The review of the play can be held for a day or two and remain of news value. Human interest stories involving a pet that can do unusual tricks or the person with a fascinating hobby also are examples of news situations that can be held for days or, in some cases, for weeks.

THE LEVELS OF NEWS

The relative importance of news, as decided by reporters and editors, determines *whether* a particular story is vital enough to be used and *where* it will appear in the newspaper. Journalists, weighing the value of news situations, subconsciously classify items as "hard" or "soft."

Hard News. Stories of primary or urgent importance rate the "hard" news classification. Examples would include articles concerning a key vote in the United Nations, Congress approving or rejecting controversial legislation, the police department breaking a crime ring, the city council approving a substantial tax increase or decrease, or plans for a facility that would greatly increase the quality of living in the newspaper's community. These situations would provide "must" stories that readers would *expect* to see.

Soft News. News of secondary importance is labeled "soft" news and might concern such items as a school or church social meeting, reports of minor crimes, a city council meeting that produced routine action, or a "human interest" story concerning a pet, hobby, personality sketch, or club activity. Such articles would lack great consequence and would be "optional" stories that readers probably would not miss if omitted.

While few people would debate the assignment of the "hard" news category to a tense or controversial international situation, there can be much disagreement over what constitutes important news at other levels. A battle for a baseball pennant can be "hard" news for a baseball fan but of little interest to one who does not follow the sport. A parents'

Figure 5–5 "Nancy" rates among the nation's highly popular comic strips. This is the strip's creator, Ernie Bushmiller, at work. (United Features Syndicate Photo)

Figure 5–6 Marv Myers, creator of "Zody," works alongside an example of his comic panel. (United Features Syndicate Photo)

meeting to discuss school problems will be of major importance for those involved in the turmoil but of no interest to those who have no children or reside in another neighborhood.

The referees who ultimately decide what is "hard" or "soft" news are the reporter, who decides what facts are worthy of placing in a story, and the editor, who selects the stories to be published.

TYPES OF REPORTING

Within the framework of "soft" or "hard" news, "timely" or "timeless" stories, and reporters who deal with beats, general assignments, or special assignments, there are different approaches for writing stories.

Objective News Writing. The journalist's traditional goal is to "just give the facts," or in other words produce "objective" stories presumably devoid of personal opinion or bias.

The "straight facts" story would exclude, in keeping with the traditions of objectivity, any explanations or opinions. In a story from the police beat, for example, the reporter would rely on the officers' report and make no effort to obtain auxiliary information. Stories, in effect, would deal only with basic and superficial information without "digging" for important dimensions. Here is a hypothetical example of an objective news story:

Mayor John Jones today proposed that the city finance construction of a $20 million resort hotel on the shore of Lake Pleasure and lease it to private interests. The City Council will consider the proposal at its next meeting.

Interpretative Reporting. A great deal has been written advocating "interpretative" reporting, but most good news stories of any consequence have been using this technique for years. Since reporters are human, it is virtually impossible for them to be "objective." They can, however, be fair and serve their readers better by gathering auxiliary—or "explanatory"—information for their stories. They thus "interpret" or explain a story situation. Readers, who obviously lack the time and ability for research, consequently are better informed. For a story involving the police, the officers' written report would be supplemented by *oral* interviews with the officers as well as the victims and the alleged wrongdoers. The hypothetical story of the mayor, too, could be projected to the "interpretative" level and would read something like this:

Mayor John Jones, whose family controls a hotel chain, today proposed city financing of a $20 million resort hotel on the shores of Lake Pleasure.

A similar proposal was defeated a year ago when City Council members determined Jones's company was the only firm interested in leasing the giant hotel.

Council members will consider the new proposal at their next meeting.

Campus newspapers are publications where interpretative reporting can and should be used frequently. An example of such journalism is illustrated by a hypothetical story involving a new method of grading. The "objective" article would provide facts regarding how grades would be assigned and the effective date of the new system. The skillful reporter, however, would produce an interpretative story with much greater depth and meaning by using information from a series of interviews: a college official commenting on the reason for the changes, teachers in regard to what the system would produce in the quality of classes, students discussing their expectations, and even representatives of other colleges where similar or radically different grade programs were used.

The reporter in such a story situation in a sense "manages" the direction or slant of the article, but he does so fairly in order that readers can more accurately interpret the news.

Another example of interpretative reporting at the college level is in the story dealing

with the student body budget. The "objective" article probably would list the organizations receiving funds and the amount of their allocation. A more meaningful story, however, would be the interpretative one comparing individual allocations to those of the previous two or three years to show whether pressures were at work, and to quote high points of arguments presented for or against giving the individual funds.

Digging into old newspaper files, checking legal documents, looking at lists of corporate directors, conducting interviews and asking questions—and then conducting more interviews and asking more questions—will provide the facts that let the reporter "interpret" or explain.

While some journalists speak of "interpretative" reporting as a recent development, it is a technique used for years by reporters motivated and obligated to explain a situation. Modern journalism, serving an increasingly intelligent audience, relies heavily on interpretative reporting as a replacement for the "objective" facts which, when offered alone, can be confusing.

Advocacy Reporting. Some journalists also regard "advocate" reporting as an innovation, but it actually began when politically oriented editors "advocated" a particular party or candidate. For years, newspapers have advocated changes in tax laws, more industry for their communities, less smog, or solutions to pressing urban problems. "Advocacy," usually referring to pressing a point in the *news* column instead of in an *editorial*, has been a part of newspapers for many years.

Two factors, however, have brought increased focus on advocacy reporting in recent years. The first has been the use of advocacy writing in the underground and antiestablishment newspapers as they seek to correct social injustices ignored by the traditional media. The other has been the fact that conventional newspapers have given staff members more freedom in personal advocacy.

The most dedicated proponents of advocate reporting—who can be found on the extreme right as well as the extreme left—require the writer to abandon all pretense of

EDITORIAL

School principal must be powerful figure

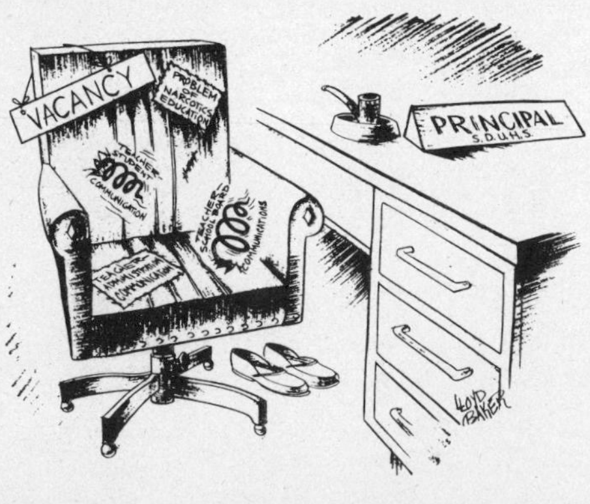

The Not-So-Easy Chair!

Fact: Dr. John Clark has resigned his position as principal of San Dieguito High School.

Fact: San Dieguito High School District board of trustees must act within the next several weeks to find a suitable replacement.

Fact: High school principals must be tough birds to survive these days.

Clark has done a commendable job as principal, but in the time he has been in San Dieguito, the area has begun a transition from rural to (pardon the word) suburban. Things have changed, people have changed, philosophies of education have changed.

Nobody stays in one place forever if he is to consider his life a success. John Clark feels a need to explore other facets of the educational process.

But who will be his successor?

Who will deal with the types of problems school principals face in these changing times? The new principal will naturally have to be a good administrator. He must advise others in choosing the best curriculum possible.

The new principal will also have to be aware of student problems and be able to deal with them effectively.

There have been charges that Clark is leaving because of student unrest at the school. The board tells us, however Clark's intentions were known before recent controversial student body elections.

Reasons why Clark has chosen the end of this year to end his association with San Dieguito High School District are not of great concern.

The concern expressed by students, parents and teachers should be directed toward selection of Clark's replacement.

School trustees will have to make a choice before this summer in order to allow enough preparation time for the new man. There will be criticism from quarters to the extent that the board should wait until after the election April 15 which will determine new board makeup and then wait until the new board is seated July 1.

The district doesn't have that kind of waiting time. The principal must be selected before July 1 to insure enough preparation time for the fall semester.

Principals are dealing these days with the types of problems which involve far more than watching the students at milk break or developing curriculum or advising the superintendent on policy matters or talking with student leaders or working with teachers.

The principal must be tough, ready to take criticism, equally ready to give constructive criticism. He must work with students to determine their needs and wants and then have the courage to set reasonable limits on student action in the classroom and on campus in general.

School trustees must look for a powerful figure, one with the ability to communicate as effectively with his teaching staff and students as he does with the school board and superintendent.

Finding such a person will be a difficult task at best, but it must be done.

The role of the principal has changed because the roles of the school board, teacher and student have changed in recent times.

Education is the best tool we have to offer to the youth in this nation. Educators, therefore, must be able to provide that education as best they can.

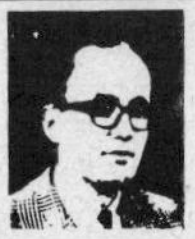

THE EDITOR'S DESK

(Editor Bruce Dillon comments on events of the past week in the San Dieguito area.)

Bond Proposal: Little To Gain

A proposal for a bond election in San Dieguito Irrigation District for "immediate" action on replacing worn pipeline isn't necessary.

Supporters believe a bond action would reduce water rates; result in a better overall construction job; bring a better system into service faster than current plans would indicate.

There is, however, little proof to substantiate any assertion that the bond proposal, if approved, would be more beneficial to the majority of district residents than present plans of the district to replace the pipelines within the next four and a half years.

This really is what must be considered — whether a bond proposal to get the work done in a shorter period of time (in reality probably as little as two years shorter) would be most beneficial to the majority of water users in the district. We don't agree that the bond proposal would benefit the majority and therefore oppose it.

It should be pointed out that Dr. L. Wainwright, a district resident, has spent months working on a plan which he believes in the best interests of the people. His work is an example of public interest and concern often lacking in San Dieguito.

The proposal would mean interest paid over a 30-year period; a special bond election and necessity of establishing the mechanics to put through a bond election which takes time.

San Dieguito Irrigation District water users are being asked if they favor a bond election at this time. SDID board members will then study the results of that poll and decide if an election should be held. In this case, a bond election will not mean gaining something otherwise impossible to get.

The pipelines will be replaced without a bond election in as little as three years but no more than four and a half years. The saving of time by holding a bond election will not amount to very much and the interest paid over a 30-year period on bonds will undoubtedly exceed any saving on materials.

The best interests of the majority of district residents must be kept in mind. Quite a few residents will be here for a long time and a bond proposal as outlined would serve only short term residents.

More On Moonlight

Encinitas Chamber of Commerce has taken up the challenge issued by Coast Dispatch for getting some action on Moonlight Beach. Chamber directors agree with us that the state must get off the dime and start work instead of constantly delaying the project.

Supposedly, improvement work is now scheduled to start in October on the first phase which will include construction of lifeguard towers, restrooms and restoring the beach area.

Can the state keep its promise and get the project going instead of stalling? We will know the answer to that question in October. In the meantime, pressure should be applied to insure an October starting date.

Bouquet For Fire Department

San Diego County Fire Chiefs' Association has thanked Encinitas Fire Protection District for providing flowers for an installation dinner recently. Any method of advertising the San Dieguito area is valuable.

Keep Cool, Real Cool

Plans are currently being formulated by a steering committee representing all major community elements for discussion which may lead to a study of possible incorporation of the San Dieguito area.

It would be foolish at this time to sample public opinion on the subject. The question: Do You Favor Incorporation?" would, at this point, bring an uneducated "yes" or "no" answer.

It's only common sense that the steering committee should proceed with determining the feasibility of such a study; that if such a study is fundable, it should be made; that the people then be contacted for reaction to factual unbiased information and that after all of this, direction for the area be recognized for whatever it turns out to be.

In short, keep cool. Don't start old fights. Wait until you are able to make an educated statement based on a report made by an unbiased, outside firm skilled in studying unincorporated areas.

Coast Dispatch

1968
PRIZE-WINNING NEWSPAPER of the CALIFORNIA NEWSPAPER PUBLISHERS ASSOCIATION

ARCHIE J HICKS, JR., Publisher
BRUCE DILLON, Editor
PAUL MARSHALL, Advertising Mgr.

Second and F Streets
Encinitas, California
Telephone 753-6543

Entered as second class matter Feb. 19, 1925, at the post office at Encinitas, California, under the Act of March 3, 1879

Decreed a legal newspaper of general circulation by the Superior Court of San Diego County, Calif., Feb. 19, 1932 · No. 70135

ISSUED EVERY THURSDAY AT ENCINITAS, SAN DIEGO COUNTY, CALIFORNIA

Subscription Rates — Payable in Advance
LOCAL
Mail — $5.00 year Mail — $4.00 six mos.
OUTSIDE SAN DIEGO COUNTY
One Year — $5.50 Six Months — $4.50

AAUW survey results given

(The following survey was taken by American Association of University Women and is presented as a public service to our readers.)

The AAUW community survey of attitudes toward elementary school education was taken between the months of June and September 1968. Twenty-one poll-takers did door-to-door surveying in 23 prescribed areas of Solana Beach proper plus the outlying areas of Marine View, Montecillo, and Sun Valley. The object of this survey was to obtain a comprehensive view of community attitudes toward the expanding needs of our growing school system.

AAUW interviewers received replies from 446 Solana Beach households. These families were raising a total of 817 children: 19% at the pre-school level, 46% at the elementary level, 26% at the secondary level, and 9% in the undesignated status. The age distribution of the adults answering the questionnaire was as follows:

20-30, 14% 40-50, 28% over 65, 7%
30-40, 36% 50-65, 15%

(Pollsters experienced some reluctance among older people to answer the survey on the grounds they were too far removed from the educational experience; therefore the over 65 category may not reflect true population percentage.)

The distribution of occupations among those answering the surveys was as follows:

Housewife, 33%
School affiliated, 7%
Professional, 13%
Business, 7%
Skilled worker, 7%
Nonskilled worker, 2%
Retired, 5%
Military, 1%
Unspecified, 25%

Question 1

Responders to the questionnaire indicated their preferences for additional school space as follows: A **library** was heavily preferred, followed by a **cafetorium**, followed closely by a **multi-purpose room**, followed by other (undesignated); trailing substanially was a **music room**.

Questions 2 and 3

Given a list of special programs, responders checked those programs they had heard of and indicated those programs they felt important, as follows:

Program	Heard of	Important
Compensatory Education	44%	56%
Educable Mentally Retarded	77%	79%
Elementary Guidance Counselling	57%	57%
English as a Second Language	49%	63%
Instrumental Music	78%	51%
Mentally Gifted	62%	69%
Neurologically Handicapped	36%	53%
Physically Handicapped	49%	58%
Remedial Reading	64%	81%
Speech and Hearing Therapy	68%	74%
Vocal Instruction	60%	41%

Opinion Page

4 — Coast Dispatch, Thursday, February 27, 1969

LETTERS TO EDITOR

Need for SDID bond argued by reader

(Letters To The Editor are invited but must be brief and to the point. Unsigned letters won't be printed under any circumstances since the editor feels those expressing an opinion must be willing to stand behind letters with a signature. Letters should be typed and will be used on a space available basis.)

Editor,

As regards the proposed water bonds, many people who are considering the advisability of supporting them are afraid that the bonds would mean higher taxes. This is not true at all. While the bonds would be technically "general obligation," the kind carrying the most favorable interest rate, they would be repaid from revenues. They would thus be tantamount to "revenue" bonds. So far as higher taxes go, the SDID recently reduced its tax rate from $1.66 per $100 assessed value to $1.50, and there is no indication whatever that there will be an increase in the foreseeable future. This case is quite distinct from school bonds, for schools have no revenue for repaying their bonds.

Your front page article last week, "Residents must decide if water district needs bond election," besides quoting from the inquiry which the district is now mailing along with our individual bills, devotes a majority of its space to information attributed to Mr. Stanley T. Mills, SDID Manager. Much of this information needs to be considered very critically to avoid its giving a false impression, an impression that the proposed bond issue with the resulting piping repair will be a slow and unduly expensive operation. Actually, given competent management, the bonding of the costs with early completion of the work by contract, will be quicker, cheaper, and better.

The times which Mr. Mills gives are definitely on the pessimistic side, and he fails to consider that some of them can run concurrently. In other words, some of his time estimates are high, and the several steps which he lists do not all need to follow in turn; some of the steps can proceed together. Overall, he sees it taking about a year to do the bonding and have the work completed. Realistically, the whole operation should be finished well before year's end, if it is pursued with proficiency and alacrity. Who wants to wait even three years for decent water service or smaller bills? Bonding would definitely get the job done quicker.

Bonding would also get the job done cheaper. Handled as a complete package, not on a piecemeal basis, there would unquestionably be economies materials and in labor.

L. Wainwright
Encinitas

Editor,

The reappointment of Herbert Marcuse for another year at the University of California at San Diego meets with the high disapproval of the Encinitas Republican Assembly.

Taxpayers should not be expected to support an institution which persists in hiring instructors such as Marcuse. The Chancellor offers only the thin excuse that this will be the last year of extension of his services; in our viewpoint even one more year of poison to our students is intolerable.

Therefore be it resolved that the Encinitas Republican Assembly is unalterably opposed to the extension given to Herbert Marcuse and demands that the Legislature act in deleting from the budget, the amount necessary to finance Marcuse on the University of California, San Diego Campus for another year.

Phyllis E. Lorang
President
Encinitas Republican Assembly

Figure 5–7 The newspaper also presents an editorial or opinion page. This one has an editorial (top), comments on events by the editor (left), a report from another publication (center), and letters to the editor.

objectivity as he presses for a particular side. Proponents of this approach would make no attempts at fairness, emphasizing only the information that fortifies their stand. A police beat story would be handled by the "advocate" reporter according to his persuasion: the police or accused viewpoints, depending on the writer, would be given to the detriment of the other side. Projecting the "advocate" approach to the hypothetical story regarding the mayor, the article might read like this:

Mayor John Jones again is pressuring the city into financing a $20 million hotel which no one wants but his family—and it would probably lease the building for almost nothing at the expense of the taxpayers.

Jones apparently didn't get the message last year when the City Council laughed at his scheme to build by Lake Pleasure and is again seeking to bamboozle the city fathers into contributing money for a hotel.

Advocacy reporting, while widely and effectively used in antiestablishment newspapers of varying persuasions, has yet to gain any degree of acceptance by dailies except in rare instances.

The "New" Journalism. Many practicing journalists are unable to agree on a definition for the New Journalism, but in varying forms it is becoming a part of the reportorial scene.

Figure 5–8 Syndicate-distributed comic panels add interest to newspapers. Jim Berry, creator of "Berry's World," pauses during his work. (Newspaper Enterprise Association Photo)

One of its forms was the book *In Cold Blood*, in which author Truman Capote used fiction techniques to recount a tragic murder case in great detail.

A second application of the New Journalism uses a different form of fiction techniques to present news situations. For example, assume that a story involved the rehabilitation of paroled convicts. The traditional way of handling the article would be to present the material, either (1) identifying the convict by his real name, (2) using initials to protect the subject from public contempt, or (3) explaining that a fictitious name was substituted. The "new" technique typically would be to consolidate experiences of several convicts and tell the story with one fictitious name—without advising the reader that it was being done. This method often gives more "punch" to an article and gives the reporter more freedom for the dramatic than if he were dealing only with facts.

This application of the "new" has been used for years by newspapers and magazines. It is moving into the spotlight as an "innovation" only because it is being used more often and frequently with more impact and writing skill.

A third technique of the New Journalism also has been used for years: the involvement of the reporter himself in a news event. Elizabeth (Nellie Bly) Cochran was practicing the New Journalism in the 1890s when she pretended insanity to get committed to Blackwell's Island for an exposé published in the New York *World*. Modern journalists involve themselves in stories by assuming disguises or masking their identity to infiltrate secret organizations, to test antidiscrimination laws, to determine the honesty of public officials, or to measure the way members of the general public *really* are treated when dealing with public or private bureaucrats.

Practitioners also apply the label of New Journalism to almost any other technique—old or new—which departs from traditional handling of the news. Pages devoted exclusively to photographs or free-hand art, sections devoted entirely to letters from readers, presentations of lengthy pro and con articles by dis-

Figure 5-9 "Why Subscribe?" This mail carrier takes a break in a mail storage box—and provides a photographer with a picture that helps the newspaper give a light touch along with the day's serious news. (*Oakland Tribune* Photo by Lonnie Wilson)

sidents of the right or left, or departures from news into poetry and fiction also have been labeled as examples of the New Journalism.

Journalism really is always "new," with innovations becoming traditions which eventually must be broken to make way for new developments that meet the public's always growing and changing tastes.

EDITORIALS AND COLUMNS

Two other areas that belong in the news category are editorial and column writing. Editorials are the opinions of the newspaper management regarding situations that have been aired in news stories, and columns are regular contributions by an individual.

The editorial "we," indicating the collective opinion of the newspaper, often is used in editorials. While some columnists prefer to

write in the third person, many prefer to use "I" or a poetic "we" to add a personal feeling to their material.

A REVIEW OF THE WRITING FORMS

A single news situation would inspire varied approaches according to writing styles. Here is what might be expected with the announcement that the Soviet premier planned to visit the United States:

The objective news writer would confine the story to the information that the premier planned a visit and would provide available details pertaining to the dates and itinerary.

The interpretative reporter would supplement the basic information of the projected visit with background data drawn from Russian-American experts on what the tour might mean to international relations.

Figure 5–10 Writing a column is a much sought-after position because of the latitude and recognition coming with the job. Mrs. Novella Williams presents a Citizens for Progress Award to Claude Lewis, columnist for the *Philadelphia Bulletin*.

The advocate reporter would write an outspoken news story lauding or condemning, according to personal feeling, the proposed visit.

The editorial writer would produce a contribution weighing the relative values of the trip, concluding with an opinion as to whether the visit would or would not accomplish its goals.

The columnist would have leeway to handle the situation in a number of ways: a satire of how the premier might tour America as an average traveler; recollections of people who traveled to Russia; comments on the expectations of the visit, perhaps with background information on tours by foreign officials.

EXERCISES

Using a copy of your local newspaper, find examples of the following:

1. "Soft" and "hard" news stories, by standards suitable for readers in your community.

2. An editorial.

3. "Timely" and "timeless" stories.

4. Objective, interpretative, and advocate news stories; if you are unable to find examples of the latter in your regular newspaper, check others.

5. An "entertainment" feature.

6

What Is News?

One exercise that professors and editors often give prospective journalists calls for providing an answer to the question, "What is news?" Such exercises are excellent for developing an awareness of news, which has many definitions. News has dimensions and perspectives according to time, place, type of publication, and interests of the audience.

Dictionary definitions say that news is something "new and notable," but it is difficult to agree on what really is "new" or "notable" for different audiences. For example, the election of five new city council members in New York City obviously would hold great interest to readers there who watched hotly contested races, but people in Los Angeles wouldn't even recognize the names of the winners. Instead, they would expect to read about victors in elections for Los Angeles city offices.

You would be interested in reading the news of your neighbor getting married, but you would hardly be interested in a list of brides and bridegrooms from a city miles away.

Neighbors instinctively would smile at the couple down the street celebrating 50 years of marriage and nod in approval when a paragraph on the social pages noted the anniversary.

Everyone would expect front page coverage, however, of the episode involving the newlyweds who argued so furiously that they proceeded to settle their dispute with guns.

News, in a great sense, is the breakdown of human relationships and the occurrence of events which are unexpected and even surprising.

Journalists, who are decent human beings, dislike to see tragedies occur, but they must be ready to report such events when they do happen.

Most people are law-abiding, well-adjusted, and happy and enjoy seeing good things happen to others. Yet these people will pass "good news" items in their papers to dwell on stories reporting the breakdowns and tragedies of society.

THE INGREDIENTS OF NEWS

Numerous factors affect what can be called "news." Seasoned journalists would never consciously attempt to classify news by categories, even though they do so automatically as they gather and write stories. They frequently, however, compile lists to help aspiring reporters recognize the ingredients of news. Here is one such list.

PROXIMITY

The geographic nearness or distance of an event can make a story more or less attractive to the reader. People like to read about what is near them. The city council increases taxes in the community where the reader resides. Naturally, the reader wants this news because of the effect on his pocketbook. Such action is hardly news to people in a town miles away whose homes are not covered by the increase. A tragic auto accident in the reader's community will receive attention because subscribers are familiar with the terrain and may even know the injured. An accident in another state would hold little interest because few readers would know the area.

In a weekly or neighborhood newspaper, the factor of proximity may narrow the scope of stories holding readership attraction. Editors may emphasize articles regarding nearby schools, churches, clubs, and political events, knowing they are meaningful to readers, while occurrences a few miles away are meaningless.

SELF-IDENTIFICATION

Closely allied to proximity as a news value is the factor of self-identification, or the impact that a development will have personally on the individual. The news of a property tax boost is of primary concern to the property owner who must pay it and of secondary interest to the person who owns no property. News of farm prices would find high readership in an agricultural region but would attract little attention in an industrial community. Families with children would carefully read story situations concerning half-day sessions or reduced school services, while those without youngsters would be less concerned. The wealthy individual would focus his attention on the article reporting income tax increases for those in the upper brackets, while the person without a job would give bare notice to the story.

The story situations logically might have eventual meaning for all levels of readers: the property tax boosts could cause rent increases, the farm prices might be reflected at the grocery store, reduced school services might bring a demand for more taxes, and the income tax increases could result in a change in economic factors affecting job potentials.

The fact of the situation, of course, is that people read news with emotion instead of logic.

PROMINENCE

Names always make news, but stories about well-known people have a higher readership than those about persons in the rank and file. When a teller in a local bank sprains her ankle, friends may express condolences—but the injury is not news. If the star of the nation's No. 1 television program injures her ankle, newspapers will note the event, even though briefly, because of her fans' interest. If the President of the United States plays a round of golf or visits a church, his high office elevates the event to newsworthiness.

People who are prominent or well known locally also rate coverage in the community newspaper. The episode of the mayor who elopes with his secretary is of interest to his constituents. The pastor awarded a church promotion is probably well known to community members outside of his congregation. Last year's high school football star remains a notable worthy of a news story when he wins a college scholarship. The schoolteacher who is known to hundreds of students and parents will rate a news story when she retires after years of service, while the instructor who resigns after only a year will not.

Some dimensions of the prominence factor will lap over to "proximity" values. A mayor or businessman may be a notable in his own community but unknown and therefore of no news value in a city a few miles away.

CONSEQUENCE

One important duty of journalists is to keep readers advised on matters of consequence and importance that are developing around them. For example, if a large college announces that tuition fees will be doubled and enrollment is expected to drop one-third, there are consequences for prospective students, society, the faculty, and a community whose economy may be geared to the education. A pending strike may affect not only the involved workers but also the supply and prices of vital goods.

The daily weather reports, so often taken for granted, are consequential for their effect on environment, business, fuel consumption, and leisure activities. News of medical or scientific advancements is of great consequence because of the hope they offer.

News of Washington, D.C., is of immense consequence to readers throughout the world as officials deal with war, peace, justice, aid, monetary problems, and so many other things. Similarly, legislators in every state and community are dealing with important matters that people expect to know about.

DISASTER AND PROGRESS

Two important news values, disaster and progress, are at opposite ends of the scale. With human psychology as it is, disaster or *bad* news usually triumphs over progress or *good* news. When an earthquake rocks a city, newspapers devote pages to stories and pictures describing the loss of lives and property. An explosion rips a building, and readers eagerly consume the news stories detailing the tragedy. By contrast, plans to build a skyscraper or the dedication of an important flood control project rate relatively small space and only passing reader interest. One factor, of course, in many "good news" stories is the lack of human elements that help develop emotional involvement.

The "bad" news, unfortunately, usually outdraws the positive in exciting reader interest. While the public complains that editors overemphasize news with negative or violent overtones, few people would bother to read the publication that failed to print the news of society's efforts and failures in minority relations, war and peace, fighting poverty, or slowing the crime rate.

A few "progress" stories manage to capture headlines and readers' attention. Among the "good news" situations that received immense readership were Charles Lindbergh's flight over the Atlantic in 1927, Jonas Salk's development of polio vaccine in 1953, the U.S. Supreme Court's decision for desegregation in 1954, and the landing of the American astronauts on the moon in 1968. Some positive aspects of the latter two stories were marred, respectively, by resistance to enforcement and controversies over the wisdom of using funds for space programs in view of widespread poverty.

Most readers will skip the 20-inch story telling how 2,000 young men and women successfully completed high school and earned diplomas to read the 10-inch article reporting that 20 youngsters were arrested for using narcotics. Few people will read the article on how the community welfare organization uses contributions to help the needy, but virtually all readers will eagerly consume details of how the agency's trusted executive embezzled funds. The article reporting how someone provided parties for invalid children will rate little space or readership compared to the story situation involving a person on trial for sex crimes.

Readers expect the news of tragedies, disasters, violence, and breakdowns in human relationships.

Journalists, too, wish the world were filled with good news and that their audiences wanted to hear about it.

CONFLICT

The element of conflict is present in many daily situations: sports events, elections, debates, control of a corporation, and arguments among legislators at the national, state, or local levels, for example. Conflict exists when an individual attempts to scale a forbidding mountain or brave nature by crossing the ocean in a small vessel.

People identify with the personalities or issues involved in conflicts and want to know about them. One of America's biggest "conflicts" comes every four years with the Presidential election. Try to imagine news stories and the level of reader interest if one person were running for the office without competi-

WINDY, RAIN
Freeze warning tonight! Warm and showers today, clearing and much colder tonight. High today 70, low tonight 30, high Thursday 57. Southerly winds, 10 to 15, changing to northwesterly tonight.

Tallahassee Democrat

Wednesday Afternoon

64th Year, No. 320 — 80 Pages | Florida's Capital Newspaper | ★ ★ ★ Wednesday, November 19, 1969 10 Cents

U.S. Scores Moon Bull's-Eye

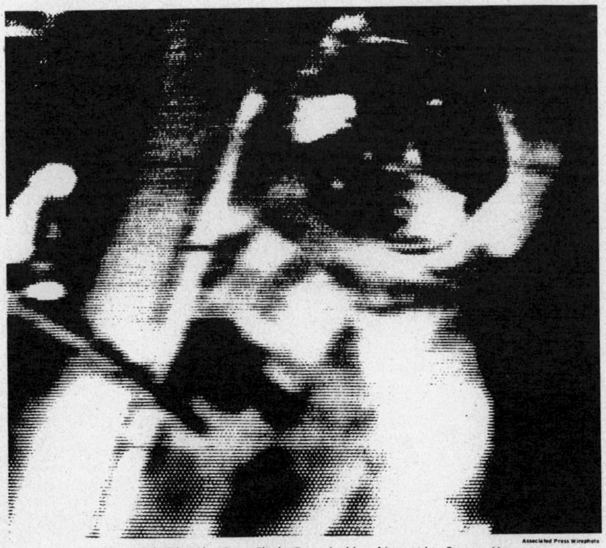

Associated Press Wirephoto

Lunar Module Pilot Alan Bean Climbs Down Ladder of Intrepid to Step on Moon
. . . he joins Commander Charles 'Pete' Conrad on second walk of discovery

Apollo Men Take Walk In Replay

By HOWARD BENEDICT

SPACE CENTER, Houston (AP) — Two American astronauts made a bull's-eye landing on the moon today, raised their nation's flag and explored a cratered surface covered with black, powdery dust.

Charles "Pete" Conrad Jr. and Alan L. Bean became the third and fourth humans to trod the moon as they carried man's quest for knowledge to that alien soil for a second time.

They steered their lunar ferry Intrepid to a perfect landing just 20 feet from the edge of their target crater at 1:54:29 a.m. EST. Just 600 feet away rests an unmanned Surveyor spacecraft that soft-landed in the crater 2½ years ago.

Conrad and Bean reported the dust in the Ocean of Storms was thicker and blacker than that in the Sea of Tranquillity where the first moon explorers landed in July.

"Your boots dig into the soil quite a bit," Bean said. "If you don't pick up your feet you really kick a load of dirt in front of you."

★ ★ ★

THEY ROAMED several hundred feet from Intrepid to explore and to set up a set of five sophisticated scientific instruments to measure such things as the solar wind, moonquakes and the moon's atmosphere and ionosphere.

To power the instruments they implanted the first nuclear generator on the surface, a unit which required delicate handling because of its hot radioactive element.

But there were early problems.

The first color television camera carried to the moon flopped after 45 minutes, and earthlings received only brief glimpses of Conrad and Bean as they moved about the alien world a white ghostly figures.

The camera did record the first steps of both on the powdery surface. Commander Conrad's first words as he placed his 13-inch boot in the soil were: "That may have been a small one for Neil, but that's a long one for me."

He referred jokingly to Neil Armstrong's first words last July when he became the first man to step on the moon: "That's one small step for a man, one giant leap for mankind."

While ground experts studied the problem, the astronauts abandoned the camera to continue their exploration.

The third member of the expedition, Richard F. Gordon Jr., orbited some 65 miles overhead, awaiting the return of his companions on Thursday after they complete 314 hours on the surface.

They were overjoyed at the landing spot, as they wondered at a variety of geological formations surrounding them.

★ ★ ★

"WE COULDN'T have picked a better spot," Conrad reported. "We could play geologists all day and we would get no farther than we are now."

The commander noted a strange-looking mound, and commented excitedly: "I've got to photograph this thing. I can't imagine what it is. There's this big mound sticking up about 300 feet at the foot of a shallow crater on the right-hand edge of the head crater. This is fantastic."

He later reported it looked like a small volcanic formation.

Twice they used a hammer to solve minor problems.

When Bean had trouble driving a tube into the ground to collect a soil sample from beneath the surface, he pounded it with a hammer.

"That's skilled craftmanship," he quipped.

Later, he had difficulty removing a canister containing the radioactive element, Pluto-

(Continued on Page 16)

Oh Well— It's Same Temperature

SPACE CENTER, Houston (UPI) — The Temperature in the arid lunar Ocean of Storms was about the same today when Alan L. Bean and Charles "Pete" Conrad landed as it was for Neil A. Armstrong and Edwin E. "Buzz" Aldrin in July.

Lunar temperatures are measured by surface heat and the figures today were the same because the sun angle was the same at the Ocean of Storms as it was three months ago in the Sea of Tranquillity when Apollo 11 set down.

But, it will be warmer when Apollo 12 leaves the moon than it was for Apollo 11, because Apollo 12 will stay longer, giving the sun more time to heat the lunar surface.

The surface temperature was between 40 and 50 degrees on landing and the sun was at an angle of 15.5 degrees. It will bbe near 100 degrees when Conrad and Bean leave the lunar surface.

I Declare!

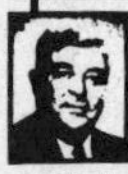

By Malcolm Johnson

A Color Book For the Snobs

Out of the mail, for publicity purposes, comes a "Spiro T. Agnew Coloring Book" which pretty well proves the Vice President was right when he referred to an "effete corps of impudent snobs who characterize themselves, as intellectuals."

It is about as effete and snobbish a collection of gags about the Vice President, the President, their wives and such American symbols as the city policemen and the National Guard as you could find.

In black and white, with a little package of crayons attached, it invites the intellectual to take his impudent color in hand and fill in the lines.

There are two well-known ladies. "This is my wife, Judy, and my boss's wife, Pat. Color them . . . colorless?" it suggests with no concealment of snobbishness.

And there is a man with two Nixon heads. (Oh how they love that characterization!) "This is by boss," the caption says. "Color both his faces." (This effete punch certainly will convulse the anti-Nixon crowd which now is engaged mainly in trying to get him to face backward away from the whole Vietnamese war policy on which he campaigned and was elected.)

Another picture of Nixon throwing out a league-opening baseball carries the suggestion, appropos of nothing but sure to get a titter: "Color him tainted."

And the book closes with an indirect slur at the vice president by showing Nixon having a physical examination: "This is my boss's heart. Color it and his doctor very healthy."

★ ★ ★

All in all, it's a crude hatchet job "created" by someone named Mel Baily and Jamie Jameson and published by the reputable house of Grosset and Dunlap to be sold at $2.95 per copy to the Smart Alec trade.

With characteristic snobbish inability to distinguish between humility and humiliation, they dedicate their little poison crayon work to "the man who said, 'I have difficulty imagining myself as a national leader and I sometimes have difficulty imagining myself as a state leader.'"

Now, it isn't likely that Vice President Agnew, nor the President, nor their wives, will go off and sulk about this book. They are used to such needling.

Agnew, particularly, took a whole lot before he started dishing it out. And it is to his credit that he never has yelled "foul" or publicly groused about the "undignified" language of his critics the way Senator Fulbright, for instance, did when Agnew sounded off about the Fulbright crowd.

Of course, you may say that Mel Baily and Jamie Jameson and Grosset and Dunlap aren't part of the political opposition to Agnew and Nixon, and therefore we shouldn't blame their literary product on the administration's political opposition.

★ ★ ★

Nonsense. This is the jaded line of opposition to Nixon and Agnew that has been carried from the beginning. It was used against Nixon in campaign after campaign — and against Eisenhower, and Tom Dewey and Bob Taft and so on back through all the Republican conservative contenders since the New Deal.

And it never has failed to

(Continued on Page 16)

Chuckle

Perfume saleswoman to customer: "This one has been banned by Planned Parenthood."

In Helsinki

A Large Party Due at Talks

HELSINKI, Finland (AP) — The U.S. and the Soviet ambassadors are giving a precedent-shattering joint party today during the one-day recess in the strategic arms limitation talks.

The reception being given by Ambassadors Val Peterson and A. E. Kovalev is the first in Helsinki—and diplomats believe the first anywhere—to be given jointly by Soviet and American ambassadors.

The idea—understood to have been proposed by Peterson and willingly seconded by his Soviet counterpart—was to stage a get-acquainted social for the disarmament delegations, their staffs and leaders of the Finnish government hosting the conference.

★ ★ ★

ABOUT 200 guests were invited to the reception at a restaurant-nightclub neutrally located between the U.S. and Soviet embassies.

The two ambassadors drew up the invitation list—and agreed to split the cost 50-50.

The joint reception underscored the air of cordiality which has surrounded the negotiators since they first met Monday.

Conference sources said there have been no procedural disputes so far like the long argument in Paris last year over the shape of the table for the Vietnam peace talks.

A toss of the coin, for example, gave Soviet negotiator Vladimir S. Semenov first place in the speaking lineup at the ceremonial opening. The Russians readily agreed in turn to hold the first business session Tuesday at the U.S. Embassy, and the Americans agreed to hold the next session Thursday at the Soviet Embassy.

Whether this show of cooperation means the two superpowers will make any progress in the main aim of the talks—to slow down the nuclear arms race—remains to be seen.

The shortness of the first negotiating session—only 45 minutes of business time since half the 90-minute meeting was spent in translations—indicated neither side presented its position in detail.

'Something Quite Normal for U.S.'

LONDON (AP) — Persons around the world were interested in the Apollo 12 landing on the moon today, but there was little of the excitement that the pioneers of Apollo 11 set off.

"Something quite normal for America," said a Polish student in Warsaw.

Morning newspapers in London put the story well down on the front pages in contrast to the banner headlines for the first men on the moon.

Japanese newspapers which published extra editions during the Apollo 11 landing this time only delayed their deadlines to carry stories on the landing.

The Japan Broadcasting Corp. said its switchboard was clogged with calls in the first minutes after the landing, inquiring about the success of the mission. Some callers expressed their happiness at the success, a spokesman said.

Tokyo television dealers, after a run on color sets in July when Apollo 11 landed, complained because the demand wasn't repeated.

"Business was awful," said one, "and we were heavily stocked."

A Moscow telecast announced the landing with a one-sentence report from Tass, the Soviet news agency; about 20 minutes after the landing. No telecast from space was planned until evening, about 10 hours after the landing.

Foreigners in Moscow monitoring the BBC reported its news of the landing was blasted off the air just before the touchdown by two stronger stations.

The Vote On Judge Is Friday

WASHINGTON (AP) — Administration forces, facing a Senate vote Friday on the Supreme Court nomination of Judge Clement F. Haynsworth Jr., have been buoyed by what one Republican leader calls "the way things are going."

Announcements Tuesday by two freshmen senators brightened the outlook for the Haynsworth backers.

The Senate's newest member, Republican Ralph T. Smith of Illinois, said he had changed his mind and will support Haynsworth. Sen. Mike Gravel, D-Alaska, said he too will vote for confirmation.

★ ★ ★

THIS CAME on the heels of word Monday from Sens. Winston L. Prouty, R-Vt., and William B. Spong, D-Va., that they would vote for Haynsworth.

Sen. Gordon Allott of Colorado, chairman of the Senate Republican Policy Committee, said "the way things are going" he expects more announcements backing Haynsworth before Friday's 1 p.m. vote.

Democratic Leader Mike Mansfield obtained agreement on the timing of the vote after Sen. Birch Bayh, D-Ind., a leader of the opposition, withdrew a proposal for a showdown Thursday.

Smith's decision to vote for confirmation tipped the balance in an Associated Press survey to 41 senators supporting the nomination compared to 40 against. The other 19 remain publicly uncommitted.

Smith, who was appointed to the Senate to succeed the late GOP leader Everett M. Dirksen, said last month that a "shadow had been cast" on Haysworth's record as chief judge of the 4th U.S.Y Court of Appeals and he could not vote for confirmation.

Flu Warning

BUDAPEST (AP) — Dr. Ferenc Gacs, Hungarian public health official, has set up an early warning system in an effort to head off and combat flu epidemics. It gauges the spread of flu by student and worker absenteeism and provides anti-flu inoculations.

'Son of a Gun, It's the Moon'

By HARRY F. ROSENTHAL

SPACE CENTER, Houston (AP) — Apollo 11 had history, uncertainty and danger. Apollo 12 had pure exuberance and excitement. So much that you almost forgot about the danger.

Across 240,000 miles of space you could almost picture Pete Conrad jumping up and down with joy as the lunar lander Intrepid bore down on the Ocean of Storms exactly the way it was supposed to.

"There it is!" he shouted. "Son of a gun. Right down the middle of the road."

And Alan Bean, standing beside him reading out the computer's figures, joined in: "Outstanding!"

Down, down, came the Intrepid. And the excitement mounted. Conrad like a kid seeing his first circus elephant.

"Hey, it's right down the center of the crater!" he yelled. The moon's horizon was coming up in the Intrepid's little windows.

"Forty-two," Bean said, calling out the degree of the ship's bearing. "Look out there."

Conrad again: "I can't believe it! Amazing! Fantastic!"

"Forty-two degrees," Bean said again. "Ride it in. Forty-two. We're passing 3,500 feet."

It seemed superfluous, but Mission Control had to say it: "Intrepid, Houston. You're go for landing."

"I just want to land to the right a little."

"Forty degrees, Pete, 40 degrees," said Bean.

"That's so fantastic, I can't believe it," Conrad said.

"We're at 2,000 feet." Bean again.

Then the dramatic final minutes, with Bean narrating:

"Thirty-eight, 38 degrees. 36 degrees. You're 1,200 feet, Pete. Thousand feet coming down at 30. You're looking good. Got 14 per cent fuel. Looks good out there, Babe, looks good."

Down, down came the Intrepid; 800 feet . . . 680 feet . . . 600 . . . 530. Bean counted them off.

"Four-seventy-one" he said. "You are all right. 426."

It was the signal for Conrad to take over from the computers, his hand on two airplane-type controls.

"I got it, he said."

"Four hundred. You're at 366,

(Continued on Page 16)

★ ★ ★

On Inside Pages

Bridge	19
Comics	18, 19
Crossword	31
Editorial Columns	4, 5
Food News	31
Obituaries	16
Sports	41, 42, 43
Television	18
Theaters	19
Want Ads	43-47
Weather	16
Women's News	14, 15

877 6141 The Democrat's ACTION LINE

Please Turn To Page 2

Highlights of Apollo 12

SPACE CENTER, Houston (AP) — Here are highlights of the sixth and seventh days on Apollo 12's flight to the moon, all times Eastern Standard:

Wednesday, Nov. 19

6:02 a.m.—Astronauts Charles Conrad Jr. and Alan L. Bean, on the moon's Ocean of Storms, begin first of two moon walks. Conrad exits through hatch, then a television camera is activated to show him descending to surface. Astronaut Richard F. Gordon Jr., meanwhile, continues to orbit the moon, taking care of Apollo 12 command ship.

6:32 a.m.—Bean exits Intrepid lander craft and descends to the surface. He and Conrad spend the next three hours taking pictures, deploying scientific experiments and gathering rocks.

9:18 a.m.—Bean, then Conrad, re-enter Intrepid and close hatch.

10:20 a.m.—Astronauts begin one-hour eating period, put new batteries and oxygen in life-supporting backpacks in preparation for second moon walk, then string up hammocks inside Intrepid for rest period.

12:14 p.m.—Start of nine-hour sleep period.

9:17 p.m.—Conrad and Bean end sleep period, start one-hour eating period, then prepare for second moon walk.

Thursday, Nov. 20

12:32 a.m.—Lander's hatch is re-opened and Conrad, then Bean, exit to start the second moon walk. During next three hours and 15 minutes, they gather rocks—documenting photographically the position of each on the surface—and walk to Surveyor 3 spacecraft to clip off pieces of it to return to earth.

3:47 a.m.—Astronauts re-enter Intrepid and close hatch.

5:02 a.m.—Cockpit is depressurized again so backpacks and other unnecessary gear can be tossed onto surface of the moon to reduce weight inside Intrepid, then the cockpit is repressurized.

5:47 a.m.—Astronauts begin one-hour meal period, then check Interpid's systems for launch back into moon orbit.

9:23 a.m.—Conrad and Bean trigger the landing craft's ascent engine for critical seven-minute, 10-second burn to propel them into lunar orbit.

1:02 p.m.—Intrepid and Yankee Clipper command ship dock.

2:26 p.m.—Conrad and Bean rejoin Gordon in command ship.

3:19 p.m.—Unmanned Intrepid's jettisoned from nose of Yankee Clipper, then the command ship maneuvering rockets are triggered to pull a safe distance from Intrepid.

4:46 p.m.—While astronauts aim a camera at Intrepid, the lander craft's engine is triggered to send it on a collision course toward lunar surface. Maneuver will rid it from lunar orbit, making it safer for future flights, and perhaps send sound wave to a seismometer experiment at Apollo 12's landing site some six miles away, giving scientists a better idea of the moon's interior structure.

5:15 p.m.—Intrepid crashes.

5:22 p.m.—Conrad, Gordon and Bean begin 7½ hour rest period.

Figure 6–1 Man's first landing on the moon is regarded as one of the century's major news stories.

Figure 6–2 This 1971 revisit to the moon was news—as will be all other moon flights until they become a daily occurrence. (Wide World Photos)

tion. Mankind's relationships seem to abound with conflict and competition. These elements are found in court cases, winning scholarships, awards for motion picture and television excellence, prizes for outstanding journalists, and a host of other daily activities.

HUMAN INTEREST

Editors assign or select many stories not so much for their impact on the community or the world as for their ability to arouse sympathetic interest in the reader. The article may involve a child's unusual pet or a senior citizen's success in a field usually reserved for younger people. Journalists classify such situations as "human interest" stories, even though all articles presumably are of interest to people.

The "human interest" category covers the myriad of subjects that may lack story elements such as prominence, real consequence,

disaster, conflict, or timeliness. The story situations are worthy because they deal with such elements as youth or senior citizens, pets, adventure, attractive girls or women, success formulas, the problems of illness or poverty, overcoming handicaps, romance, strange places, or merely unusual people. Another term for them is "feature" stories.

These stories often are timeless and can be held with the photographs that usually accompany them until the newspaper has the space to display them properly.

A well-handled human interest story can be like dessert: a pleasing touch added to the menu of heavier and more serious articles.

TIMELINESS

A newspaper itself has a certain urgency about it. The reader must consume it before the next copy arrives with new, fresh information. News, like dairy products, is a perishable commodity that must be used before it is worthless. The radio or TV news report of an hour ago or yesterday's newspapers are of little value.

People of a century and a half ago were content to read news three or four weeks or more after it happened. Today's electronic transmission of news provides the audience with the logical expectation of receiving almost instantaneous news. The public expects its telecasts to be literally up to the minute and expects that day's issues of the newspaper to provide details.

Modern society is one of rapid changes and developments, and the increasingly alert and intelligent public has the right to receive its news with all speed possible so that decisions can be made promptly.

EDITORIAL "POLICY"

An important news determinant often not recognized outside of the news department is "policy," or an order by the publisher or editor that certain subjects *must* or *must not* be used or featured. Publishers and editors are human and have strong opinions and biases; they also can be of a determined nature and use the power of their positions to rule on particular types of stories.

One publisher feels so keenly about a public project that his newspaper publishes little criticism, even from responsible parties, regarding the endeavor; this policy does not change even after a rival newspaper documents the questionable spending of millions of public dollars on the project. Another publisher so intensely dislikes the present philosophy of public schools that their failures are given substantial space and their successes are seldom recognized.

The opposite policy comes from another publisher, who endorses public education so heartily that he discourages editors from using stories so much as hinting at controversy in the schools for fear that it would crumble their

Figure 6–3 Campuses presumably are a place for study. News was made, therefore, when demonstrators rushed the president's office at San Francisco State College and officers drew their guns. (*Oakland Tribune* Photo by Lonnie Wilson)

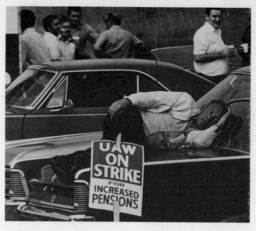

Figure 6–4 Airplanes usually land without incident. News develops when they do the unexpected—and crash. (*Oakland Tribune* Photo by Lonnie Wilson)

Figure 6–5 Pickets are supposed to march. When one rests—at least in an unusual place—that is news. [*Ypsilanti (Mich.) Press* Photo by Summer W. Fowler]

support. One publisher backed construction of a large theater center, and his editors let staff members know clearly that maximum space would be devoted to its programs despite the facility's inconvenient site and admission prices so high that the average reader could not afford to buy tickets.

One editor, on close terms with the city's police chief, rebuffed reporters who sought to investigate apparent irregularities in the police department, only to have his newspaper beaten by a neighboring rival after a task force of investigators unearthed the situation and the chief was forced to resign.

Other news policies may dictate such matters as covering a large advertiser's service club despite lack of general reader interest, reviewing a musical concert presented by a friend of the editor, or overplaying a series of stories to help raise money for a community agency instead of using in-depth reports on how the funds are spent.

Reporters and lower-level editors can do relatively little to alter most policies. If their approach is right, they may be able to convince editors and publishers that policies should be changed. Most often, staff members must accept these doctrines as they accept the other good or bad parts of their jobs.

Journalists do well to accept employment on newspapers with a minimum of policy re-strictions or with policies of which they basically approve.

NEWS VIEWPOINTS

Classifications for news ingredients help beginners recognize basic elements, but experienced journalists would not take the time to categorize stories except subconsciously. Indeed, it would be virtually impossible to assign classifications because most story situations are a blend of elements.

SMALL-TOWN VS. BIG-CITY REPORTING

The yardstick for new values obviously varies according to the community's size and the nature of its social and economic life. The measurement also varies if the newspaper is a daily or weekly, and it depends on the amount of space available for news.

It should be emphasized that there are good and bad big-city dailies, just as there are excellent and poor small-town dailies and weeklies. Regardless of his newspaper's circulation, every editor wants to produce a publication reflecting high standards. Part of publishing a good newspaper revolves around judicious use of available space and news.

The largest cities usually have newspapers with not only bigger circulations but also more

Figure 6–6 Being where the action is often can put journalists in dangerous positions. Jim Kean of the *San Rafael Independent Journal* took this picture of San Quentin convict James McClain holding a revolver and home-made weapon on Judge Harold J. Haley during an attempt to escape. The judge and three others were shot to death; the photographer was not injured. (*San Rafael Independent Journal* Photo by Jim Kean via United Press International)

use news stories of minor interest to metropolitan daily newspapers.

Reporters and editors must attune themselves to the audience and the availability of stories for their newspapers.

The reporter moving to a small-town newspaper from a large city daily would need to adjust his outlook, writing relatively minor items previously discarded but expected by his new audience. Similarly, the reporter who works for a metropolitan daily after beginning on a smaller newspaper would need to learn the new outlook.

Despite many differences, both reporters would be dealing with similar news values and the same qualities of fairness and expectations of skill in writing.

VARIABLES IN THE NEWS

While the basic ingredients of news would remain the same in various cities, different values would govern the emphasis of stories according to the nature of the newspaper's community.

Here are examples of how story situations could be played according to small-town or big-city standards.

The opening of the first five-mile stretch of freeway at a small city in a relatively isolated area probably would command front page treatment in the community's newspaper. Such a freeway would make the city more accessible and perhaps open it for industrial or residential growth. By contrast, completion of five miles of freeway in a metropolitan area could hardly rate more than a paragraph because the region normally would have so many freeway miles that the new artery would have little impact.

A proposed subdivision of 2,000 homes could command a headline in the newspaper of a small community, which could well double because of the project. Plans to build the same number of houses in a metropolitan area would hardly rate a sentence, since many such projects probably would be under way.

For many cities snow on Christmas Day is expected, but when it falls in Los Angeles or Phoenix, where such weather is virtually unknown, real news occurs. The newspapers

pages and space for news. This is because there are more stores that are potential advertisers to reach the many subscribers. The numerous advertisements are spread over more pages, making more room for news. Yet more news usually develops in a larger city, and even editors with much space to fill find many items competing. Editors must decide which stories are the more interesting and meaningful for the readers.

Newspapers in smaller cities have less space because there are fewer stores to buy advertising, and their smaller circulation is less attractive to the merchant. Smaller cities often have fewer activities than large ones, and as a consequence news items which may be routine in a large area develop into important ones for the community daily. Weekly newspapers, usually serving smaller areas and frequenty supplementing dailies, also find that they must

Figure 6–7 Dramatic sidelights often illustrate big stories. This photo of a crying baby in a bombed Shanghai rail station helped millions sense the pathos of the war in China in 1937. (United Press International Photo)

would cover the freak weather profusely with stories and photographs.

Large or small, most newspapers play Washington, D.C., or international news because of its general interest. They carefully weigh, however, the proximity of other news items according to local interest as the following examples illustrate:

A small-town newspaper ignores the opening of a freeway in a city 100 miles away, since the story would have only vague interest for readers. The metropolitan newspaper would run the story, even though briefly, on the basis that the widespread interests of many of its readers would include the project.

The election of a new mayor for metropolitan areas typified by Los Angeles, San Francisco, New York City, Boston, Philadelphia, Chicago, Detroit, St. Louis, or Cleveland would rate some degree of coverage in medium-sized to large newspapers. For the small-town election to warrant coverage in newspapers in distant cities, the story situation would require unusual ingredients such as violence or involvement of a nationally known personality.

The proximity factor would result in much greater coverage for an earthquake centered in a community 40 miles away than for one 1,500 miles away.

Readers would be interested in reading details of how the local high school football team achieved victory over arch-rivals, but even the most avid grid fan would find little

Figure 6–8   Journalists should never attempt to anticipate or guess the end of a story. This newspaper headline, based on early returns, brought a smile from President Truman. (United Press International Photo)

Figure 6–9   Conflict—represented in its extreme by war—is a major ingredient for news because it is a departure from mankind's normally expected patterns. Combat photographer Steve Northup made this dramatic picture during the Vietnam conflict. (United Press International Photo by Steve Northup)

merit in the conflict between schools situated 2,000 miles away.

THE NEWS PACKAGE

There are many factors to be considered in writing and editing a newspaper. The approaches to be weighed are as numerous as the personalities of the people who will read it. Editors must include material for all tastes, providing news that the reader *should* know about as well as the new situations he *likes* to read about. Ideally, the editors will be able to include items which help to expand the reader's horizons. The ideal news package is the one that carries an array of stories for many interests.

Reporters and editors find it impossible to please everyone on every day. There is no satisfactory explanation for the enraged sports fan who complains that the score of his favorite team, even though miles away, is never reported. The luncheon club members will never be convinced that their speaker, who already has appeared for most of the community's other clubs, is "not important enough" to cover. Nor is there any satisfactory way to advise a sorority that a belated account of a meeting is "old news."

In a society that is becoming both increasingly stratified and sophisticated, with segments aware of issues holding personal interest, news can be important to one group and valueless to another.

Reporters and editors must sort and choose the news situations to be published according to their understanding of the wants and needs of their readers.

Figure 6–10   Journalists, by the nature of their job, are in the midst of what is happening and are with the people who make important decisions. President Nixon, seated at his oval desk, talks to newsmen and newswomen in the White House. (United Press International Photo)

EXERCISES

1. Take an issue of your daily newspaper and tabulate the number of "good" and "bad" news stories to determine their proportionate usage.

2. Find the longest positive or "good" news story in the newspaper and note how it was handled from the writing and make-up standpoints.

3. Locate a "human interest" story in the paper.

4. Using your local newspaper, select examples of stories evidently used because of the following news elements: (a) prominence; (b) conflict; (c) disaster, and (d) proximity.

7
Stylebooks: Their Purposes and Uses

Most casual readers of newspapers, magazines, and books are probably unaware that virtually all publications follow "style" rules of one type or another. If writers did not follow a given style consistently, the reader would subconsciously feel that something was "wrong" because of variations. Even though few readers would consciously notice, seasoned journalists quickly would note such variations as "one dollar," "I dollar," "$1," or "$1.00," or "goodby," "goodbye," or "good-bye."

The various styles or usages would be similar to a speaker using a host of different accents, each time pronouncing the same word differently.

Most newspapers have rules that set the style for everything that goes into print. Editors may set style by designating the use of a particular dictionary, specifying which of alternate spellings in that dictionary must be used, or even by overruling a dictionary and arbitrarily specifying their own spellings. These standards of preference, or "style," are defined by the dictionary as the "manner of dealing with spelling, punctuation, word division of a particular press."

"Style" for newspapers, magazines, and books extends past spelling to capitalization, abbreviation, punctuation, the form of titles, and whether numbers will be figures or spelled. These matters are established by editorial executives and distributed to the staff as a "stylebook." Individual newspapers vary considerably in their style, just as they are unable to agree whether the collections of style shall be called "style books" or "stylebooks," although dictionaries prefer the latter form.

STYLE HELPS CONNOTE CARE

The reason for expecting reporters to adhere to a stylebook is not an arbitrary one. If a newspaper is careless and inconsistent in its rules of style, the reading public subconsciously will think that the publication is careless and inconsistent in gathering the news.

Frank R. Ahlgren, then editor of the Memphis *Commercial Appeal*, explained it this way in that newspaper's stylebook:

A newspaper's physical appearance reflects the thinking of its creators. If it is slipshod or inconsistent, then the reader forms that idea of its character.[1]

Lewis Jordan, news editor of the prestigious New York *Times*, summed up the problem in these words:

> Style for a newspaper was no problem in the days when one man owned it, wrote it, edited it, and printed it. By doing things in his own way, he achieved consistency, whether he sought it or not. When dozens, or hundreds, do the writing, editing, and printing, a kind of anarchy will arise unless there are rules to follow.[2]

Stylebooks establishing rules for writing and editing copy have become a standard part of the equipment for good newspapers. It must be acknowledged that some publications, notably smaller newspapers with low standards, do not use stylebooks. Good newspapers, including many small ones, do adopt and religiously follow stylebooks to help produce readable, consistent copy.

While stylebooks follow basic rules and patterns, they vary between different newspapers. Some are neatly printed booklets bound and trimmed to fit into a shirt pocket, while other "books" are large mimeographed sheets so bulky they must be stored in a desk drawer. A reporter going to work for a newspaper traditionally receives a copy of that publication's stylebook to use as a reference in writing. When a person understands how a stylebook functions, it is easy to adapt to other stylebooks since generally they are more alike than they are different. Seasoned journalists become so familiar with their stylebooks through daily use that they refer to the contents only when unusual situations arise.

TRENDS TOWARD "UNIVERSAL" STYLEBOOKS

The newspaper-produced stylebooks allowed individual editors to decide such matters as preferred spelling, capitalization, abbreviations, and the form for use of numbers. A trend to standardize stylebooks, and even to reduce the number of individual stylebooks, began with the advent of the Teletypesetter (TTS) in 1951. TTS, furnished with the Associated Press or United Press International wire news services, did exactly what its name indicated: it set type, using a perforated tape threaded onto typesetting machines. By using this tape, newspapers could set their type much faster than by manual operation. They could, in fact, save up to 40 per cent of the cost of typesetting—a major savings for newspapers facing increases in salaries and the price of new equipment.

The TTS tape at that time could not be edited, which meant that one stylebook would be required if all stories in a newspaper were to conform with a set of style rules. AP and UPI agreed on basic usages and produced the "Joint Wire Services Stylebook," identical for each agency except for cover and introduction. This compact volume is sold for a nominal cost, and many newspapers, discarding their locally edited stylebooks, use it for all stories.

Some newspaper editors objected to the joint book because of disagreements over style, while others expressed dissatisfaction over alleged lack of clarity in the volume. The majority of editors endorsed the book for the economies afforded by automatic typesetting and the ease in obtaining it in quantity for staff members.

Many large newspapers, because of their higher circulation and consequently bigger budget for setting type, could afford the luxury of not using the typesetting tape or the joint stylebook. Among the newspapers that have been using their own stylebooks are the New York *Times*, Seattle *Times*, Oakland *Tribune*, *Christian Science Monitor*, Los Angeles *Times*, Providence (R.I.) *Journal-Bulletin*, Santa Barbara *News-Press*, Miami *Herald*, St. Louis *Post-Dispatch*, Indianapolis *Star* and *Tribune*, Garden City *Newsday*, *Wall Street Journal*, and New Orleans *Times-Picayune* and *States-Item*.

Technical advancements in the late 1960s and early 1970s permit local newspapers to edit or make changes in the wire services'

---

[1] Memphis Commercial Appeal, *Style Book of the Commercial Appeal*, Memphis, 1967, p. iii.
[2] Lewis Jordan, editor, *The New York Times Style Book for Writers and Editors*, New York, McGraw-Hill Book Co., 1962, p. 5.

Figure 7–1 The chief copy editor (in "slot") and the copyreaders (around the "rim") check stories to be sure that reporters follow the newspaper's stylebook. (*Des Moines Register and Tribune* Photo)

punched tape, thus allowing even publications with comparatively low typesetting budgets to again use individual stylebooks and still retain TTS advantages. Many newspapers, however, are keeping the AP-UPI joint stylebook as their guide because of its convenience.

Familiarity with the wire services stylebook and its use by reporters and editors on the campus newspaper is recommended because of the practice provided in practical journalistic techniques. The public may obtain copies of the stylebook from AP or UPI offices in New York City. There is a per copy price reduction for bulk or large orders.

STYLE RESPONSIBILITIES

Following stylebook rules is a responsibility of all members of a news staff. Reporters adhere to the rules as they write their stories, and copyreaders make style changes in the articles with style violations. Copyreaders are busy with other duties, of course, and re-

porters who regularly fail to follow the stylebook become unpopular.

Journalists, being human, occasionally let style mistakes creep into the newspaper. The publication with numerous and regular style errors is probably one that also contains sloppy unreliable reporting and editing, and the one with few mistakes usually is excellent in many ways.

WHO DECIDES STYLE RULES

The AP-UPI stylebook is produced jointly by the services, with revisions made on the recommendation of newspaper editors.

Newspapers electing to use their own stylebooks can obtain one in several ways. One is for a staff member with experience and interest in style standards to produce the rules as a one-man project. A more popular and effective method, because of the participation, is through a stylebook committee, composed of editors and representative staff members who discuss approaches and problems while deciding the rules. An individual is assigned to organize the group decisions into book form.

In all approaches, the AP-UPI stylebook and those of newspapers noted for excellence in style are used as models.

Stylebooks are revised at intervals so that changes and trends in editing and reporting can be included in order for the rules to remain current and usable. The use of a loose-leaf format is an excellent way to provide for deletions or additions to the stylebook.

THE CONTENTS OF STYLEBOOKS

The organization of a stylebook can be as informal as a mimeographed sheet of paper with the rules given in no particular order. Most stylebooks, however, are longer, and their authors organize and index the rules for ready reference by reporters and copyreaders. The two most popular methods of organization are alphabetically, which requires no separate index since each entry is in fact part of an index, and by category of subjects such as capitalization or abbreviations. An index refers to individual points.

In stating rules, stylebooks usually provide sentences containing examples of the points covered in order to make it easier for reporters and copyreaders to apply the rules to their daily work.

As indicated, most newspaper stylebooks are basically similar in the way they give rules. Here is a listing of the categories generally covered and of typical rules:

CAPITALIZATION

Journalists regard conventional writing as abounding in *overcapitalization*, although those involved in high school or college composition consider newspapers guilty of *under-capitalization*. In fact, the trend in journalism for more than a half century has been to what is known as "modified down-style," or limited use of capital letters as compared to more formal writing.

This calls for the usual capitalization of all proper names (John Jones, France), but

Figure 7–2 Service and trademarks are capitalized, according to stylebooks. This organization purchased an advertisement in a journalism trade magazine to remind editors and reporters.

for changes in many other usages. For example, titles are capitalized when they precede a name: Secretary of State John Jones; they are not capitalized when used after a name *or* alone: The secretary of state visited the office.

The full names of committees, legislative bodies, commissions, and similar organizations are capitalized: The City Council will meet to discuss decisions by the Senate Judiciary Committee and the Interstate Commerce Commission.

When portions of organizations' names are used, they are lowercase: The council discussion involved action by the committee and commission.

Common nouns are capitalized when part of a formal name: Hoover Dam, Missouri River, Allegheny Mountains, Pacific Ocean, or Empire State Building. These nouns would be lowercase when used alone in subsequent references: the dam, river, mountains, ocean, or building.

ABBREVIATIONS

High school or college conventional composition more often *overabbreviates* than does journalistic writing, where abbreviations are less arbitrary and more likely to conform with those widely accepted and recognized.

For example, abbreviations are used in the full names of business firms: Brown Implement Co.; Amalgamated Leather, Ltd.; United States Steel Corp.; Smith & Co., Inc. [*Note:* most newspapers use the ampersand (&) *only* in company titles and *never* in conventional sentences.]

Complete spellings would be used for other references to business firms: the company, the corporation.

The name of a firm, agency, or other organization on first mention in a story is spelled, followed by its initials; thereafter, the initials are used.

Example:

Students at Central Valley College (CVC) are organizing a program to study the impact of the European Economic Cooperation Organization (ECCO). John Smith will direct the ECCO project.

Some stylebooks caution journalists not to "overinitial" stories with excessive "letter" abbreviations nor to use, without prior identification, letters alone that have no meaning to local readers.

The names of states, except Alaska, Hawaii, Iowa, Ohio, Maine, and Utah, are abbreviated *only* when they appear after a city and then according to standards specified in the stylebook.

Titles are abbreviated only *before* names and in compliance with a list provided by the stylebook. Days of the week usually are abbreviated *only* when used in tabular matter such as financial or weather reports.

The use of "Mr." in news stories is often misunderstood by beginners, who are accustomed to using the title as a matter of respect. Journalistic custom and most stylebooks decree that "Mr." can be used only in conjunction with "Mrs." or in clerical titles or in verbatim quotations.

Example:

Among those attending were Mr. and Mrs. Thomas Jones. After introductions, Jones said, "I want to introduce Mr. Smith, who will speak." The Rev. Mr. Young offered the benediction.

The journalistic rationale behind not using "Mr." is related to the objectivity or "fairness" endeavor. It may be well, the journalist would hypothesize, to accord the "Mr." prefix to the bank president or a wealthy depositor, but what about the teller, small depositor, janitor, or man accused of robbing the institution? In fairness, no one is called "Mr."

This rule does *not* apply to women, who are identified as "Miss" or "Mrs." Many publications are beginning to use "Ms.," the women's liberation movement substitute.

Most newspapers spell out months when used alone, but abbreviate them when used with dates.

Example:

Columbus Day, to be celebrated Oct. 12, will be the only holiday during October.

March, April, May, June, and July are usually abbreviated only in tabular matter because they are already short.

PUNCTUATION

The rules of punctuation for journalistic writing are the same as for other forms of composition except that newspaper usage has in most cases eliminated the comma before "and" and "or" in a series of three or more items.

In conventional composition, for example, a sentence would be constructed this way: The speaker's stand was painted red, white, and blue.

Journalistic construction, deleting the final comma, would have it like this: The stand was red, white and blue.

Many stylebooks make it a point to note a widely misunderstood difference in the British and American usage of quotation marks. In British usage, for example, the construction would be this way: "You're late for the meeting", he said. The comma would be *outside* the quotation marks. American usage, for conventional writing as well as for journalism, would be: "You're late for the meeting," he said. The comma would be *inside* the quotation marks.

NUMERALS

Rules pertaining to the usage of numbers are an important part of most stylebooks because numbers are used so widely in stories filled with times, finances, ages, and scores.

The general rule in most stylebooks is to spell numbers below 10 and use Arabic figures for those of 10 and above. One basic exception is that when a number begins a sentence, it must be spelled even though it is 10 or more. This presents the problem of avoiding the start of a sentence with an involved number such as 1,017.

Example:

A total of 1,017 students won prizes. The four children with the top scores had 25 points each.

Stylebooks usually vary from the "spell" mandate to require figures for statistics, records, election returns, times of day, speeds, distances, dimensions, heights, ages, military units, betting odds, and dates.

Example:

The vote was 6,345 for and 4,300 against, making an approximate 6–4 ratio. The girl, 23, started at 1 p.m. and dug a 5-foot-2 trench. The man, 6 feet 2, was given 10–1 odds for the Sept. 1 race.

Note that a comma usually appears with four or more numerals (1,000) and that 1 p.m. is used without the "00." If minutes were involved, they would be included: "1:15 p.m." Incidentally, 12 p.m. or 12 a.m. are seldom used because of possible confusion. The designation would be "midnight" or "noon" in the interest of clarity. Stylebooks also caution against such redundancies as "8 p.m. tonight," since "p.m." "means "night." Note also that the form is "Sept. 1," not "1st" or "4th."

Most stylebooks call for use of the dollar sign but rule against using an abbreviation for cents.

Example:

The price of the tickets ranged from $1 to $10.50, plus 60 cents for reserving seats.

Note that the "00" is deleted from dollar amounts unless "cents" are concerned. Terms such as "10 dollars" are not used.

In amounts of a million or more, numbers are rounded when possible and take the dollar sign and million, billion, or trillion; decimalization is carried to two places. Exact amounts are handled as in mathematics.

Example:

The $6,585,217 contract was considerably more than the $4.75 million estimated.

SPELLING

When there are alternate spellings for words, most stylebooks specify the shorter version in a specific dictionary (although most dictionaries vary little). Stylebooks also list spellings preferred by their compilers (and hence, editors of the newspaper).

Stylebooks usually favor "employe" over "employee," "goodby" over "good-bye," and "Vietnam" over "Viet Nam," but often are split over using "cigaret" or "cigarette." Editors prefer shorter spellings because they are easier to use in headlines, where space is at a premium.

Spelling sections often list words frequently used and misspelled. These may include judgment (no "e"), occurred (two "c's" and two "r's"), subpoena (a "b" and a "p"), and under way (two words instead of one). Incidentally, American spelling prefers "theater," even though many motion picture and legitimate play houses call themselves "theatres." It is not uncommon for a news headline with the word "theater" to appear in a column adjacent to an advertisement for a "theatre."

Locally produced stylebooks customarily also have sections listing area places and organizations that might be easily misspelled.

OTHER ITEMS

Stylebooks also become a depository for miscellaneous information, some of it not applying to style, that editors wish to make known to staff members. Policy matters advising how individuals are or are not to be treated in stories sometimes are included. Other inclusions may cover definitions of libel, directions for writing, procedures for giving by-lines, or samples of type used for headlines.

EXERCISES

1. Contact your local newspaper and determine whether it uses the AP-UPI joint stylebook or its own; if it has its own, endeavor to secure a copy to examine.

2. Using the joint stylebook and a locally produced stylebook, determine the rules that would and would not be applicable for use in your campus newspaper.

3. By examining copies of your local newspaper, determine its policies regarding the usage of "Mr.," "Mrs.," "Miss," and "Ms."

4. Examine copies of your local newspaper for one week and determine how closely it adheres to a style in regard to capitalization, abbreviations, punctuation, numerals, and spelling.

8

The Format for News Copy

The ability to type, even though it be with one finger, is a requirement for the journalist since editors and typesetters must be able to read the stories easily if they are going into print. There is also a preferred format for preparing articles, which are known in the profession as "copy."

The format outlined here is basic in preparing copy for most newspapers, and it is used in principle by writers for magazines, radio and TV stations, public relations organizations, and book publishers. The reason for this standardization is that wherever a writer may practice, editors, copyreaders, and printers can, with a minimum of confusion, edit it and set it into type.

Here are the standards used by most newspapers in preparing copy.

THE PAPER

The standard paper size of 8½ by 11 inches is preferred for stories. (Smaller paper sizes are utilized for the cutlines to photographs and for writing headlines; other chapters deal with these specialties.) Reporters do *not* use onionskin or other lightweight paper because flimsiness makes it difficult to copy-read. Most newspapers provide copy paper cut from the ends of newsprint. This paper obviously has the rougher texture identified with a newspaper, but no one really cares. The reporter's copy will be handled by very few people before being transferred to type. Since this paper comes from the roll ends that ordinarily would be discarded, its cost is virtually only the labor of cutting it.

This type of paper has one disadvantage: it requires time to insert carbons (see below), and a reporter's time is valuable. Some newspapers therefore provide commercially produced "books" of manifold copies with pull-out carbons to save the time of assembling the forms. Special paper treated to produce multiple copies without separate carbon sheets is also used in situations where the staff does not have the time to assemble "books" with carbons for stories.

CARBON COPIES

Many newspapers, particularly the larger ones, require that the reporter produce at least one carbon of each story. One copy is edited and sent to the typesetters, while the other is retained, at least temporarily, while the story is in the mechanical department. Some newspapers require multiple carbons for numerous purposes: the editor, master permanent files, reporters handling related stories, and for the reporter's reference in handling additional stories on the same subject. Such situations are the ones where the commercially produced "books" containing carbon prove economical.

THE HEADING

Contrary to widely held public opinion, reporters do not write the headlines to their stories. These headlines are composed by copyreaders. Reporters, however, do have certain obligations. While "theme" papers for conventional English classes contain introductory material in the upper right-hand corner, the opposite is true for journalistic copy: it appears, single-spaced, in the upper left-hand corner. These items are as follows.

THE REPORTER'S LAST NAME

If problems or questions develop regarding a story, the last name quickly advises the identity of the staff member to be contacted. Since editors, not the reporters, make the decisions regarding which stories shall have bylines, the required name is readily available without someone shouting, "Who wrote this?"

On papers large enough to have more than one reporter with the same last name, the writers obviously would need to identify themselves with initials or first names.

THE "SLUG"

One or two words expressive of a story's contents constitute the "slug," the purpose of which is to help people "follow" the story on its way into print. For example, slugs such as "hotel fire" or "mayor election" indicate the subjects involved; when determining whether stories are with editors, copyreaders, or typesetters, staff members can use the slug words instead of lengthy descriptions. Different

machines usually set the smaller type in the body of stories and the larger type in headlines. The use of the same slug with the story and the headline serves to bring the two kinds of type together on the proper page in the newspaper.

The reporter's responsibility is to devise the slug, being certain that it is reasonably expressive in order to avoid confusion with those that logically could be coined by other writers on the same newspaper. It is important for the slug to be concise and therefore easily written or used in oral discussions.

Caution: Do *not* use derogatory, obscene, humorous, or other extraneous or needless words in the slug or elsewhere in the story, assuming that they will be seen only by staff members. These words, through mechanical or editing errors, could be set in type and result in a libel action if printed.

THE DATE

A time element in a story makes it important to know when it was written. Without the date, "tomorrow" or "today," as expressed in the story, could confuse and mislead the reader. The subscriber, logically believing what is printed, could arrive at the place of a program on the wrong day if the editors had no way of knowing the writer's intention. The date at the top of the story enables editors to make appropriate changes in the article according to when it will appear.

WHERE TO BEGIN

After placing the above information on the copy paper, the reporter moves to a point approximately half-way down the page to start the story. This white space serves a number of purposes: it provides room for directions for the style of headline, instructions for the width and size of type, the number of the page in the newspaper where the story will appear, or an editor's questions regarding some fact in the copy.

ABOUT TYPING

The typewriter is customarily set to provide 1-inch margins on each side of the paper, with pica typewriting giving 50 to 60 spaces per line. While newspapers traditionally have required that copy be double-spaced, many now demand triple spacing. The reasons are obvious. Reporters may wish to add a word or phrase on top of a line, and time is too valuable to allow typing an entire sheet over. Editors require the space between lines to correct spelling, make style changes, or interject words or phrases they believe will help the story.

Great emphasis must be placed on the requirement that reporters type their stories. Newspapers can't afford the luxury of stenographers to type handwritten stories.

It should be noted, however, that reporters are hardly expected to be as proficient at typing as a secretary. All reporters make typing errors and change their minds regarding words or phrases, but few would consider erasing errors. Instead, writers "x" out the mistakes or changes and retype. While this technique is acceptable, strike-overs are forbidden: the typesetters might misread such letters, and therefore prefer to have the word or letter clearly legible.

Reporters must remember that their typing must be readable, but that it hardly must achieve the perfection that would be expected for a business letter in a typing class.

BRIEF PARAGRAPHING

Each paragraph is indented five to ten spaces, depending on the newspaper's requirements or the reporter's preferences. The typewriter indentation signifies only that a new paragraph is desired. The actual indentation of type in the newspaper is determined by mechanical instructions during typesetting.

Beginning journalists usually have backgrounds essentially involving conventional English compositions, where ideas may develop in paragraphs as long as two pages of double-spaced typing. They are therefore frequently surprised and even disbelieving to learn that paragraphs in newspapers *average* approximately four lines of typewriting, or 40 to 50 words. In fact, some paragraphs are even shorter. Experienced reporters and editors usually regard six lines of typewriting as the

maximum. There are three reasons for this construction.

Readability. People who begin reading a book or magazine often have subconsciously committed themselves to completing their selection, and despite interruptions will finish. Mr. and Mrs. Average read newspapers, in contrast, during spare moments and with interruptions such as drinking coffee, looking from a window while commuting, or conversations.

Brief paragraphs (1) permit them to return to their reading point without searching through long paragraphs, and (2) allow them places to abandon reading if they are not interested in one story and wish to skip to another.

Ease in Typesetting. If the typesetter makes the mistake of dropping words or phrases, he needs only to return and reset a few lines of type when the paragraphs are short. If the paragraphs were lengthy and the errors occurred early in them, it probably would be necessary to reset a substantial part of the story to include the missing words. Despite care, typesetting mistakes are made, and newspapers seek to keep costs down by correcting them as easily as possible.

Making up the Newspaper. Fitting stories on top of advertisements and around photographs and other articles is an art. Printers and the news department's make-up editors work together on this problem. Dropping a few lines from a story often will make it fit the desired space on a page, and it is easier to delete one paragraph with a few lines than to break into a large one. Cutting lines from a large paragraph usually requires extensive resetting of type, thus boosting costs.

In analyzing the journalistic mandate for short paragraphs, emphasis must be placed on the fact that the main reason for this construction is its service and convenience to the habits of the reading public. The benefits for typesetting and make-up are subsidiary ones, even though important.

Writers accustomed to the long paragraphs associated with conventional composition may find it difficult and at first uncomfortable, but they must discipline themselves

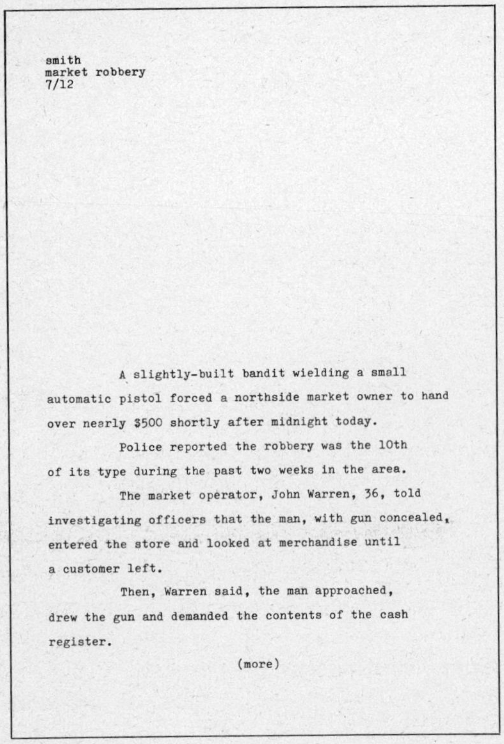

```
smith
market robbery
7/12
```

> A slightly-built bandit wielding a small
> automatic pistol forced a northside market owner to hand
> over nearly $500 shortly after midnight today.
>
> Police reported the robbery was the 10th
> of its type during the past two weeks in the area.
>
> The market operator, John Warren, 36, told
> investigating officers that the man, with gun concealed,
> entered the store and looked at merchandise until
> a customer left.
>
> Then, Warren said, the man approached,
> drew the gun and demanded the contents of the cash
> register.
>
> (more)

```
smith
market robbery
7/12
add 1
```

> Warren told officers that the robber
> was approximately 5 feet 3, thin and was wearing
> a blue business suit and white shirt without a tie.
>
> The bandit escaped in a car apparently
> parked in a nearby alley.
>
> Police Lt. William Morris, in charge
> of the robbery detail, said officers are investigating
> to determine if the same man committed all hold-ups
> in the area.
>
> -30-

Figure 8–1 Most newspapers use this basic format for the first page of news stories. The reporter's last name, the story slug, and the date the story was written appear at the top. The story starts halfway down to allow room for instructions to printers. At bottom, (more) indicates there is another page.

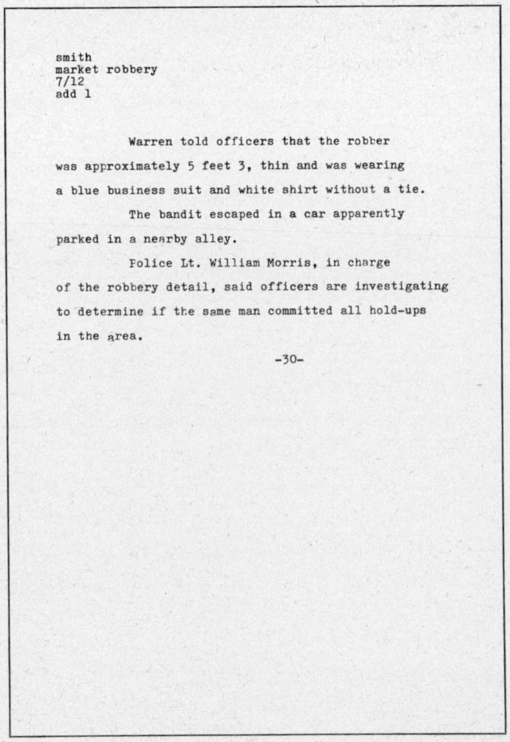

Figure 8–2 This is the general format for the second (or ensuing) page of a new story. "Add 1" indicates that this page is to be added to the first. The final "30" signifies the end of the story.

to use shorter ones to achieve journalistic style.

SPLITTING WORDS, SENTENCES, AND PARAGRAPHS

Journalists avoid hyphenating words at the end of lines because typesetters, working speedily, are slowed by hyphens, which they may set almost automatically in the center of a line. To avoid hyphenation, reporters either stop short of a full line if a word may not fit in its entirety or press the margin release to complete the word.

Some newspapers go as far as to direct reporters to complete a sentence or paragraph on one page instead of continuing to another. The reason for this is that typesetters work more efficiently when they can read copy to logical breaks at the end of pages. Other newspapers have no such rules, but eliminate unnatural breaks by requiring reporters to paste the pages of copy together in consecutive order.

STORIES WITH MORE PAGES

Journalists use several techniques to achieve clarity with stories consisting of more than one page.

ENDING PAGES

On reaching the end of a page, the writer types "more" at the bottom to advise editors or typesetters that there is more to the story. Unlike fiction, news stories may logically end at various points; without indicating that there is "more," the reporter could cause others to stop after the first page and not handle the balance of the article.

NEW PAGES

Unlike the first page, the second starts approximately an inch from the top. Starting in the upper left with single spacing, the reporter types his last name and the same slug used on the first page. He then types "Add 1," meaning that this page is the first addition to the first. Some reporters prefer simply to use "Page 2." The story is double- or triple-spaced in the same fashion as the first page.

END OF THE STORY

When the reporter reaches the conclusion of an article, he shifts to a new line and in its center types "30"—the symbol made so famous on TV shows and fiction relating to journalism. It traditionally ends stories so that editors and typesetters will not be expecting more pages. Researchers debate the origin of the symbol, tracing it variously from telegrapher's terms in the 1800s to phrases used in printing. Regardless of how it originated, "30" is used almost universally in journalism as an abbreviation for "The End."

AIDS TO CLARITY

The reporter frequently is absent when his story is being handled by editors or typesetters. The thoughtful reporter anticipates questions that could arise and provides their answers. There are several widely used ways to accomplish these goals.

DAYS AND DATES

If the reporter writes that a program will be held "tomorrow," it is wise to add the date, i.e., "4/15" or "April 15" over the "tomorrow" to assure editors that the information is current. The precaution is better even though the date appears at the top of the page. Accuracy and reliability are commodities that readers are entitled to expect from their sources of news.

UNUSUAL NAMES OR SPELLINGS

News stories often involve situations providing unusual or unfamiliar spellings. Instead of the traditional "Smith" the name may be "Smithe," or it may be "Briwn" rather than "Brown." Without the reporter present, conscientious copyreaders may debate whether the reporter hit the wrong key or was accurate in spelling an unusual name. The reporter should verify unfamiliar spellings by typing "ok" *over* the word; placing it after, on the same line, possibly could result in the "ok" being set in type. An alternate to "ok" is "cq," derived from an early telegraphic term meaning that the transmission was correct.

UNUSUAL OR INCORRECT MATERIAL

To produce an effect, a reporter may use Old English phrases that contrast present-day spelling and usage, or even material that is grammatically incorrect; writers also may quote from illiterate ramblings. These situations call for alerting an editor or typesetter not to make "corrections" which would ruin the effect. To accomplish this, the reporter writes "follow copy" on the story, thus indicating that the unusual writing is purposeful and not intended to be corrected.

The Latin term "*sic*," meaning that what might sound surprising or incorrect is true, is seldom used in newspapers because of the belief that the average reader would not understand the term.

EXERCISES

1. Set your typewriter margins to provide 50 to 60 spaces, and then copy typical news stories from your local newspaper. Note where the reporters started new paragraphs and the lengths of the paragraphs.

2. Select 10 stories from your local newspaper and assign "slugs" of not more than two words that would be descriptive and not easily confused with other articles in the issue.

3. Choose stories from the newspaper containing unusual names or spellings and mark where "ok" might be used for clarification to the editor and typesetter.

4. Contact an editor at your local newspaper and ask for samples of "copy" produced by reporters; study these stories for format.

9

The Basic News Story

Illusions to the contrary, journalistic writing requires a working knowledge of correct English usage and a good vocabulary. The myth that news stories can be sloppy and ungrammatical probably stems from two factors: the old movies, still alive on television, where the reporter was more brash than brainy, and the irreverent staccato of newspaper headlines.

Even during the early twentieth century such caricatures of real reporters probably never existed outside of a few large cities, and the handful that inspired those fascinating movies undoubtedly began searching for jobs in other fields when newspapers and the general public started demanding better writing during the 1930s. Headlines, which are written by copyreaders and not the reporters, are a special field to be discussed later in this book; the liberties permitted in them are not allowed in stories.

For decades good reporters have been masters of good English, but the emphasis on craftsmanlike writing is being intensified as readers become better educated and as salaries continue to increase, attracting and retaining skillful writers. Moreover, reporters are not only good writers, but they know how to use words and phrases in the journalistic style and organization.

THE JOURNALIST AS AN "INTERPRETER"

Although journalistic writing utilizes the fine points common to all English usage, it is a particular type of writing. We recognize as specialties such fields as essays, poetry, short stories, novels, and technical writing for a factory manual. Journalistic writing is a form of expression that seeks to interpret a group of facts—frequently highly technical or confusing—for the understanding of the reading audience.

Journalistic writing, therefore, is a way of using words that is considerably different from other kinds of English usage. It is a technique, however, that can be readily learned through practice and that brings great pleasure to the writer through his contacts with fascinating people.

The reporter becomes the interpreter or translator linking the words and actions of diverse groups of people—police, scientists, sociologists, lawyers, members of ethnic minorities, businessmen, educators, athletes, philosophers—with Mr. and Mrs. Average, who read newspapers to keep posted on local and world events. The reporter is the first editor to sift a story, weighing facts to determine whether all sides of a situation are being presented, seeking the truth, and discarding material which could be confusing because it is irrelevant.

THE "INVERTED PYRAMID"

Journalistic stories can and do follow numerous formats, but one is basic. It is commonly called the "inverted pyramid" or "summary lead" story because it presents the pertinent facts in the earliest paragraphs. Its popularity and usefulness are evident in that it is used in approximately 90 per cent of all news stories. The summary lead is widely used on radio and TV newscasts because it enables the broadcaster to give the facts concisely in the brief time allocated.

The analogy of the "upright" pyramid explains the format. A short story or novel follows the format of an upright pyramid, where the base is at the bottom. The reader begins with preliminary or introductory facts, and in

the case of a murder mystery he finds out "who did it" in the last chapter.

Invert the pyramid to create news style: you learn the identity of the slayer (presuming it's known) in the first paragraph. The reader then continues to the preliminary or introductory facts that developed before the conclusion.

The "summary lead" label is also given to the inverted pyramid format because important points in the story are digested or summarized in the first paragraph or two.

The origin of the summary lead can be debated, as can many journalism techniques. One logical theory dates it to the early days of telegraphy, when reporters gave the basic facts in the first paragraphs of their stories for fear that the transmission would be broken prior to completion of the message.

To develop the technique of writing summary or inverted pyramid leads, the beginner can pretend that only 50 words have been allocated for the entire story. Those 50 words must summarize the vital points, since the reader will get no additional information. This exercise will help the novice reporter develop the skill of eliminating preliminaries and getting to the point of a story.

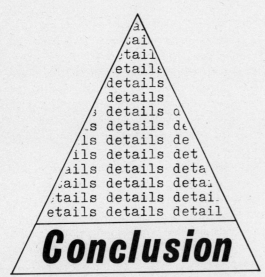

Figure 9-1 The pyramid format, with the conclusion at the end, serves as the basis for most fiction and many magazine articles. The reader must continue to the end to learn the conclusion or major points.

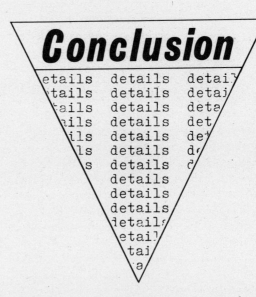

Figure 9-2 The inverted pyramid is the basic format for news stories. The reader learns the conclusion or major points in the first paragraph or two; introductory points are at the bottom of the story.

For example, in using the summary format to report a speech, the writer would hardly waste words on the master of ceremonies, the title of the talk, or the fact that the speaker began by reviewing generalities. Instead, the reporter would digest the startling or unusual remarks and later recapitulate the incidentals surrounding the gathering.

The beginning of the story, or the first paragraph or two, is what journalists call the "lead."

Years ago, reporters attempted traditionally to crowd as many facts as possible into a lead. The effect was burdensome and difficult to read, because all the facts were not necessarily the pertinent ones. Modern journalists recognize that the lead should be confined to the facts vital for telling the reader the story's contents. If interested, the reader can continue the article; if not, his eyes will move to another item.

Leads, it must be emphasized, not only give a good idea of the story's contents but also are brief.

America's leading wire services, Associated Press and United Press International, usually begin news stories with a paragraph containing only *one* sentence.

That one important sentence is easily readable, to the point, informative, and accurate.

While some newspapers allow the use of lead paragraphs with two sentences, many follow the wire services standards by encouraging reporters to develop the habit of writing a single sentence.

OTHER PURPOSES OF THE INVERTED PYRAMID

Readers do not consciously realize it, but they expect to see basic facts in a story's first two paragraphs. If the story begins with preliminaries or unimportant facts, their interest never develops; they turn to an article with a lead offering provocative facts. Leads which lucidly digest a story give the reader an opportunity to decide which articles to pursue from start to finish. If the salient facts were in the closing paragraphs of stories, readers would never find them because it would be impractical to consume every article in its entirety.

Aside from its service for readers, the structure of the inverted pyramid or summary lead format implements other goals.

The copyreader who writes the headline can quickly determine the point of the inverted pyramid story and transfer this idea to type for display to attract readers. His duties, of course, obligate him to read the story entirely to make corrections.

Another attribute of this format is that the copyreader can easily cut the story from the bottom and yet retain its readability. With the important facts at the top of the story, and those of decreasing interest closer to the end, such deletions cause no harm.

Moreover, this format is the delight of the make-up editors and printers who must trim stories to fit over, above, and around other articles, as well as advertisements. Since the least important facts are at the bottom of the story and the competent journalist uses short paragraphs readily discarded, trims can be made quickly without damaging the basic message of the story.

Conclusion

Figure 9–3 If the bottom of a news story written in the inverted format were cut, the top should still provide enough facts to give the reader pertinent information.

NEWS STORIES AND ESSAYS

Returning to considering what information should go in the lead, let's compare a news story with the essay that students learn to write in composition classes.

Everyone recognizes the importance of writing compositions, which facilitate the handling of every writer's tools: words, phrases, sentences, commas, and other punctuation. There is a major difference, however, between the audiences that read essays and those that read news stories. In the case of an essay, the instructor (or an assistant) is obligated to read the contribution from start to finish for the purpose of assigning a grade or other evaluation. On the other hand, most news stories must attract and interest a reader not later than the second paragraph. Otherwise, they are failures.

The inverted pyramid or summary construction, therefore, represents a major difference in organization as compared to the typical essay for a composition class.

Most material written for English composition classes follows a format that begins with generalities and then develops into specifics. One paragraph may run as long as two pages of double-spaced typing, and, as discussed in Chapter 7 (Stylebooks), there is much overcapitalization as far as journalists are concerned. The theory of this type of writing is that the dedicated reader will, at a single sitting, read the essay—unbothered by such distractions as other essays, television, books, radios, or noises which normally plague commuters.

In contrast, news stories begin with specifics and end with generalities.

As previously mentioned, paragraphs are short (remember: four typewritten lines are a good "average" length) and to the point. If a reader doesn't find a story informative or interesting by the second paragraph, he turns to another part of the newspaper or discards it for television, a book, or some other activity. The reader attracted by the first two paragraphs will continue, but only so long as the material in the story is engrossing. A start does not guarantee that he will finish the article.

Earlier, we discussed the emotional and intellectual ingredients that make news. The

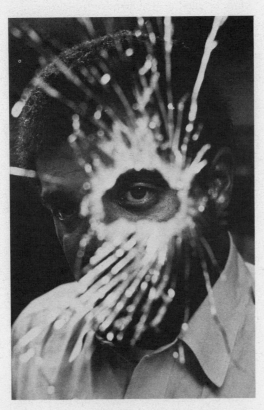

Figure 9-4 A barrage of bullets fired at a San Francisco police substation, killing an officer, made news. This officer, who survived, looks at a bullet hole in a window. (*Oakland Tribune* Photo by Lonnie Wilson)

Figure 9-5 Love vs. Guns: This young woman embraced a National Guardsman during a demonstration at the University of California, Berkeley. The photographer took this picture to add an unexpected touch to the story situation. (*Oakland Tribune* Photo by Lonnie Wilson)

leads for spectacular stories are obvious. If an earthquake kills 50 people, a bank is robbed of $2 million, an assassin kills a prominent governmental official, or the local high school beats its traditional rival for the first time in a football game, few reporters could miss in determining the leads that would specifically and concisely tell people the facts that would be the most important.

But let's face reality: how many times a year—or a decade—would there be such earthquakes, robberies, slayings, or high school victories? For the few times that such events occur, there would be more than adequate assistance to cover the stories at virtually any newspaper.

The spectacular stories are relatively easy to handle. The mark of a successful journalist is the ability to cover and write the events which on the surface appear routine, but yield fascinating stories. For every "big" story, even the skilled reporter will handle hundreds of lesser stories; yet, through thoughtful interviewing, organization, and writing, he will develop these situations into entertaining and provoking stories.

Craftsmanlike handling of "routine" stories prepares the reporter for the big assignments.

Figure 9–6 Reporters and photographers often find they are in the midst of news as it happens. This picture was made during a demonstration at the University of California, Berkeley. (*Oakland Tribune* Photo by Lonnie Wilson)

NEWS VS. SEQUENTIAL STYLE

To illustrate the handling of a typical story situation, let's look at the facts presented two ways. The material in the first example is treated in conventional narrative style, while the second is the way the facts might be treated in the inverted pyramid or summary style.

NARRATIVE:

Fred Jones was the speaker at a meeting of the XYZ Club today in the Lakeside Hotel. He is the author of the bestselling book, "Memories of a Writer." He was introduced by Robert Smith, club president. William Arnold led the salute to the flag, and Ted Burton gave the invocation. Jones told how he got started as a writer. He began covering

Figure 9–7 This dramatic picture of a Coast Guard helicopter making a rescue at Land's End, San Francisco, was shot by a photographer who sped to the scene with the rescuers. (*Oakland Tribune* Photo by Lonnie Wilson)

sports events while in high school and then attended Central University, where he earned his B.A. He then went to work for the Central City Daily Globe, eventually becoming city editor. "Hard work helped me succeed," he said. "Ideas are fine, but they mean little unless you work at them. For a writer, that is writing and more writing. Write, write, write, and if you enjoy it, write some more. You'll finally write that novel that will be a success. But you'll find that perseverance in writing is as important as ideas."

The End

INVERTED PYRAMID:

A best-selling author told a local audience that perseverance as a writer helped him succeed as much as did ideas.

Fred Jones, author of "Memories of a Writer," advised potential writers to "write, write, write, and if you enjoy it, write some more."

Then, Jones said in a talk before the XYZ Club in the Lakeside Hotel, "You'll finally write that novel that will be a success. But you'll find that perseverance in writing is as important as ideas."

Robert Smith, club president, introduced Jones.

The writer, a graduate of Central University, was city editor of the Central City Daily Globe before becoming an author.

He began his writing career covering sports while in high school.

—30—

EXERCISES:

1. Select new stories at random in your local newspaper. Covering up all but the first two paragraphs of the articles, observe which do and do not conform to the inverted pyramid or summary-style lead.

2. To determine the extent of usage of the inverted pyramid format, make a count of the stories in your local newspaper of the articles that do and do not follow this organization.

3. On stories using the inverted pyramid style, cover up the final paragraph to ascertain whether deleting it materially alters the article's meaning.

4. Cover the first two paragraphs of stories using the inverted pyramid format and determine whether the reader would still understand the meaning.

10
Other Types of Leads

Despite its usefulness, the inverted pyramid lead is not suitable or desirable for all news situations. There are numerous types of stories where varied leads can give sparkle and flavor, adding to the mood of the article.

USING OTHER LEADS

Reporters, like their readers, enjoy variety. Some news events by their very contents seem to cry for different treatment. Working journalists would seldom consciously attempt to categorize leads, despite their ability to handle many varieties, any more than they would take the trouble to compile classifications of news ingredients, although they are acutely aware of them. This list is provided to help beginning reporters develop an awareness of the latitudes in writing stories.

PEOPLE TALKING

Using various forms of quotations is one general method of creating variety. *Writing for the AP*, a booklet prepared for Associated Press, to guide its staff members, cites leads opening with a quotation as being among the most effective for attracting attention.[1] They can be handled in several ways.

THE "DIRECT QUOTATION" LEAD

Starting with a verbatim quotation that is meaningful is an excellent way to stop the reader.

Example:

"I didn't know it was a real gun!"

This sobbing statement came from Randy Doe, 10, as he told investigators how his 7-year-old brother was wounded during a game of cops and robbers with weapons found in their father's closet. Police reported . . .

A word of caution must be added to emphasize that quotation leads must be composed of words that add an element of inter-

---

[1] *Writing for the AP: The Second AP Writing Handbook*, The Associated Press, New York, 1959, p. 4.

est such as drama, pathos, humor, astonishment, or some other factor that will reach out to the reader. A direct quotation that is "wordy," contains abstract ideas, or is unclear will turn the reader away whether used in the lead or body of a story.

Direct quotations alone do not always make good leads. Sentences that sound fine when given orally by a speaker can become uninteresting in print because of unnecessary phrases. Some quotations are better when paraphrased.

Example:

Direct Quotation
"Last year, more juveniles than ever before were arrested in this city, and investigations show that laxity on the part of parents is the major cause," Juvenile Court Judge Warren Jones reports.

Paraphrased Quotation
The juvenile crime rate is rising rapidly in this city, according to Juvenile Court Judge Warren Jones, who blames the increase on parental laxity.

In this case, paraphrasing the verbatim quotation permitted the removal of unnecessary words and got the message over to the reader more quickly. If the speaker had chosen more forceful and quotable words, a reporter could have fashioned a more dramatic lead with a direct quotation.

Example:

"I'd like to jail parents themselves who are so lax their kids are boosting the crime rate!"
This statement came from Juvenile Court Judge Warren Jones, in releasing a report...

THE "DIALOGUE" LEAD

Closely allied to the direct quotation lead, the dialogue beginning can add flavor to many stories with a human interest or other strong "people" angle.

Example:

"The snow was 10 feet deep and it was so cold that the coffee froze almost as soon as we poured it."
"Sure, and the trails were so covered over that it was weeks until word reached us that the Spanish-American War was over."
"But the laugh was that, for all the hardships, the only gold we really saw was in an assayer's office."
This was the exchange today when two one-time Alaska sourdough prospectors, both 100 years old, met for a reunion.
Fred Williams and Robert Thompson saw each other for the first time in 60 years during the Pioneer Association annual gathering being held...

THE "DIRECT ADDRESS" LEAD

Although quotation marks are not used, the second-person ("you") approach reaches out to involve the reader and capture his attention.

Example:

Ski fans, here's your opportunity!
The recent storm deposited five inches of powder snow on Pleasure Mountain and the public ski lift is being operated...

While occasional direct-address leads help add sparkle, overdoing them can create monotony and cause them to lose the impact of involvement.

VARIATIONS OF THE SUMMARY LEAD

So reliable is the inverted pyramid or summary lead that journalists have developed variations to emphasize a single situation or to encompass several news items.

THE "PUNCH" LEAD

One method for attracting attention is concentrating with a brief, to-the-point lead sentence and developing details later in the story.

Example:

An attractive 35-year-old woman executive was arrested today on charges of being the "queen" ruling a multi-million-dollar narcotics ring.

Unfolding a bizarre story, police said . . .

THE "1-2-3-4" LEAD

Often a story situation contains a number of news-making elements which the reporter would like to emphasize. By listing them in "1-2-3-4" order, the writer accentuates them all.

Example:

Acting on proposals to alleviate growth problems, the City Council today approved these measures:

1. The $1 million widening of Main Street to four lanes from two.

2. Opening a branch police station at Broadway and 45th Street, in the western area.

3. An option for the $750,000 purchase of a 20-acre civic center site two blocks east of City Hall.

4. Contracting with a city planning consultant to study revision of zoning and building codes.

The actions were approved by a 4-0 vote following a morning-long hearing attended by approximately 1,500 people.

The next step will be . . .

THE "CROWDED" LEAD

An alternate way of handling material similar to the above would be to "boil" a portion of it into a single but crowded paragraph.

Example:

The City Council, acting to alleviate growth problems, today voted the $1 million widening of Main Street to four lanes from two, opening a western area branch police station at Broadway and 45th Street, engaging a city planning consultant to study revising zoning and building codes, and an option for the $750,000 purchase of a 20-acre civic center site.

The 4–0 council vote came after a morning-long hearing attended by approximately 1,500 people.

The advantage of crowding a great deal of information into a lead is the use of less space. Its disadvantage is the loss of impact for important material that would be more readable in shorter sentences.

THE "SHIRT-TAIL" LEAD

An alternate to the above two methods of handling situations containing several news elements is including them in two or more brief paragraphs, or adding a "shirt-tail" for the information.

Example:

A $1 million project for widening Main Street to four lanes and opening a branch police station at Broadway and 45th Street won City Council approval today in a series of moves to alleviate crowded conditions.

The council also okayed an option for the $750,000 purchase of a 20-acre civic center site two blocks east of City Hall and a contract with a city planning consultant to study revision of zoning and building codes.

The council vote was 4–0, following a morning-long hearing attended by approximately 1,500 people. The next step will be . . .

This type of lead can be used as a compromise to the "crowded" and "1-2-3-4" leads; it permits the combining of a number of news elements without using a great deal of space.

THE "CARTRIDGE" LEAD

This "bang" lead is brief and contains one single news incident, to be expanded later in the story. Its impact makes it a lead to reserve for important stories, and using it for minor news can magnify an article, causing the reader to lose interest—as well as faith in the newspaper's integrity—when he reads the full article.

Examples:

The German news agency Transocean said

today in a broadcast that the Allied invasion has begun.

(AP, June 6, 1944)

President Kennedy was slain by an assassin today in a burst of gunfire in downtown Dallas.

(UPI, Nov. 22, 1963)

STRUCTURED LEADS

The reporter should develop his ability as a "word-smith" and learn to structure sentences so that the phrases are arranged for more impact. The skillful reporter can arrange phrases so they will relate or contrast ingredients in a news story.

THE "CONDITIONAL CLAUSE" LEAD

When a reporter wishes to combine a feature dimension with a news development, a conditional clause helps weld them for a lead.

Example:

Because Phillip Arnold has a photographic memory, he was able today to spot the man who six years ago allegedly robbed the bank where he is assistant manager.

Police have charged John Doe, 35, with the robbery following Arnold's identification . . .

THE "SUBSTANTIVE CLAUSE" LEAD

A substantive clause, usually starting with "that" or "when," helps achieve variety and usually contains interpretive elements.

Example:

That traffic conditions will improve was assured today with City Council approval of projects for widening Main Street and installing sophisticated traffic signal systems.

The council vote came after civic leaders declared that . . .

THE "CONTRAST" LEAD

News stories often involve a situation offering the opportunity to vary leads by contrasts.

Example:

Richard Roe, who started 47 years ago as a $10-a-week janitor for Consolidated Corp., today took office as the firm's $263,000-a-year chairman and chief executive officer.

THE "DESCRIPTIVE" LEAD

Eyewitness accounts can provide the background for writing lucid descriptions which help the reader to visualize a news situation.

Example:

An ominous silence, broken only by the call of a faraway bird, hung over the battle-scarred hills when suddenly an explosion followed by the yells of charging troops smashed the stillness.

The loyalist offensive, launched to clear roving guerrillas . . .

THE "STACCATO" LEAD

A series of phrases or words separated by periods or ellipses also can set the mood for a story.

Example:

Mining pans . . . hip boots . . . picks and shovels . . . snowshoes . . . guns and holsters . . . fur-lined jackets . . . dog sleds . . . heaps of memories.

These items formed the background for the Pioneer Association's 67th annual convention, which started today at the City Hotel. Delegates included . . .

THE "PREFACE" LEAD

A brief quotation or a few appropriate lines from a poem or familiar saying preceding a story can form a background that helps increase enjoyment of the article.

Example:

"I am a farsighted man, and I believe Los Angeles is destined to become the most important city in this country if not in the world. It can extend in any direction as far as you like."—Henry Huntington, 1850–1927

Rail tycoon Henry Huntington's early twentieth-century prediction is approaching truth, and an exhibition of historic photographs saluting his contributions to Southern California's growth will be held at . . .

"PLAYING" WITH WORDS

The reporter with a background in the arts and literature can use his knowledge to develop leads that connect familiarities with current stories.

THE "LITERARY ALLUSION" LEAD

Paralleling the construction of a nursery rhyme or part of a well-known literary creation can add variety to the newspaper.

Example:

Mary had a little camera, and everywhere that Mary went the camera was sure to go.

Mary Richards' perseverance in carrying her camera on every trip with her anthropologist husband has resulted in the publication of her first book, a collection of photographs of natives in seldom-visited areas of South America.

THE "FAMILIAR SAYING" LEAD

A familiar quotation or saying can be woven into a story to help create a light touch. Care must be taken that the effect comes naturally and is not trite or strained.

Example:

There's gold in them there hills, Richard Roe discovered today when he sold a 10-acre parcel on Pleasant Mountain to a real estate syndicate for $1 million.

Roe said he thought the property had little value until . . .

THE "PARODY" LEAD

Brightness can be added to appropriate stories with leads parodying well-known motion pictures, songs, or books, or sayings by noted people.

Example:

It was "How Dry I Am" today for the 81 residents of Two Palms when the desert village's only well quit working, with the nearest water supply 100 miles away.

Jim Doe, a mechanic, borrowed a tank truck . . .

STORIES THAT CAN'T BE CUT

Most of the alternate leads discussed can be used with stories constructed so that the last paragraphs can be cut from the bottom by editors or printers. The stories using the following leads cannot be cut; to do so would deprive the reader of the endings.

THE "UPRIGHT PYRAMID" OR "SEQUENCE" LEAD

Some stories can be told effectively in the order in which the events occurred, that is, the opposite order of most newspaper articles. The subject matter is usually feature material.

Example:

Fred Williams and Robert Thompson left their Ohio farm homes in 1898 to try their luck in the Klondike Gold Rush.

They made their headquarters in a log cabin surrounded by snow 10 feet deep, with outside temperatures so cold that coffee poured from a cup froze before hitting the ground.

Communications were so bad that they didn't hear about the end of the Spanish-American War until four months after the cease fire.

They didn't find gold and in 1901 parted company.

Today they met each other for the first time in 60 years during a Pioneer Association annual gathering at the City Hotel.

Williams and Thompson, both 100, said that . . .

THE "CUMULATIVE INTEREST" LEAD

Beginning with a brief news fact, reporters lead the reader's interest to the end of the story.

Example:

Bill Turner, 8, has been found and so has his wagon.

When he was leaving for school, the youngster discovered that his new coaster wagon was missing from the front yard and told his mother, Mrs. John Turner. She said she would look for it.

Two hours later, school officials called to ask why Bill was not at school. Shocked and fearing that he had been hurt or kidnapped, she called police.

Officers contacted hospitals and searched on the banks of Red River. They were about to drag the waters when they saw a youngster pulling a red wagon through a nearby field.

Bill explained to his mother and police that a friend told him other boys had taken the wagon to a field two miles from his house. He planned to get it on his way to school.

The youngster said he went to the wrong field and lost track of time because he was so intent on finding the wagon.

Bill promised officers that hereafter he would "garage" his vehicle nightly.

THE "SUSPENDED INTEREST" LEAD

Unlike the previous construction, the "suspended interest" lead contains no news element. The reader must obtain the news by reading to the end of the story.

Example:

Bill Turner, 8, received a red coaster wagon for Christmas and it led to problems.

This morning, while leaving for school, he noticed that it was missing from his front yard.

Two hours later his mother, Mrs. John Turner, received a call from school officials asking why Bill was absent.

Shocked and fearing that her son was hurt, she called police, who contacted hospitals and searched the banks of the Red River. They prepared to drag the waters.

At that moment, they saw a boy pulling a red wagon through a nearby field.

Bill explained . . .

MORE VARIETY

When reporters are aware of writing techniques, they skillfully use various approaches according to the flavor of individual news situations. Here are two other leads that help achieve variety.

THE "COLON" LEAD

Phrases separated by a colon are another way of attracting attention.

Example:

Wanted: A master or mistress.

Approximately 100 puppies and 135 kittens are awaiting "adoption" at the City Animal Center, according to Supt. Charles Henry, who says the animals will make lovable Christmas presents . . .

THE "QUESTION" LEAD

A lead that comes easily and is highly popular with beginning journalists is the one that starts with a question addressed to the reader.

Examples:

What is the first thing that a woman buys when she is advised that she won $250,000 in a jingle contest?

Mrs. Jane Roe, informed by XYZ Soaps that her entry took top prize in the nationwide contest, said that she will buy a rhyming dictionary that . . .

Or:

Do you enjoy motion picture classics?

If so, "Gone with the Wind," the Civil War drama starring Clark Gable and Vivien Leigh, will be shown at 7:30 p.m. tomorrow at the Harmony Theater.

The first lead probably would arouse curiousity, since a great many people would be interested in her buying plans. The second lead would undoubtedly attract only those having an interest in older motion pictures.

Question leads therefore can be good or bad according to the news situations involved and how the questions are phrased.

While these leads can lend variety when used occasionally, many editors frown on them on the basis that people read newspapers to get answers—not to be asked questions.

They argue, with great merit, that unless the question used in the lead is provocative, it may bring a subconscious "no" retort from readers, whose eyes would skip to another story.

Opponents of "question" leads contend that the reporter tempted to use such a beginning should ask *himself* the question silently and write the reply as the lead to be submitted to the editor.

AVOIDING "DRAB" LEADS

Journalists develop a habit of avoiding leads using "dead" verbs that say little and have no action, or which drag because they contain needless past perfect verbs.

This lead, for example, lacks impact because the past tense is emphasized needlessly:

The burglars had been climbing through a hole in the roof when the police had arrived and caught them.

By using "action" verbs and deemphasizing the past tense, the sentence could be rephrased to attract more interest:

The police caught the burglars climbing through a hole in the roof.

Forms of the verb "to be" (was, is, are, has been) also carry little action and therefore tend to slow interest in a lead.

This lead lacks impact:

The warehouse was destroyed by flames that left $1 million damage and endangered hundreds of homes.

Re-phrasing the lead by deleting the passive "was" helps build the news values:

Raging flames destroyed a $1 million warehouse and endangered hundreds of homes.

The use of direct-action, expressive verbs invariably will make a lead more readable and understandable.

EXERCISES

1. Using your local newspaper, find a story with direct quotations that would be attractive if used in the lead. Write your own "quotation" lead for the story.

2. Count the number of question leads appearing in your local newspaper during a one-week period.

3. Using your local newspaper, clip and label examples of direct quotation, dialogue, direct address, punch, 1-2-3-4, shirt-tail, cartridge, conditional clause, substantive clause, contrast, and "crowded" leads.

4. Again using your local newspaper, find a story with material that could be used for a "shirt-tail" lead, and rewrite the material to that format.

11

Writing the Balance of the Story

While a story's lead attracts a reader and provides a summary, the remainder of the article must hold that interest by furnishing details clearly and concisely. The reader will lose interest in the article—and the newspaper, too, if all stories are handled without skill—when the details fail to justify the lead or if the reporter neglects to fill his role as "translator" of intricate and involved situations.

After an appropriate lead, the body of the story should be accurate, use names, qualify sources, follow the rules of good grammar, and, above all, be understandable.

THE USE OF THE THIRD PERSON

All news and feature stories are written in the *third* person. The main reason for doing this is to maintain the air of fairness and objectivity which would not be present in a first-person story.

News stories therefore do not use "I," "mine," "my," "we," "us," "me," "our," or similar personal references. The exception to not using these words would be in direct quotations, where the writer cannot, of course, alter a speaker's exact words.

Note: "We," "us," and "our" are used in editorials and refer to the newspaper's staff or owners. Along with "I," "mine," "my," and "me," these words are also appropriate for *regular* columns or letters to the editor. *They are not used in news or feature stories.*

These paragraphs demonstrate the *incorrect* usage:

We will elect a mayor and four city councilmen today, with officials predicting a 75 per cent turnout at the polls. Mayor George Hatfield told me that he expects to win reelection despite stiff opposition.

I estimated at 9 a.m., following a spot check of polling places, that 25 per cent of the voters already had cast ballots.

Here is one way of rephrasing those paragraphs to eliminate the first person:

Voters will elect a mayor and four city councilmen today, with officials predicting a 75 per cent turnout at the polls. Mayor George Hatfield said that he expects to win reelection despite stiff opposition.

A reporter estimated at 9 a.m., following a spot check of polling places, that 25 per cent of the voters already had cast ballots.

WRITE FOR THE READER

Readers, not the subject of the story, will be the audience for the news story. A good reporter naturally wants to please the person concerned in the story, but he can't go to the extremes of playing down or concealing pertinent information.

The reporter must remember that he will not be present with the reader to explain any vagueness, confusion, conflicts, or references to "private" jokes in his story. The reader's understandings and impressions will come only from that story, unless there is an unusual situation where he may have an independent knowledge of material in the article. Reporters write, of course, not for that isolated knowledgeable reader but for the bulk of the subscribers.

USING TECHNICAL INFORMATION

Most readers, even though they are educated, have little knowledge of numerous fields of technical subjects. The reporter must serve as "middleman" between the technician and reader to put information into meaningful words. Stories should be *fair* and *understandable* as well as *accurate*.

Writers sometimes yield, to the disadvantage of the reader, to the temptation of using technical but confusing language. For example, quoting a law word for word may be *accurate*, but it is not understandable to the average reader. Instead of lengthy quotations with legalistic terms, the skillful reporter will contact a lawyer and then write a meaningful summary using everyday words.

In writing a scientific story, the reporter —even though versed in science—will use layman's terms so that the reader will not be forced to consult a dictionary.

News stories, the reporter should remember, inform and entertain *average* people. They are not intended as technical trade articles. People who excel in one field may be only *average* in other areas, and they enjoy news stories to help round out their knowledge.

READABILITY

The reporter thus avoids words, phrases, quotations, or sentences that he does not understand; if the writer lacks comprehension of his own story, it is doubtful that the reader will fathom the meaning. The reporter gathers many facts and sorts the meaningful ones, translating this information into words and sentences that the average reader will understand and enjoy.

WRITING "FORMULAS"

There are guidelines for good writing, and numerous studies show that unfamiliar words or involved sentence structure can confuse readers. Few journalists would go as far as to prescribe "formulas" for understandable writing, but most would urge numerous "cautions" for clarity.

This book already has emphasized the need for short, concise paragraphs. To reiterate, four lines of typing are a good *average*, and except for infrequent exceptions six lines should be the *maximum*. The person conditioned to writing conventional compositions finds it difficult to abandon long paragraphs, but do it he must to produce readable stories. Reporters on virtually every daily and quality weekly find that the first requirements of their jobs include "breaking" long paragraphs. The news writer must develop a "habit" of almost automatically terminating one paragraph when it becomes lengthy and starting another.

Four lines of typewriting is a good average for a news paragraph, and six lines, with rare exceptions, is a maximum.

Avoiding "Wordy" Sentences. Involved or lengthy sentences also are undesirable for journalistic writing because they create difficulty in reading. Skillful reporters can delete unneeded words from a sentence and, instead of altering the meaning, strengthen it.

Here is an example of a "wordy" sentence:

John Green, who is the instructor, said that the course is being aimed at persons interested in commercial art, journalism stu-

dents, printing buyers and purchasing agents, public relations personnel and all persons interested in the graphic arts.

A "tight" version provides the same information with fewer words:

Instructor John Green said the course is for purchasing agents, printing buyers, and those interested in commercial art, journalism and public relations.

Removing unneeded or pointless words and phrases from stories not only makes individual articles more readable; it also helps provide more room for other stories. "Tight" story construction is an art that writers can develop by being conscious of "wordiness" when they write and read. An excellent way to form an awareness of the possibilities for dropping words and phrases is by checking one's own copy and that of others.

The Importance of Shorter Sentences. Readers of news stories represent a much greater spectrum of education, intellect, ages, and interests than do the consumers of the more specialized magazines and books. Reporters seek to point articles *to* the reader, being careful neither to offend him with a simplistic approach nor to lose him through involved sentences. The art of successfully reaching readers distinguishes the skillful journalist.

In general, the *average* newspaper reader is not as sophisticated as most people may believe. A survey, covering 118 major newspapers throughout America, was published in the September 1971 issue of *Direct Marketing* and showed that the median completed by readers aged *25 years or older* ranged as low as 9.2 years to a top of 12.1 years of schooling. The report by Dr. C. L. Jain, assistant professor at St. John's University, Brooklyn, explained that half of the readers had completed more than the medians listed, while the other half finished less than the medians of the newspapers listed.

Even prestigious and well-edited newspapers such as the New York *Times* and Los Angeles *Times* had medians of only 10.9 and 12.0 years of schooling respectively.

Many newspaper readers obviously are considerably younger than 25 years old since entire families compose the audience.

In its *Writing for the AP* booklet distributed to staff members, the Associated Press emphasizes studies by its consultant, Dr. Rudolph Flesch, showing that short sentences with an *average* of not more than 19 words each have the maximum readability. This standard assumed that there would be some longer and some shorter sentences.

Editors do not expect reporters to count words or follow formulas for writing, but they rightfully demand that their writers construct sentences so they will be readable.

The AP booklet explained it this way:

Our first duty is to tell what has happened in language the average reader can grasp at first reading. Every lead—and every subsequent paragraph—should be clear, incisive and interesting, so that he will be impelled to continue. We must not delay him with wordiness, confuse him with imperfect sentence structure or discourage him with dull, technical phraseology. We must give him the drama and color that come from judicious selection of detail, and a relaxed, conversational technique. We must not overfeed him by forcing who-what-why-when-where into a single sentence.

The Associated Press also said, summarizing the report:

Flesch urged the use of short words. Why? The main trouble with long words, he said, is that they make the reader work harder. Every unfamiliar word is an obstacle. But even a familiar *long* word takes more time and effort to understand than a short one.

In almost every news story there are certain long words that are essential to the story. But, to balance these, the writer can keep the rest of the words shorter.

It is better to use words that are generally used in everyday conversation. But, if you have to use a word that is unfamiliar to an ordinary reader, explain it.

Reporters, becoming involved with the many facts they have, may subconsciously produce lengthy sentences. Good writers develop the habit of writing readable sentences by examining their copy for logical sentence breaks. They soon are able to write a readable sentence almost automatically.

Here is an example of a sentence which is too long:

Students will study nomenclature, processes, type, paper, layout, basic estimating, rotary offset and color processes in workshop sessions which will meet 7 to 10 p.m. Tuesdays at the ABC Printing Co. offices, 127 E. 20th St.

The reader can better absorb the information when words are simplified and it is broken into the two sentences:

Students will study terms, techniques, type, paper, layout, estimating, rotary offset and color processes in workshops. The meetings will be 7 to 10 p.m. Tuesdays at the ABC Printing Co., 127 E. 20th St.

Writers justifiably are proud that they have above-average vocabularies, but they resist the temptation to over-display their attainments in news stories. Here is an example of using words that might not be clear to the average reader:

John Smith, 24, suffered contusions and lacerations when involved in a mishap today after he lost control of his car and ran into a telephone pole.

Using the words and phraseology that people would choose in ordinary conversation will make the sentence more understandable:

John Smith, 24, suffered bruises and cuts when he lost control of his car and struck a telephone pole.

USE PREFERRED GRAMMAR

To construct a good story, journalists must skillfully use the tools of their trade—words, phrases, punctuation, and sentences—just as any craftsman or technician will master his instrument. The standards that apply to conventional grammar also hold true for journalistic writing.

The Active Voice. All writing loses emphasis with the passive voice, but the offense grows greater in journalism where readers expect vibrant, lively writing. The passive voice involves forms of the verb "to be," with the subject seemingly *receiving* the action instead of *giving* it.

Here is an example of the passive voice in which the reader doesn't even learn who is speaking:

It was said that property taxes would decrease approximately 25 per cent, and the crowd could be heard cheering when the news was announced.

This example uses the speaker's name, but still contains the objectionable passive voice:

It was said by Jim Jones that property taxes would decrease approximately 25 per cent, and the crowd could be heard cheering when the news was announced.

Rephrasing this information to the active voice not only gives more life and readability, but also eliminates unneeded words:

Jim Jones announced that property taxes would decrease by approximately 25 per cent. The crowd cheered.

The passive voice makes the reader wait to find out who is speaking:

The banquet's main speaker was John Jones, port manager.

Putting the subject (or name) *first* eliminates the passive voice and adds interest through use of an active verb:

Port Manager John Jones gave the main speech for the banquet.

The writer who attempts to defend "passive" sentences on the basis that the reader will "understand" merely apologizes for careless construction. The reading or listening audience consciously expects and subconsciously recognizes skillful writing with to-the-point sentences. While a few passive-voice sentences will not ruin a newspaper, numerous ones will make a publication dull.

The reporter who is aware of good construction can easily develop the habit of *always* writing vibrant sentences by being aware of the pitfalls. Passive-voiced or other types of confusing sentences discourage readers and force them to other stories—or to competing newspapers with higher standards.

Use of Active Verbs. One way to add color and heighten interest in a story is by using active, expressive verbs in order to dramatize aspects of an article.

Here is an example of how a paragraph could use verbs that, while acceptable, might lack impact:

A fire destroyed the ABC warehouse last night, leveling the 100-year-old downtown landmark. Firemen fought the blaze during a snowstorm.

For more interest, the paragraph could be rewritten this way:

Flames roared through the ABC warehouse last night, leveling the 100-year-old downtown landmark. Firemen braved a snowstorm to battle the blaze.

Subject and Verb. Most college students understand that a correct sentence requires a subject and a verb. Journalists put them close together to increase the understanding of sentences.

Here is an example of a subject and a verb being too far apart:

City voters, moved by a controversy-packed race between Mayor John Jones and challenger Richard Smith, and unseasonably warm weather, turned out in heavy force today.

A better effect is achieved by moving the subject and verb closer together:

City voters turned out in heavy force today, prompted by unseasonably warm weather and a controversy-packed race between Mayor John Jones and challenger Richard Smith.

The direct approach is always the best. "Backing in" to a news situation may fascinate a reporter, but the reader finds it difficult to follow the events.

This paragraph loses its effectiveness because the writer "backed in" to the news:

One pilot parachuted to safety but the other fought for control of his plane before also bailing out after jet fighters collided.

Rephrasing the sentence for a more direct approach adds punch:

After jet fighters collided, one pilot quickly parachuted to safety. The other fought to control his plane before bailing out.

Matching Adjectives and Pronouns. Inexperienced writers commonly violate the rule that possessive adjectives must agree with their pronouns.

The underlined words show the misuse of this rule:

The City Council approved the $1 million sports arena at <u>their</u> meeting Tuesday. The football team will play <u>their</u> first game next fall in the new facility.

The underlined words show the corrections:

The City Council <u>members</u> approved the $1 million arena at their meeting Tuesday. The football team will play <u>its</u> first game next fall in the new facility.

The council, being *singular*, would require *its*; when *members* is added, the possessive adjective *their* can be used correctly. *Team* also is singular and takes *its*; if *members* were added, *their* would be justified.

Participial Phrases. A participial phrase starting a sentence must refer to the grammatical subject.

This sentence shows the incorrect usage:

Running across the finish line, the crowd cheered the horse.

The *crowd* did not run across the finish line; the horse did, despite the confusing construction. The sentence should be rephrased for clarity. This is one way to do it:

The crowd cheered as the horse ran across the finish line.

When a conjunction or preposition precedes a participial phrase, the adjectives, adjective phrases, and nouns in apposition must be treated as though they begin a sentence.

Here is an example that violates the rule:

Without an audience to hear the arguments, the council's vote was postponed for a week.

Rephrasing the sentence makes it grammatical and more to the point:

Without an audience to hear the arguments, the council postponed its vote for a week.

This example shows another way the rule frequently is violated:

Vibrant and easy-going, the meeting appeared easy for John Jones to handle.

John Jones, *not* the meeting, was vibrant. This would be a more correct way of phrasing the sentence:

Vibrant and easy-going, John Jones appeared easily able to handle the meeting.

Here is another example of how phraseology can lead to confusion:

A city manager of long experience, they appointed him to the position.

They is an incorrect reference to *city manager*. For clarity and better grammar, the sentence could be phrased this way:

A city manager of long experience, he won the position.

This example shows another pitfall in sentence construction:

On leaving the plane, the mayor's supporters greeted him.

Assuming that it was the *supporters* who greeted the mayor alighting from the plane and *not* the supporters who arrived, the sentence could be restructured this way:

When the mayor left the plane, his supporters greeted him.

Use of Quotations. Quotations, whether verbatim (word for word) or indirect (paraphrasing or using parts of statements) are vital for newspaper stories. They help bring the human element to an article and identify the source.

Direct quotations. What people say is important, and often they express themselves so succinctly and forcefully that reporters want to quote them verbatim. Word-for-word statements properly go between quotation marks, and the reporter breaks into them as soon as possible for attribution.

Here is the structure for handling direct quotations:

"This is the biggest and best fair that Center County has ever held," declared John Smith, chairman of the event. "Attendance hit the 100,000 mark at noon today, indicating the growth that this area is experiencing.

"It's strange to note that the ranches so numerous when I came here have given way to farms, and that these are now yielding to subdivisions where I never would have expected them 30 years ago.

"People who have been here for years," he concluded, "wonder sometimes what eventually will replace the tract homes with the growth continuing."

Note that the quotation marks are not used at the end of a paragraph if the quotes continue.

Another point that frequently can confuse is that in American usage—for conventional writing as well as in journalism—the commas and periods go *inside* the quotation marks, as opposed to the British method of using them *outside* the marks.

This is an example of the American usage:

"There will be five more ways," he said, "to save money during the production program."

The British construction would be this way:

"There will be five more ways", he said, "to save money during the production program".

Unless the reporter were writing for a British publication, of course, he would be obligated to follow the American usage—or cause his editors a considerable problem in making changes in the story.

Journalists normally use only verbatim quotations that add to the interest or meaning of a story. Some word-for-word quotes do not fit in with the facts of an article, and reporters do not use them just because they have them.

Indirect quotations. Sometimes a speaker's exact words are not as clear when written as they were orally. Rather than use unwieldly or cumbersome quotations that fail to give the message clearly, the reporter paraphrases them into indirect quotations. The writer may delete some phrases and select words that are more easily understood. Indirect quotations appear without quotation marks because they are not the speaker's *exact* words. They *do* relay his meaning.

Here is an example, given earlier, of using indirect quotations:

Center County is having the biggest and best fair in its history, according to John Smith, event chairman. He said that attendance hitting the 100,000 mark at noon today reflects the area's growth.

Smith said that farms cut from ranches a few years ago are now being developed into housing tracts to contribute to this growth. Pioneers such as himself, he mused, wonder what will replace the homes under continued growth pressures.

The use of "said" is permissible and expected even though the information is not in the speaker's exact words. The speaker did "say" the information being digested.

Using "said" numerous times can be monotonous if a story is lengthy. Here is a list of synonyms that can be used, as appropriate, for "said" with direct or indirect quotations:

acknowledged	alleged
added	announced
admitted	answered
admonished	argued
advised	asked
advocated	assented
affirmed	asserted
agreed	assured

attested	entreated
avowed	enunciated
babbled	estimated
bantered	exclaimed
bargained	explained
barked	exposed
began	expressed
begged	faltered
bellowed	feared
beseeched	foretold
boasted	fumed
bragged	giggled
called	granted
cautioned	grinned
charged	groaned
chided	growled
cited	grumbled
claimed	grunted
commanded	haggled
commented	hedged
complained	held
conceded	hesitated
concluded	hinted
confessed	howled
confided	implied
contended	implored
contradicted	indicated
counseled	inferred
countered	informed
cracked	inquired
cried	insinuated
cursed	insisted
debated	instructed
decided	interjected
declared	intimated
decreed	itemized
demanded	jested
demurred	lamented
denied	laughed
denounced	lectured
described	lied
dictated	lisped
directed	maintained
disclosed	mimicked
divulged	moaned
drawled	mumbled
droned	murmured
elaborated	mused
emphasized	muttered
enjoined	nagged

narrated	reported
noted	reprimanded
objected	requested
observed	responded
opined	restated
orated	resumed
ordered	retorted
petitioned	returned
pleaded	revealed
pointed out	roared
prayed	ruled
predicted	sanctioned
proclaimed	scoffed
professed	scolded
prompted	screamed
pronounced	shouted
proposed	shrieked
propounded	snapped
protested	sneered
proved	sobbed
publicized	solicited
queried	specified
questioned	sputtered
quoted	stated
rambled	suggested
ranted	taunted
raved	testified
reaffirmed	threatened
reasoned	told
reassured	twitted
recited	upbraided
recommended	urged
recounted	vowed
referred	wailed
refuted	warned
reiterated	went on
rejoiced	wept
rejoined	whimpered
related	whispered
relented	whistled
remarked	whooped
reminded	yawned
remonstrated	yelled
repeated	yelped
replied	

To emphasize, the replacements for "said" should be used appropriately, and not merely so that the reporter can prove that he has built a good vocabulary. "Said" is often per-fectly appropriate and not the overworked word many people think.

CARE WITH WORDS

The reporter, using his tools of words, phrases, and sentences to build stories, constructs stories to give readers maximum information and understanding. "Padding," or adding words merely to lengthen an article, wastes valuable space. Journalists develop the habit of selecting the most expressive words and cutting extraneous phrases. Readers want facts, not speculation, and generalities always yield to specifics.

Don't Make Readers "Guess." Reporters avoid using words that are unfamiliar to the *average* person. If the writer has more to say, he should give it to the reader but should not expect his audience to imagine what was left out of the story.

Here is an example that could make a curious reader wonder what the reporter omitted:

James Jones told how his engineering firm planned the Trust Building, Smith Warehouse, Main Street Center, South Fork Towers, etc.

Readers have no way of learning what the "etc." means, and probably reporters who use the term are equally in the dark. Unless there are more *facts* to add, the writer should end the sentence this way:

James Jones told how his engineering firm planned the Trust Building, Smith Warehouse, Main Street Center and South Fork Towers.

Be specific. Subscribers buy a newspaper for facts, not generalities. The underlined words in this example demonstrate poor writing that the reader could interpret in different ways:

Mayor John Smith presided and several city councilmen attended to hear a number of complaints from residents.

Reporters presumably have facts. The sentence should be revised with specific information:

Mayor John Smith presided and underline{eight} *city councilmen attended the gathering to hear* underline{10} *complaints from residents.*

While the *exact* number of councilmen and complaints may not be vital, the reporter should have and give definite information instead of leaving it to the readers to guess. Reporters, after all, are paid to have and use facts.

Avoid Unnecessary Words. Journalists pride themselves on "tight" writing, or being able to delete unneeded words. One can develop this skill by carefully reviewing his own copy and by having others check it. A reporter also can note the "wordy" writing of others to see how extraneous words and phrases can be deleted. The beginning writer must think and consciously "strain" to cut wordage, but soon he will develop the habit of writing concisely by second nature.

These underlined words could be eliminated without substantially changing the meaning:

Many of the men *who arrived at the* building were those who *had been given tickets. Fifty* who had been *admitted* were among the ones who *paid* for the seats.

Edited, the paragraph would read:

Many who arrived at the building had been given tickets. Fifty paid.

Deleting words and phrases that say little or nothing will make room for more facts in that story and more stories for the reader.

Spell Correctly. Misspelled words block understanding of stories and slow reading time. They also cause the reader to question accuracy of facts since they indicate carelessness. Most stylebooks name the specific dictionary that is the source when there is a question over spelling. Many stylebooks also list *preferred* spellings when there are choices, but few newspaper manuals would recommend spellings that are not in dictionaries.

Using "manufactured" abbreviations not given in dictionaries or stylebooks also can cause confusion. Do not, for example, use "nite" for night, "thru" for through, "bi" for buy, or "&" for and (except in company titles).

When there is a question over spelling, seasoned journalists instinctively consult a dictionary. After looking up a problem word once or twice and using it, the spelling thereafter comes almost automatically.

Avoid Repeating Words. An elementary rule for writing is not to use the same word (or name) twice in a sentence, but substitute a synonym on the second usage. Journalists go a step farther to avoid repeating words or *parts* of the same words in a paragraph. This makes for less monotony and smoother reading.

This paragraph contains repetition:

The 10th Annual Western Jazz Festival will be held Jan. 10 in the Municipal Stadium, according to John Samuels, president of the sponsoring City Music Association. The stadium seats 15,000, and Samuels said the association will make 15,000 tickets available through stores.

To avoid repetition, the paragraph could be rephrased this way, with underlining showing the replaced words:

The 10th Annual Western Jazz Festival will be held Jan. 10 in the Municipal Stadium, according to John Samuels, president of the sponsoring City Music Association. The amphitheater *seats 15,000,* he said, *and* the group *will make* that number of *tickets available through stores.*

Use the Correct Words. As stated, writers usually have excellent vocabularies but avoid words that the average person would have difficulty in understanding. They use to-the-point words that convey the correct meaning.

About means "around"; *approximately* refers to a number that is "not exact."

A *banquet* is a rather formal affair, and the word should not be used to describe a conventional supper or dinner held in conjunction with a meeting.

Affect means to influence; *effect* means to cause.

Girls and *boys* attend high school; *women* and *men* go to college.

Everyone dies *suddenly*; some people die *unexpectedly*.

Over means "above"; *more than* means "in excess."

There are nothing but *true facts*; if they weren't true, they wouldn't be facts.

Unique means the *only* one; *unusual* means that something is "different" but that there may be others.

Virtually is a more forceful way of saying "almost"; by using this qualifier before something that the writer believes is the biggest or smallest, or tallest or shortest, more credibility is given the story.

Avoid "Overworked" Words and Phrases. Slang and figures of speech can add punch to a story *if* they are not overdone or so aged that they are no longer effective. In an era where television popularizes "cute" phrases but kills them with use in a few months, the writer must be on guard.

Words and phrases such as "police dragnet," "raining cats and dogs," "raining buckets," "sorry about that," "as thrifty as a Scot," "combing the area," and "wild and woolly"—to name just a few—have become so trite that they detract, rather than add, to stories.

"Very" is also a *very* overworked word which no longer has great meaning. If a story deals with "very high attendance," the reporter would do better to substitute an estimate of the number present. Often "very" means *very* little: "a *very* new car," "a *very* good example," "*very* fresh paint," or "*very* interested." The use of "very" frequently does little more than clutter sentences, which usually are already crowded. Ordinarily by removing "very" there is *very* little change in the meaning of the sentence.

"Interesting" is another word that says little. People may be "interested" in a story or they may receive "interest" from a bank, but beyond those uses the word is virtually meaningless. A play that is "interesting" can be described better and more specifically as "funny," "hilarious," "frightening," "dramatic," or "well-structured," for example. Each descriptive word tells the reader that it is "interesting" and why it is.

A poorly written news story may describe a pending program abstractly as "interesting," which really tells little. The reader is served better with specific information pertaining to the event: a motion picture with its title, a speaker with his name, a panel discussion naming the participants, a game identifying the teams, or whatever the subject may be.

Readers will be intelligent enough to judge from the facts whether or not the program is "interesting."

THE USE OF NAMES

People, not inanimate objects, make news and usually are involved in most story situations. Journalists therefore use names generously in their articles. Stories without names lack interest. People are important and so are their names, even though they may not be famous.

THE FORM FOR NAMES

Names are used in their entirety when initially used in a story: *John P. Jones.* Note that the middle initial is included, when available, to help differentiate that person from others. In subsequent uses in the same story, people are identified only by their last names. If the man or woman has a doctor's degree, "Dr." would be used. In other cases, "Miss," "Mrs.," or "Ms.," as appropriate, would precede the name. Men are identified only by their last names, with no "Mr." being used. The use of last names only is being extended more and more to women, due greatly to the Women's Lib movement. No disrespect is intended by the deletion. This last-name usage is simply the custom with most newspapers.

Example:

Mrs. Mary Anderson, Thomas Smith, Dr. William Taylor and Joan Williams today won election to the City Council. Mrs. Anderson had only nominal opposition, but Smith, Dr. Taylor and Miss Williams fought strong opponents.

The Use of First Names. Using first names after complete identification may be well for high school newspapers or those produced by fraternal organizations, but few college or commercial publications would follow this format. Even though the reporter might be on a first-name basis with a news subject, he would avoid the usage because it connotes overfamiliarity or even rudeness which subconsciously makes the reader uncomfortable.

Where does "first name" usage, if it is to be condoned, begin and end in news stories? The office boy may be called by his first name, but can the president of the corporation? Newspaper usage of first names gives many readers the same feeling of disrespect that comes with the television caricatures of police officers calling frightened suspects by first names.

There are rare exceptions when using first names helps, rather than hinders, news articles. One situation would be where children are involved in a story, and another could be a "human interest" feature that could be more sparkling if handled with first names.

ATTRIBUTION

Every news story has a source and must be attributed to the person who provided the information. Otherwise, the reader may assume that the newspaper is vouching for the accuracy of the information instead of only publishing it. If the story is lengthy, the attribution should be reinforced by quoting the source every three to four paragraphs. This attribution is particularly important when dealing with controversial material.

Beginners may feel that a single attribution is enough, but readers have been conditioned to having their credibility bolstered at intervals so that they need not return to the point in the story where the source is initially given.

Statements that are controversial, dubious, or questionable should be attributed to their sources, thus permitting the reader to weigh their validity and not credit the information to the newspaper or writer. Care should be taken to credit *each* such statement so the reader will know the source.

The reader does *not* know who provided the story unless the reporter tells by attributing the source, using either direct or indirect quotations.

While one or more individuals must be the source of every story, there are circumstances when for various reasons the person is not identified. One instance may be in a *routine* story, often developed from a publicity release, from a public or private agency. If the story was not routine or involved controversies, the reporter would be negligent not to give names. Using names instead of inanimate agencies as sources even for routine stories will make the article more readable, since names add a human and lively element.

Brief stories pertaining to motion picture or play performances, club meetings, or other routine activities are among the few areas where the attribution can be deleted. The assumption is that the information came from the organization involved, and quoting the source merely consumes space.

IDENTIFY AND QUALIFY

Closely allied to attribution is the need to identify and qualify the story source and those involved in a news situation. People want to know who other people *are*, and why they are in the news.

Identification. People can be identified by many factors. These include the community or specific address where they reside, their job or title, height, weight, age, and sex.

A number of these factors could be mentioned appropriately in a story dealing with an automobile accident. Age would be of interest in the case of an injured person, whose chances of survival could be adversely affected by being extremely young or old. Giving the addresses of those involved would increase readability, since subscribers would wonder if those injured resided nearby.

News that an 80-year-old woman or a 16-year-old girl earned a bachelor of arts degree has more readability than a story reporting that a 22-year-old woman earned one. If a news story can correctly describe the writer of a forged check as a bank official, the article will draw greater attention than the same crime involving an outsider.

Good journalists never use national, racial, or religious designations—or any other identifications, for that matter—in a derisive, discriminatory, or derogatory manner. Designations are intended to add perspective to a story.

Here is an example of their *meaningful* use:

Those attending included John Thompson, first white man to head the city's NAACP, and Fred Schultz, who discussed social developments in his native Germany.

Others at the meeting were John Adamson, Fred Burnside and William Fields, representing the Protestant, Catholic and Jewish viewpoints respectively.

Qualification. Identifying a story source or person involved in a news situation frequently *qualifies* them and establishes the article's credibility. Readers are entitled to know *why* a person is quoted in a story. Qualification obviously comes in many forms. If a story source is requesting a neighborhood improvement program, the individual's address should show him able to speak with—or without—authority on the basis of place of residence. An individual speaking on a school problem would be qualified to speak as a student, teacher, administrator, or parent, and thus be qualified according to identification.

Identification can add to a story's credibility. What is lacking in this paragraph?

William Smith predicted today that subterranean formations in the Berkshire Cliffs area will cause landslides that probably will result in severe damage to homes.

Identifying the source helps understanding and gives the reader more background:

William Smith, State University geology professor who two years ago correctly forecast landslides at Point Thomas, predicted today that formations in the Berkshire Cliffs area will cause landslides that probably will result in severe damage to homes.

Readers are entitled to know the backgrounds and qualifications of the people to whom opinions are attributed. This is particularly true of people speaking on controversial or technical subjects. For example, if a reporter is handling a medical story, he should advise the readers where the physician received his training and how his specialized field qualifies him to speak. A feature on problems in the postal service would be more meaningful if it quoted an expert in the field qualified to discuss such matters instead of the carrier a reporter happened to know personally or who delivered the mail to the office. An article on ecology would carry more weight to the reader if the story quoted a source qualified in a pertinent scientific field rather than someone concerned about it but lacking an expert background in the area.

USE OF UNUSUAL TYPES

Journalists usually do not use italics, all capitals, underlined words, or other special faces of type. Instead, they give emphasis by relying on their ingenuity and skill to phrase and construct sentences.

Italics ("slanting" type) are used in books and many magazines to designate titles of books, magazines, plays, songs, and similar material, or to emphasize words. When a typesetter sees a typewritten line underlined, this indicates that italic type is to be used. Because of technicalities involved in automated typesetting and the cost and time of changing "fonts" or kinds of type, most newspapers do not use italics except for special material in magazines or feature sections.

Newspapers therefore place titles in quotation marks. The names of newspapers, magazines, or other periodicals do *not* take quotation marks.

Example:

"Gone with the Wind," the motion picture classic, will be screened at 8 p.m. Friday at the Main Theater. When first released, the film won plaudits from the New York Times, New York Daily News, Time Magazine, Newsweek and other publications.

All capitals are intended to give emphasis because they appear larger than capitals and lowercase letters. Most newspaper editors rule against using them because their appearance in numerous stories would cancel any special effect. Using all capitals also makes reading more difficult and actually distracts from the interest. To emphasize points, skillful writers restructure sentences to accomplish their goals.

Underlining words with a typewriter is a simple matter. One need only to backspace the words and punch the "line" key. Creating such an effect on a typesetting machine would present a problem: the printer would need to take time to place a font composed of underlined type, since there is no way to backspace the machines.

Underlined or other special types may be used for advertising, where the buyer pays the cost of the extra labor involved. Newspaper deadlines, however, prohibit the use of unusual types except in magazines or special sections where more time is available.

Incidentally, a layman may believe that a line under typewriting means the material will be set in underlined type, but printers universally have a different interpretation. To them, underlined typing means that the material is to be set in *italics*.

ENDING THE STORY

When a reporter has used all of his facts, he simply ends the story.

Assuming that the story is written in the widely used inverted pyramid format, the article could end even before *all* of the facts are used. The presumption is that an editor might need to cut the story, which he logically would do from the bottom, to make it fit a space.

Beginners often are tempted to end a story with an admonition or command. Editors dislike such endings because they say little.

A typical "command" ending reads something like this:

Be sure to attend the meeting. Have a good time!

The earlier part of the story should have given pertinent information so that the reader could decide for himself whether or not he wanted to attend, and the admonition to enjoy oneself has nothing to do with news.

The experienced reporter, after exhausting his facts, simply ends the story.

EXERCISES

1. Interview an individual dealing in a scientific area, and write an article, using layman's language, in a form that the average person could understand.

2. Associated Press studies recommend 19 words as an *average* length for a sentence. Take a group of news stories that you have written and count the words in each sentence, averaging them to note their readability by this formula.

3. Interview a subject or attend a speech for the purpose of writing a story using quotations. Selecting *understandable* and *lively* statements, use both direct and indirect quotations in your article.

4. Exchange copies of news stories with classmates, and edit the articles to cut unneeded words and phrases without *substantially* changing the meaning.

12

A Few Comments About the Five W's

Laymen traditionally advise journalists always to include the "who, what, when, where, why, and how" in the story. A more meaningful admonition would be for reporters to consider the relative values of these news ingredients and emphasize the ones which are pertinent.

These "five W's and an H" are good questions for a reporter to ask himself as he gathers information for a story. The extent to which these items will affect the completed article depends on several considerations.

RELATIVE VALUES

An automobile accident serves as an excellent example of how different values or interests can shape a story.

If two ordinary citizens are involved in the collision, the "who" fails to generate the impact that would be present if a well-known name happened to be in one of the vehicles. In the case of an accident involving someone whose name was relatively familiar, the "who" would be a factor to be logically emphasized in the lead. The name of the person relatively unknown to the general public would be played down.

Here is an example of a lead when the "who" is someone familiar to many people:

Sen. Robert Burns (R-N.Y.) escaped with minor injuries when his auto was involved in a collision with another car early today on State Highway at Main Street.

The other driver, Phil Kelly, 30, of Center City, suffered cuts and bruises in the 2 a.m. crash.

The "what" ordinarily constitutes the most readable factor in most accidents involving ordinary citizens, with all due respect for reporters' and editors' concern over the victims' personal well-being.

Example:

A head-on crash of two cars blocked traffic briefly early today on State Highway at Main Street.

The drivers were Phil Kelly, 30, of Center City, who suffered cuts and bruises, and William Anderson, 35, of Metropolis, who escaped injury.

FACTORS VARY

The "when" element would be important when the time added importance to a story. In this case, a reference to the hour makes the article more readable:

Traffic was blocked during the 5 p.m. rush hour yesterday when two autos collided on State Highway at Main Street.

One driver, Phil Kelly, 30, of Center City, suffered minor injuries. The other, William Anderson, 35, of Metropolis, was not hurt.

The "where" ingredient would add interest in certain situations. Here is an example:

Two cars collided at this city's busiest intersection, Speedway Highway and Broadway, attracting hundreds of curious spectators who created a monumental traffic jam at noon today.

Twelve officers directed traffic for nearly two hours before vehicles were flowing again in normal patterns.

The drivers, George Thomas of Crestview and Fred Overton of New City, escaped injury.

The "why" facet in this story involves a cause of an accident:

A car swerving to miss a small child collided with another auto today on State Highway at Main Street. One driver suffered injuries.

Ann Smith, 2, wandered through an open gate in her yard and into the path of an auto driven by Martin Jacobs, 34, of New City. Swerving, he lost control of his car and hit an auto driven by Mrs. Nell Guiness, 36, of Metropolis.

Jacobs suffered facial bruises. Police said the child was frightened but not injured.

The "how" often makes an important part of a story. Here is how it could be featured in a lead regarding an auto accident:

A car driven by a Center City motorist smashed into a light post early today after its steering gear failed, careening into a passing auto and stopping only after breaking a fire plug that flooded the neighborhood with water.

This lead, incidentally, has far more than the 19-word *average* recommended by the Associated Press studies. Editors would justify its use on the basis that its words are familiar and the sentence sustains itself with action.

What does a journalist do when a number of the "W's" seem newsworthy? While often they would be placed in separate paragraphs, here is a way they could be placed in one:

U.S. Sen. Robert Burns suffered minor injuries today when his car swerved to miss a child. His careening auto smashed into another car, downed a lamp post, hit a fire plug that flooded the area and blocked downtown traffic for three hours.

EMPHASIZING IMPORTANT POINTS

While all of the W's are important ingredients of stories, individual news situations will make some more or less important than the others. The reporter must weigh and evaluate so that the most important ones go into the lead. Unimportant ones only confuse and do not belong anywhere in the story.

It is not enough to include the pertinent W's in a story. The reader deserves explanations.

Names Are the "Who." Names are important and are part of the who. The other relevant part is proper identification of the "who" and of his qualifications to speak. If John A. Jones is announcing a $10 million hospital construction program, the reader has a right to know his association with the hospital: board president, director, general manager, treasurer, or whatever identification qualifies him to be quoted. If Thomas B. Smith presents the results of a poll showing prospective winners in an election, the reporter should tell his qualifications for speaking: his record of accurate predictions in the past, a résumé of his training to conduct such polls and how he arrives at results, association with a well-known firm that has achieved accuracy in polling, or whatever explanation adds to the credibility of the results.

"Who" determines where the story will be played. If the situation involves the President of the United States, the article will be a candidate for Page 1. If the story pertains to the head of the local button collector's club, it may not rate a line on the deepest inside page.

Without a doubt, "who" rates as probably the strongest factor in making a story readable. Whether the name is famous nationally or known exclusively in the community, it helps add sparkle and life to an article: names make news.

Don't Be Afraid to Use Names Generously. Long lists of names may appear as a waste of space on the surface, but actually they are not. Instead, they increase readability and make friends for the newspaper. Weeklies and dailies in small communities print "who"

received high school diplomas, much to the pleasure of the students' families and the interest of neighbors. In larger cities, the number of schools and graduates are so large that newspapers lack the space to use names. Editors frequently receive letters indicating disappointment that those involved cannot clip lists for their scrapbooks.

Lists of names, whether the subjects attended a convention, won scholarships, joined a club, or received an honor, attract readers.

Incidentally, most newspapers handle lists of names with a summary paragraph explaining the situation. Long lists are broken into paragraphs of four to six lines of *typing* to help printers in making corrections and to allow the reader pauses while reading.

Figure 12–1 News elements can vary in fire stories: sometimes the angle may be *what* burned, while often it can be *where* it burned or *how many* viewed the disaster. Even small blazes lend themselves to news photos. [*Alma* (Mich.) *Daily Record-Leader* Photo]

THE IMPORTANCE OF TIME

The "when" is highly relevant when a reader wants to attend or participate in a program. For example, when a theater production is scheduled, advising that it will be on Wednesday is not enough. The exact time—say it is 8 p.m.—is essential to serve the reading public. Everyone doesn't know: they read the newspaper to find out. Even though a program is always held at 3 p.m. Fridays, a story announcing details should still include the time for the thousands who haven't been attending but who might if they notice that a particularly interesting meeting is planned.

The information is more to the point when the time is inserted *before* the day: "at 7:30 p.m. Saturday." Putting it *after* the day makes more awkward construction: "on Saturday at 7:30 p.m."

"When" can be a perishable commodity. Few people are interested in reading about the *time* of an event *after* it has happened. After the event, therefore, the "when" becomes of secondary interest. For example, the *review* of a play or an *account* of a speech is of greater interest after the event than exactly when it happened. The reader is still entitled to know the "when," but the time can reasonably be placed lower in the story since it is no longer possible to attend the event.

Journalists often revolve their stories around the pertinent and readable facts more than the time or day when they obtained the information. When dates are "stale" and have little meaning, there is no sense in featuring them. They can be "hidden" deeper in the story where they will not add to wordiness or confusion.

TELLING A STORY'S "WHERE"

Depending on circumstances, "where" can be an important or subsidiary element. When an event is being held, the "where" is important to those who may attend. The name of a well-known meeting place may be enough; if the general or average reader probably would not know it, then the street and number should be furnished.

In this example, the meeting place obviously is so well-known and even massive that most people would know where it was situated or could find it through directional signs:

Thomas Young, president of the Community Chamber of Commerce, will discuss plans for a new auditorium at 8 p.m. Thursday in the Civic Center Amphitheater.

This example shows the treatment for a meeting to be held at a lesser known place:

Thomas Young, president of the Community Chamber of Commerce, will speak on re-

Figure 12–2 This story was unusual because burglars smashed through a wall to reach valuable coats. This picture, taken through the hole, helps give perspective. (*Orange County Register* Photo by Clay Miller)

Figure 12–3 On-the-spot crime pictures are difficult to obtain. This photo, made during the 1965 Watts riot, was taken during the peak. The riot was initially news because of its size and later because of social implications. (*Los Angeles Herald-Examiner* Photo)

gional planning at 8 p.m. Wednesday in the Green Derby Restaurant, 10521 N. Adams St.

The reporter must decide how detailed the "where" descriptions must be. The experienced journalist provides the more complete details when there is a doubt.

Other Aspects of "Where." The "where," like the "when," often becomes of secondary importance in "follow" stories. An account of what a speaker said usually relies more on high points of his talk than on where he said it. The name of the place might well be midway in the story without spoiling the effect. The obvious exception would be the situation where the speaker was mobbed or involved in a riot, thus opening new dimensions for the article.

The "where" can be a fascinating part of many stories. Examples include the marriage that takes place in skindiving suits at the seashore, the student who receives a diploma in a hospital because of sickness or injury, the temperance meeting held in an auditorium belonging to a brewery, or the play presented in a prison.

OTHER APPLICATIONS OF THE "W's"

The "why" of a story frequently is the most important element and is akin to interpretive reporting. The journalist must be intelligent and curious enough to continually ask himself "why" in gathering stories. He also must be brusque enough, in a nice way, to ask

questions: the replies may not be obvious, and they may help make even a better story.

If the city or county tax rate is increasing (or decreasing), what is the cause? If traffic accidents are going up (or down), what started the trend? If there has been an increase (or decrease) in juvenile arrests, what triggered this situation? If officials predict a radical change, up or down, in school enrollment, what is setting the pattern?

The intelligent reader will wonder why many things are happening, and curious reporters must anticipate the questions that give the pertinent five W's.

EXERCISES

1. Using a story from your local newspaper, mark the "who, what, when, where, why, and how" elements, and note how they are played in the article.

2. Do the same with a story that you wrote before reading this chapter.

3. Gather facts and write a story that lends itself to emphasis on the "when" element.

4. Using your local newspaper, examine the stories to determine the importance of the "when" element by noting its position in the articles; make a count of those that contain *no* time element, and observe whether this detracts from one's understanding of the story situation.

13

How Beats Are Covered

The "beat" reporter is the backbone of the news department. Beats cover the important sources that newspapers rely on regularly for stories: this is true for commercial weeklies and dailies, and it is true for campus newspapers.

DEFINING A BEAT

A beat is an individual or place where a reporter is assigned to make regular contacts: daily, weekly, or other intervals, as the situation may require. Merely *covering* sports, therefore, is not a beat. Covering a *specific* sport on a small newspaper or a *particular* team on a large one would constitute a beat. Other examples of beats would be covering courts, the police, City Hall, schools, medicine, ecology, consumerism, or science.

The reporter assigned to a beat is responsible for the news that develops on it. If a competitor gets it first or someone complains legitimately that a beat's news is not being covered, the editor will want to know why. Reporters usually cover their beats so that they become the trusted eyes and ears of their editors as well as of the readers.

Different reporters could be sent to a beat from day to day, but editors prefer to assign one regularly so that he will develop an intimate knowledge of the people and subjects he contacts and will be familiar with the stories and their backgrounds. The reporter becomes an "expert" on matters on his beat and can deal with them authoritatively.

LARGE AND SMALL CITIES

The amount of news and techniques of handling a beat vary greatly according to the nature of the community and size of the city. In a smaller community, the City Hall reporter would write stories on many situations that would be of minor interest in a large city. The reporter covering city government in a metropolitan area could write stories only on matters of relatively high or general interest, since limited space would prohibit editors from printing everything that happened.

A community's geographical location and its interests also help determine the beats to be covered. In a farming community there would be an agricultural beat producing stories of great local interest. Farming would be of secondary interest in an industrial area, but labor relations and the dominating industries would provide beats yielding important local news.

A port city would have a harbor beat, and a community where a college dominated would require a campus beat. A city with a large ethnic minority logically needs one or more reporters assigned to the beat of covering its activities of interest within the group and to the general public.

DUTIES OF THE BEAT REPORTER

Reporters covering a beat develop genuine friendships with the people they meet. Some individuals may be daily news sources, while others may provide information only occasionally. The reporter's value includes knowing news sources, so that if a need arises, they will respond because they know and trust the writer's integrity and reliability.

Aside from regular coverage of day-to-day news, the beat reporter usually provides regular feature or "human interest" stories. Examples include an employee on the beat who is retiring after a half-century on the job,

one who has a fascinating hobby, background on technicalities involved on the beat, or stories analyzing trends.

"SYNDICATING" THE NEWS

Some beats offer so much news that a reporter would have difficulty in covering everything and might wish for a helper. Other reporters on the beat, obviously, feel the same way. In these cases reporters often share or "syndicate" news facts. If four important meetings happen at the same time on a beat, reporters from different newspapers or TV stations each cover a session and then share notes with the others.

While sharing *facts*, the reporters would write individual stories. Even though they used the same set of facts, the articles would vary substantially because of different approaches or evaluations of the news elements.

The beat syndicate is an "honor" operation. If a reporter handling news under the system withheld facts from the others, he would find himself boycotted and unable to obtain information that fellow reporters gathered.

REGIONAL BEATS

While in the traditional sense a beat indicates coverage of a particular news source in a community, some reporters are assigned the

Figure 13–1 Many beats develop as a result of area interests or industries and provide important stories regularly. Farming is of great importance in the Midwest, and Don Muhm, farm editor of the *Des Moines* (Iowa) *Register and Tribune*, takes notes as he interviews farmer Elmer Carlson.

Figure 13–2 An entire nation or even a group of neighboring nations can be a reporter's beat. This Associated Press photo shows East Pakistani refugees in Calcutta, India. (Wide World Photos)

Figure 13–3 A war can be a beat. This Associated Press photo shows a South Vietnamese trooper holding to a helicopter during an evacuation. There was no room for him inside. (Wide World Photos)

"beat" of covering an entire city or county for a newspaper a substantial distance away. These reporters are also known as "correspondents." Their assignments are to cover *all* the news from a specific community that would be of interest to readers.

Editors expect this reporter to use judgment in covering his community beat and to use his time in gathering news stories that will be of maximum interest to readers.

PRESS ROOMS

In the larger cities, most beats include a press room, or office, provided by the organization or agency being covered. Reporters from the media have desks, usually furnished by their company, and use the press room as headquarters. Here they type their stories, have telephones, meet people, and keep files of story materials. Since many beat reporters phone stories or dispatch them by messengers, they infrequently visit their offices.

TYPICAL BEATS

Specialized training and interests obviously help a reporter cover a beat, and ed-

itors consider these factors when making staff assignments. We can discuss covering beats, but to detail techniques is virtually impossible: a reporter, armed with subject information in the field, can learn more during two weeks on a beat than during months in a classroom.

Newly assigned beat reporters therefore often accompany their predecessors for a breaking-in period even though they are grounded in writing techniques. This allows them to meet key people and learn details regarding story sources, since seemingly identical beats vary according to state, regional, and even community differences in laws and customs.

Here are representative beats, and what the reporter covering them might expect.

POLICE

This is probably the best-known beat. It customarily covers not only crime and auto accidents, but also reports on missing persons, industrial accidents, and other breakdowns in normal living. Many of the news media's biggest stories break on this beat. The reporter covering it should have good judgment, take

pride in accuracy, recognize news values, and be able to handle stories quickly and thoroughly.

The press rooms provided by police departments in most cities often are headquarters for regional correspondents assigned to cover all activities in a community. The press room usually includes a communication system monitoring both sides of police radio calls to keep reporters alert to developments. Each reporter customarily has a telephone connected to the police master switchboard and another to his office. The latter is necessary in deadline situations to provide quick access to the newspaper city desk.

Contrary to popular belief, beat reporters do not go out on every police call. While most incidents are momentous to those personally involved, the majority are routine from a jour-

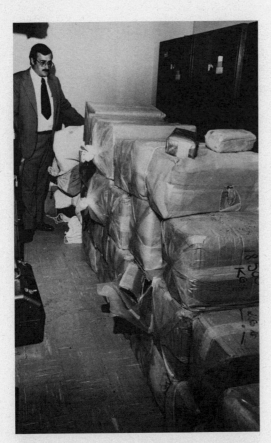

Figure 13–4 The police beat produces pictures as well as stories. This officer checks bales of marijuana seized in a raid. (*Orange Coast Daily Pilot* Photo)

nalistic standpoint and can wait until officers file written reports. On situations apparently involving an event of major interest, the beat reporter alerts the office to send a reporter. There is so much crime in the larger cities that one reporter could not begin to cover all potential stories alone. In smaller communities, there is relatively less crime, and the area is smaller; one reporter then can handle the chores.

Going to the scene of a crime or accident seldom gives the reporter an advantage unless the story is a major one or a deadline is approaching. Instead, reporters wait for written reports. Many incidents require hours to investigate, and a reporter who sped to the scene not only would be in the officers' way but in many cases would be forced to wait for completion of the investigation.

Most police or sheriff departments maintain a "log" with brief digests of the officers' reports. Reporters beginning a shift scan this record to determine which incidents are worthy of stories. The digests provide the key for the detailed reports needed to write news stories.

In many smaller communities, newspapers frequently print the police log in its entirety as a matter of public interest. Entries may range from a report of a lost child found minutes later to a bank robbery. The police log, with its newsy details, can be a well-read feature in a community newspaper. Printing a large city's police log would be impractical because its length would consume several pages every day.

Dailies in large cities screen police stories more finely in order to use only those of top interest. Crowded streets and freeways produce so many accidents in metropolitan areas that the one which appears in the newspaper must be an unusual one. A wreck involving an unusual object, such as a boat being towed, or an airplane making an emergency landing would be featured in a newspaper; conventional collisions, even though they involve major injuries, unfortunately are becoming so commonplace that they lack news impact.

Unless there are unusual circumstances, big-city dailies confine themselves to stories regarding major thefts or those with unusual angles. Police beat reporters soon learn the nature of the stories their editors do or do not want to run.

Medium-sized or smaller dailies and the weeklies use proportionately more police beat stories.

Obtaining Information. In most states, the official police, sheriff, or other law enforcement reports are available to reporters. Journalists can use these documents to substantiate their stories in case those involved dispute the news coverage. Except under unusual or special circumstances, reporters would be reluctant to use information from onlookers unless it could be substantiated independently and the witnesses, through identification, appeared reliable.

The wise reporter, unlike TV prototypes, lets the police officer do the investigating except under extraordinary situations, and then after clearances with editors. The fair reporter also may handle stories of exceptional interest by contacting victims, arrested persons, or their attorneys to present all sides.

Conflicts can develop between law enforcement authorities and the police beat reporter: officers sometimes feel that their side is not presented enthusiastically enough. When newspapers publish stories of acquittals, they look on the publications as the pharaohs did on messengers who brought bad news and were put to death. Many officers feel that newspapers should play down this court news to avoid "encouraging" criminals. Reporters whose stories are not greatly "enthusiastic" in giving the police viewpoint often feel that officers are not as forthright as they might be in providing information.

Newspaper reporters are the eyes and ears of the public, which is interested in a police department's successes and failures. In most communities, police cooperate with journalists and withhold only that information that would enable a criminal to escape detection. In cooperating, officers recognize that they are employees of the public and not a power unto themselves.

COURTS

Coverage of the courts is allied to the police beat in that persons accused of crimes arrive there for trial. Many civil, or noncriminal, cases also develop into stories. Laws and many legal procedures vary from state to state. The reporter assigned to cover the courts can become a well-informed layman by asking questions of court attachés, attorneys, and judges, all of whom usually are pleased to clarify technicalities to assure fair stories.

In most states, local courts are divided into two classes. They are (1) the justice, municipal, or *inferior* court, where civil cases involving smaller amounts of money, small claims, misdemeanors or relatively minor crimes, including parking citations, and associated matters are settled, and (2) the upper, or *superior*, court where civil cases involving larger amounts of money, felonies or major crimes, requests for restraining orders or injunctions, and appeals from lower courts are heard. This higher court often is the one that issues marriage licenses and grants divorces or dissolutions of marriage.

Figure 13–5 The trend is for reporters, particularly on larger newspapers, to specialize in their fields of coverage. Seated at their desks at the *Fort Worth Star-Telegram* are Linda Pavlik, federal reporter, and Charlotte Guest (right), medical writer. (United Press International Photo)

Whether a crime is a misdemeanor or felony is set by statutes that vary from state to state. Individual states also legislate the amount of money involved which lifts a civil suit from one level of the judicial system to another. Jury trials are held at both court levels. Decisions can be appealed to district courts, a state supreme court, or the United States Supreme Court.

Crimes involving alleged violations of selective service, postal, customs, internal revenue, or other federal laws are tried in United States district courts, which are situated in major cities.

Photographs in the Courtroom. Section 35 of the Canons of Judicial Ethics of the American Bar Association bans the use of conventional or television cameras in a courtroom. The reason for this prohibition probably goes back to the early twentieth century when cameras were bulky and used flash guns illuminated with a blast of powder. Despite today's modern small cameras and fast film that can be used in natural light, the bar association holds steadfast in its refusal to lift the ban.

The bar in recent years has reiterated its fear that the use of cameras would upset the dignity of the courtroom and expose participants in a trial to sensational publicity that could defeat justice.

Judges vary in their interpretation of the bar's injunction against photographs. The most lenient will permit picture taking once they have left the room, while those who are the most strict refuse to permit a journalist to so much as carry a camera, even though it contains no film, into the courtroom.

Courts also ban tape recorders because of potential damage to dignity.

Teamwork in the Courts. The previously mentioned "syndicating" whereby competing reporters share basic information because of many things to cover on a beat often is used by those assigned to the courts. Attending several trials simultaneously would be impossible, but when a reporter is responsible for individual sessions or courtrooms and shares information, each journalist can furnish complete coverage.

Members of the court press room "syndicate" often rotate the duties of preparing carbons of marriage licenses issued and divorces filed or granted.

LOCAL GOVERNMENT

Among the important beats is covering those who make decisions and laws at the local level. Depending on the state and the size of the community, the local government is called the city, town, village, or county, and its elected officers may serve on a council, commission, board of trustees, or other agency designation. This unit produces important news stories because it sets the tax rate, decides road-building programs, sets building standards, and passes laws affecting the quality of living.

The reporter covering this beat attends the governing body's meetings, where the pros and cons of important matters are aired. He also meets frequently with city officials while producing stories and often develops an expertise on governmental affairs equaled by few in the community.

SCHOOL ACTIVITIES

Education, involving so many people because they are students or are related to students, also is an important beat. A single district covering all grades sometimes serves a community, while others have separate agencies for various school levels. These districts also have a publicly elected governing body known, according to state, by varying names: board of trustees, board of education, board of schools, or board of governors.

A reporter covers the school board's meetings, where teachers are hired, contracts are awarded for constructing new buildings, and other business is conducted. Some activities may be worth stories, while others may be routine. The good beat reporter will extend activities into other fields, however, by writing stories pertaining to unusual developments in education. Such feature articles could include explanations of innovations in teaching mathematics, the progress students are making through a new learning machine, unusual clubs

Figure 13–6 Kathi Miller of the *Fort Worth Star-Telegram* conducts an interview in her position as education writer.

Figure 13–7 Governmental news is an important beat because of its impact on people. Here is Gloria Sneed of the *Detroit News*' city-county bureau interviewing Mayor Roman S. Gribbs.

for teachers or students, or social problems that develop because of controversial styles in hair or wearing apparel.

The reporter who, with interest, covers any beat will note trends and problems which he can translate into words that the average reader can understand.

RELIGION

Church news can be routine, or it can furnish one of a newspaper's most fascinating beats. Many writers handling religious news let this beat degenerate into nothing more than a weekly listing of churches with pastors' sermon topics. These listings really are not news and have virtually no readability except for those associated with a particular church or minister; the latter would probably go to church anyway even though the listing did not appear.

Many newspapers, both large and small, build the religion beat into one that holds the reporter's and the readers' interest. These newspapers discard the weekly church "roster" in favor of news and features pertaining to all dimensions of religion, with emphasis as much as is practical on local aspects. One example is taking an issue of international interest, such as the Dead Sea Scrolls or a revision of the Bible, and interviewing representative religious leaders for their views as to impact. Other current social issues in which churches are—or should be—involved also provide subjects for stories that subscribers will read even though they may not be churchgoers.

This beat also permits development of many features. The reporter, after interviewing those involved, can write stories giving the perspectives on new formats of services, unusual projects sponsored by church-related organizations, backgrounds of guest speakers, and insight into the beliefs of the lesser-known religious groups.

Regular features can include articles in which ministers digest their "favorite" sermons or tell what challenged them to enter the ministry. Other features that could help build reader interest are histories of individual churches and "guest" articles contributed by local laymen.

The reporter covering this beat should remember that Jewish and some Christian groups observe their Sabbath on days other than Sunday, and should make it a point to accord these organizations adequate coverage.

Nontraditional religious groups, including those outside the Judeo-Christian area, usually have relatively small memberships in America, but their ceremonies and beliefs, when treated respectfully in stories, often generate greater reader interest than the activities of the larger churches.

POLITICS

The political beat is associated with local government coverage on small to medium-sized newspapers but is often a separate one on larger papers. The decision to cover or not to cover a political candidate or meeting is in effect "slanting" the news, and the political writer therefore may work closely with the editor or publisher. Since this reporter develops an intimate knowledge of the newspaper's policies, this position frequently is a stepping-stone to an appointment as an editorial writer.

The newspaper's size helps determine the scope of the political beat. On smaller newspapers, the beat would encompass only community or regional candidates; on larger ones it could include traveling with candidates seeking such offices as a state governorship or the presidency of the United States.

The person selected for this beat usually is one who has a knowledge of political science and probably a person who has been on the local scene long enough to recognize the various factions and personalities involved in campaigns. Stories covered range from "background" articles on current developments to descriptions of political club meetings, conventions, rallies, and conferences.

OTHER BEATS

Journalists discover that many beats develop according to the nature of their community or changing social interests. Larger newspapers usually have more beats and can allow the reporter to specialize to a greater degree. Smaller papers have the advantage of

being able to use more stories from individual beats rather than choosing from the most newsworthy of the many written. One great encouragement for every writer, as well as the people on his beat, is seeing stories displayed in the newspaper.

Areas such as ecology, consumerism, drama, science, aerospace, agriculture, labor, medicine, television, books, art, travel, shipping, boating, and finance provide beats according to a newspaper's size and locale.

Whatever beat a reporter is assigned, he will cover it best when he has or can develop a genuine interest and expertise in the field. He then can earn the friendship and respect of his contacts, and will be a valuable staff member.

ROTATING BEATS

To produce lucid and meaningful stories, reporters must remain alert to the challenges of their beats. While friendships are important, writers must resist the temptation to withhold controversial or negative news. Most reporters are intelligent and ethical enough to reject writing for people on the beat instead of the newspaper's readers. Reporters who enjoy their beats also keep abreast of developments in their writing field so they recognize news values and do not become "stale" or cynical regarding their job.

Those who develop false loyalties or whose stories reflect boredom often find themselves transferred to other reportorial duties. Some newspapers, as a matter of policy, attempt to avoid such possibilities by rotating reporters at one- to four-year intervals.

BEATS ON A CAMPUS

Most college campuses offer many beats for coverage by student newspaper staff members. On even the smallest campus, the average student does *not* know everything that is developing and wants to read *accurate* details regarding things that affect him or his friends. One obvious beat would be the student government meetings, where a student reporter can develop the skills of reporting debates

Figure 13-8 The police beat is one of the basic beats on almost every newspaper. *Detroit News* reporter David Grant interviews Inspector Harold Smith, a police commissioner aide, while making his rounds of police headquarters.

Figure 13-9 Governmental offices provide beats with stories telling the community of the activities. Here is Cecil Johnson, city hall reporter for the *Fort Worth Star-Telegram*.

among various groups and at the same time serve the general student body by providing news that can affect their welfare. The administrative offices also provide a beat yielding stories pertaining to students.

Various colleges provide different beats, according to their organization and student interests. Aside from student government and administration activities, typical beats can include individual sports and coaches, clubs, political and social organizations, the library, the student treasurer, the lost and found, the student employment office, the scholarship office, and chairmen of academic divisions. Special circumstances and individual colleges will offer other beats.

College beats, like those anywhere else, will produce stories when the reporter uses intelligence and imagination while interviewing informants and writes stories fairly but without fear of dealing with controversies.

EXERCISES

1. Invite a reporter who covers the police, court, city government, or another beat for a local newspaper to attend a question-and-answer session with student journalists.

2. Make a list of the beats that could be assigned to reporters covering your campus; compare the list with those actually assigned by the college newspaper editor.

3. Select one of the recommended campus beats, and cover the stories on it that develop for two weeks.

4. Analyze a local newspaper for a week, and list stories that apparently came from beats you can identify as being covered.

5. If two or more newspapers or other publications serve your community, analyze their coverage of a beat of your choice for a week. Compare the extent and effectiveness of their efforts.

14

Covering Interviews and Speeches

Contacts with people provide the information for most stories in a newspaper or for radio-TV newscasts. Even seemingly "non-people" sources originate with people—examples are court and other public records; police reports; plays, films, records, and books to be reviewed; and story material received in the mail. These situations often require personal contacts to obtain information to write a good story.

TYPES OF CONTACTS

Names big and small—and what their owners say—make news. News can develop in few ways without involving people. These contacts normally come through personal interviews, telephone conversations, speeches or public meetings, or press conferences. The techniques of handling people vary considerably according to the situation, and so do the methods of taking notes.

THE "INTERVIEW"

An interview is not necessarily a formal event, but covers any situation where the re-

porter talks with someone face to face to obtain information. An interview, therefore, can range from a conversation with a local club official who calls at the newspaper office to tell about a meeting to the formal event where a reporter assembles with others to ask questions of the President of the United States.

A Few Precautions. Most people involved in news are meeting reporters for the first time, and as a result may be nervous and apprehensive. They may hesitate to talk, fearing that their words may be "wrong" and reflect against them in a story. This can be true in a relatively harmless situation, where they have committed no wrong or are not even involved in a controversial matter. They are frightened simply because they are doing something for the first time: meeting a reporter.

People who have met reporters before are not so apprehensive. They know that journalists do not bite, and that most are good ones who only write what people say. Reporters, however, must put the uninitiated at ease. Even using the term "interview" can frighten some story subjects because it connotes a formal event or even, if they believe TV or old movies, an inquisition. Reporters should create a relaxed and informal atmosphere. One way to do this is to suggest a "talk," which really is an "interview" although it lacks the formal implication or urgency that the latter indicates. Another is to postpone any suggestion of taking notes until after the reporter establishes rapport with the subject.

THE TELEPHONE INTERVIEW

Personal interviews, which give the reporter a better chance to achieve rapport and watch facial reactions, often are impractical or impossible because of such obstacles as deadlines, difficulty in reaching the subject, or distances. Sometimes there is little to be gained in a face-to-face meeting.

Reporters achieve a great deal, both in time saved and information gained, by using the telephone. A practical way to conduct phone interviews is by avoiding preliminaries or lengthy explanations. The reporter simply identifies himself, digests the problem, explains the deadline or other problem, and asks the questions. In some situations, reporters may make an appointment for a personal interview after obtaining the information needed for a deadline. The need would vary according to the completeness of the telephone interview and the importance of the story.

COVERING SPEECHES

Among the important sources for stories are meetings in an auditorium or in conjunction with a dinner where there may be one or more talks of news interest. Many organizations provide journalists with seating near the speaker, and those giving talks often provide carbons or digests of their talks. The careful reporter will follow the actual speech to determine whether the subject departs from the text and ad libs material that may be more news than the prepared text.

Often a reporter may chat with a story subject before or after a speech. If the speaker makes "off-the-cuff" remarks that are more newsy than the formal talk, the writer owes it to his editors and readers to feature this material in the story. The reporter, *not*

the speaker, should decide what is worthy of news coverage.

When a reporter covers a speech or meeting, his duty is not to prepare a "transcript" of all that is said. The reporter's obligation, instead, is to tell the important points in the story and discard those that are of comparatively little interest.

PRESS CONFERENCES

When a person or organization wishes to make an announcement of importance, the press conference frequently is chosen as the vehicle for reaching the media. Journalists from newspapers, radio, TV, magazines, and other media are invited to the conference, usually held in a reserved room at a hotel or other central location. A printed release or an oral announcement regarding the subject of the meeting often precedes a question-and-answer session.

Press conferences can involve presidents, governors, mayors, or visiting celebrities who are accustomed to this means of reaching the media. Conferences also may center on individuals who unexpectedly find themselves in the news spotlight and want to give their viewpoints to the press. These individuals might be,

Figure 14–1 Tape recorders can help ensure accuracy in reporting speeches or interviews. The late Orrin C. Evans, veteran reporter for the *Philadelphia Bulletin*, uses one while interviewing Clarence Farmer (left), chairman of the Philadelphia Commission on Human Relations.

Figure 14–2 Press conferences are epitomized in the heavily covered meetings of journalists with the President of the United States. President Nixon faces newspaper, radio, and TV journalists at a press conference in the East Room of the White House. (United Press International Photo)

for example, accused of a crime, presenting results of an investigation, answering charges previously aired publicly, or otherwise making an announcement of public interest.

The more sophisticated principals of press conferences may, because of their status, arrive with an entourage of public relations attendants to help answer questions or serve refreshments.

Journalists share in the replies to each other's questions at press conferences, but give individual treatment to the stories.

There are occasions when individuals or organizations call press conferences for announcements that are not newsworthy in an attempt to capitalize on the results of legitimate ones. Most journalists can screen "phony" press conferences and boycott them.

HINTS FOR INTERVIEWING

As indicated, the most productive and newsy interviews develop when the subject is

at ease with the reporter. People are naturally tense because most are not accustomed to the prospect of having their words taken down for a news story that thousands will read.

PREPARING FOR THE INTERVIEW

One way to help create a good atmosphere and make the interview go better for all concerned is for the reporter to brief himself on the background of the story subject. This is not always easy when the interviewee is involved in a spot news situation with an impending deadline. One readily available place to look for all subjects is the clipping file or "morgue" maintained by most newspapers.

When the person is nationally known or has been in the news frequently, the reporter can consult reference books such as *Who's Who*. If the subject wrote a book, the reporter should examine a copy to gain perspective.

This research can help the reporter to frame meaningful questions and avert such catastrophes as asking an expert on Latin-American affairs questions pertaining to the effect of household detergents on river pollution, or quizzing an expert on Indian affairs about what is being done to relieve congested transportation in Southern California. While these analogies may seem ridiculous, experienced reporters who fail to check backgrounds often make such mistakes.

The reporter who takes the time to familiarize himself with backgrounds will gain the respect of the subject and add more depth to the interview when he demonstrates a knowledge of the individual's background. By skipping time-consuming preliminaries, the reporter and interviewee can delve into important questions and to-the-point discussions.

Research into the subject's background also gives the reporter material for giving depth and more interest to a story.

STARTING THE INTERVIEW

The reporter must judge when the story subject is at ease and ready to answer questions. If he or she appears tense, the wise reporter chats leisurely about other things before leading into the areas of concern. This procedure often is necessary even with people involved in noncontroversial situations. On the other hand, some subjects are eager to talk, but their conversation wanders to areas that have nothing to do with the matter at hand. The journalist must politely, but firmly, provide questions to direct the person into the area to be covered.

Reporters have few problems with "professionals," or those who because of their place in life frequently meet journalists. These individuals usually are cooperative, even in unfavorable situations, because they are accustomed to talking with reporters.

TAKING NOTES

Since few people have "photographic" memories that retain substantial amounts of information, some method is required for accurately preserving the important points an individual makes during a contact with a journalist. Unless an accurate record is made, the news story obviously will be wrong—to the unhappiness of all concerned from the interviewee to the reader.

Whatever method is used, the reporter should strive to maintain a relaxed setting by having a preliminary talk with the story subject before making any move to take notes. While everyone wants his words taken down accurately so the story will be correct, the average person has never had such attention. He may "freeze," refusing to say anything of importance. Seasoned journalists overcome this fear by talking without attempting to make notes; when the story subject appears at ease, the reporter suggests that taking notes will help accuracy. By this time the interviewee should be relaxed and trustful, and the conversation can be continued with notes being taken.

USE OF SHORTHAND

The ideal way to take notes is in shorthand, and the journalist who masters this skill will find it much easier to handle stories. Few reporters, unfortunately, have achieved this; they are consequently forced to devise their own shorthand symbols and combine them with conventional writing or printing. In making hasty non-shorthand notes, journalists often find that the quality of their handwriting suffers. They must transcribe the jottings promptly to ensure the accurate story that all concerned expect.

The prospective journalist who expects to achieve success and ease in performing his work should do what many veteran writers failed to do: learn shorthand. The skill is invaluable to a reporter, and, moreover, will distinguish him from others who have not done so and may be competing for a job.

Reporters usually take abundant notes but base their stories only on those they decide are pertinent. During an interview, reporters have no way of knowing the major story element and must have adequate notes for "insurance" when they sit down to write the story and make that determination.

USE OF TAPE RECORDERS

Many newspapers and radio stations equip staff members with tape recorders, an increasingly valuable tool for the reporter. Recorders not only eliminate the burden of taking detailed notes, but they also help assure the story subject that his speech or replies to questions will be reported accurately.

While tape recorders help accuracy, a disadvantage is that the reporter must go over lengthy tapes to find important segments of a talk. Some writers take notes while using a recorder and after completing the story listen to the tape to check for accuracy.

Just as the sight of a notebook and pen requires preliminaries to reassure the interviewee, the plan to use a recorder also should be explained to avoid distrust from those not accustomed to dealing with the press. The reporter who begins an interview by thrusting a microphone in front of the subject is almost certain to terminate the talk before it begins. One way to win the interviewee's confidence is to begin a discussion and develop rapport. When the interview is going well, the reporter suggests the use of a tape recorder to avoid any possibility of misquoting.

The recorder then can be placed into operation, with the interviewee's full knowledge and consent.

Those accustomed to dealing with the press prefer using a tape recorder for the interest of accuracy. These "professionals" know from experience that they shouldn't tell secrets to a reporter, and realize what they say will be used, if it is newsy, whether or not a recorder is used.

Those in the spotlight at public meetings and press conferences usually are accustomed to tape recorders, just as they are to TV cameras. Many city councils and other public agencies not only expect recorders but even make their own tapes of meetings for the use of reporters and to compose their official minutes.

Reporters or their editors usually retain tapes at least until the story is published. If there is a likelihood that a controversy could develop, tapes are retained indefinitely.

Hidden Tape Recorders. The "speak-into-the-flower" approach, or taping interviews without the subject's knowledge, suggests something less than forthright in most situa-

tions. For conventional interviews, it is far wiser to bring the recorder into the open or not use it at all than to lose the subject's respect if he finds that it was hidden. The reporter dealing with honorable people has more to lose than to gain with hidden recorders.

In the case of the controversial interviewee or investigations, the concealed tape recorder may be necessary. These exceptions should be weighed carefully in view of state or federal laws and in consideration of personal and journalistic ethics.

Taping an ordinary telephone interview after the reporter has identified himself can be justified on the basis that there are no implications of "surveillance," and the recording helps, just as do written notes which the subject does not see being taken, to produce an accurate story. The lack of a face-to-face meeting that allows explanations is a disadvantage to any phone interview. To discuss the use of a recorder, in view of these disadvantages, probably would cause most subjects to refuse to talk.

Concealing a tape recorder during a personal interview is another matter. Reporters who defend the practice, in many cases with great merit, contend that the technique helps to arrive at the truth with individuals involved in questionable activities who would deny statements made to a writer carrying only a notebook. This, they argue, serves community interests by shedding light on situations which otherwise would never be brought to public attention.

Those who oppose the use of concealed recorders argue that the instruments constitute an invasion of privacy and deprive the interviewee of his rights, even though the subject may realize that he is talking with a reporter.

Question-and-answer Format. Tape recorders afford the opportunity for question-and-answer stories giving the entire text of an interview. This technique usually is reserved for subjects of considerable interest because of the large space involved.

The "Q-and-A" format has the advantage of providing more depth by letting the subject speak at length. A disadvantage is that it forces the reader to consume the entire story to learn the main points instead of providing a digest given in a conventional news article.

OFF-THE-RECORD STATEMENTS: WHEN?

Story subjects occasionally confide information to a reporter only to add, "Don't print that!" The decision as to whether or not to follow such an admonishment has ethical implications relating to the interviewee, reporter, reader, and the newspaper.

PERSONAL INTERVIEWS

The story subject unaccustomed to dealing with journalists often becomes engrossed in talking and provides information that may or may not be pertinent to the story but which he, the interviewee, views as harmful. The reporter must decide whether to use the material. Often such statements have little to do with the story, and the writer can produce a good article by ignoring the item. If the statement has a bearing on a situation of reader interest, the reporter has a moral obligation to his newspaper and its readers to ignore the request and print the information within the bounds of good judgment.

PUBLIC MEETINGS

There are circumstances when reporters *cannot*, in good faith, honor an individual's request to place statements "off the record" or otherwise suppress them. One example is when a speaker makes the request after making a statement before a public audience. All of the people present could not conceivably keep such a secret, so why should the reporter conceal news from his readers? They eventually would hear it, particularly if it had news impact, from someone in the audience. This version could very well be distorted and the reader would wonder why the newspaper attempted to "hide" the information.

The reporter, confronted by such a demand, should advise the speaker of the incongruity of the request or simply write the story without comment.

PRESS CONFERENCES

A different set of standards prevails at a press conference, usually attended by several journalists but not open to the public. If the speaker at a conference announced he was making an "off-the-record" statement, the reporters would feel indignant since the gathering was called to give news—not conceal it. If there was belief that the speaker would give information of substantial news interest, some reporters would leave the room before he spoke. This would allow freedom to publish the news if they learned it from another source.

Story subjects defend making "off-the-record" statements on the basis that they thus give background information to help the reporter in writing the story even though he does not use the forbidden facts. Journalists prefer, obviously, having the option to use all information. Many would agree that there are occasions when "off-the-record" facts are helpful. Seasoned journalists would caution the person agreeing to the injunction too frequently to remember that he, the reporter, is on the job to get information on—not off—the record.

PRESS "BRIEFINGS"

A favored technique among many high officials in Washington, D.C.—as well as in other circles—is to meet journalists for press "briefings." The understanding for all attending such meetings is that stories may be written on the information but reporters are ethically bound *not* to quote the source of the material.

Public officials and journalists who defend this method of providing news argue that the public gets valuable information which otherwise would not be released. Opponents contend that the technique only allows officials to test theories anonymously before publicly committing themselves. There are instances when reporters—believing that the news situation is so important that it transcends their agreement to keep sources "faceless"—name the sources of the information. The story source, as well as others who give "briefings," can retaliate by banning these reporters from future meetings.

HANDLING QUOTATIONS

The reporter is morally bound to see that a story reflects what a speaker said. To use a quotation out of context and thus distort the meaning would be unethical and possibly libelous.

DIRECT QUOTATIONS

The use of word-for-word or direct quotations can add sparkle to a story *if* the speaker's exact words are clear and to the point. Verbatim quotations with punch and zest can help tell the story, but there is no point in using the ones which are involved or difficult to read.

There is no validity to the reporter's excuse of "that's what the speaker said" when asked why he used confusing or pointless direct quotations. The speaker's personality may make oral statements understandable when *heard*, but the same words may be confusing in print.

Meaningful and clear quotations, however, can add zest to the story.

The subject during a personal interview may use awkward words to express a sparkling idea. Rather than use the confusing phrases, the alert reporter may counter with the request, "May I quote you?..." and state the idea lucidly. If the subject agrees, the information can be used in direct quotations and thus add to the story's readability.

Reminder: In American usage, the punctuation—including commas, periods, question marks, and exclamation marks—goes *inside* the quotation marks, except under unusual circumstances such as a quotation within a quotation.

INDIRECT QUOTATIONS

Condensing a quotation by removing unnecessary words or using better ones is not only permissible but *preferred* to using a word-for-word statement that is involved. In paraphrasing a direct quotation, the journalist must take care to retain the subject's intention and not produce a wrong or distorted meaning.

Quotation marks are removed when the statement is an indirect quotation, or not in the speaker's exact words.

ALTERNATING DIRECT AND INDIRECT QUOTATIONS

News stories seldom use large blocks of direct quotations. One reason is that verbatim quotations often are too "wordy" and do not read as well as they sound. Another is that readers want a digest of the story situation, and direct quotations tend to be more lengthy.

Unusual speakers and subjects do lend themselves to more lengthy direct quotations. Reporters and editors must decide the merits according to the situation.

One technique to avoid monotony in handling a speech or interview is to alternate paragraphs of direct and indirect quotations. Here is an example:

Mayor Thomas Jones announced today that he will seek election as a state senator from this district.

"I have the backing of mayors in 11 neighboring cities," declared the mayor, who was elected by a 2–1 majority two years ago. "With such community backing I think I can win."

Jones said Fred Thomas, a former mayor, will serve as his campaign manager and Mrs. Mary Smith will be general chairman.

"Substantial campaign pledges are assured," said the candidate, a 35-year-old attorney, "and with the office being vacated I expect wide support."

He added that branch campaign offices will be opened next Monday in eight neighboring cities.

EXERCISES

1. Attend a speech in your community; take notes and write a story based on the talk. Check the style and accuracy by comparing your article with one in a local newspaper and by having one or two persons who also attended the meeting read it.

2. Find examples of stories based on speeches, press conferences, personal interviews, and briefings in your local newspaper.

3. Invite a representative of your local city government or student body government to hold a press conference for student journalists; write a story on the session.

4. Interview a person of interest and write a story, interspersing direct and indirect quotations.

15
Developing Feature Stories

Feature stories are becoming an increasingly important part of newspapers and television news broadcasts. Audiences expect their menu of news to be "spiced" with features, which in varied ways provide a light touch of humor or added perspective for the important news of the day.

A group of journalists would define "features" in different ways, depending on their own backgrounds and working experience. Some would maintain that features are largely intended to "amuse" and could not be classified as "hard" news. Others would argue that features can be "soft" or "hard," citing examples of background stories helping people to understand a world crisis or community problem as examples of important articles best approached with the "feature" treatment.

There is, therefore, no way of categorizing feature stories by standards agreeable to all journalists. Even those working side by side on one newspaper probably would give various definitions.

Some journalists would regard features as a stepping-stone to being assigned a beat, while others would regard the opportunity of handling feature stories exclusively as a highly desirable career milestone.

GENERAL CONTENTS

A feature story, despite its name, is not fiction but a nonfiction article tailored for consumption by a newspaper or television audience. Its peculiarities in newspaper usage include ordinarily being shorter than its magazine counterpart. This is because the person reading a newspaper consumes it in a day, while the magazine reader has the periodical for a week or month and can spend longer reading it.

While more liberties in story construction are allowed, features follow the newspaper stylebook in regard to its requirements covering capitalization, abbreviations, numbers usage, preferred spelling, and other standards.

Features usually are relatively *timeless*, meaning that they can be held for days or weeks and still be usable. Those related to current events, of course, are *timely* and must be published before their information is valueless.

While the term "features" generally applies to written articles, it is also used when referring to columns, comics, information or "how to do it" articles, and puzzles. This chapter is concerned with reporter-produced written features.

THE LENGTH

A newspaper, to give the reader variety, requires different types and lengths of features. For example, the "cutie" or clever feature can be an amusing single paragraph placed on almost any page in the newspaper as a brightener.

Here is an example of the "short" feature:

Horses, mules and donkeys are banned from streets and sidewalks in Mid City unless they are properly "lit."

Municipal Attorney John Wright said that while examining old laws he discovered a 1925 ordinance that requires animals to have a light visible from 300 feet.

He said the highly industrialized city's law does not exempt Rudolph the Red-nosed Reindeer.

Some subjects can be treated better in a long article or even a series of several related stories used on consecutive days. While newspaper feature articles are shorter than similar stories in magazines, they can be longer than conventional news items and are usually written to be read in their entirety.

WHO WRITES FEATURES?

Virtually anyone on a newspaper's editorial staff presumably is qualified to write features, and most writers do produce them from time to time. On smaller newspapers there is more pressure on the staff, and writers produce features along with their other stories. Larger newspapers, with proportionately more staff members, assign some writers to full-time work producing exclusively feature stories. Reporters on beats write features based on the people and things they encounter.

Preparation for Writing Features. The best feature writers usually are those who are well grounded in conventional news. They know how to gather facts and recognize those that have the elements that can make readable features.

Writers accustomed to working under deadlines in handling conventional news learn almost automatically how to structure sentences to yield the most impact. On feature assignments, they can write more leisurely and refine these skills to make a story say more.

THE FORMAT FOR FEATURES

While journalists favor the inverted pyramid or summary format for news stories, features are more interesting when they follow the narrative or fiction outline. Unlike the news story, which is digested in the first paragraph or two, the feature may have its conclusion at the end.

With this consideration, editors try to place features on pages providing enough room so they will not need to be cut.

STORY CONSTRUCTION

The editor and writer expect the feature story to hold the reader's interest from beginning to end. The lead should be provocative to capture the reader's attention, and ensuing sentences and paragraphs must hold that interest.

Paragraphs, even in feature stories, are short when compared to those in conventional English composition. They can range longer, however, than the four-typed-lines average most news stories follow, but the reporter should recognize that paragraphs running longer than eight lines of typing are less readable.

More colorful descriptive phrases can be used in feature stories than in conventional articles, but the writer must remember that long sentences lose and confuse readers. Whether straight news or features, news stories, it must be emphasized, are consumed before the next issue arrives.

Straight news stories end when the writer uses all facts, or where an editor must cut to make the article fit. Feature stories often build to an ending that concludes with an ironic, humorous, tearful, or summarizing statement that is necessary to achieve the impact of the article's total effect.

Feature stories also lean more to interpretative reporting than do run-of-the-mill news stories. While the ideal "fair" news article attempts to tell *what* is happening, features have more room to develop the *why* and *how*, thus giving more perspective. This treatment gives a more human approach to news.

Photographs frequently are an important part of features, both from the standpoint of helping to display the article on a page and giving the readers a visual understanding.

Some story situations are covered best when the reporter and photographer work together, while others call for the writer to complete the article to give a better idea for picture possibilities. Features are an area where the "combination man," or reporter-photographer, can operate efficiently since deadline pressures are not so strict.

FEATURE IDEAS

Ideas for features come from many sources. Readers contact the newspaper office, those on beats make suggestions, editors assign subjects, or reporters "spot" ideas as they move around.

Most good reporters could stroll down a street for an hour, chatting with people, and produce a feature on some facet: their opinions of the weather, a sports event, national politics, or the chances for a successful rocket excursion to Mars.

Feature stories come in many sizes, shapes, and forms. People, of course, fascinate people the most.

Profiles. Stories giving the background of an individual make good news features. These articles develop through interviews and may have "news pegs" connecting them to a current event.

The "famous" or well-known person. The individual who has achieved note nationally or locally is a natural subject for a profile. Readers who have heard of this person would be interested in sidelights telling how he achieved his position. Visiting motion picture celebrities, executives of major firms whose decisions have a local or national impact, holders of public offices, or visiting foreign dignitaries are just a few of those that the reporter could "profile."

Figure 15–1 This touching photo illustrated a story about plates attached to redwood trees to unfold the names and stories of the trees to the blind. (*Oakland Tribune* Photo by Lonnie Wilson)

Figure 15–2 Skillful journalists develop ways of producing unusual pictures to illustrate feature situations. This picture noted the first day of sunshine after two weeks of rain. (*Oakland Tribune* Photo by Lonnie Wilson)

For example, an individual whose name is associated with a large local business enterprise may be little more than a name to the average reader. The public would be interested in a profile telling how he reached his position or how business interests helped him develop side activities such as charities or unusual hobbies. The newly elected mayor is a logical subject for a feature unveiling details of his background lost during the heat of the campaign. The woman who has risen to a key executive position and at the same time reared a family would also provide material for a readable feature, as would a foreign dignitary's contrasting background and his impressions of your city.

The little-known individual. People need not be famous to be interesting. Fascinating feature stories can be built around virtually any individual after an interview. The student on an exchange program from another nation, or even a different part of this country, would have interesting comparisons. The problems of a housewife who manages to rear a family and go to school at the same time make a readable feature not only for other housewives but for any person who can appreciate the situation. The janitor in a large building can tell his observations of the offices and departments that are or are not clean, and what he thinks when people do not notice him. The salesman can relate his observations of human behavior from the vantage point he occupies. Stories about people have few limitations.

Places. Stories about unusual places or little-known facts about familiar places make readable features. The article about the expedition into the Arctic or the jungles of South America gives the reporter an opportunity to delve into material that captures the attention of the person interested in faraway places—and most people are fascinated by authentic articles on unusual locales. The story playing up little-known facts about communities in the newspaper's own circulation area also is readable.

Historical. Many fact-filled articles dealing with local history can be developed with

Figure 15–3 Illustrating and writing feature stories can offer challenges that are not present in spot news situations. This posed photo illustrated the problems of a boy with parents who argued. (*Oakland Tribune* Photo by Lonnie Wilson)

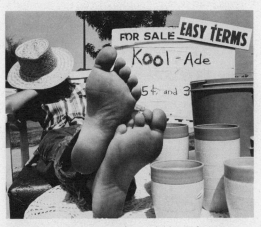

Figure 15–4 Stories involving children's business ventures are always good. This article was enhanced when the photographer caught the "easy terms" sign to show that young merchants were keeping pace with their elders. (*Orange County Register* Photo by Clay Miller)

the assistance of community historians, historical societies, and the files of early-day newspapers. These feature stories serve a real need: while the public can find many books on state and national history, there are few sources outside of newspaper articles for presenting fascinating local history.

Occupations. Unusual occupations intrigue people, most of whom have (or think they have) routine jobs. The candlemaker, crime laboratory expert, astronomer, teacher of the blind, dog trainer, or deep-sea diver only touch the surface of off-beat jobs that can make stories.

Stunts. Reporters involving themselves in stories can make fascinating features. Examples include attempting sky-diving, spending a night in a police patrol car, "joining" a questionable club or other organization to determine its legitimacy, or wearing a blindfold for a day to report the problems facing a blind person. Stories telling the results of these involvements help give the reader new perspectives.

The "Precede." Many feature stories revolve around a coming event. The special aspects of preparing for space flights could inspire numerous articles adding to understanding of the actual event. Other advance stories might tell of preparations being made for a major parade, a visit of the President of the United States, or a community festival. The behind-the-scenes activities of main events invariably produce stories with the human elements that help to illuminate the big news.

Pets. Stories involving pets that are unusual because of their breed or how they were trained invariably produce readable "human interest" features. The person who has a pet fox or other infrequently domesticated animal or who managed to train a cat or bird to perform tricks can provide material for a feature.

Calendar Events. Holidays produce opportunities to develop features. Veterans' Day is a good time to interview the community's oldest veteran, and Valentine's Day or Easter can give opportunities for articles on child art projects. A feature writer can interview Santa

Claus at Christmas, or list the resolutions that community leaders make for New Year's Day. Almost every week there is an official designation ranging from "Cotton Week" to "Dental Health Week," and features can be tied into the serious or humorous aspects of these occasions.

The Technical. The average person today learns a great deal regarding science and technology beginning early in school, and this knowledge brings an appetite for more information. Features explaining, in layman's language, the advances in medicine, electronics, mechanics, and man's understanding of natural sciences attract great readership.

Hobbies. Almost everyone has a hobby, whether it is an indoor one such as stamp collecting or an outdoor pursuit like hiking. People enjoy reading about the hobbies of others, particularly when they are off-beat or unusual. The person who collects picture postcards, spikes from different railways, antique toys, early-day movies, or vintage books, or who

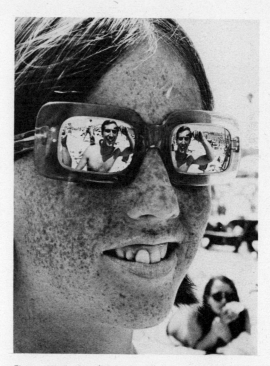

Figure 15–5 Beaches and other recreational facilities usually offer feature story ideas. This photo illustrated an article on summer activities. (*Orange County Register* Photo by Clay Miller)

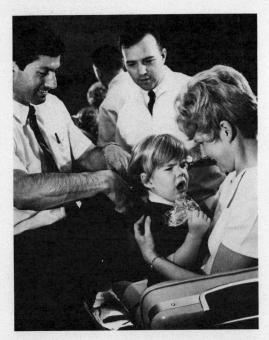

Figure 15–6 First haircut. Little other explanation is needed for this photograph illustrating a feature on a youngster's first formal meeting with a barber. (*Orange County Register* Photo by Clay Miller)

goes on archaeological expeditions will be the source for a feature story. An important part of the article, of course, will be adventures or humorous incidents connected with the hobby, and how the person got interested in the field.

People: Young or Old. The very old and very young make good features because of their accomplishments: the youngsters who prove they can adapt themselves to society, and the oldsters because of their contributions, large and small, to mankind. A good reporter can sit down and chat with a person and later translate this conversation into a readable feature. If a reporter enjoys talking with people, readers will enjoy his account of that conversation.

Academic Journals. Many natural scientists, archaeologist historians, political scientists, medical researchers, and other scholars regularly record their findings and observations in learned publications intended for those in their field. The reporter with an understanding of a specialized area can, with the aid of the researcher involved, translate many aspects of technical articles into feature stories appealing to the general public. Those in the academic world usually appreciate the opportunity of bringing their work to the attention of the public in this manner, since the average person cannot understand technical writing and the average researcher cannot express himself in layman's language.

Education. More and more people are attending schools and spending more years in obtaining an education. Most young people and their parents, knowing the increasing value of education, are planning ahead to college days and want to know about developments. New techniques in elementary and high schools also make good features, because people are curious about the programs offered their children and about the changes made since they attended school. Most educators at all levels eagerly cooperate with reporters to help inform the public, which ultimately pays the bill and is entitled to know of the programs.

EXERCISES

1. Analyze a local daily newspaper for a week and note the variety of feature stories used.

2. Select a current topic and discuss it with the first 10 people you meet on the campus; write a feature story in the third person reporting your conversations.

3. Interview an instructor in a field in which you have an interest; emphasize questions pertaining to developments in his field. Write a feature on the interview.

4. Select a faculty member or student who has an interesting background and interview him. Write a profile on the information you obtain.

16

Ethics and Libel

A newspaper, carrying the printed word to thousands of homes, wields a great deal of influence and power. It also has the obligation to use integrity and fairness in editing and publishing stories because of its power. In America, the first amendment to the Bill of Rights guarantees Freedom of the Press. That freedom is restricted only by ethics, the legal rights of the individual, and the government's right for protection against sedition and espionage.

Many of the ethics involved in journalism developed through the years as traditions and are observed voluntarily. The individual's rights are protected by laws giving him damages if he is libeled or his privacy is invaded.

LIBEL

A major legal aspect of journalism is libel, an area of which every reporter and editor should be aware. Newspapers retain attorneys to judge the fine points of libel when necessary, but the elements are simple.

DEFINITION

Libel is the printed or visual defamation of an individual, while slander is the oral or spoken defamation. Stories, headlines, pictures, the cutlines or other explanatory material under pictures, cartoons, signs, editorials, or letters to the editor containing defamatory material are potentially libelous. Defamatory material used on television or radio, particularly when a script is used or it is recorded, also constitutes libel.

Defamation is that which tends to expose an individual to ridicule; diminish the respect, confidence, esteem, or goodwill which the person enjoys in the community; provoke adverse and derogatory feelings against him; or deprive him of the right to earn a living.

Any individual can be libeled, and so can a company, partnership, joint venture, or corporation if a story casts doubts on its credit, honesty, efficiency, or integrity in doing business.

Three Types of Libel. Stories can be libelous *per se*, meaning that a statement alone caused injury and no additional proof is needed to show damages. An example of this type of libel would be if a newspaper ran a story stating that John T. Smith of 2345 Main Street was arrested for robbery when the man held by police actually was John T. Smith of 2345 Mound Street. The Smith on Main Street was *not* arrested and therefore has been libeled. If a story identifies Mary White as a shoplifter but she has *not* been convicted of such a crime, she is libeled and can collect damages. When an article charges that football player William Young accepted money to lose a game, the publication will lose a libel suit unless it can *prove* without question that he did so. The publication that charges a doctor with malpractice, a woman with being a prostitute, an individual with being a robber, a professor with selling grades, or a city official or student representative with stealing from the treasury will lose a libel suit unless it can *prove* its statements in court.

To emphasize, the publication or reporter must *prove* the charges. The person charged does *not* need to prove himself innocent.

Libel *per se* therefore involves statements which in themselves could cause injury to the person named.

Libel *per quod*, on the other hand, pertains to statements that would be harmless except for special circumstances that could cause damage. If a newspaper used a story, for instance, branding a specific hotel as a fire trap and thereby frightening guests away, it would face a libel suit because the *circumstances* would be damaging to the building's operators. If the structure cited as dangerous was an empty warehouse whose owners were not soliciting business, there would be little likelihood of a loss or a damage suit.

The third type, *criminal libel*, involves the government taking action against an individual or company for publishing material that could result in a riot or other breach of the public peace. A prosecuting attorney representing some level of government would initiate court action involving this libel.

When Libel Is Suspected. Editors and staff members of most newspapers, magazines, and radio-TV stations stand alert for possible libel in stories. The standard procedure with most reporters and editors is to *hold*, rather than publish, any story that contains unverified or questioned material. This avoids the unnecessary risk of a libel suit and possible damage to an innocent person's reputation.

Deleting Names Does Not "Forgive" Libel. Naming specific names in conjunction with a libelous statement is an almost certain way to bring a lawsuit. "Inferring" or hedging on positive identification, however, does not excuse the newspaper from the responsibility for libel. If a newspaper hinted that a "certain" (but not named) member of a three-man police vice squad was taking bribes, all of these officers might sue the newspaper for libel on the grounds that their reputations were slurred. The newspaper reporting that a student who left school recently had taken student body funds could face a suit by a student who withdrew and claimed that, because of the story and his action, friends believed him to be a thief.

The Average Person's Understanding Counts. The yardstick for whether words or phrases are libelous is the interpretation placed on them by the average person in the community. Dictionary definitions are secondary, therefore, to what readers *think* the article says. Regional customs and variations in speech and thinking can have a great deal to do with whether a judge or jury will decide a statement is libelous.

DAMAGES FOR LIBEL

A person found guilty of criminal libel would face a jail sentence, a criminal fine, or both. In other types of libel, three kinds of damages can be awarded. The amount, and whether one or all three types of damages would be allowed, is decided by the judge or jury deciding the case.

General damages are those given when libel is proved and it is obvious that the individual suffered some injury.

Special damages can be awarded additionally when the injured person proves specific losses. A doctor or dentist, for example, could collect these damages by showing that the libel resulted in a loss of patients.

Punitive damages are those awarded when the injured party can prove that the reporter or editors were guilty of malice, gross negligence, repeating the libel even when advised it is false, or purposely distorting the truth.

THE DIMENSIONS OF DAMAGES

Persons in professions or trades are more likely to be injured by unfavorable statements than those employed, for instance, in a factory or department store. To say that an assembly-line worker or salesman was not efficient obviously would be libelous if untrue. The amount of damages would probably be nominal unless the individual could show that he lost a job or promotion over the incident. To brand a physician a "quack," a lawyer a "shyster," a TV repairman a "chiseler," or an auto repair mechanic a "crook" would damage reputations and could cause a substantial decline in income. These people would be able to collect monetary damages on proving their losses in court.

Such appellations as "alleged" or "it is charged" do not undo a libel, nor do attempts to "infer" or "hint" that someone is dishonest, incapable, untrustworthy, unreliable, etc. As previously stated, dictionary definitions are *not* acceptable as defenses: libel is based on what the average reader *believes* a word or statement to mean, and not what the reporter or newspaper intended.

WHO IS RESPONSIBLE?

Technically, everyone connected with producing and distributing a libelous statement is guilty. This includes the person who said the words, the reporter who wrote the story, the editor who copyread it and wrote the headline, the printer who set it into type, those who operated the presses, the driver who carried the papers on a truck, the carriers who delivered the newspapers, the publisher, and the newspaper's owners.

The person who filed a damage suit would name all as defendants, identifying those whose names were unknown as "John Does" or "Jane Does." The plaintiff actually would be attempting to reach the publisher and stockholders, who would have the funds to pay damages if awarded.

THE DEFENSES OF LIBEL

Damages for libel can be high and can financially cripple the newspaper so unfortunate as to lose a suit. There are a number of defenses to be offered in fighting libel suits.

Truth. The best defense against libel is proof that an objectionable statement is true. This requirement rules out publishing unprovable rumors or hearsay and is an important reason for identifying story sources and attributing statements. However, the fact, that a speaker is quoted does not exempt the newspaper from libel if that person utters a libelous statement. Even though truth usually is accepted as a defense, some states call on a newspaper to provide good reasons for publishing derogatory material. To publish an account of a degrading incident that happened years ago may contain only truthful material, but its use may serve no good purpose.

Privilege. Material a reporter obtains through public hearings or from public officials *speaking in their official capacities* is *privileged,* or exempt from libel, assuming there is no malice in writing the story. Such public officials include members of the United States House of Representatives and of the Senate, judges, state legislators, and county or municipal trustees or commissioners. Official records, including the *Congressional Record,* court transcripts, minutes of public hearings, and minutes of committee or commission meetings, are also privileged and may be used for stories.

Official utterances and records are privileged because the public is entitled to know what is happening in government. If the press could not report events because of the fear of libel, the reader would have no way to keep abreast of developments—except by attending all meetings and inspecting all documents.

Police reports in most states are open records which reporters can use as story sources. Even here, the reporter must use good judgment. He can write that "John Smith was arrested in connection with a robbery *investigation,*" but to say that he "was arrested *for robbing* a market" would be libelous unless the reporter could prove, in court, that he did rob a market. People arrested are *suspects* until they are convicted.

If a congressional investigating committee issues a report stating that a contractor used inferior materials or violated the principles of a "cost plus" contract, the statements are privileged and could be used in a news story. If a private citizen stopped at the newspaper office and made the same charges, they would be libelous, if published, unless proved true.

A congressman or other authority who would be privileged in making charges when speaking officially loses that immunity when he speaks as a private citizen. The reporter who quotes the official speaking privately would have no *privilege* but would need to use other defenses if sued for libel.

Fair Comment. People in public life not only expect public attention, but frequently thrive on it. Comments on the quality of their endeavors, therefore, are *fair comment* even though they may not be entirely laudatory. The right of fair comment, however, does not extend to the personal lives of politicians or celebrities, nor does it permit a writer to imply dishonesty—unless the reporter can prove the charge in court.

The doctrine of fair comment applies to actors, authors, playwrights, politicians, and others who are in the public eye. A reviewer would have the protection of fair comment if he wrote that an actor gave a poor or unconvincing performance, or that an author's book was pointless and difficult to read. If the writer cast doubts on the actor's personal morals or the author's honesty, he would be subject to libel unless he could prove his points in court.

A reporter could analyze an architect's sketches for a public building by describing them as unimaginative and be covered by the doctrine of fair comment. If he wrote that the architect copied the drawings from another person, he would face a libel suit for inferring dishonesty. An editorial writer could criticize as "unwise" a city official's vote for a building project, but if he implied that the person's action was dishonest he would face a libel suit.

Other Responses to Libel. The above are defenses to help prove that a story did *not* contain libel and thereby defeat a damage

suit. Good newspapers and good reporters meticulously try to avoid libel not only because of the monetary damages but also because of needless injury to an individual's reputation. Sometimes libels are published because of inaccurate or sloppy reporting, or because of misunderstanding or misinformation. In these circumstances, several steps can be taken in an effort to mitigate or reduce the damage to the person libeled and the cost to the newspaper.

Publication of a retraction. On learning that a libel has been committed, a newspaper can publish a retraction. This act of good faith possibly will soothe the injured party and possibly convince him to drop plans for a libel suit. If the libeled person sued and won, the fact that the newspaper showed good faith by retracting the statement could induce the judge or jury to reduce the amount of damages and skip the "punitive" award.

Some states have passed laws which hold that publishing a retraction "forgives" a newspaper and cancels the possibility of the injured person collecting damages. These laws usually require that the demand be made under a certain format and that the newspaper publish the retraction promptly, on approximately the same page where the libel appeared, with the same length of story, and with the same size of headline.

This procedure precludes, of course, the newspaper's printing the libel in large type on page one and running the retraction in small type on an inside page where few readers would see it.

Stories with errors that are not libelous but nevertheless are offensive to those involved sometimes creep into newspapers despite precautions taken by reporters and editors. When the errors are of sufficient magnitude, most newspapers voluntarily print a correction in the interest of goodwill. Some newspapers use a regular heading such as "We Goofed" or "Setting the Record Straight" to list corrections, thus pleasing those offended and eliminating the credibility gap of readers who think journalists are too proud to admit errors.

Absence of malice. The newspaper that can prove there was no malice or ill will connected with publishing a libelous statement may avoid the "punitive" damages and also convince the judge or jury to reduce the amount of general damages. Malice can be *in fact*, meaning that ill will is present, or *in law*, which is a disregard for a person's rights even though there is no malice.

If the person libeled could prove that the reporter or newspaper management printed the story with malice or the *hope* of damaging his reputation, the monetary damages would be much higher than if the writer showed that the statement came from a presumably reliable source and was printed in good faith.

INVASION OF PRIVACY

Another important area in the relationship between a newspaper and the public is invasion of privacy. In a society that is more and more segmented and aware of civil rights, this area is becoming increasingly vital.

DEFINITION

In a democracy, the individual has the right to be let alone, and violation of that right constitutes invasion of privacy. Journalists are often accused of this fault, and there is a great "shadow" area between the black-and-white of what really is or is not an "intrusion" into private lives.

Invasion of privacy includes window peeping, wire tapping, the unauthorized use of personal letters, eavesdropping, the use of names or pictures for advertising without written permission, and trespassing to obtain pictures or interviews.

In regard to photographs, a newspaper could use a picture of a person involved in a current news story or a nonfiction article recapitulating, without defamation, a news event. If a photo were used in an advertisement or with a fictionalized story, the individual's written permission would be required to avoid invasion of privacy. If a portrait were obtained from a house, apartment, or other private property and used without permission, this also would constitute invasion of privacy.

People in the public eye—actors, authors, performers, politicians, and social figures—have less protection against invasion of privacy than individuals in conventional employment, just as their public acts are subject to fair comment. These individuals, however, would have even more protection against having their photos used in advertisements because many charge sizable fees for endorsements and thus earn part of their living.

PENALTIES

A person who believes his privacy has been invaded can file suit for general, special, or punitive damages, the amount of which would be decided by a judge or jury on proof of the charge. Courts also can restrain photographers or reporters from harassing individuals, and there can be criminal fines or jail sentences for disobeying these orders or trespassing to obtain photos or stories.

Even a legitimate news story can produce an incident involving invasion of privacy. A principal in a news story, for example, may flee journalists into the sanctity of his home and plead to be let alone. A reporter or photographer entering the house or its yard would be invading the individual's right of privacy.

OTHER LEGAL ISSUES

The journalist, being in the mainstream of history with its frenzies and human elements, can hardly avoid contact with legal points as he does his work. These areas include relationships with the courts and judges, copyrights, protection of sources providing stories, and censorship.

JUDGES AND THE COURTS

Most judges want to cooperate with journalists in order that they may legitimately depict all aspects of justice. There are limitations, of course, such as doing no harm or prejudice to courtroom participants, including defendants, plaintiffs, witnesses, attorneys, and court attachés.

A judge, to maintain the decorum and respect required for justice in a court of law, may hold an individual to be in contempt for disorderly or disrespectful conduct that may interrupt proceedings. A contempt citation can be appealed to higher courts. When upheld, contempt proceedings can result in a fine or jail term.

Areas of Contempt. There are four general areas where journalists could wittingly or unwittingly risk being cited for contempt. Some areas are "gray" in nature and will vary not only in different states but also in individual court jurisdictions or with different judges.

Use of cameras and recorders is banned. Photographic and recording equipment is banned under American Bar Association canons because of the fear that an individual's right to a fair trial will be violated and because of the contention that the equipment will reduce the courtroom's dignity. These rules stem from the era when large-view cameras and flash powder truly could disrupt proceedings.

While now there are minicameras that use fast film and take pictures without flash, the bar continues its opposition to courtroom photography. One reason is that sensational coverage with pictures would turn trials into circuses and intimidate witnesses.

Violating the rules can result in a contempt citation.

Judges almost universally enforce the rule, and some interpret the bar association injunction as forbidding so much as the presence of a camera, even on the floor or in a pocket, in the courtroom. Other judges take a more lenient view, permitting cameras in the courtroom and picture taking after they have adjourned proceedings and departed.

Journalists should be aware of the rules and determine the local interpretations when they deal with courts.

Material hampering justice. In special cases, judges may forbid witnesses or attorneys to talk with members of the press because of fears that publicity pertaining to the case will interfere with the course of justice. Violation of these judicial orders can result in contempt citations not only for the principals but also for the involved journalists.

Some judges attempt to "gag" or silence the press by forbidding stories on special cases. These efforts usually are cast aside when appealed to higher courts on the basis that they violate the first amendment to the Bill of Rights.

Use of prohibited material. In cases dealing with matter the judge believes grossly obscene or crimes dealing with children, the court may issue an order prohibiting the use of stories on the grounds of offense to the public morals or injury to the youngsters. The reporter who used such material in a story would face a contempt citation.

The news media may challenge such an order to a higher court if the judge's ruling is regarded as unreasonable.

Critical remarks. A newspaper may disagree with a court decision and print an editorial questioning its wisdom. If the criticism impugns the integrity of the judge or otherwise casts aspersions on the court, the judge may cite the newspaper and its editors for contempt. The judge may also be able to win a libel suit. Criticism of judicial actions is a hazy area and one where caution is necessary. Many newspapers have appealed contempt citations, however, on the basis of fair comment when honest criticism was involved and have won on the grounds that comment is permitted after a decision is reached.

Appealing Contempt Citations. Carrying an appeal for contempt to a higher court requires substantial attorney's fees, just as does any legal action. While generally the newspapers or radio-TV outlets that fight contempt citations are the larger, and therefore better-financed, organizations, many smaller news outlets also appeal to higher courts in the interest of freedom of the press.

A FAIR TRIAL VS. A FREE PRESS

A current debate between journalists and attorneys involves the extent of the coverage of crime trials in newspapers and over TV. Many attorneys favor the British system whereby newspapers note that an arrest has been made, but forgo additional stories until the trial concludes. They argue that immense amounts of publicity result from a "trial by press" and that it is difficult to select an impartial jury.

Journalists, arguing against voluntary or enforced restrictions, note the Bill of Rights guarantee of freedom of the press and the United States Constitution's guarantee of freedom of the press. They also express fear that closed-court proceedings could result in inequities to the rank and file or in special treatment for a favored few if the press did not "oversee" proceedings for the public.

PROTECTION OF SOURCES

Because of incriminating or other special circumstances, some news story sources will give information only if they receive guarantees that their identity will be concealed. While attribution and qualification of news sources are important, there are cases where the mere availability of material overwhelms these factors. It is to the advantage of the newspaper *and* the reader to obtain the information even though the anonymous source must be protected.

Whether a newspaper reporter should be *forced* to reveal the identity of a story source by a judge or investigating agency presents legal and ethical problems. Ethically, the reporter alone must decide the question on the basis of his promises and values. Legally, the problem is solved in some states by granting the reporter the privilege of keeping a story source secret just as a priest is entitled to hold confessions confidential.

CENSORSHIP

The first amendment to the Constitution guarantees freedom of the press. Despite this guarantee, which generally is interpreted in its broadest sense, there are variables according to time and geographical areas.

World War II, against which there were few public demonstrations, found the media restricted only by a "voluntary" censorship program at home and a military censorship in the battle areas to protect movement of forces. The undeclared war in Vietnam brought no domestic censorship, although its backers attempted to silence critics by contending

that dissent aided enemies. Massive antiwar demonstrations throughout the nation were covered in the planning stages and as they took place.

Local Restrictions. Much censorship in the 1960s and 1970s was aimed at the "underground" press or newspapers championing unpopular causes, and a great deal of this suppression came in small communities against underfinanced publications. Many stronger dailies supported, in the interest of freedom of the press, the constitutional rights of unpopular publications to be circulated.

Most of the antiestablishment or "underground" publications with funds to fight restrictions in court have been victorious under the free-press guarantee.

"Self"-censorship. Editors occasionally take it upon themselves to "blackout" certain types of news: a racial conflict on the contention that publicity will flame it, a riot over radio on the basis that more people will join it, the activities of an unpopular group for fear that people will join it, or a method of crime that unscrupulous readers might imitate.

The argument against news suppression is that it is like an ostrich putting its head in a hole. The people involved in a racial conflict know about it, and word spreads quickly without newspapers in a ghetto; suppression of a story could indicate to those people that the newspaper or society cares little about minority problems. News of a riot over the radio probably encourages people to avoid the area to escape injury more than it attracts others to the scene.

Hiding the fact that an unpopular group is growing serves no purpose. If the Ku Klux Klan or American Nazis are recruiting members, the community should be advised of the situation because of the impact that the organizations have had on other cities. Suppressing a story about crime would be more apt to let the reader, through ignorance, fall victim to a criminal than to encourage the average person to embark on a life of crime.

Self-censorship serves little purpose except to deprive readers of information to which they are entitled, and may very well obtain elsewhere, thus questioning the credibility of their news source.

Use of Obscenities. What is "obscene" can be debated and can vary according to the times and the community. As far as legal aspects are concerned, the United States Supreme Court decisions in recent years have tended to extend the doctrine of freedom of the press. This is particularly true when the "obscenities" are the incidental, rather than the primary purpose, of publication.

One gauge on using obscenities hinges on a publication's readership. Journalists should remember that a daily newspaper is read by entire families, including children. "Underground" or specialized publications are not nearly so available to youngsters, and therefore logically can contain more "adult" material without criticism.

COPYRIGHTS

Copyrights are an area of interest to the reporter from the standpoints both of protecting his own stories and of using those of others. A copyright protects the owner, whether it be the writer or publisher, from having others use a literary creation without permission. Normally, the publisher obtains the copyright. This is done by (1) publishing a copyright notice, including the year of publication, in the book, newspaper, or pamphlet; (2) filing a completed copyright form and two copies of the literary creation with the Library of Congress; (3) making the creation available to the public; and (4) paying a nominal fee. There are individual forms for newspapers and other periodicals, books, music, motion pictures, and plays or scripts.

The copyright is granted for 28 years and could be renewed only for another 28 years until the year 1966. At that time, Congress began deliberations to liberalize provisions by extending the copyright limit to the writer's life plus 50 years. The Congressional action, still being studied, included extending copyrights that would have expired in 1966 until the revised legislation is adopted.

Magazines and newspapers in major cities usually are copyrighted; the latter do so by placing the copyright notice on the front page with the date. Smaller dailies and weeklies are not copyrighted unless they contain stories of special interest. They then insert the copyright notice atop the article to be protected.

A person cannot copyright *facts*, but one can copyright the *treatment* or wording of a story.

Using copyrighted material without permission can result in a fine and/or imprisonment on conviction. In addition, the copyright owner can sue the violator for damages.

When the right to use copyrighted material is obtained, the material is published with a note stating that the copyright owner gave permission. This notice protects the copyright owner from subsequent infringement and advises that the user is within the law.

Written permission is not required for using *brief* quotations from a book being reviewed or from other publications that are quoted only incidentally to the reporter's original material.

ETHICS

What is or is not legitimate news has long been an area of contention among journalists and the public. Many journalists are unable to agree on what should be printed.

Laws pertaining to libel and invasion of privacy limit the press to a great extent, but there are many areas open to ethical consideration. For example:

How important is crime news?

Are sensational divorce cases worthy of press coverage?

Do newspapers covering court trials create sensationalism that interferes with the administration of justice?

Is it right to protect "confidential" news sources even though they may be criminals?

What is the obligation of the press in regard to the education of readers as opposed to amusing them?

How fair, in general, are daily newspapers in covering minority and antiestablishment viewpoints?

Is the press leading, or following, the

changes in society, including ecology, peace, consumerism, and sociology?

Should a newspaper "make" news to attract circulation or otherwise serve selfish motives?

Consumers of newspapers, TV, radio, and magazine news can make their preferences known by using and buying only the media that genuinely fill their needs.

The great strides in the quality of news and press ethics, however, can be made only by the journalists of today and tomorrow who shape the profile of the media. Hopefully, a young man or woman entering journalism will attempt to find a position with an organization where reporters, editors, and publisher share a mutual respect for integrity.

These canons of the American Society of Newspaper Editors, adopted in 1924, remain an excellent guide for ethics:

I. Responsibility

The right of a newspaper to attract and hold readers is restricted by nothing but consideration of public welfare. The use a newspaper makes of the share of public attention it gains serves to determine its sense of responsibility, which it shares with every member of its staff. A journalist who uses his power for any selfish or otherwise unworthy purpose is faithless to a high trust.

II. Freedom of the Press

Freedom of the press is to be guarded as a vital right of mankind. It is the unquestionable right to discuss whatever is not explicitly forbidden by law, including the wisdom of any restrictive statute.

III. Independence

Freedom from all obligations except that of fidelity to the public interest is vital.

1. Promotion of any private interest contrary to the general welfare, for whatever reason, is not compatible with honest journalism. So-called news communications from private sources should not be published without public notice of their source or else substantiation of their claims to value as news, both in form and substance.

2. Partisanship in editorial comment which knowingly departs from the truth does violence to the best spirit of American journalism; in the news columns it is subversive of a fundamental principle of the profession.

IV. Sincerity, Truthfulness, Accuracy

Good faith with the reader is the foundation of all journalism worthy of the name.

1. By every consideration of good faith a newspaper is constrained to be truthful. It is not to be excused for lack of thoroughness or accuracy within its control or failure to obtain command of these essential qualities.

2. Headlines should be fully warranted by the contents of the articles which they surmount.

V. Impartiality

Sound practice makes clear distinction between news reports and expressions of opinion. News reports should be free from opinion or bias of any kind.

1. This rule does not apply to so-called special articles unmistakably devoted to advocacy or characterized by a signature authorizing the writer's own conclusions and interpretations.

VI. Fair Play

A newspaper should not publish unofficial charges affecting reputation or moral character without opportunity given to the accused to be heard; right practice demands the giving of such opportunity in all cases of serious accusation outside judicial proceedings.

1. A newspaper should not invade private rights or feelings without sure warrant of public right as distinguished from public curiosity.

2. It is the privilege, as it is the duty, of a newspaper to make prompt and complete correction of its own serious mistakes of fact or opinion, whatever their origin.

VII. Decency

A newspaper cannot escape conviction of insincerity if while professing high moral

QM 'cost plan' order issued

By BOB SCHMIDT
From Our State Bureau

SACRAMENTO — Four state agencies have been directed to cooperate with the City of Long Beach in the preparation of a "cost allocation plan" for Queen Mary expenditures, it was learned Thursday.

The order was given by Assemblyman Willie L. Brown Jr., D-San Francisco, chairman of a lower house subcommittee on tideland oil revenues, to representatives of the attorney general, legislative analyst, auditor general, and State Lands Commission participating in a closed-door meeting of the subcommittee.

Long Beach City Manager John Mansell and City Attorney Leonard Putnam also participated in the executive session, which lasted about 90 minutes. Also present were Assemblymen Mike Cullen, D-Long Beach, and Ken Cory, D-Garden Grove.

The press and public were excluded.

BROWN LEFT immediately after the meeting for San Francisco, but an aide said that another subcommittee meeting had been scheduled for Feb. 10, at which time the cost allocation plan will be discussed.

The purpose of the plan, the aide said, was to help establish how much, if any, of the tidelands oil funds had been spent for commercial facilities on the ship.

Mansell said repeatedly during the hearing, the aide said, that no tidelands money had been spent on conversion projects directly benefitting commercial interests.

Putnam reportedly pointed out one technical exception, resulting from work which had to be redone after a former commercial lessee had withdrawn from the project.

The state law pertaining to public tidelands oil revenues limits the uses to which it may be put, and prohibits any use for commercial purposes.

Long Beach Sets Study of Funds Spent on Queen

SACRAMENTO (AP) — Long Beach city officials promise a cost breakdown plan to help determine whether turning the liner Queen Mary into a tourist attraction involved illegal use of tidelands oil revenue, a legislative consultant says.

During a two-hour closed door meet Thursday with members of an Assembly Ways and Means subcommittee probing the $50 million conversion project, officials said the plan would be delivered Feb. 10, committee consultant Bob Connelly said.

Under state law, tidelands oil revenue may be used by the city to build a maritime museum aboard the old liner, but not for commercial purposes. $3.5 million in such funds were spent in buying the vessel from Cunard Lines in 1967.

The ship was also converted to a convention center to be run by Pacific Southwest Airlines.

A subcommittee report Aug. 2 said the project was "an unconscionable use of public money for a project which is purely local in benefit, does not qualify as wise and economical, and on which large sums of money may have been illegally spent."

Under a 1964 agreement, the state is to get 85 percent of the tidelands oil revenue with the city getting 15 percent.

Figure 16–1 Which is fair? These stories pertain to the identical situation, but vary in their slant. The article in the *Long Beach* (Calif.) *Independent* (left), which favored spending millions on converting the *Queen Mary* into a tourist attraction, makes it sound as though the state must cooperate, while the Associated Press dispatch reports that the city of Long Beach must provide the information. (The latter was true.)

purposes it supplies incentives to base conduct, such as are to be found in details of crime and vice, publication of which is not demonstrably for the general good. Lacking authority to enforce its canons, the journalism here represented can but express the hope that deliberate pandering to vicious instincts will encounter effective public disapproval or yield to the influence of a preponderant professional condemnation.

EXERCISES

1. Attend a session of a local court and take notes on proceedings that appear to be of news interest. Write a news story on the material.

2. Invite a reporter who covers the courts to be a guest for a question-and-answer session in your class.

3. Contact the local bar association, and request an attorney to attend a class session to discuss "a free press vs. fair trials."

4. Analyze a local newspaper for a week to determine how it handles "corrections" or retractions; contact an editor to determine whether the paper has a formal policy when it makes errors.

17
Copyreading and Proofreading

Producing newspapers, magazines, books, or other printed matter involves *copyreading* and *proofreading*, two skills which seemingly overlap in nomenclature but which are considerably different in application. Journalists must understand both of these skills.

PROOFREADING

Even working writers and editors differ in their understandings of the definition of proofreading. People involved in writing or reading high school or college compositions use "proofreading" to describe the changes made with pen on a typewritten manuscript before submitting it to the instructor.

By contrast, staff members of most magazine, book, and newspaper publishing companies use "proofread" to describe corrections or changes they make on proofs of stories *in type*. They explain their definition of proofreading on the basis that "proofs" or impressions of type are taken to "prove" it was set correctly, or to make changes in *type*, as opposed to changes on the *manuscript*.

Book, magazine, and newspaper journal-

ists would agree on the use of "proofs" to identify material *in type*. These groups might disagree on what each meant by "proofreading," although the majority would define *proofreaders* as those whose jobs were checking galleys of type to determine whether typographical or printer's errors were made. A few book and magazine journalists describe the duties of a *proofreader* as checking a writer's manuscript for *writing*, not printing, errors.

WHEN JOURNALISTS "READ PROOF"

Journalists would check galleys, for example, to determine whether changes must be made in stories set in type. Among the changes might be a new time or day for an event, new facts to update a story so that it will be "current" if it misses an edition, correcting the misspelling of a name, or deleting material that might be libelous.

Journalists do *not* edit stories after they are in type. Editing must be done on the writer's copy before it is set into type, and attempting to make these changes *after* typesetting would result in printers doing their

Proofreading Symbols

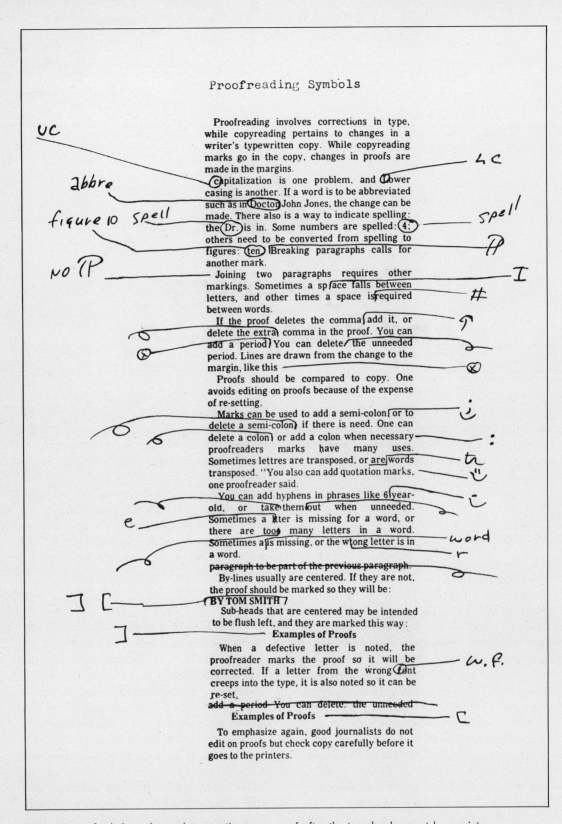

Proofreading involves corrections in type, while copyreading pertains to changes in a writer's typewritten copy. While copyreading marks go in the copy, changes in proofs are made in the margins.

Capitalization is one problem, and lower casing is another. If a word is to be abbreviated such as in Doctor John Jones, the change can be made. There also is a way to indicate spelling: the Dr. is in. Some numbers are spelled: 4; others need to be converted from spelling to figures: ten. Breaking paragraphs calls for another mark.

Joining two paragraphs requires other markings. Sometimes a space falls between letters, and other times a space is required between words.

If the proof deletes the comma, add it, or delete the extra comma in the proof. You can add a period. You can delete the unneeded period. Lines are drawn from the change to the margin, like this

Proofs should be compared to copy. One avoids editing on proofs because of the expense of re-setting.

Marks can be used to add a semi-colon, or to delete a semi-colon if there is need. One can delete a colon, or add a colon when necessary proofreaders marks have many uses. Sometimes lettres are transposed, or are words transposed. "You also can add quotation marks, one proofreader said.

You can add hyphens in phrases like 6 year-old, or take them out when unneeded. Sometimes a letter is missing for a word, or there are too many letters in a word. Sometimes a is missing, or the wrong letter is in a word.

paragraph to be part of the previous paragraph.

By-lines usually are centered. If they are not, the proof should be marked so they will be:

BY TOM SMITH

Sub-heads that are centered may be intended to be flush left, and they are marked this way:

Examples of Proofs

When a defective letter is noted, the proofreader marks the proof so it will be corrected. If a letter from the wrong font creeps into the type, it is also noted so it can be re-set.

add a period. You can delete. the unneeded

Examples of Proofs

To emphasize again, good journalists do not edit on proofs but check copy carefully before it goes to the printers.

Figure 17–1a Symbols used to make corrections on a proof after the type has been set by a printer.

Copyreading Symbols

[BY JOHN SMITH [BFC	boldface black, centered
[Copyreading marks go in the body	paragraph
of the story. ¶ They are used in	paragraph
all ~~all~~ types of printing. One	delete word
can delete a word or letter/s.	delete letter
You can also close paragraphs	close paragraph
or add letters when o^n e is missing.	add letter.
You can ^add^ words. You can change	add words
a number, (sixty,) to a figure, or	use figure
spell when it is a figure, (5.)	spell number
Spell states, (Calif.,) if alone;	spell word
abbreviate cities: Taft, (California.)	abbreviate
Capitalize new york this way	capitals
or this way: new york. This is	capitals
the /method to lower case. Broken	lower case
wo⌐rds can be joined. Those running	join
together can⌐be separated. If a word	separate words
is ~~mistakenly deleted~~ ^stet^, this keeps it.	retain
]Smith and Co.	flush right
Jones and Co.[	flush left
"You can add quotation marks,⟨"	add quotations
or commas^when desired, or add	add comma
periods when needed⊗There are two	add period
ways to do this⊙One can also	add period
use marks/for/deletions.	deletions

Figure 17–1b Symbols used to copyread and make changes in a story before it is sent to the printers.

work twice. The extra cost of resetting type would be substantial.

Figure 17-1a shows the standard proof-reading symbols used universally in handling copy which has been set into type. These symbols are standard, regardless of whether the copy is intended for newspapers, magazines, books, advertising, or other matter. Note that the symbols and marks are used in the margin *outside* the copy. The reason for placing them there is because the typesetter does not wish to take time to read the entire story, but only the portions requiring changes.

In making changes, the typesetter will reset only those lines with errors unless it is necessary to revise other lines to include all of the material.

COPYREADING

Newspaper journalists use "copyreading" to describe the task of making changes and corrections in the body of a story *before* it is set in type. In this respect, newspaper copy-readers perform the duties that "copy editors" do for most book and magazine publishers. If you visited a newspaper office and asked to see a proofreader, you would probably be escorted to the mechanical department to meet a person working with the *proofs* of typesetters.

Figure 17-1b shows the standard copy-reading symbols, which are universal for marking copy before it goes to the typesetters for newspapers, magazines, books, or other matter. Note that the symbols go *inside* the copy and not in the margins. The reason for placing them there is so that typesetters can note the changes as they follow the lines of the copy. If the marks were in the margins, typesetters would be forced to move the eyes from the flow of copy and thus slow their work.

Reporters use copyreading marks to make minor changes in their stories before giving them to an editor. When a reporter wants to make a major change, he does so by retyping an entire paragraph and pasting it in place of the section removed. This technique saves the time and effort of retyping an entire story and avoids numerous copyreading marks which could make reading difficult.

Figure 17–2 Typical copy desk arrangement for newspapers. In the center is the chief copy editor, or "slot man." Facing him are the copy editors, or "rim" men and women. Copy editors, also known as copy-readers, check reporters' stories and write headlines. (*Chicago Sun-Times* Photo by Howard Lyon)

READING ONE'S OWN COPY

A virtually universal rule is that a reporter does *not* read his own stories. The reason for this injunction is that a writer is not likely to note his own mistakes or recognize how his own story can be improved.

ORGANIZATION OF THE COPY DESK

News stories go from the reporter to the editor, who passes them to the copy desk for copyreading, heads, directions for typesetting, and dummying on a particular page. The copy desk is an important phase of newspaper production because it involves the coordination of so many segments of the news operation.

The "Desk." The copy desk itself is often a large horseshoe-shaped table made especially for a newsroom—and because of its size frequently assembled there. The inside is called the "slot," and the chief copy editor sits here. The outside is the "rim," around which are seated the copyreaders (or "copy editors"). The number of editors on the rim can range from 4 to 15, depending on the size of the desk and of the newspaper.

When a unique horseshoe-shaped desk is not used, newspapers create the same effect by arranging conventional desks in the same general pattern so that the copy chief can readily communicate with the copyreaders.

On smaller newspapers, those in the women's and sports departments often operate their own copy desks because of staff limitations and the specialized nature of their stories. Another copy desk handles wire news and local stories other than sports and women's news.

The larger newspapers use the "universal" desk, or one that handles *all* stories. On the largest newspapers, story volume is so great that the "universal" operation actually involves several copy desks, each handling specialized fields: wire, local, sports, financial, or other news areas.

Duties of the Copyreader. In general, a copyreader prepares the story and its headline for typesetting after a reporter clears it through an editor. A *competent* copyreader must walk a tightrope between leaving the reporter's writing style individualized and yet "polishing" the story for maximum readability.

Reporters, half-joking and half-serious, often accuse copyreaders of "wrecking" their stories.

Copy editors, in turn, with a mixture of humor and seriousness, frequently claim that they "save the reporter's job" by making the proper additions or deletions on a story.

Both copyreaders and reporters can be alternately right and wrong, and they must remember that they are working on a team to produce readable stories. Most reporter-copyreader conflicts can be resolved by friendly discussions and a mutual understanding of the problems each job involves. If a real dispute should develop, it usually (but not always) would be settled by an editor deciding in favor of the copyreader. The reasons for such a decision would include the fact that journalists must accumulate considerable skill and experience before becoming copyreaders, and once in such a position they must retain the authority to make decisions to be effective.

Copyreaders fill important positions at newspapers because of the judgment they exercise and the skills they practice. Here are some of their duties:

1. Check the story for grammatical, spelling, stylebook, and related errors, correcting any that are found. Well-trained reporters keep errors at a minimum. If a reporter continually makes the same errors, copyreaders must gently advise him.

2. Check the article for facts and logic. While the copyreader relies on the reporter's ability and skill, he also uses his own memory to ascertain whether familiar names are used correctly and draws on his knowledge of many subject areas to determine credibility.

3. Note any parts of stories that may contain libel, and query the reporter or chief copy editor to determine whether consideration has been given to these points. When material is obviously libelous, copyreaders delete the references immediately.

4. Refer the story to the reporter or his editor for remedy if pertinent facts are missing, or if important information is "hidden" toward the end of the article when it should be near the lead.

5. Write a clear and meaningful head (see next chapter) according to the size directed by the chief copy editor. The person who copyreads the story traditionally writes the head because he is most aware of its contents.

6. Indicate the size of type to be used and whether the head will be one, two, three, or more columns wide. While this information frequently is given by the chief copy editor, the decision may be made in situations where copyreaders design specific pages.

7. Write the page number, when known, on the copy so that the printers can dispatch the type more readily to the correct page form.

8. Advise by marking the copy ("with art" or "w/a") if an illustration will be used with the story. This expedites handling by the printers and the editorial make-up editor.

9. Initial the story so that editors or typesetters can contact the reader if there is a question.

Qualifications of the Copyreader. While the layman regards reporting as the "glamour" job of journalism and tends to dismiss copyreading as a secondary position, this is untrue. Outsiders are unfamiliar with the organization and line of command in a newspaper office. A talented and respected individual, the copyreader actually has one of journalism's coveted jobs and may be in line for promotion to a position as an editor. In job seeking, one's credentials as an experienced copyreader carry more prestige than one's experience as a reporter in landing a position when there are several applicants.

Copyreaders usually win these jobs after being successful reporters for four or more years. They have demonstrated the ability to recognize news ingredients, write clearly, understand stylebook usage, spell, punctuate, and understand the problems of libel.

Some copyreaders are pleased with the challenges of their positions and are not interested in promotions. Those who tend to be introverted enjoy copyreading because it limits their contacts to a few familiar people rather than the large number of contacts a reporter typically makes. Some journalists regard copyreading positions as an opportunity to demonstrate abilities that will help them move into editorships at higher levels.

Few journalists skip from a position as a reporter to an editorship without an interim period in copyreading or a related position.

Training for Copyreading. While some schools of journalism and newspaper-sponsored workshops have successfully produced copyreaders through training programs, most copyreaders learn the craft by working as reporters and observing techniques. While entire books have been devoted to the methods of copyreading, one must do the job under supervision to master the skill. The good copyreader must be a word-smith, a grammarian, and a story organizer and must enjoy the conciseness in phraseology that is so important for news stories. The person with these attributes can refine them through long hours of supervised practice.

Incidentally, copyreading is a journalism area where handicapped people can achieve a great measure of success. Confinement to a wheelchair or deafness are not handicaps to good editing. While reporting ordinarily is regarded as preliminary to copyreading, many individuals have bypassed these positions

n248

d lbyluivryyr

334

handyman

LOS ANGELES AP -A 39-year-old man who drove a Rolls Royce while reporting income of only $7,000 over two years as a elf employed handyman pleaded quilty to income tax evasion Friday in Fedeal Court. U.S. District Court Judge C. Aery Crary sentenced Ulysses J. Hicks of suburban Baldwin Hills to 2½ years in federal prison.

The Internal Reverse Service said Hicks was now serving a six-year sentence at McNeil Island, Wash. federal prison for the illegal sale of cocaine.

Hicks listed a combined income of $7,000 for 1969 and 197 while he was living in an expensive suburban home, owned a Rolls Royce and other expensive cars and carried a mobile telephone in an attache case," the IRS said. It said he had a net worth of $32,000 during the period.

He pleaded guilty to evading federal income taxes in 1969.

09-22-72 05.11ppd

Figure 17–3 An Associated Press wire story after being copyread and before going to the printers. Its narrower width comes from a punched tape (attached) for automatic typesetting.

Figure 17–4 Copyreaders Lyn Wilson (left) and Kara Rogge of the *Fort Worth Star-Telegram* check over stories in an early edition.

through enrollment in specialized college courses.

The Specialists. Whether a newspaper is large or small, copyreaders develop their own specialties: aerospace, City Hall, sports, Washington, D.C., European, Asiatic, or other news areas. Major newspapers consciously employ experts as copyreaders for special-interest stories. While most copyreaders can handle any copy, those with specialized backgrounds can handle stories involving subjects they know best more authoritatively. This pleases the involved reporter, who is assured that an understanding hand will help his story, and it serves the reader by having touches that make an article more understandable. Copyreaders develop their specialization through academic studies and on-the-job training.

Emphasis must be placed on the fact that writing a head for a story is an important part of the copyreader's job. Because of the specialized techniques involved, this skill is covered separately in the next chapter.

EXERCISES

1. Invite a copyreader from a local newspaper to attend a class question-and-answer session regarding his duties.

2. On a separate occasion, ask a reporter from the same newspaper to discuss the writers' relationships with copyreaders.

3. To acquaint yourself with copyreading symbols, check over your own stories to make them comply with the AP-UPI or other standard stylebook and to eliminate unneeded words; keep in mind that a reporter does *not* copyread his own stories in commercial newspaper operations.

4. Do the same with stories written by other journalism students.

5. Obtain "raw" (or uncorrected) proofs of stories from a local newspaper, and practice proofreading as compared to the newspaper definition of copyreading; be sure to correct only typographical errors, and do *not* edit.

18

Writing Heads

Heads, the abbreviation for "headlines," are often called titles by laymen. They play several important roles in a newspaper. They (1) give readers an idea of what the story concerns; (2) provide variety in the newspaper's design and make pages attractive; (3) make a person select the paper from a newsstand in preference to a competing publication; and (4) create an identity or character for the publication through the use of distinctive types.

Make-up itself, while related to heads, will be discussed in the next chapter. This discussion is concerned with the styles of heads and the problems of writing them.

WHO WRITES THE HEADS?

Contrary to the layman's opinion, the reporter does *not* write the heads. The writer may finish his story at noon and be away from the office while his story is on the way to the printers. The procedure is for an editor to assign a head size and give the story to the copyreader to process. As previously explained, copyreaders work at a desk around the chief copy editor. The latter distributes stories according to specialties or to which readers are available for work at the moment.

While checking the story for readability, stylebook adherence, libel, and other factors, the copyreader notes the facts that might be used in a head. He then writes a meaningful and informative head of the assigned size.

TERMINOLOGY

A *head* refers to a headline ranging from a single line across only one column to several lines stretching over an entire page. A *line* (once called a *bank*) is one line of a head. A *deck* has two or more parts, each with different kinds of type. A *drop*, *dropout*, or *readout* refers to the decks in different columns below a head stretching over several columns. The *banner* or *streamer* is the main headline. The *skyline* is the head at the top of page one. A *combination head* is one that serves more than one story, each of which usually has a *readout*.

CAPITALS VERSUS LOWERCASE

The style or preference concerning the use of capitals changes with the years as well as with the choices of individual editors. The "traditional" or early-day preference was for an emphasis on capitals, but there has been an increasing tendency to use lowercase letters since the 1920s with its development of tabloid newspapers and more informal journalistic techniques. If given a choice, copyreaders probably would vote for the system offering the fewest capitals, since larger letters mean less space, therefore making it more difficult to write a head.

While all systems have merit, it is important to realize that one system should be adopted so that the reader, even subconsciously, will not be annoyed by a change in style. *Note:* the "all capital" system can be mixed with others to achieve variety.

All Capitals. Even newspapers that use heads with lowercase letters still favor achieving variety with "all caps" heads which were traditional with early journalism. Editors believe that such heads give the illusion of more type faces because capitals look larger. Example:

> MAYOR TO HELP
> DEDICATION
> OF L.A. CLUB

Capitals Followed by Lowercase. An earlier method for writing heads still favored by many newspapers calls for capitalizing the first letter of *every* word. Example:

> Mayor To Help
> Dedication
> Of L.A. Club

Capitals and Lowercase. A highly popular method provides for capitalizing all words except conjunctions, prepositions, and infinitives. The latter *are* capitalized, however, when they *begin* a line. Example:

> Mayor to Help
> Dedication
> Of L.A. Club

Lowercase Emphasis. A style that is becoming increasingly popular requires capitalization only of (1) the *first* letter of the *first* line; (2) the *first* letter of proper names; and (3) letters abbreviating a proper name. Example:

> Mayor to help
> dedication
> of L.A. club

TYPES OF HEADLINES

Newspapers of a half century or more ago featured heads composed of many layers or decks, each developing different phases of the story. Today's newspapers use simpler heads with a minimum of decks. Head styles vary according to newspaper and may even change with editors. Readers subconsciously become familiar with the styles, which help identify the newspaper. Radical changes in head styles are therefore made infrequently.

Once a newspaper adopts an array of head styles, it clings fairly tenaciously to the standards because of reader identification. When a decision is reached to change styles, the entire paper adopts the heads so that readers will not be disturbed, even subconsciously, by having mixed standards.

Flush Left. Among the most popular, this style of head has been gaining in usage since the 1920s. They are easier to write, and typesetters can work more easily with them. They often can tell more, since the copyreader is not confined with rigid mechanical requirements. Example:

> Mayor to speak
> at dedication
> of main library

Stepline. Another popular head is the *stepline*, which also is called the *dropline* or *stagger*. It can be (1) two lines, with one flush left and the other flush right, or (2) three lines, with the top and bottom flush left and right respectively, and the middle one centered. A disadvantage is that the lines cannot be filled, or the "step" effect is ruined. Examples:

Mayor to speak   Mayor to speak
at dedication   at dedication
of new library

Flush Head. This head is difficult to write and causes problems for the printer who sets it because of its mechanical requirements: it theoretically must *fill.* the column so it is flush left *and* right. The copyreader therefore must work longer with words to accomplish the goal. Because of the difficulty in writing them, *flush heads* are seldom used in modern newspapers. Example:

Mayor will speak
at library rites

Inverted Pyramid. This head, sometimes two but usually three lines long, steps down with successively shorter lines. The mechanical requirements make it difficult to write, and it requires more time in typesetting. Relatively few modern newspapers use it. Example:

Mayor to speak
at library
rites

Crossline. Early American newspapers relied heavily on this head, and it continues to be widely used for short stories. The head is a single line of type, originally centered but now popularly used flush left. Example:

Mayor to speak

Hanging Indention. This head is composed of two or three lines, with the top one filling the space and the bottom ones indented flush left. Because its format makes it relatively difficult to write, its use is limited today. Example:

Mayor to speak
at dedication
of library

Kicker. A single line above the main head produces the *kicker*, which adds a new thought but does *not* repeat the words or information in the lines below. This line usually is (1) in type approximately one-third to one-half the size of the main head; (2) underlined; (3) in the opposite kind of type from the main head; (4) in all capitals if the main lines are in capitals and lowercase, or in capitals and lower-

case if the main lines are in all capitals, and (5) one-third to two-thirds as long as the main lines. For example, 12- or 18-point italic (slanting) capitals would be used over a main line with 30- or 36-point roman (straight) capitals and lowercase. While kickers are frequently used with feature stories or those with humor, editors also put them over straight news articles. Example:

3RD BRANCH OPENING
Mayor to speak at dedication
of eastern regional library

Reverse Kicker. The general effect of this head is similar to the above, except that the overline is larger than the two lines of type below it. The kicker overline, for instance, might be in 30-point italic capitals, while the two lower lines would be in 18-point roman capitals and lowercase. This head is essentially for feature-type stories. Example:

NEW LIBRARY TO OPEN
Officials planning gala events
to salute eastern area facility

IDENTIFYING THE HEADS

When a newspaper's editors adopt the style of type and kind of heads they will use, examples are provided in a booklet or on printed head-style sheets. These samples show how the different sizes and kinds of type look in various column widths. The two most widely used means of identifying heads are (1) by an assignment of numbers and (2) by the "column-size-lines" designation.

The first method involves using a number for every kind of head that the newspaper ordinarily uses. If a copyreader receives a story with instructions to write a "No. 5 head," he refers to the sheet and sees that it is, for instance, one that is two columns wide, contains two lines, and uses 24-point Vogue italic type.

The other way uses a designation such as "1-24VI-3." Copyreaders, through habit, "decode" this as follows: the first number indicates the number of columns (in this case, one), the middle number gives the kind and size of type (24 Vogue italic), and the last number advises the number of lines (three). A sample of this head would be included on the head-style sheets so that the copyreader could visualize his work.

HEAD "COUNTS"

Along with samples, head schedules show the "count," or how many letters (or units) of a particular size or kind of type will fit in a line stretching over one, two, three, four, or more columns. Types vary: some are extended, meaning that the letters are broad and require more room, while others are condensed, enabling the copyreader to use more letters. Fewer letters of a larger type will fit into the same space as a smaller size, even when the styles are identical.

While a typewriter makes an equal space regardless of the letter, printing does not. For instance, "i" takes just half the space required for "e" and a capital "M" will cover approximately twice the space of a lowercase "a." The relative proportions of the letters remain the same whether the type size is 12, 18, 24, 30, 36, 42, 48, 60, 72, 96, etc., point.

Those who write heads therefore use a "count" schedule to compensate for letter variances. These "counts" are standard regardless of the size or style of type used.

Standard "Counts." Copyreaders use the following table in writing heads:

Capitals

M and W	2 units
I	1/2 unit
Other letters	1 1/2 units

Lowercase

m and w	1 1/2 units
f, l, i, t	1/2 unit
Other letters	1 unit

Other elements

Symbols ($, &, %, #)	1 unit
Punctuation (. , ; :)	1/2 unit
Single quotes (')	1/2 unit
Hyphen (-)	1/2 unit
Dash (—)	1 unit
Numeral 1	1/2 unit
Other numerals	1 unit
Space between words	1 unit

Counting the Heads. There are at least four ways to count heads, or to determine whether the words will fit in the allocated number of units. The number of units may be 10, 15, 18, 24, or whatever is indicated by a particular sample on the head schedule.

The "count" is given by the line. For example, if a particular head counted 10 units, the copyreader would have room for 10 units *per line* and could *not* put six units on one line and four on another. Neither could he *exceed* 10 units even by so little as a half unit; all above 10 units would intrude into the adjoining column.

The method used by many veteran copyreaders in counting heads is to go over each letter with a pencil and add the number of units mentally. Practice builds proficiency in using this technique.

A second method is to place a mark *over* a *full*-count letter and a mark *under* a *half* count. The copyreader counts the marks to determine whether the head will fit without the need of mental arithmetic.

A third way is the *key words* method, which uses words matching the number of units in a specific head. For instance, an 11-unit head may use the words *Eddie Gives*, containing 11 units, as its key; these key words would be on the head schedule. The copyreader types the key words, then types the proposed head beneath it. Adjustments necessarily must be made for half, one-and-a-half, or double-unit letters. Each head used by the newspaper would have key words of varying length according to its units. This system is an adaptation of writing heads on a typewriter after setting margins. Its advantages are that the key words eliminate the need for looking at calibrations, and there is no need to count manually or in one's head.

The fourth method is using sheets printed with squares having small numbers above them. The squares are utilized according to the headline count, with the copyreader compensating for half-unit or one-and-a-half-unit letters. A disadvantage for this method is the necessity of having relatively costly printed forms for the heads.

To emphasize, the first or "mental count"

Below: A mark above the letter indicates a full count
and a mark below the letter means a half count.
The copyreader counts the marks to determine
the number of units in each line of the head

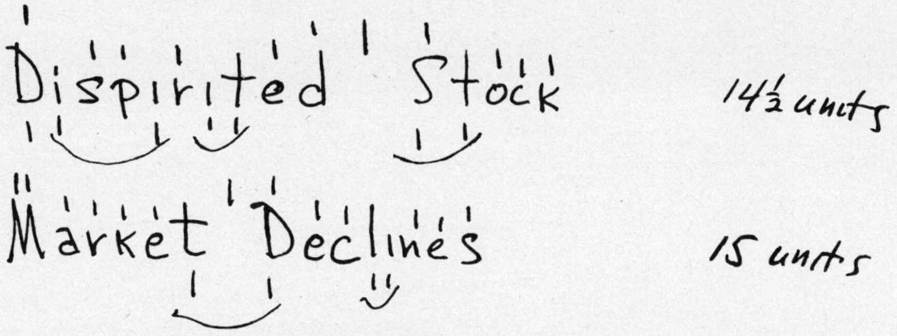

Dispirited Stock   14½ units

Market Declines   15 units

Below: An alternate method is to write the unit count
above each letter and total them.

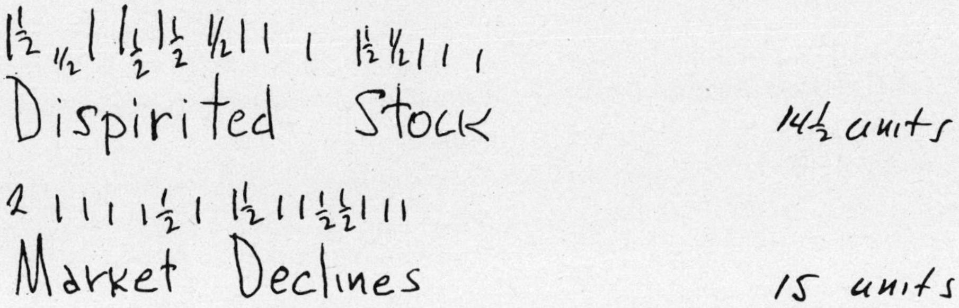

Dispirited Stock   14½ units

Market Declines   15 units

Below: The "key words" method of counting uses a phrase
that contains the exact number of spaces in a specific head.
Here, "write your head" are the "key words" for a 15-unit
head. The copyreader spaces ahead or backwards
on the typewriter to compensate for half units
or more than one unit.

                write your head
                Dispirited Stock   (14½)
                Market Declines   (15)

The Head in Type:

Dispirited Stock
Market Declines

Figure 18—1   Three methods of "counting" heads. Below is the head after being set in type.

method is the most popular with veteran journalists. After writing heads for several months, many copyreaders are able to judge whether a line will fit almost by looking at it.

WRITING HEADS

One reason why many copyreaders do not enjoy working crossword puzzles is that they are playing just such a game daily when they write heads. Only so many units of letters will fit in headlines, and copyreaders grope for synonyms or for shorter or longer words, as the need may be.

Skill in the art of headline writing grows as the copyreader develops experience. Part of this experience is reading newspapers and noting how heads are phrased. "Headlinese," the art of selecting understandable words and phrases that will fit in the limited space of particular head counts, is a skill that can be mastered best through supervised practice.

THE AMOUNT OF LEEWAY

Heads do not need to *fill* a line, but most editors like to have them cover the allocated space—whether it is a column or five columns—as much as possible. To have a head fall greatly short of the specified units produces a "jagged" effect and excessive white.

A rule of thumb is to *try* not to let heads fall more than approximately 15 per cent below the allocated number of units: for example, a 12-unit line would pass the chief copy editor with as little as 10½ units, or a 20-unit head would be acceptable with 17 or 17½ units. The subjects of some stories obviously make it more difficult to write a head than others. Editors therefore would prefer a head that made sense and was readable even though short in preference to one of the correct length that was misleading.

Successful copyreaders have a good command of English and are able to interchange words so that heads approach the allocated length.

Note: A head will *not* fit if its length is so much as one-half unit over the allocated count. Long heads, if they mistakenly pass the chief copy editor, will cause more problems than

short ones because they must be rewritten and set when the mechanical department is on a deadline. The seasoned copyreader invariably will make a head a half unit or a unit *short* of the required count instead of even a half unit too long.

WORD USAGE

The copyreader tells the substance of a story in the head, using ground rules that have developed over the years. The techniques are based on the assumption that readers are "conditioned" and would stumble subconsciously if faced with unfamiliar headlinese.

Heads must be punchy and appealing, and yet meaningful and truthful. They must be brief, but not so "telegraphic" in their brevity that they are annoying. Beginning copyreaders easily can spend an hour, at their student level, composing their first usable head; experienced journalists develop the skill and proficiency to write good ones in a matter of minutes.

Verb Usage. Active, meaningful verbs are vital in heads to reflect the freshness of news. *Important:* all forms of the verb "to be" (is, are) and particularly the past tenses (were, has been) are avoided because they are passive and tell little. When there is a need for some

Figure 18–2 Campus newspapers can offer practical work in their production. Here is Rosemary Ushiro planning a page for the Orange Coast College publication.

Figure 18–3   Reverses (white on black) help create interest but lose their effectiveness if done too frequently.

form of "to be," it is usually deleted and inferred to be in the head. Example:

Last of magazines
now for sale
at college store

In the above head, "are" before "now" is understood. Parts of the verb "to be" are also implied when they would be used with other verbs. Example:

Cheerleaders chosen
for winter programs

Figure 18–4 The large type in this newspaper made it attractive to street buyers. Modern readers would be more interested in "depth" or interpretive coverage.

Prime Rate Cut Boosts Stocks

★ ★ ★ ★ ★ ★ ★ ★ ★ ★ ★ ★ ★ ★ ★ ★ ★ ★ ★

2 Airlines Talk Merger

GOLDEN GATE HANDICAP, RESULTS

Oakland Tribune 6 PM

A RESPONSIBLE METROPOLITAN NEWSPAPER

97th YEAR, NO. 84 | G | WEDNESDAY, MARCH 25, 1970 | 10c DAILY, $3.25 A MONTH

Air Traffic Disrupted By 'Sick-in'

Airline flights were being canceled at Bay Area airports today as the nationwide air traffic controllers' "sick-in" gathered impetus.

Controllers at the big Federal Aviation Administration centers in Oakland and Fremont joined the work stoppage.

The controllers have been campaigning for higher wages, additional staff and modernized equipment, but today's slowdown was triggered by the proposed transfer of three controllers from Baton Rouge, La.

A spokesman for the Professional Air Traffic Controllers Organization in Washington, D.C., said "initial indicators" pointed to a widespread walkout by its members and that "there would be a severe dissipation of air traffic as predicted."

A spot check of airlines showed that flights to and from the Bay were being scrubbed and passengers booked with one line were sometimes placed on competing lines to reduce the number of planes in the air.

American Airlines canceled 11 of its 14 scheduled flights from San Francisco International today and 138 of its flights from three New York area airports were washed out.

Western Airlines called off its San Francisco to Minneapolis-St. Paul run, transferring the passengers to a Northwest Airlines flight.

The same procedure was to be followed for two Los Angeles-San Francisco schedules.

Some special services will be discontinued, according to an FAA spokesman.

These include local airline training flights, student flying and radar advisories for private pilots not filing flight plans.

Don Torchio, spokesman for the Eastbay PATCO members, said:

"Some controllers are quite upset about inaction on their major complaints," including the petition for a nationwide representation election and improved working conditions.

At the Oakland Air Route Traffic Control Center 35 of the 75-member day shift of controllers called in or sent telegrams saying they would

See Back Page, Col. 6

ROBERT E. JENKINS
Takes new post

S.F. School Boss Quits His Post

Robert E. Jenkins today announced his resignation as superintendent of San Francisco City Schools effective July 31.

He announced at a press conference he would leave the $38,500 a year job to accept the presidency of a new business firm which he declined to identify.

Jenkins, who was hired in July, 1967, said his recent differences of opinion with Mayor Joseph L. Alioto over school busing had no effect on his decision to leave. He maintained he and Alioto had gotten along well until the busing problem brought to the surface a "sincere difference of opinion."

School Board President Alan H. Nichols, who sat beside Jenkins through the press conference, said Jenkins' leaving will have no effect on school district plans for busing. He added the board will try to find a replacement for Jenkins by May 10 and indicated the new superintendent will have to favor the busing proposal to the Park South and Richmond complexes.

Nichols said a special school board meeting will be held Tuesday to establish criteria for selection of a new superintendent.

Jenkins said he had received five specific offers from private business, none of which he identified. He said he had also been urged to become a candidate for public office but that he turned thumbs down on the suggestion. He did not identify the office. He described his job with San Francisco schools as "three busy and hectic years."

Jenkins was superintendent of Pasadena public schools when he was hired in San Francisco in 1967. He was selected for the job over a field of 40 candidates.

HAPPIEST SIGHT IN A QUEENS NEIGHBORHOOD — THE MAILMAN
Victor Oleoga was greeted by women with open arms today.—(AP)

Nixon Asks Death Law in Bombings

Compiled from AP and UPI

WASHINGTON — President Nixon asked Congress today to increase penalties—even to the death penalty—and to extend federal jurisdiction to deal with the rash of bombings by "potential murderers."

Nixon said actual and threatened bombings have "sent fear through many American communities" and tough new legislation is needed to deal with the perpetrators, whom he called "political fanatics, many young criminals posturing as romantic revolutionaries."

"They must be dealt with as the potential murderers they are," Nixon said.

"The anarchic and criminal elements who perpetrate such acts deserve no more patience or indulgence," he declared. "It is time to deal with them for what they are."

Nixon's proposed legislation mainly would provide stiff new federal penalties for anyone convicted of being involved in a bombing, transporting explosives or threatening a bombing.

He said proposals being sent to Congress ask that:

—Anyone transporting or receiving explosives, intending to use them unlawfully, be made subject to imprisonment for 10 years or a fine of $10,000, or both. The current maximum penalty is a single year in prison or a $1,000 fine or both.

—The maximum penalty be doubled to 20 years in prison or a $20,000 fine or both if anyone is injured as the ultimate result of such transport of explosives.

—Penalties for bomb threats be raised from one year in prison to a maximum of five years of a $5,000 fine or both.

—Incendiary devices be included in the category of "explosives," bringing such devices under the anti-bombing provisions.

—Use of explosives to damage or destroy any building, vehicle or other property owned or leased to the Federal Government be made a federal crime.

—Possession, without written authorization, of any explosive in a building be made a federal crime.

—Use of explosives to damage or destroy any building or property used for business purposes by any person or firm engaged in interstate

See Back Page, Col. 1

Postal Pay Hike Talks Started

WASHINGTON (AP) — Government officials and union leaders today began efforts to resolve issues that disrupted mail service and, at one point, threatened a complete breakdown of the postal system.

The government's negotiating team was headed by Postmaster General Winton M. Blount. The postal union forces were led by James C. Gildea, acting for George Meany, president of the AFL-CIO.

Earlier, Blount told reporters he was optimistic about the outcome of the talks.

"I would expect we will deal with this matter very rapidly," he said.

In New York City, virtually coincidental with the start of the negotiations here, the executive committee of Manhattan Branch 36 of the National Association of Letter Carriers agreed to accept a proposed bill that would give the workers a 12 per cent pay increase.

The measure would make the increase retroactive to October, 1969. In addition, the bill provides that the government would pay the full cost

See Back Page, Col. 2

A's Jackson Signs--$45,000

See Sports

My Lai—3 More Charged

WASHINGTON (UPI) — Three more GI's have been charged with murder in connection with the My Lai massacre in Vietnam on March 6, 1968, the Army announced today.

The announcement brought to 25 the total of suspects against whom charges have been brought by the Army in connection with the reported slaying of several hundred civilian men, women and children in the Vietnamese village of Song My on March 16, 1968.

Fourteen of those are officers — including two generals — accused of failing to report and investigate the incident.

The men charged today were identified as Spec. 4 William F. Doherty, 21, Readville, Mass.; Cpl. Kenneth Schiel, 22, of Swartz Creek, Mich., and Spec. 4 Robert W. T'souvas, 20, of San Jose.

All three of the men were charged with "murder in violation of the Uniform Code of Military Justice," but there was no indication that they were accused of more than one slaying.

All three are now at Fort McPherson outside Atlanta, where they will undergo pretrial investigations to determine whether they face courts martial.

Doherty, a high school graduate, was a private first class at the time of the alleged massacre. He was at Fort Hood, Tex., before being moved to Fort McPherson for the investigation.

Schiel, also a high school graduate, was a sergeant and a squad leader at that time. He was at Fort Bragg, N.C., before being moved to Georgia on March 8.

T'souvas had only a 10th grade education and was also a private first class at the time of the massacre.

Earlier story, Page 4

The Turned Off Hippie Culture

By JIM HAZELWOOD
Tribune Science Writer

If there is one dominant puzzlement in the minds of middle-aged America today, it is the baffling behavior of the hippie generation.

A Canadian psychiatrist offered some explanations in San Francisco yesterday and, if he is right, the hippie situation may be even more serious than it seems.

Dr. Andrew I. Malcolm, of the Addiction Research Foundation of Ontario, Toronto, said the alienated subculture loosely referred to as hippies is turned off, not on.

His remarks were directed to the annual meeting of the American Orthopsychiatric Association.

Dr. Malcolm said the conversion of a hippie often leads to an altered state of consciousness (ASC) which is similar to the experience of religious zealots, the trance-like state of primitive dancers and the political brainwashing of prisoners of war.

ASC can be caused in a variety of ways, he said, ranging from the use of hallucinogenic drugs to hypnosis.

"The ASC will also appear when there is a greatly increased sensory bombardment of the brain," he said.

"Sophisticated brainwashing techniques, the third degree, and revivalist religious meetings exemplify this means."

Dr. Malcolm said immature

See Back Page, Col. 8

Merger Talks By Airlines Revealed

HONOLULU (UPI) — Pan American World Airways is in the market for a merger, and the most likely candidate is United Air Lines, the Honolulu Star-Bulletin reported today.

It learned from "reliable sources" that preliminary merger talks have been held between the two, the newspaper said.

A Pan Am-United merger would create the world's largest air carrier and one of the largest corporations in the travel and hotel industry.

Both airlines already are in the hotel business. Last week, UAL Inc., the holding company for United, announced plans to purchase Western International Hotels.

The Star-Bulletin said Pan Am was "leaving no stone unturned in its quest for a

See Back Page, Col. 2

Angel Held In Altamont Knife Death

Alan David Passaro, 21, an itinerant Hell's Angels motorcycle club member, was indicted on a murder charge by the Alameda County Grand Jury yesterday for the fatal stabbing of Meredith C. Hunter, 18, at the Altamont Speedway rock concert last Dec. 6.

The indictment followed nearly four months of exhaustive investigation by Lt. James Chisholm and Det. Sgt. Robert Donovan of the Alameda County Sheriff's Department.

Their work, which included trips to Los Angeles and San Diego, drew praise from Dist. Atty. Lowell Jensen.

The case was presented to the grand jury by Deputy District Attorney Clayton Da Vega.

The key evidence shown the jury was a film strip taken by a New York movie company under contract to the Rolling Stones, and a closeup of the actual stabbing.

Jensen described the se-

See Back Page, Col. 1

POLITICS AND POVERTY

Struggle Within Struggle

By BOB DISTEFANO
Tribune Staff Writer

The struggle to control the Oakland war on poverty being waged between Percy Moore, poverty chieftain, and his foes obscures a far greater struggle:

Decisions made now, may in turn decide political control of the city.

That control is inexorably complicated by racial feelings and controversies — unfortunate though this may be.

The non-white population of Oakland has soared from 14.5 per cent in 1950, to 26.4 per cent in 1960, to 34.9 per cent in 1966.

The Congressional Quarterly now estimates 39 per cent of the population is black.

In 1966, whites with Spanish surnames and nonwhites other than blacks made up 15 per cent of the population. From 1960 to 1966, Oakland's total minority group population, Spanish-surname whites, blacks and other nonwhites—climbed from 33 to 44 per cent.

Even if all trends completely reverse, the federally-sponsored 701 planning study of Oakland predicted that at least 43 per cent of the city's population will be black by 1985.

If those trends do continue, 64 per cent of the city's population will be black then.

"The city's political institutions, including both the city government and the Oakland Board of Education, will undoubtedly reflect this racial makeup. Public recognition of these trends may well alle-

Last of a Series

viate tensions that may result from this political transition," states that same report, "Options for Oakland," a summary of 38 studies.

Robert Pitts, immediate past regional administrator of the U.S. Department of Housing and Urban Development, is the first black to rise to that position throughout the nation.

Pitts, a Mill Valley resident, believes it is time to stop fixing cost values on the effectiveness of various poverty programs and time to face up to the realities:

The black population is growing. Urban problems cannot even approach solution until blacks and whites come to some understanding, some sharing of power.

"Somewhere a line of mobility has to set in," said Pitts, a lecturer in the University of California at Berkeley School of Business Administration.

"We may be a little ahead of our time but those of us who are taking the leading role in the cities have got to stop playing games with each other. Everyone's out to push his own little cart. We're just beginning to realize the intricacies of urban living do not permit all this game-playing," Pitts said a while ago in his faculty office while students waited impatiently outside to talk about their projects.

Pitts, 58, recalls his own youth in Pittsburgh, Pa, when he could find a job by just walking the streets and popping into a shop and asking the merchant.

"How many times can you get employed today, doing that? Somebody would call the cops," he said.

Past belief in representative

See Back Page, Col. 3

Golden Gate Results

GOLDEN GATE FIELDS—Wednesday, March 25. Clear and fast.

FIRST — Purse $2,600, 6 furlongs, 4-year-olds and up, claiming.
Mortal Coil, Iwai $31.00 $14.20 $12.60
Ansgar, Tierney 5.00 4.20
Taillevho, Hall 31.20
Time — 1:10⅖. Also ran — Here Comes George, King Joaquin, Reserve Power, Sorrento Wave, Rubbish Man, Rickety Wrack, Perugino, Renown's Pal, Willow Rod.
Scratched — Larry Lin, The Scrambler, Nictate, Doreen's King.

SECOND — Purse $3,500, 6 furlongs, 4-year-olds and up, claiming.
Via Venuto, Hall $3.80 $3.00 $2.60
Tommy Kid, Peichoto 4.60 3.60
Goofy McGenty, Cantarini 5.40
Time—1:10⅘. Also ran—Son Of Mosque, Lord Agile, Martial C., Tommy Tickle, No Hurry, Fighting Farmer, Roaring Rapids, Baron Charlie, Joe's Hawk.
Scratched—Rapid Fleet, Nechao's Risk, Look In, Chesty Rob.
DAILY DOUBLE — Mortal Coil to Via Venuto paid $84.60. DD Nos. 2 & 8.

Santa Anita Results

SANTA ANITA—Wednesday, March 25. Clear and fast.

FIRST—Purse $4,500, 7 furlongs, chute, 4-year-olds and up, claiming, $4,000-$3,500.
Freewave, Pincay Jr. $7.00 $4.00 $2.?0
Alooraido, Velasquez 17.40 7.80
John Van Milwood, Harris 3.80
Time—1:23. Also ran—First Salute, Captain Lex, Defler, Dark Tie, Peace Signal II, Bit O Dell, Mr. Flower, Sonapanoma, Ken Dee.

SECOND—Purse $5,000, 1⅛ miles, 3-year-olds, Calif. bred, claiming. All $6,2?0.
Faithville Litz, Pineda $12.60 $6.80 $3.60
Peek Ahead, Wellington 8.20 4.00
Act On Time, Teiera 2.60
Time—1:45. Also ran: Bettys Envoy, Prowling Prince, Rosy Sphere, Sonic Shower, Sonny Dress, Long Pants, Bella Lady.
DAILY DOUBLE—4 and 7 paid 78.20.

Prime Rate Cut Hoists Stocks

NEW YORK (AP) — The Bank of America, the nation's largest, cut its prime interest rate to 8 per cent from 8½ today as it and others quickly followed a move announced by Irving Trust Co., one of the nation's major banks.

Other banks included Wells Fargo, Crocker-Citizens, and Central Valley National Bank. Stock market trading picked up, and the Dow Jones average of 30 industrials closed up 16.37 points.

Details on Page 11

Figure 18–5 The head at the top of this newspaper is the "skyline." Below it is the "banner," or main headline. Ears on each side of the nameplate note the inclusion of race results and the time the edition reaches the streets. Note that even though some heads "bump," there is no distraction because the style of type and number of lines vary.

Figure 18–6 The front page of this modern medium-sized city daily obviously was intended for home delivery, where purchase in effect was made in advance via subscription. The photos are smaller, and relatively smaller type is used in heads.

Weather
Nice
Details on Page 6A

The Detroit News

THE HOME NEWSPAPER

Financial
Pages 2-4B
Races
Page 4D

MONDAY, AUGUST 17, 1970 — 97th YEAR No. 360 10 CENTS

Hopes for peace fading in Mideast

From UPI, AP, Reuters Dispatches

Hopes for peace in the Middle East continued to be edged in gloom today. There was one brighter note: United Nations negotiator Gunnar Jarring was meeting today to hasten substantive Egypt-Israel talks.

Israeli Premier Golda Meir said it would not surprise her if shooting resumes across the Suez Canal before the expiration of the 90-day, U.S.-engineered cease-fire, now in its 10th day.

Israel's Foreign Minister Abba Eban today said his government had definite proof that Egypt violated the new cease-fire not long after it went into effect. Other sources in Tel Aviv said Egypt was continuing to fortify missile sites in the Suez Canal zone covered by the cease-fire.

These sources said that after Israel first charged such fortification work, the Egyptians moved up another missile battery and resumed work on other incomplete missile sites in the "frozen" military zone extending 32 miles from each side of the canal.

In Jordan, Palestinian guerilla chieftain Yasir Arafat said he expects renewed fighting between his commandos and the Jordanian army of King Hussein. Arafat said four brigades of government troops are ringing the capital of Amman in preparation for a new crackdown on guerillas.

"But we shall turn Jordan into a graveyard for plotters," Arafat said. "Amman shall be the Hanoi of the Middle East."

The guerilla newspaper Al Fatah claimed Lebanon was collaborating with Jordan in preparations "for an anti-guerilla showdown."

Independent sources in Amman claimed to have seen armor being moved from the Israeli frontier to the Amman vicinity. But a

"I would not be surprised if firing resumes." — Meir

"Could happen tomorrow or the day after."

Lebanese spokesman denied the two governments have had any contacts regarding the guerrillas.

Hussein will begin a three-day visit to Cairo on Thursday, it was announced today.

Past attempts by the Jordanian and Lebanese armies to curb guerilla operations in their countries have resulted in hard fighting, government shake-ups and only slight, temporary checks on the guerillas' activities. Now the guerillas are continuing their attacks on Israel in defiance of the Israeli-Jordanian-Egyptian cease-fire, and Israel has already made two attacks on Jordan in reprisal.

Jarring's meeting in New York today with Egypt's peace negotiator was aimed at getting substantive Arab-Israel talks under way within a week.

The Egyptian diplomat, Mohamed H. Al-Zayyat, arrived in New York during the weekend for his first meeting with Jarring since the UN peace mission was reactivated.

Informed sources said Al-Zayyat brought with him detailed proposals from President Gamal Abdel Nasser to present to Jarring for submission to Israel.

It was understood that a key element is Egypt's demand that Israel withdraw from all territories seized in the 1967 war if a peace settlement is to be achieved.

Al-Zayyat was also to see UN Secretary-General Thant, U.S. Ambassador Charles W. Yost and delegates of Russia, France and Britain.

Israel's Mrs. Meir told the Labor Party central ccommittee in Tel Aviv that Egypt's alleged movement of Soviet - made anti - aircraft missiles closer to the Suez Canal after the start of the cease-fire "was not an encouraging beginning to peace talks."

"Considering what they did with the missiles, I would not be surprised if shooting were to resume before expiration of the 90-day temporary truce," she said. "It could happen tomorrow or the day after."

U.S. Defense Secretary Melvin R. Laird said in Washington yesterday it would be "difficult to prove or disprove" Israel's charges the missiles were moved after the truce began.

Laird said reconnaissance indicates both sides are now abiding by the cease-fire terms, and he urged them to forget the argument and begin peace talks.

Israelis expressed disappointment with Laird's remarks.

Eban yesterday indicated Israeli's continued resistance to Arab demands that any peace settlement be accompanied by Israeli withdrawal from all territory occupied during the 1967 Middle East war.

In another development, Israel has decided to release the two Algerian passengers of a British airliner who were detained in Tel

(Concluded on Page 10A)

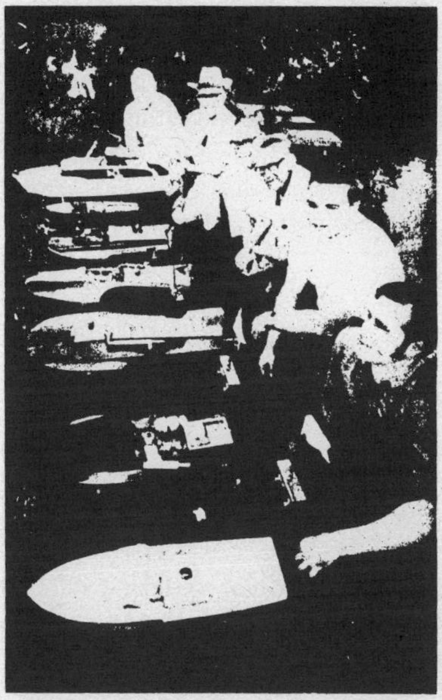

—News Photos by Joseph F. Wiedelman

MODEL BOATS AND SKIPPERS—Racing radio-controlled model boats ranging from cruisers to hydroplanes is a favorite diversion for this group of Detroiters. Arrayed alongside the sleek little jobs before they take to the water are (from top) Earl Jagger, Richard Gaskell, John Pomeroy, Emery Bocz, Richard Kuzma and Richard Dumas.

Dynamite trap kills policeman

From UPI and Special Dispatches

OMAHA—One police officer was killed and seven others were injured early today when they were lured into a dynamite trap here.

Police said they received a telephone call reporting that a woman was screaming in a house. Eight officers went to the house, which turned out to be vacant.

An officer found a suitcase inside and, as he was moving it, it exploded. The officer, Larry Menard, was killed.

A second policeman was blown through a back door and another halfway across the front lawn. A resident standing across the street was felled.

The seven officers were taken to a hospital. None were in serious condition.

Half of the house was "shattered to kindling," a witness said. He said the rest barely was standing and a heavy odor of "shotgun shells" permeated the area.

Police sealed off the area and brought in floodlights to illuminate the scene. They expressed apprehension over another vacant house nearby. Bomb experts were called in to inspect it.

In Minneapolis, an explosion rocked the Federal Building in the downtown area early today, causing considerable damage to the two-story structure and injuring a police officer.

The front of the building received extensive damage, with the steps uprooted and most of the windows blown out. Rubble was scattered over a parking lot across the street.

Police and FBI agents sought to determine whether the explosion was caused by a bomb.

A woman who was sorting mail in the main Minneapolis Post Office, a block away, reported that the post office vibrated from the explosion.

Widow can keep her bushes

U.S. hedges on a ban

BAD AXE —(AP)— Mrs. Byron Watson learned today that bureaucracy has a heart and the federal government will not take away her barberry bushes.

The decision ended weeks of anxiety for the 86-year-old woman.

Mrs. Watson's barberry bushes grace the entrance to her home in this Thumb community.

But barberry bushes are under a federal ban in major crop areas because they are a source of stem rust, a disease which is devastating to grain. The prickly barberry bushes, however, are common in suburban areas, where they are often used as hedges.

The U.S. Agriculture Department office in Lansing ordered Mrs. Watson to cut down her bushes or officials would come and do the job.

Mrs. Watson wrote M.E. Turner, the department supervisor, and begged for an exemption.

She asked that the bushes be allowed to remain until her death.

That won't be long, she assured Turner, because "never in my four-years-short-of-90 span of life have I been so near the end."

She pointed out that no grain grows near her home.

Turner announced today that agriculture officials will visit Mrs. Watson's home, where they threatened originally.

But they will not chop down the bushes. Instead they'll pick the berries.

That way, Turner said, the bushes will be prevented from reproducing and possibly spreading—with the help of birds—to areas where they would threaten crops.

And the bushes will remain to brighten Mrs. Watson's remaining years.

Lifeguards save scores

Coast riptides kill 2

NORFOLK, Va. — (AP) — Two person drowned as riptides spawned by an Atlantic storm chased hundreds of swimmers ashore yesterday along 300 miles of beach from Maryland to North Carolina.

Lifeguards up and down the coast reported saving scores.

Mrs. Susan Jones, 23, a Cinicinnati housewife, drowned at Cape Hatteras, N.C. At virginia Beach, Julo Fajardo, 19 a Guatemalan visiting his brother, was swept to sea.

Police at Virginia Beach attempted to close off the shore to swimmers after the weather bureau issued riptide warnings shortly before noon. But they found the only thing they could legally do was to warn swimmers of the danger and stand by with rescue equipment.

Hobbyists keep their feet dry

Boat race in a pond

By CHARLES MANOS
News Staff Writer

The two hydroplanes, one carrying the General Motors' colors and the other representing the Ford Motor Co., roared across the water at top speed.

"Watch the turn," yelled Richard Kuzuma, 43, at the control of the Ford boat.

Richard Gaskell's boat skims over the water as he controls speed from shore.

"Don't worry," countered Jack Pomeroy, 56, pushing his GM special ahead as both crafts made the far turn and headed back at top speed.

Suddenly the Ford boat flipped over and the GM boat sputtered. Finally it stalled.

"Oh, well," said Kuzma to his rival, "let's push the rubber raft out and get them."

Both pilots had their feet firmly on the ground.

For this was another "fun time" session for a group of men whose hobby is building and racing radio-controlled model boats.

Called the Ford Motor Tri-Modelers Club, their operation headquarters is the twin ponds, on Ford property near Greenfield Village.

A majority of the two dozen members are Ford engineers. The rest are "outsiders" like Pomeroy who works for the GM purchasing department.

"I drove by this area several times a couple years ago and became curious," he said. "I stopped one day and chatted with the boys here. Then the model boat bug got me."

Pomeroy is now a vice-president of the club.

The model boats range from trim speedboats to cabin cruisers.

The boats are about 36 inches long and each is controlled by a short-wave radio on a licensed Federal Communications Commission citizen's band.

Initial investment in the hobby is costly as the radio unit alone is about $500. or more.

Plans or kits for model boats start at $40.

Earl Jagger, 43, said he had invested about $500 in his 42-inch model cabin cruiser.

An assistant manager at City National Bank, Jagger said he built it from a kit.

"It is the nearest I could get to the real thing which would cost about $50,000," he said.

The men, often accompanied by their wives and children, said the hobby provides year-around recreation.

TV tips help boy defuse bomb

BIRMINGHAM, England — (Reuters) — Schoolboy Ian Hughes, 15, astonished the experts by defusing a dangerous mortar bomb by himself—with just a few clues from television.

Ian found the live wartime bomb on a building site during the weekend. He took it home and calmly sat on the back doorstep unscrewing the rusty detonator.

By the time his father saw what was happening, Ian had wrenched out the fuse with a pair of pliers.

"I've seen bombs defused on television," Ian said. "It's always fascinated me. I like messing about with anything mechanical."

He said he was worried about leaving the bomb where he had found it because children were playing nearby.

Today's index

AUGUST
17 18 19 20 21 22
23 24 25 26 27 28 29
30 31
SEPTEMBER
1 2 3 4 5
6 7 8 9 10 11 12

Amusements	4C	Magazine Page	14A
Bridge	17A	Movie Guide	3C
Classified	7-17D	News Summary	2A
Comics	6D	Obituaries	7D
Crossword	17D	Sports	1-5D, 7D
Editorial	18A	TV-Radio	16-17A
Experience	3C	Weather	6A
Finance	2-4B	Women's	1-3C
Horoscope	8A		

A buyer's guide

LONDON — (Reuters) — A trendy Carnaby Street boutique is offering a free man to every free-spending girl customer.

At least the boutique is promising a free blind date—matched by computer—to any girl spending moer than $24. The offer goes for married women as well.

Owner Harry Fox said, "We'll be handing out the computer dating forms to every girl, whether she's got a ring on her finger or not. Then it's up to her whether she takes it up."

Red prof bought gun that killed judge, U.S. confirms

From AP and UPI Dispatches

—SAN FRANCISCO — The search for Angela Davis broadened today after a federal attorney confirmed that the self-professed Communist teacher bought the shotgun that killed Judge Harold J. Haley.

The judge and three other men were killed Aug. 8 in a gun battle that followed a courtroom kidnaping in San Rafael, across the Golden Gate from San Francisco.

Miss Davis, 26, is charged with one count of murder and five counts of kidnaping under a California law which holds that anyone who aids a major crime is as guilty as the direct participants.

Jerrold Ladar, assistant U.S. attorney, said yesterday a serial number check showed the shotgun was purchased at a San Francisco pawnshop Aug. 5 by Miss Davis, a former UCLA instructor whom the regents had refused to rehire.

The search for Miss Davis ranged from the West Coast to Birmingham, Ala., and abroad after Ladar disclosed that she had a passport.

Early reports about the possible whereabouts of the black educator, who has a high, bushy afro hair-do, had included Canada. Ladar said a passport is not needed to enter Canada, but would be necessary to go from there to any other country.

As the FBI jined the search on a federal fugitive warrant charging unlawful flight to avoid prosecution, reports persisted that Miss Davis might be in Birmingham, her birthplace.

Maj. David Orange, head of the Jefferson County (Ala.) sheriff's intelligence force, said he is convinced she is still in Birmingham.

An informant told officers Miss Davis had attended a Black Panther Party meeting in Birmingham last Friday night, Orange reported.

But Sheriff Lt. Dan Jordan said he believes Miss Davis left Birmingham about 20 minutes before simultaneous raids raids by federal, local and state officers on her parents' home, her father's service station, a local Black Panther headquarters and the home of a Panther member.

"We put out an all-points bulletin arrest order for her as soon as our raids didn't produce her," Jordan said. "I feel the reason we didn't get her was because Saturday morning when we learned of her presence we had to telegraph the San Rafael courthouse and be sure they had warrants for her arrest."

There was an eight-hour delay in obtaining the warrants, he said. By the time the warrants had been obtained, Jordan added, Miss Davis probably had been warned that officers were seeking her by a story in a local newspaper.

In San Francisco, Ladar said Miss Davis was reported to have been a frequent companion of Jonathan Jackson, 17, one of those killed in the shoot-out at the Marin County Civic Center.

Investigators said Jackson went into Haley's courtroom with a bowling bag full of weapons and interrupted an assault trial by brandishing guns and shouting, "All right, everybody freeze!"

Taking the judge and four others in the courtroom as hostages, Jackson and three San Quentin convicts—one on trial for assaulting a guard and two present as witnesses—marched the hostages to a parking lot.

In a gun battle that erupted as the abductors tried to leave the area in a small van with their hostages, Jackson and two of the convicts, James McClain and William A. Christmas, were killed.

The third convict, Ruchell Magee, and two of the hostages were wounded.

A sawed-off shotgun, which had been taped around the judge's neck in the courtroom and which later was used to kill him, is the one

(Concluded on Page 10A)

Figure 18–7 Editors of this newspaper "weighted" the front page with large type and relatively long stories at the top and bottom for eye-appealing effect. Note the ears on each side of the nameplate directing the reader to specific pages. This standard-sized newspaper provides an "open space" look with five columns (instead of eight) with wide margins.

The "are" in front of "chosen" in this head is deleted, and the reader, conditioned to headlinese, understands the meaning.

While most editors frown on using forms of "to be," some nevertheless will use them occasionally.

Tenses in headlines. Journalists differ from other writers in forming the tenses for headlines, and over the years readers have been conditioned to understand. For example, consider the tenses for a story referring to a speech.

Using the *infinitive* form indicates that the event *will* take place:

**Chief to speak
on crime rate**

A head with the *gerund* infers that the event is continuing as the newspaper is issued:

**Chief speaking
on crime rate**

The use of the *present* tense denotes that the event *was* held:

**Chief speaks
on crime rate**

There is little usage, therefore, for the past tense in heads.

Unneeded Words. Journalists do *not* use articles (the, an, a) in heads. The reason is that they say little and take up valuable space. Here is an example showing how articles contribute nothing to heads:

**The chief speaks
on a crime report**

Removing "the" and "a" would save space for more expressive words and at the same time make the head easier to read.

"And" is another word that consumes valuable space. Headlinese has conditioned readers to accept a comma as the substitute for "and." Example:

**Chief, assistant
to name suspects**

Do Not Overabbreviate. Despite limited space in heads, arbitrary or rare abbreviations are not acceptable. If they were used, the average reader would need a code book to decipher the meanings; consequently the heads would have little meaning. Here is an example of abbreviations that would be confusing:

**Coll. assoc.
to hold conf.**

To produce an understandable head, the copyreader would use better-known abbreviations and rephrase it. Here is one way it could be done:

**College assn.
plans parley**

The stylebook standards for stories do not apply to abbreviations or other style matters in heads. Instead, editors develop a set of rules—written or oral—pertaining to style for heads. These standards seek to produce usage to help readers understand. Head styles usually give more variation and flexibility than those for stories. For example, despite the spell-below-10 injunction for stories, numbers in heads can be figures or spelled according to the copyreader's needs.

Initials can be used to abbreviate, as long as the letters are meaningful to the readers of a particular newspaper. Virtually everyone understands the meaning of AFL-CIO, N.Y., L.A., or NATO, but other letter combinations may not be recognizable outside a particular region, and some vary according to locale. The use of the abbreviation "OCC" would mean Orange Coast College in Orange County, California, while it would stand for Oklahoma Christian College in Tulsa, Oklahoma.

Do Not Hyphenate. Splitting or dividing a word between lines is not permitted because of the difficulty that would come in reading heads quickly. This usage would *not* be permitted:

**9 profes-
sors win**

This is one way of redoing the head:

**9 profs
honored**

High and Dry

Sunny today and Saturday. High today 75-80. Northerly winds 10-15 mph becoming northeasterly 15-20 mph Saturday. (See map, Page 2A.)

HOURLY TEMPERATURES

7 a.m.	64	1 p.m.	74	7 p.m.	69
8 a.m.	67	2 p.m.	74	8 p.m.	67
9 a.m.	67	3 p.m.	74	9 p.m.	65
10 a.m.	70	4 p.m.	74	10 p.m.	63
11 a.m.	72	5 p.m.	74	11 p.m.	63
Noon	73	6 p.m.	70	Midnight	63

The Miami Herald

Friday, December 12, 1969 No. 12 *Florida's Complete Newspaper* 60th Year 166 Pages 10 Cents

Two Latin American Editions Published Daily

CITY EDITION

13 SHOPPING DAYS 'TIL CHRISTMAS

$20-Billion Hike Urged to Fight Social Ills

By SAUL FRIEDMAN
Of Our Washington Bureau

WASHINGTON — The National Commission on the Causes and Prevention of Violence is about to recommend huge slashes in defense spending and massive increases in funds for social programs.

The commission's final report, delivered to the President Thursday by Chairman Milton Eisenhower, is officially a secret until Sunday. A copy was obtained by Knight Newspapers.

"When our participation in the Vietnam war is concluded," the commission said, "we should increase annual general welfare expenditures by about $20 billion, partly by reducing military expenditures and partly by use of increased tax revenues resulting from the growth of the Gross National Product.

"We suggest this only as an initial goal; as the Gross National Product and tax revenues continue to rise, we should keep military expenditures level, while general welfare expenditures should continue to increase until essential social goals are achieved."

THE COMMISSION included in the phrase "general welfare" all programs to eliminate hunger and poverty, and to provide adequate housing, health care and education.

In one of its strongest sections, the commission said: "We . . . solemnly declare our judgment that this nation is entering a period in which our people need to be as concerned by the internal dangers to our free society as by any probable combination of external threats.

"We recognize that substantial amounts of funds cannot be transferred from sterile war purposes to more productive ones until our participation in the Vietnam war is ended.

"We also recognize that to make our society essentially free of poverty and discrimination, and to make our sprawling urban areas fit to inhabit, will cost a great deal of money and will take a great length of time.

"We believe, however, that we can and should make a major decision now to reas-

Turn to Page 34A, Col. 1

Violence Report: What Commission Asks

Here are the principal recommendations in the final report of the National Commission on the Causes and Prevention of Violence:

● **INCREASE** welfare spending by $20 billion a year, partly by cutting defense outlays and partly by use of increased tax revenues coming from the growth of the Gross National Product.

● **ISSUING** an "Annual Social Report" comparable to reports on the economy and the nation's defense posture, on progress in housing, education, health care and public safety.

● **FORMATION** of a "council of social advisers," like the Council of Economic Advisers, to check on effectiveness of social programs.

● **LEGISLATION** to permit federal courts to grant injunctions against attempts to interfere with rights of freedom of speech, press, peaceful assembly and petition for redress of grievances

Milton Eisenhower
. . . final report

—United Pressinternational Telephoto

Back Again

White House police hold back crowds as President Nixon shows former President Johnson to his limousine after the two held a two-hour breakfast meeting. It was Johnson's first return to the Executive Mansion since he left office. (See story, Page 35A.)

Next Step: Compromise

Senate OKs Tax Bill, Ignoring Veto Threat

House OKs New Voting Rights Bill

By DAVIS MERRITT
Of Our Washington Bureau

WASHINGTON — The House dealt the civil rights movement a major setback Thursday as it voted to junk the tough 1965 Voting Rights Act and replace it with a softer administration bill.

Shepherded through a divided and sometimes embittered House by Republican Leader Gerald Ford of Michigan, the bill passed by only five votes, 208-203.

REPUBLICAN loyalists and southerners cheered as they handed the President his first victory on a civil rights issue. Liberals and blacks viewed it as a major setback and another indication of Nixon's wooing of the South — the so-called "southern strategy."

One liberal opponent of the administration measure called it "a sheep in wolf's clothing." The description comes because while the administration bill wipes out literacy tests nationally and eases some voting restrictions it also pulls the teeth of the Voting Rights Act.

That act, which centered its force on seven southern states, expires next August. The House Judiciary Committee, headed by Rep. Emanuel Celler of New York, had approved a straight five-year extension of the 1965 act with the support of civil rights forces.

FORD, ON behalf of the administration, introduced a version which did away with the 1965 provision for federal registrars in the seven affected states.

The bill now goes to the Senate, where civil rights backers were startled and thrown into confusion by the House vote.

Sen. Phillip Hart of Michigan, floor leader on civil

Turn to Page 2A Col. 3

—Herald Staff Photo by BATTLE VAUGHAN

Clownettes

The clown fraternity, formerly an all-man's world, will be invaded this winter by two women. Vernice Klier, 24, left, and Jane Shirley, 18, in a Raggedy Ann costume, are in training in Venice at the College of Clowns. They had to take all the training the men did — yoga, juggling, unicycle riding, stilt-walking, tumbling, acrobatics and pantomime. The two young women were in a graduating class with 27 men and are expected to join one of the traveling units.

Exemption Would Go To $800

Bills Compared .. *28A*
Florida's Man *38A*
Roll-Call Vote *38A*

WASHINGTON — (UPI) — The Senate brushed aside a threatened veto and Republican talk of "economic collapse" Thursday and approved 69-22 a tax bill that would affect every American taxpayer.

Eighteen Republicans ignored President Nixon's opposition and joined 51 Democrats in voting for the bill, the biggest tax measure since the adoption of the income tax in 1913. Two Democrats and 20 Republicans voted no.

AS CHANGED in a three-week floor debate that Republicans said raised the bill's price tag for the government to $11 billion, the measure would cut everybody's income tax starting next year by boosting the $600 personal income tax exemption to $700 in 1970 and $800 in 1971.

It also would give special relief to 12 million poor, and grant 25 million retired Americans a 15 per cent boost in Social Security benefits effective Jan. 1. It would raise taxes on the wealthy and on corporations through $5 billion-a-year worth of tax reforms — including a cut in the 27.5 per cent oil depletion allowance to 23 per cent.

But friends and foes alike predicted that a far different measure — with more severe tax reforms and less generous tax cuts—would emerge from the House-Senate conference committee which now receives the bill.

THAT COMMITTEE must reconcile the Senate's bill with a bill adopted by the House last summer which is far closer to President Nixon's tax reform goals.

House managers of the tax

Turn to Page 38A, Col. 1

Patrol Puts $12,000 a Month Into Guarding Dade Witness

By JAMES SAVAGE
Herald Staff Writer

The Florida Highway Patrol is spending more than $12,000 a month to guard Charles R. Celona, the ex-policeman whose testimony has led to 33 Dade County indictments.

Eleven troopers have been guarding Celona on a full-time basis since Sept. 17 and to date it has cost the patrol more than $36,000 according to patrol executive Eldredge Beach.

The cost of the Celona guard detail was cited by patrol officials questioned by legislators about their request for an emergency appropriation. The Legislature Wednesday passed the $700,000 appropriation to bail out the patrol budget.

CELONA, a former deputy, has been under police guard since October 1968, when he became a voluntary state's witness testifying about alleged police corruption.

Since then Celona's testimony before the Dade Grand Jury has led to the indictment of 33 persons. Eight of the accused are former sheriff's deputies.

Sheriff E. Wilson Purdy, who has directed the over-all Celona probe, has described the indictments as a "long needed housecleaning."

PURDY'S detectives guarded Celona from the beginning of the investigation until September, when an aide to Gov. Claude Kirk requested that the Highway Patrol supply the necessary manpower.

A single Dade deputy is still assigned to Celona to

Turn to Page 2A Col. 4

Now It's Spiro, Film Star

WASHINGTON — (UPI) — The government is producing a $20,000 biographical film about Vice President Spiro T. Agnew for viewing overseas, but it probably won't include scenes of his headline-making speeches criticizing war protesters and the news media.

The 10-minute film, produced by the U.S. Information Agency, will be ready for shipment to more than 100 USIA posts abroad by the end of January, officials said. It will be the agency's first such film about a vice president.

Officials said the purpose was to provide a sketch of Agnew for foreign audiences, concentrating on his career prior to his emergence as a national figure and glossing over domestic political controversies.

For this reason, they said, his recent critical speeches probably will be omitted, although there might be scenes from his post-Christmas Asian tour.

Plans for the film were initiated by USIA executives in charge of planning, who recalled the difficulty in putting together a film on President Lyndon B. Johnson immediately after President John F. Kennedy was assassinated and his vice president was sworn in.

Notable Quote

"I regard myself as having been eased out, not fired — a subtle distinction but an important one."

—Dr. Herbert Ley, who was replaced as chief of the FDA, announcing that he was leaving government

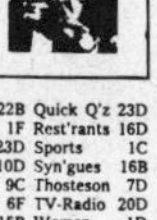

See Story, Page 20B

INDEX

Today's Chuckle

A gourmet is a man who is invited for an evening of wine, women and song — and asks what kind of wine.

LUBY CHEVROLET CITY
Service-Parts 'Til 9 Mon. and Thurs.
Sales 'til 9 PM Mon. thru Fri.
9200 N.W. 27th Avenue —Adv.

Medina Recalls Order to Stop Casualty Count

Did General Halt My Lai Death Probe?

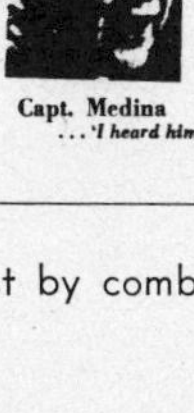

Capt. Medina
. . . 'I heard him'

Probers Argue *11B*

By JAMES McCARTNEY
Of Our Washington Bureau

WASHINGTON — A two-star general stepped in personally to halt an investigation of civilian casualties the day of the alleged My Lai massacre, Capt. Ernest Medina told Knight Newspapers Thursday.

It was the first time that any of the principals in the case suggested publicly that the top general in the area may have been aware — almost from the start — of the possibility of a massacre.

Capt. Medina, commander of the company involved in the incident, placed Maj. Gen. Samuel Koster, commander of the Americal Division, firmly in the My Lai area.

"I heard his voice on the radio," Medina said.

KOSTER is now superintendent of the U.S. Military Academy at West Point, one of the most prestigious jobs in the Army.

A special Army board plans to question Koster here in an attempt to determine whether there was a coverup of the incident.

The general has declined to discuss his role, although West Point officials acknowledge he was in the "habit" of staying close to combat operations by helicopter at that time.

Medina, who insisted he knew nothing about the alleged massacre, said that Koster personally rescinded a lower-level order for a check on civilian casualties.

He said that Koster's inter-

Turn to Page 2A Col. 7

Gen. Koster
. . . a cover-up?

Figure 18–8 This front page attracts interest by combining a reverse (white on black), a kicker (at bottom), a "box," and photos.

Garden Grove
THE ORANGE COUNTY EVENING NEWS

WEATHER
Mostly fair today through tomorrow but increasing early morning fog and low clouds near the coast. High today 78. Low tonight 58.

Vol. 61, No. 56   13 Published in Garden Grove —Since 1909—   20 PAGES   GARDEN GROVE, CALIFORNIA, MONDAY, OCTOBER 13, 1969   10c   JEfferson 7-7510

War Moratorium Rallies, Boycotts Loom in County

IWO JIMA FLAG RAISING REENACTED? NOT HARDLY
...group of McKinley school students give assist to brace holding building

Santa Ana School Election 'Crisis'

Story, photo by BRUCE YOUNG

General Pleaded: 'Destroy Receipts'

WASHINGTON (UPI)

IN THE NEWS
	Page
Ann Landers	B-3
Astrognide	B-1
Bridge	C-5
Classified	D3-4
Crossword Puzzle	B-3
Editorial Page	A-4
Entertainment	C-4
Sports	C1-3
TV	B-4
Weather	C-5
Women's Section	B1-2

Action Line
GETS THINGS DONE!

RUSS PUT 3 CRAFT IN ORBIT
First Step in Construction of Space Station
MOSCOW (UPI)

Rising G.G. Cafeteria Costs to Be Aired

Students to Picket Base at El Toro
By PHYLLIS CANNON

Moratorium Opposition Increasing

By United Press International

Schmit Will Press Smog Hearing Plan

WORLD NEWS
By United Press International

3 Women Wait Call from N. Viets
PARIS

Yorty Raps Vietnam Moratorium
LOS ANGELES

B52s Bomb Near Cambodia Border
SAIGON

Chicago Appears Back to Normal
CHICAGO

15 Nabbed on Stolen Car Charges
BISHOP

Front Page

Union leaders here appealed to striking mail carriers to return to work so that negotiations can begin.

Several mail carriers unions across the country voted to continue the strike.

President Nixon's most pressing domestic problem — the mail strike — is all his fault, according to union leaders.

The premier of Laos was handed a letter from the leader of the Communist-dominated Pathet Lao as the battle for a key base continued.

Some saw a turning point in American-Israel relations in the expected negative response the United States is to make to Israel's request for more jet aircraft.

College student suicides have less to do with drug use and academic pressures than was believed, suicide experts learned.

A 75 mm cannon capable of blowing up a tank or a police station was stolen over the weekend from a Tahoe ski resort.

Inside

Mayor Alioto said he will fight to insure that recent State action does not cripple new construction in the city. Page 2.

John Lennon said the Beatles smoked marijuana before meeting the Queen in Buckingham Palace. Page 2.

The paddlewheel steam tug Eppleton Hall will puff into the Bay Area this week to become a prize exhibit of the Maritime Museum. Page 3.

TOP OF THE NEWS

A three-alarm fire gutted the abandoned Schwabacher-Frey warehouse in the Yerba Buena Renewal Project. Page 3.

Young people turned garbage into sculpture in Civic Center Plaza, to greet spring and to offer art in the streets. Page 3.

The city's top union officials and Mayor Joseph Alioto are credited with the swift settlement of the city employees' strike. Page 4.

The ladies are getting more militant. They have made plans for a national strike in August. Page 4.

The Golden Gate Bridge District board will consider cutting tolls in half for car-pooling commuters. Page 5.

A wrecking ball smashed its way through the old Hotel Plaza to make way for a new hotel and shopping center. Page 5.

A recent Gallup Poll reveals that George Wallace still retains strength with American voters. Page 6.

Five actors preparing for a play about prison inmates took a tour through San Quentin. Page 7.

The Rincon Annex Post Office was picketed again, but most of the employees chose to cross the line. Page 8.

Telephone and telegraph lines hummed with extra weekend activity while small businessmen worried about the mail strike. Page 8.

Pope Paul IV renewed his appeals for peace in his Palm Sunday address at St. Peter's Square. Page 10.

The anxiety of U.S. military commanders over the widespread smoking of marijuana has brought about a time-consuming pot search and destroy mission. Page 11.

Three recent Harvard graduates have started a national humor magazine poking fun at such American institutions as Julie Eisenhower. Page 13.

The deb business is booming again. Page 18.

A Sausalito husband-and-wife team has designs on everything from sheets to chairs. Page 20.

Sports

Dale Douglass and Don January tied for the Jacksonville golf title and will meet in an 18-hole playoff today. Page 49.

The Warriors dropped a 132-112 decision to Philadelphia, ending a most dismal season. Page 49.

Gaylord Perry pitched the Giants to a 6-3 win over Lotte Orions, the San Franciscans first win on a two-week tour of Japan. Page 49.

Weather

Bay Area: Fair today except for some morning low cloudiness. High, mid-60s to low 70s; low, in the 40s. Northwesterly winds to 20 m.p.h. Page 39.

San Francisco Chronicle

★★★★ FINAL

106th Year No. 82 ★★★★ MONDAY, MARCH 23, 1970 10 CENTS GArfield 1-1111

U.S. Replies To Israel on Planes Today

By James Feron
New York Times

Jerusalem

The modified negative response that Secretary of State William Rogers is expected to announce today in response to Israel's request for more jet aircraft may, in the view of some observers, mark a turning point in American-Israeli relations.

These observers are saying, for example, that it is apparent that tight secrecy will be imposed on future arms talks.

The day of publicly announced weapons agreements is probably over.

SIGNAL

It is also expected that the long-awaited reply by Washington to Israel's request will serve as the signal for the most crucial re-examination of Israel's security requirements in her 22 years of existence.

The Israeli cabinet met yesterday to determine its response to the statement promised by Rogers to Premier Golda Meir's six-month-old military and economic requests.

During her visit to Washington last October, Mrs. Meir is believed to have asked for an additional 25 Phantom jet fighters and approximately 80 Skyhawk reconnaissance jets. Israel is at present scheduled to receive 50 Phantoms which were sold to Mrs. Meir's predecessor, the late Levi Eshkol, by the Johnson Administration.

NEGATIVE

Although the wording of Rogers' delayed reply remained the subject of last-minute negotiations, it is expected to be generally negative as far as the jets are concerned, although coupled with assurances of review.

Israeli officials will probably demand that this review begin immediately, especially against a background of disclosures that the Soviet Union is installing and planning to operate antiaircraft missile sites in Egypt.

It is likely that this call for a review of security requirements will be made quietly and that the talks themselves

See Back Page

A Cannon Is Stolen

Tahoe City

A 75-millimeter artillery piece has been taken from the Alpine Meadows ski resort, where it was used to bring down potential avalanches from surrounding mountainsides.

The Placer County sheriff's office said yesterday the cannon and four or five rounds of ammunition were missed Saturday by Norm Wilson, mountain manager for the resort.

A sheriff's spokesman said the cannon and its high-explosive shells "could blow up any kind of armored car, bank or police station from a half mile away. If it was a prank, why take the ammunition?"

The cannon, one used for the 1960 Olympics at nearby Squaw Valley, was on loan from the United States Forest Service. The shells were in a locked gun locker below the weapon. Deputies say the cannon was taken between Wednesday and Friday night.

Associated Press

Red Peace Proposal To Souvanna

Vientiane

Premier Prince Souvanna Phouma yesterday received a presumed peace proposal from his half-brother, Prince Souphanouvong, head of the Communist-dominated Pathet Lao.

No one would divulge the contents but it was believed a move for a political settlement of the Laotian war.

It was also presumed that the proposal was couched in terms of the five points advanced as a basis for settling the war by the Pathet Lao earlier this month.

STUDY

A press release from the premier's office called it a "proposition" and indicated it would be given lengthy study before a Vientiane response.

The five-point plan of the Pathet Lao calls for, among other things, an end to all foreign military aid or intervention in Laos, the setting up of a provisional coalition government that would hold elections for a government of national union, and the re-establishment of Laotian neutrality under the Geneva accords.

Included is a demand for an end to United States military aid to the Laos and a halt to government bombing of Laotian territory.

TROOPS

No mention was made of evacuation of North Vietnamese troops in Laos in support of the Pathet Lao or of an end to North Vietnamese, Chinese and Soviet assistance to the Pathet Lao.

The five points are regarded by the government here as unacceptable but Souvanna has made clear he is prepared to discuss a peace settlement with the Pathet Lao.

Loyal Laotian forces defending Long Cheng reported killing seven North Vietnamese, including six women in full combat gear, in a clash near the key government base yesterday.

Long Cheng, 80 miles north of Vientiane, is the headquarters base of the U.S.-supported clandestine army trying to halt the North Vietnamese-Pathet Lao offensive which already has penetrated deeper into Laos than any previous drive.

New York Times

The Mail Showdown-- Postal Workers Split

Union Asks S.F. Men To Return

By Elmont Waite

Work at some of the major mail-handling facilities in the Bay Area was nearly back to normal yesterday and union leaders were appealing to striking letter carriers to stop picketing and get back on the job today.

George Pieraldi, after a meeting with all union stewards of the big San Francisco Letter Carriers Local which he heads, said, "Everybody has agreed to spread the word—get back to work."

The return to work could be temporary, he added. "We're asking everyone to work for five days, during which wage negotiations in Washington will proceed. Then, if there's still a deadlock, there would be a national walkout."

OAKLAND

In Oakland, more than 200 members of that city's letter carriers' union met yesterday and voted 151 to 73 not to strike — but local President Robert Christian said he didn't know what would happen if a wildcat strike developed anyhow. A minority reportedly was still planning to attempt a walkout and picketing.

No letter carriers were on duty yesterday but many had stayed off work and set up picket lines Saturday, blocking home deliveries of mail in many Bay Area communities, including much of San Francisco.

RINCON

On Saturday, the picketing had kept many postal clerks (who work inside the postal stations and who are not on strike) off their jobs — but at some major centers most of them were back on the job yesterday, the Post Office Department's regional office here reported.

Russell E. James, regional director, reported that at

See Back Page

A PICKET OUTSIDE RINCON ANNEX
Many workers crossed the line

Deadline Today in Walkout

Associated Press

New York

Striking postal workers in cities from coast to coast made plans to ignore President Nixon's deadline for ending the mail strike.

But others voted to return and the Government indicated that enough may be doing so to permit talks to begin today.

The Government announced return to full or partial service in several areas of the East and Midwest.

LOS ANGELES

Meanwhile, however, the 3500-member Postal Workers union in Los Angeles announced it was going on strike today.

An Associated Press spot survey of local communities around the country indicated that workers in most major cities on strike were remaining on strike, that a number of the smaller cities were returning to service and that workers in many communities not on strike have voted to maintain a five-day, wait-and-see attitude.

The areas hardest hit by the strike have been New York, Philadelphia, Pittsburgh, Cleveland, Detroit, Milwaukee, Chicago, Denver and the entire states of Connecticut and New Jersey. Some cities in New Jersey have voted returns to work but the service statewide remained doubtful.

RETURNING

Among places where mailmen voted to return to work, Buffalo, N.Y., and Cincinnati did so for five days, dependent on how well negotiations proceed. Back to work unconditionally were Trenton, Camden and Atlantic City, N.J.; Madison, Wis.; Boulder, Colorado Springs and Greeley, Colo.; and Meriden and Milford, Conn.

Joining the ranks of strikers, along with Los Angeles, were locals in Albany and Rochester, N.Y.; Worcester, Mass., and Providence, R.I.

Postmaster General Win-

See Back Page

Beliefs Upset

A New Look at Student Suicides

By Bill Workman

A study of suicidal behavior among Los Angeles college students, released here yesterday, indicated long-held beliefs that academic pressures and drug usage are significant links to campus suicides may have to be thrown out.

This most comprehensive study to date on collegiate self-destruction also challenged the widely held view that college students who commit suicide are brilliant and do so at a greater rate than non-college youths of the same age.

Conclusions of the two-year study — conducted among all 52 colleges and universities in Los Angeles county — were presented by Dr. Michael L. Peck of the Los Angeles Suicide Prevention Center at the third annual meeting of the American Association of Suicidologists.

CONFERENCE

Close to 300 experts in the field of self-destruction behavior and suicide prevention from all over the nation and Canada are attending the two-day conference, which convened yesterday at the Fairmont Hotel.

Dr. Peck said the 1968 suicide rate among Los Angeles

See Back Page

N.Y. Club Bombed -- 14 Injured

New York

Fourteen persons were injured last night when a pipe bomb exploded at the Electric Circus discotheque in the East Village, police reported.

All were taken to the emergency wards of two hospitals. Most appeared to be suffering shock and the injuries that were evident did not appear to be serious, the hospitals said. Nearly 200 persons were in the building at the time of the blast.

Earlier in the day a bomb exploded at a Bronx brokerage firm, knocking out a door and twisting the facade of the building, and another device was found unexploded on the window ledge of a neighboring bank. No one was injured in those incidents.

Deputy Police Inspector Charles Smyth said of the discotheque blast: "Somebody set off a pipe bomb. What it was loaded with we do not know. The person or persons entered the building and then left."

Associated Press

An Analysis

Mail Crisis Puts Nixon in a Bind

Times-Post Service

Washington

President Nixon comes face-to-face today with his most pressing domestic crisis in a situation forced not by students, restless blacks or the New Left, but what was once the most solid and dependable corner of middle America —the mailman.

Mr. Nixon is committed today to restoring mail service virtually halted by a four-day wildcat strike. Yet the Commander in Chief's ultimate weapon, the Army, may not work.

Mr. Nixon has said he won't negotiate postal wage demands until the walkout is ended. Postal union members — defying their national leaders and Federal Court orders — have said they won't go back to work until the Administration makes a promise of prompt, and sure, pay action.

BACKLOGS

If the strikers don't come back, the President is in a bad spot. Postal officials concede that untrained military personnel couldn't do a satisfactory job of sorting mail, especially with the mammoth backlogs most offices have.

The President is also in a fix, because legally he can't give anybody a raise. Federal salary bills are in the hands of Congress, which is controlled by the Democrats. There is some speculation that members of the opposi-

See Back Page

Soviet Party Official Fired

Moscow

The Soviet republic of Azerbaijan, shaken by scandals and economic failures, has fired another top party official, the Soviet newspaper Pravda reported yesterday.

The Central Committee of the Caucasian republic at a meeting in the capital of Baku, dismissed Gambar K. Kyazimov as party secretary and member of the state Politburo, the newspaper said.

United Press

Last Magical Trip for the Zephyr

By William Moore

The California Zephyr died yesterday—and some of America died with her.

Hundreds lined the Western Pacific tracks in Northern California to snap pictures and wave good-by to the loveliest and most loved train in all the country.

And when, four hours late, she rolled into Oakland's Third and Washington streets station for the final time last night — and when her groaning engine sounded a haunting farewell whistle blast — there weren't many dry eyes among the 350 passengers.

"What a tragedy the government didn't step in — we're losing a natural resource," observed a balding, cigar-chomping gentleman who was among the crowd of 300 that greeted the streamliner at the depot.

In Sacramento more than 400 persons, some of them wearing black arm bands, gathered quietly on the station platform as the Zephyr paused briefly, then glided on.

A young man placed a black wreath on the side of a sleeping car. And a freight engineer stood sadly nearby, holding his blue denim hat over his chest.

What sort of magic did this silver train weave upon those who rode her?

It might have been the spectacular scenery she passed through, much of it timed for daylight viewing on the leisurely 2½-day run between Chicago and Oakland.

There was something irresistible about a train that each day for 21 years meandered through the Feather River canyon, snaked her way across the Colorado Rockies, and then continued her serpentine course over

See Back Page

Index

Figure 18–10 This front page commands interest by its generous use of white space around headlines, even though it uses the eight-column format and rules between columns. Note the news digest at the top of the page and the box used to break type beneath the nameplate.

In the above example, "profs" is used as an understandable abbreviation for professors that eliminates hyphenation. "Honored" replaces "win" to avoid a short line. Copyreaders gradually build their own mental libraries of synonyms to help make heads longer or shorter.

Use of Quotation Marks. When slang or a portion of a direct quotation appears in a head, the copyreader uses quotation marks. In a story, the marks would be used in double fashion like this: "Hello." In headlines, most newspapers use only *single* quotation marks. This would be the usage:

**'Hello,' starlet
yells to fans**

One purpose of using the single quote marks is to conserve space in the head. A second reason is to avoid excessive symbols which could "clutter" a head.

The Period. When a head ends, it is over —without a period.

Periods are used in many abbreviations to help make them more understandable. Here is an example of typical usage:

**Police assn.
to meet today**

On the other hand, periods are usually omitted in "letter" abbreviations. Examples:

**AFL-CIO parley   LA physician
to open tomorrow   to head clinic**

Third Person. Heads, like news stories, use the third person to carry through the idea of objectivity or fairness. This usage would be wrong:

**Our team
wins meet**

Removing the personal reference would make the head acceptable:

**City team
wins meet**

Figure 18–11 Press time nears and produces this scene in the newsroom of a major daily newspaper. Note the overhead system to rush stories to printers and the intricate phone switchboards at several desks which allow calls to be transferred to reporters and editors. (*Chicago Sun-Times* Photo by Bob Kotalik)

H. L. Hunt Excited Over Creeping as Healthy Exercise

DALLAS (AP)—H. L. Hunt, one of the world's richest men, popped a date into his mouth and smiled around it. "I'm a crank about creeping," he said.

Creeping?

"You get down on all fours and

YUGOSLAVS HIJACK JET, MAKE SWEDEN FREE 6 PRISONERS

MALMOE, Sweden (UPI)—Three Yugoslav terrorists, who hijacked a Scandinavian Airlines System jetliner and demanded the release of seven fellow countrymen, freed 30 of the 87 hostages aboard for three of the prisoners but refused to let the others go unless they got one million Swedish kronor ($200,000), Malmoe airport officials said early today.

They had threatened to blow up the plane with all aboard.

Originally the hijackers had only demanded the release of the seven

Conferees Wrap Up Fund-Sharing Bill--- Half Billion to State

BY PAUL HOUSTON
Times Staff Writer

WASHINGTON — The Los Angeles County government apparently would receive more than $80 million a year under a $30 billion, five-year federal revenue-sharing package wrapped up Friday by Senate and House conferees.

New Rules Don't Bar Souvenirs Ripped Off Craft

SPACE CENTER, HOUSTON (UPI)—Space Agency officials say the new restrictions on personal items astro-

Hart Aims To Kill Transit Giveaway

WASHINGTON (UPI) —Sen. Philip A. Hart, D-Mich., said Sunday he would wage a Senate fight to kill a proposal under which the government would guarantee repayment of $3 billion worth of loans to

"So what did the American public gain? Nothing. If anything, rail service deteriorated after 1958."

In television commercials paid for by the Association of American Railroads, former

Figure 18–12 "Bumping" heads often makes more interesting effects and gives more news than a single large headline. Here are examples of creativity produced by variances in type styles, sizes, lines, and widths.

APPROACHES IN HEADS

Headlines come in many shapes and sizes. There are, however, four basic approaches in head *messages*.

1. The summary or "digest" head serves the same purpose as the inverted pyramid or summary lead. It gives the reader an idea of what the story is about, and if he wishes to continue by reading the story, he may do so. If the head says something that is not in the story, one of two things probably happened: (a) the copyreader did not read the story carefully and made the wrong conclusion in writing the head, or (b) he wrote the head on information in the middle or bottom of the story, and those facts were cut from the article during page make-up. To serve effectively, this type of head should be based on the early part of the story so that it will be meaningful even if the end of the article is deleted.

2. Feature or "soft" news stories often have a "teaser" head which arouses the reader's curiosity, as opposed to providing facts concerning the article's contents. While over serious stories such heads would annoy the reader for their lack of information, they add variety and humor to lighter articles. They can be based on information from other than the lead, since such stories do not follow the inverted pyramid format and are less likely to be cut.

3. Columns often take the same head, known as a "standing head," each day or week. This regular head can be a design with the column's name and author, or it can simply be conventional type arranged in a block and held for regular use. Some journalists defend standing heads as an ideal way for the reader to easily identify a favorite feature. Others oppose them with the contention that they fail to show column-by-column changes in contents.

were forged and made out to Hubbard. The complaint did not mention the 11 other checks.

TWO HOURS after the federal warrant was issued, the county state's attorney's office announced it will present evidence in the case to the Cook County grand jury on Friday.

Each act was preceded by one or more serious but avoidable accidents, such as the massive oil leak resulting from the grounding of the Torrey Canyon off the British and French coasts in 1967.

* * *

"OIL SPILLS have focused public attention on the need for safety," said Coast Guard Lt. Cmdr. Gill Shaw, who was public information officer in San Francisco at the time the Arizona Standard and the

banese Army moved back into the area and the dead and wounded were removed.

Combatants Gone

And Tuesday, there were no guerrillas nor were there any army troops: just the townspeo-

Landrigan says about his position, "I'm in the center of all the big dudes. I don't like to hit so when I can, I try to run around or go underneath the big fellas. "I really psyche them out."

KIDS ABOUT SIZE

Even though the Pirate kids about his size as soon as he gets on the field his performance makes up for what he lacks. He throws effective blocks on many of his opponents that are bigger than him.

that the muscles on his hind legs atrophied. He had great trouble in later learning how to climb trees.

The Rehabilitation Center

Not all people who make pets of orangutans treat them badly or teach them bad habits. But

Figure 18–13   Examples of subheads, used to break solid areas of type.

wore a Bronze Star and a Silver Star among other decorations, said his own report

~~~~~~~~~~~~~~~~
Related Stories On A2, A3
~~~~~~~~~~~~~~~~

of the My Lai engagement was that 20 to 28 civilians had been killed. He said the total

lines set up by the letter carriers.

At a surprise news conference in his oval office — the

Ends don't meet, Page 31

first of its kind since he became President — Nixon be

soaked South Vietnamese marines raised their national flag on a 20-
~~~~~~~~~~~~~~~~
Air raid scares greet kin of POWs in Hanoi. Page A-8.
~~~~~~~~~~~~~~~~
foot pole atop the west wall of the btatered fortress, recaptured by

trainer survived.

The Colorado State Patrol said there was no chance of other survivors among

```
MORE CRASH DETAILS,
SEE SPORTS, Page 9
```

the 40 persons listed as passengers and crew on the twin-engine Martin 404.

The ill-fated plane, with one engine

Figure 18–14   Methods of inserting "refer" lines, guiding readers to related stories.

of the Balboa Island Improvement Association.

"We support this proposed law with one exception," Houston said. "We'd like to see the one-fourth lot ratio figure chang-
(See HEARING, Page 2)

Santa Ana. Down the road are excellent beaches. And Dana Point Harbor—there are plenty of slips available."

Please Turn to Page 4, Col. 1

what they wanted and Spanish authorities expressed satisfaction that

(Continued on Page A-18, Col. 3)

Injunction Orders End To Walkout

Continued from Page 1

up for work, according to Charles W. Harper, director

Swedish jet hijackers give up in Madrid

(Continued from Page A-1)

they had been able to find the hijacking without violence.

It was a peaceful end to an odys-

Israelis Shocked by Resistance

(Continued from Page A-1)

Continued from Page 1

per cent non-white.

More than half of Oakland's

---

far from earthquake danger zones to build expensive
See Back Page, Col. 6

fluid," he added. "It can change from one hour to the next."

About 300 of the Rincon Annex's 1,000 employes showed
See Back Page, Col. 4

ceded that he has his "sails up, testing the wind."

But he asserted repeatedly
Turn to Page 10, Column 1

From Page 1

HEARING . . .

ed to one-third to give a little larger area.

"I'm sure, though, that if the commission keeps to the one-fourth figure,

Order arrest of Alderman in fund theft

Continued from Page 1

"I don't think so. I think it is a good plan."

Our Man Finds a Place That Re-Orangutanizes Orangutans. Really.

Continued From First Page
the underbrush and up the giant saraya trees. Most of the orangutans sleep high up in the

deb⁺ at more favorable rates. A spokesman for
Continued on Next Page

Let the Buyer Beware---True in Some Cases

Continued from First Page

(According to marina salemen there's a waiting list for all boat mooring

ings of the Vietnamese people will continue, and dissensions and unrest in the U.S. will continue, and more American
(Turn To Page A2, Column 6)

that the guerrillas were the enemy, not the Lebanese.

After going even farther north, the Israelis arrived in

(Continued on Page A-2, Col. 6)

Hubbard's wife, Arnette, has been at home during most of her husband's absence. On Thursday, the telephone in the

More About

3 POWS Freed

(Continued From Page A1)

pilots will be killed and captured."

VNA said the young American pilot "promised that back

---

of Sandilok can be seen sitting around the clearing, peeling their own bananas and drinking a milky liquid out of large tin cups.

Mealtime over, the orangutans lope off into
Please Turn to Page 21, Column 1

Financing Business
* * *
Continued From Preceding Page
the maker of technical equipment for the aerospace, industrial, machinery and informational

---

Figure 18–15   Some of the many ways to say that a story is continued to or from another page.

By CHRIS COCHRAN Barnacle Editor	BY LIZ McGUINNESS Times Staff Writer	By FRAN TARDIFF Barnacle Cub Reporter
By GIL BAILEY From Our National Bureau	By NOEL SWANN Staff Writer	By ANNE THOMPSON SMITH Herald-Examiner Society Writer
By CHRIS COCHRAN Of the Daily Pilot Staff	BY MICHAEL KILIAN [Chicago Tribune Press Service]	By ED SALZMAN Tribune Capital Bureau
by Helen Mitchell Barnacle Staff Reporter	BY TOM DAMMANN Special to CHICAGO TODAY	By JOHN P. WALLACH Herald-Examiner Washington Bureau
By Phillip J. O'Connor and John Camper	By MIKE COLWELL Register Staff Writer	By DAVE ROSE Register Political Writer
By Arthur J. Snider *Daily News Science Editor*	By the Elko Weather Bureau Elko, Nevada	Special to CHICAGO TODAY Exclusive to The Times from a Staff Writer

BY RAY ZEMAN and JOHN KENDALL
Times Staff Writers

By a WALL STREET JOURNAL *Staff Reporter*

By THE ASSOCIATED PRESS

By STEPHEN GROVER
Staff Reporter of THE WALL STREET JOURNAL

By United Press International

BY WILLIAM TROMBLEY
Times Education Writer

A WALL STREET JOURNAL *News Roundup*

Compiled from AP and UPI

From Our Springfield Bureau

Figure 18–16 Examples of by-lines following numerous styles.

4. The compromise between a standing head and one written anew with each column is the "standing-active" head, which combines a top line or "kicker" with the column's name or author and additional lines based on material from the column below.

OTHER HINTS FOR WRITING HEADLINES

Headlines *must* fit the allocated space and give the reader a reasonable idea of the story's main contents. The journalist also observes other points in writing meaningful headlines.

Be as Specific as Possible. Give *facts* instead of abstract material as much as possible. For example, use the *exact* number instead of

"many" in a headline. When using numbers, figures are better than spelling because they are easier to read in heads.

Names. If the person about whom a story is written is reasonably well known, use the name in the head. Avoid using the names of individuals who are unknown to the average newspaper reader.

Avoid Repetition. Do *not* repeat the same or similar words in headlines. Repetition in heads, as in stories, detracts from readability and indicates sloppy writing and thinking.

Avoid "Splits." Avoid splitting prepositional phrases or infinitives between lines; doing so makes heads difficult to read and understand. Years ago, editors said *never*

Mike Royko

A hard look at sick cars

In the Wake of the News

by David Condon

Money's Worth

Proper Resume Key In Finding Best Job

By SYLVIA PORTER

"I myself have screened fr any information that will assist you.

Spouting Off!

by GALE TAUCHER

People today

By Jim Mc Cormick

RICHARD BUFFUM

Two Happy Happenings

Two potentially happy things for Orange County have happened this

Just Coasting

with Tom Murphine

A Reprieve For Landmark

ONLY IN LAGUNA DEPT. — The tranquility of pre-dawn hours around our neighborhood was broken early today by the growls of a semi-truck engine, shouts

Figure 18–17 Methods of presenting columns. The Buffum and Royko columns carry the writers' names, with the balance varying according to daily contents. The McCormick, Taucher, and Condon displays are examples of standing heads which do not change or have additions. The "Money's Worth" column title goes in a kicker, while a head tells the contents for the day. The by-line follows.

make such splits, but today the injunction has been loosened to *avoiding* them. The most readable heads do *not* split prepositions or infinitives; beginners will do well to develop the habit of taking the time—and developing the skill—to redo heads to eliminate such constructions.

Other Points. Editors prefer *not* to use heads *beginning* with verbs (and usually containing no subjects) because they are confusing. Avoid "question" heads, since people want news and information—not quizzes. Develop a knowledge of synonyms and use it to write informative heads that fit the assigned type; avoid the artificial use of dashes and colons to "cram" words into heads.

APPROVAL FOR THE HEADLINES

The chief copy editor checks copyreaders' work to determine whether stories were properly edited and have an appropriate head. If the headline is too long or short or misses the

Auburn Journal

VOL. 96 NO. 19 | 10c COPY | AUBURN, CALIFORNIA THURSDAY, JAN. 16, 1969 | 30 PAGES | PHONE 885-5656

Work Progress Assured:

$17.6 Million Is Tagged For Dam

Outgoing President Lyndon B. Johnson this week recommended that $17.6 million be budgeted for the continuation of work on the Auburn Dam-Folsom South Canal Project during the 1969-70 fiscal year.

Optimism that the President's recommendation "will hold up" was expressed immediately by Congressman Harold T. "Bizz" Johnson of Roseville, co-author of legislation authorizing the $430 million multipurpose Bureau of Reclamation development.

"I am quite confident that Congress will not trim this figure," he told The Journal from Washington, D.C. "This amount will allow continuation of the project at a good pace. I feel the sum recommended is a reasonable one when you consider how hard money is to come by."

The current allocation for the project is $10,794,000. The President's recommendation for the upcoming fiscal year would see $12,941,000 go toward work on the dam, power plant and reservoir – meaning that the money would be spent in this area. The Folsom South Canal portion would receive $4,464,000. Other items would get $195,000.

Congressman Johnson said the 1969-70 money will assure continuation of relocation of the Auburn-Foresthill Road, and the award of contracts for excavation of dam keyways, the diversion tunnel and damsite clearing. It also will provide for continuing work on access roads to the power plant and dam.

A CARMICHAEL YOUTH was seriously injured late Tuesday afternoon on Highway 49 near Cool when he was thrown from the sports car at left, as it spun out of control, hit a dirt bank and slid broadside into the vehicle at right. Above, the two drivers, Rick Terry Barber, 19, of Carmichael, left, and William John Vasil, 55, of Bellevue, Wash., exchange identification at the scene. Barber's passenger, Dave Ernest Dubie, also 19, was thrown out of the car as it careened across the roadway, landing on the pavement only inches in front of the wheels of the Vasil sedan. The two youths were taken to Placer General Hospital in Auburn by the Chapel of the Hills ambulance. Barber suffered only minor injuries. The California Highway Patrol reported the two youths had been drinking beer prior to the accident, and witnesses said the driver tossed beer cans from the car after the crash. The CHP said investigation is continuing, pending the outcome of a blood alcohol test requested on Barber.

'An Outstanding Job'

Grand Jury Report Lauds Water Agency

By JOE CARROLL

The 1968 Placer County Grand Jury, unlike its immediate predecessor, thinks that the management of the county water agency is doing a fine job.

This much was made clear this week with the publication of the grand jury's final report. The backslapping was put in these words:

"No meaningful arguments have ever been advanced against the purpose of the water agency. Most of the charges and criticism (against the agency) have come from the very complex and exacting process of accomplishing this simple purpose (sic).

"Keeping in mind the simplicity and integrity of this purpose as opposed to the multiplicity of complications involved in accomplishing this purpose, we feel that all of the agency management and directors (members of the county board of supervisors) should be highly commended for an outstanding job in our county.

"During these past 10 years they have literally cut their way through a forest of red tape, and more lies ahead. It is inconceivable that a pioneer project of this magnitude (the $115 million Middle Fork American River development) could have been accomplished without some mistakes having been made along the way.

"We feel the citizens of Placer County can be proud of their water agency. And with all of our continued confidence and assistance, we certainly anticipate that the full potential of the Placer County Water Agency will be realized."

The report made no mention whatsoever of the grand jury's closed-door hearing last July on allegations by the State Attorney General's office that a ranking appointed official of the agency had misused funds. No indictment resulted from the hearing.

In his cover letter to Superior Court Judges Leland J. Propp and Ronald G. Cameron, however, Foreman John C. Griggs Jr. of Lincoln stated, in part:

"We must admit that we were disturbed at times to note the methods used by some (individuals) to glean information concerning closed sessions of the grand jury. We heard and read reports, speculative and erroneous in content, on supposed grand jury actions during closed sessions. We are unable to ascertain any benefit or public service in such actions, and (we) want to recommend legislative action to discourage damage caused by half-truths and innuendo. . ."

In another agency-related matter, the grand jury urged the agency directors to "delay development of plans for a water and power project on the north fork of the American River" because (1) the U.S. government is considering declaring that portion of the river as a "wild river"; and (2) reservoirs at Hell Hole and French Meadows have assured adequate water for the county.

For several years the agency has been considering construction of such a project in the Giant Gap area. Nothing much has been heard about it lately.

The grand jury's bland report was in sharp contrast to that of the 1967 panel which recommended the firing of Agency General Manager John M. Bernard and the dismissal of McCreary-Koretsky Engineers as an agency consultant.

So biting were the words of the 1967 grand jury's interim report

(Continued On Page 2)

Michael Is Grand Jury Foreman

Sydney Michael

Sydney M. Michael of Auburn, a retired Pacific Gas and Electric Company executive, is the foreman of the 1969 Placer County Grand Jury which was impaneled last week by Presiding Superior Court Judge Leland L. Propp.

The other 18 members of the grand jury are:

Amy M. Amick of Roseville, Theodore C. Fowler of Meadow Vista, Laura Frediani of Roseville, Albert S. Gulliford of Lincoln, Jenny Lou Jansen of Auburn, Alton C. Jones of Lincoln, Mary Joseph of Roseville, George Lay of Meadow Vista, Phillip J. McNamee of Sunset Whitney Ranch, Reuben F. Nelson of Roseville, Robert H. Royer of Roseville, Anne Sands of Auburn, Sally F. Semas of Auburn, Mary Jane Shamhart of Sunset Whitney Ranch, Lois S. Stagner of Auburn, Richard E. Steel of Colfax, Marie H. Summers of Roseville and Lila M. Vineyard of Lincoln.

County Building Squabble Quiet

All was quiet this week in the controversy over a last minute proposal by the 1968 board of supervisors to erect an additional geodesic-domed building at the county administrative center in Auburn to house the office of Auditor - Controller Kimbuck Williams Jr.

At the request of County Executive Officer James E. Williams, who was on vacation when the 1968 board voted for the extra dome at its New Year's Eve meeting, the supervisors postponed additional discussion until next Tuesday.

At last week's board meeting, freshmen Supervisors J.B. Paolini and Ray Thompson indicated opposition to the addition which will cost more than $100,000.

The 1968 board, with the then chairman Robert P. Mahan at the helm, claimed a "lack of communication" with the auditor was responsible for the much-publicized bickering between them. The board's answer to the problem was the green light to build another dome so the auditor's office could be moved from the Court House to the center and thus be under the watchful eye of the county executive officer, the supervisors' chief attache.

In a related development this week, Robert G. Armstrong of Roseville, president of the Fidelity Title Company, stated in a letter that if such a move is to be made the board also should consider relocating the tax collector, recorder and assessor because these offices are "interrelated."

Cost Of Living Adjustment:

Placer Trustees Order Realistic Budget Policy

A cost of living adjustment of approximately three and a half per cent for all employees of the Placer Joint Union High School District was approved by the board of trustees Tuesday night, effective until the end of the present fiscal year June 30.

W.O. Francis, business manager for the district, estimated the action will cost approximately $63,000. He said additional federal and state funds which became available after the budget was prepared at the beginning of the school year, will cover the increases.

Historically, district trustees have granted a salary increase each year, in an attempt to keep abreast of rising costs and to maintain competitive salary schedules which will attract and hold qualified personnel. This year, however, the board tabled action on a requested salary hike in July, because of the dim financial outlook at that time, although it did approve district-paid health and dental plans.

Subsequently the state legislature passed a measure establishing a $6,000 minimum salary for teachers, although voting no additional aid to districts to meet the increased costs. In order to meet the state requirement, trustees voted in December to bring first-step teachers to the $6,000 level, but turned down a request that the entire teachers' salary schedule be adjusted to maintain the two-to-one policy adopted by the board in 1964, which would have spread the salary range from $6,000 to $12,000. The interim adjustment approved Tuesday night is based on the $6,000 minimum, as opposed to the previous $5,600 minimum, and provides adjustments through the six step schedule to a top of $11,601, representing a 3.57 per cent increase over the $5,600 to $11,200 schedule adopted in July.

The same 3.57 per cent cost of living adjustment will apply to salaries of administrators and classified personnel.

The adjustment will terminate with the end of the school year, and new salary schedules, based on the budget outlook for the 1969-70 school year, will be adopted, effective July 1.

With this in mind, trustees instructed Superintendent Ralph Goggins to take a long, hard look at proposed expenditures for the next school year, and to come up with a "hard honed" program realistically geared to anticipated income.

Mrs. Helen Bale of Newcastle asked for the action, pointing out that "there are only so many dollars available. . . . .we can only do so many things. Let's take a long hard look at our program and face the fact that something's got to give. We have to repair roofs when they leak, we have to maintain reasonable salary schedules. But somewhere, we must cut in order to stay within the funds available."

Trustees agreed that the en-

(Continued On Page 2)

Local Naval Reserve Unit Is Rated High

It was announced this week that naval reserve surface division 12-10 located in Auburn and serving Placer, Nevada, and Sacramento Counties had held a comfortable first position in the Twelfth Naval District for the past three months and is in eighth position in the nation.

The rating is based on competition in performance, advancement, active duty and inspection results.

The Auburn unit consists of 78 enlisted men and four officers. According to LCDR Peter Tweedt, commanding officer, the majority of the men in the unit have served two or more years of active duty with the regular navy, the exception being young men who are awaiting their two year tour to begin.

At present there are 16 men in the unit who have served in Vietnam. Navy veterans who are interested in affiliating with the unit are asked to contact the recruiter at 885-9012.

Blood Bank Seeks 200 Pint Quota On January 28th

A campaign to obtain 200 pints of blood is being launched by the Auburn Area Community Blood Bank for Tuesday, January 28, when a mobile unit of the Sacramento bank will be on duty at the Veterans Memorial Hall in Auburn.

Extractions will be made from 11 a.m. to 1 p.m. and from 2 to 6 p.m., according to Earl "Tige" Larson, secretary.

Local blood bank president Dr. Thomas Rossitto said the Auburn Area organization has used 187 pints in the past four months.

Two open heart cases, a leukemia case and furnishing a district share to Weimar Medical Center took a heavy toll of the supply here, Larson explained. He added that blood supplies are running low throughout the country.

'A Disgrace to Community'

'68 Jury Urges Cleanup Of Placer High Campus

The 1968 Placer County Grand Jury charged this week that certain areas of the campus of Placer Union High School in Auburn "are a disgrace to the community."

In its final report, the grand jury urged the high school district's board of trustees "to review and recommend provisions for school building maintenance (throughout the district), especially at Placer Union High School. Areas of this school in particular are a disgrace to the community."

The jury report stated that last October the panel's committee on schools toured the campus. It declared:

"A tour of this facility disclosed evidence of great disrepair. Painting is needed, windows need glazing, and the boys' shower and locker room is in dire need of attention. This particular area gave the impression that it has lacked attention for years. . ."

Regarding school discipline, the report stated:

"The administration staff throughout our district should continue to review student behavior and to institute the discipline of the student(sic) throughout the schools of Placer County."

Generally, however, the report was favorable to the school districts in the county and to the county superintendent's office.

Rehabilitation Emphasis Urged For Delinquents

The 1968 Placer County Grand Jury has recommended that the probation department inaugurate a rehabilitation program for youngsters lodged at the Juvenile Hall in Auburn.

In its final report, the grand jury declared:

"The Juvenile Hall appears to be operating presently as a detention facility with little emphasis being placed on rehabilitation. We feel the prime concern of the Juvenile Hall should be rehabilitation."

The report described the appearance of the facility as "depressing" and urged that it be spruced up and that a recreation room be added to the girls' section.

The grand jury also recommended that the board of supervisors "pursue the possibility of building a camp (for juveniles) on a portion of the Weimar Medical Center property as proposed by Chief Probation Officer James Nelson some time ago."

Assessment Ratio In County Still Is 25 Per Cent

Placer County Assessor Frank R. Chilton Jr. this week announced that the county's assessment ratio will remain at 25 per cent during 1969.

He noted that the Revenue and Taxation Code "makes it mandatory to announce a ratio no farther away from 25 per cent than that of the preceding year."

Placer Women Relate Memorable Journey On Foot To Mt. Everest

By BOB ELDER

Dr. Helen Strickland and Dr. Mary Lamy, both of the staff of the Placer County Office of Education, returned early this month from a six week trip to Nepal.

While on the trip, the two women walked 170 miles to the base of Mt. Everest, accompanied by a group of 12 Sherpas and porters.

The pair comprised what was probably the first expedition solely for women into this area. They described it as a memorable experience through spectacular country.

Dr. Strickland and Dr. Lamy left Sacramento by air on November 22, stopping at Tokyo and Bangkok en route. They arrived at Katmandu, capital of Nepal, on Thanksgiving Day.

Arrangements for their trip to Thyanboche, a lamasery at the foot of Everest, were made by a retired British army officer who resides at Katmandu.

In the accompanying party were three Sherpas, who served as guide, cook and waiter; and nine porters who carried baggage, packed in baskets weighing 65 pounds each on their heads and backs.

The trip was accomplished in stages of from eight to 15 miles a day over many steep ridges. There were no hotels, each night being passed in camp. No vehicles were seen on the entire trek.

The country was inhabited, Dr. Strickland said, the steep mountainsides being terraced to provide growing space for rice, corn and potatoes.

The average altitude was above 10,000 feet, rising in places to 13,000. Dr. Lamy and Dr. Strickland had conditioned themselves with walking and exercise for a year before starting the expedition.

Although accompanied only by native guides who spoke few words of English, the two women said they encountered no difficulty. The natives seemed unable to comprehend what was meant by the violence and trouble known elsewhere in the world.

The country is cut by many swift rivers, which were crossed on small swinging bridges, Dr. Strickland said. A number of these had been built by Sir Edmund Hillary, who took this route on his successful climb of Everest.

The women described the climate as warm by day, cold at night. They encountered no snow, which generally does not fall until late December.

Fifteen days were required to reach Thyanboche, hiking generally from 6 a.m. to 4:30 p.m. each day. There were two rest days, one spent at the lamasery, where spectacular views of Everest and adjoining peaks were obtained.

A slightly different route was taken on the way back, making it possible to cut four days off the trek, for a total of 30 days.

On the way home, Dr. Strickland and Dr. Lamy stopped at Calcutta and Hong Kong. They reported the principal expense of the trip was the air fare.

Dr. Strickland is curriculum specialist, and Dr. Lamy is guidance consultant in the Office of Education.

Persistent Unemployment In County, Says U.S.

The U. S. Department of Labor this week declared Placer County as "an area of persistent unemployment," thus enabling the county to qualify for additional federal financial aid.

The Department of Labor's finding was disclosed by Congressman Harold T. Johnson of Roseville, who noted that the government survey was requested last year by the board of supervisors at the suggestion of the North Tahoe Public Utilities District.

"This means that Placer County can compete on an equal footing with neighbors to the north and south for economic assistance, Department of Defense contracts and other programs tied to limiting persistent unemployment," Johnson stated.

He added that once the official designation has been made by the U.S. Department of Commerce, Placer County will be eligible for financial assistance for public works projects, including grants up to 50 per cent of each project's cost, and for loans for both public and private development.

Weather

TEMPERATURES
Maximum 54 degrees
Minimum 27 degrees

PRECIPITATION
Season (July 1, 1968):
Total season this date 20.56
Normal season this date 14.35

Suit Filed Over Tramway

Alex Cushing and his Squaw Valley Development Company went to superior court this week to find out if they are obliged to pay money for the use of air space in the operation of their spectacular $1 million-plus aerial tramway.

The Cushing litigation was filed against Paul and Shirley Rosen, owners of adjacent property at Squaw Valley, to erase an agreement calling for them to receive unusual compensation for the tramway passing over their land.

Cushing and his battery of lawyers indicated the tramway, which passes nearly 300 feet over the Rosens' acreage, has the same right to air space as any other aircraft.

A SPECIAL Statewide merit citation was awarded to the Auburn Journal last week for outstanding continuous coverage of educational news. The Journal was nominated by the Auburn Union Teachers Association and won this commendation in the John Swett Awards for the 1967-68 school year through a carefully kept news clipping scrapbook. William Pfaff, publisher, accepted the honors at an AUTA meeting held last week at Alta Vista School. The presentation was made by Mrs. Harriett Schlichting, president, and Ginna Akers, chairman of publicity.

Figure 18–18 This newspaper has the traditional eight columns but does *not* use "rules" or lines between the columns. The effect is for increased readability by providing more white areas.

The Daily Californian

HOME EDITION

Tuesday, January 21, 1969 · El Cajon, California · 16 Pages—10 Cents

Peace Talks to Start Saturday

Henry Cabot Lodge Takes Over U.S. Delegation

By STEPHENS BROENING
Associated Press Writer

PARIS (AP) — The first plenary session of the Vietnam peace talks, with Henry Cabot Lodge as head of the U. S. delegation, will be held Saturday morning, U. S. officials said today.

Lodge arrived here Monday night as the appointee of President Nixon to succeed Ambassador W. Averell Harriman.

The meeting Saturday will follow by a week the first four-way meeting on procedures in which Harriman headed the U. S. delegation.

This next meeting will finally bring together delegations of the United States, South Vietnam, North Vietnam and the National Liberation Front to discuss the substantive questions of the heart of the war.

Lodge met with South Vietnamese Ambassador Phang Dam Lam for less than an hour.

Lodge was accompanied by the outgoing deputy U. S. negotiator Cyrus R. Vance and by Lodge's own chief aides, Lawrence Walsh and Marshall Green.

On the South Vietnamese side Lam was accompanied by his deputy, Nguyen Xuan Phong.

It was Vance and Phong who led the allied delegations at the four-sided procedural meeting Saturday at which the negotiators cut through the obstacles which had held up the opening of the four-way talks for more than two months.

Some Saigon officials were left with the impression after that Saturday meeting that North Vietnam is more eager to make peace than its Viet Cong allies.

This assessment emerged today from authoritative accounts of last Saturday's first meeting of representatives from Saigon, the United States, North Vietnam and the Viet Cong's National Liberation Front.

The meeting produced a surprisingly quick agreement on procedures for substantive peace negotiations. In sharp contrast with their earlier negotiating stances, Col. Ha Van Lau and his Hanoi contingent demonstrated a business-like flexibility on the organizational questions.

U. S. delegation spokesman William Jorden remarked afterward there was more give and take at the session than at any he had attended here. Jorden was a regular participant at most of the 28 U. S. North Vietnamese meetings which led to the agreement last Oct. 31 to stop the bombing of North Vietnam and enlarge the peace talks.

Officials who attended Saturday's meeting stressed the different attitudes of Lau and Mrs. Nguyen Thi Binh of the NFL.

The South Vietnamese deputy delegation chief, Nguyen Xuan Phong, opened the session by introducing a set of procedural proposals. U. S. Ambassador Cyrus R. Vance spoke briefly, calling for speedy adoption of rules. Then Mrs. Binh took the floor, to attack "U.S. imperialism" and the "puppet clique in Saigon."

The sources said Lau and his colleagues carefully studied the South Vietnamese proposals while she spoke and paid no apparent attention to her remarks. When it was his turn to speak, Lau said in an almost inaudible monotone that North Vietnam subscribed to the NLF's views. He swiftly got down to business, agreeing with some of Phong's points, disagreeing with others and offering substitutes.

Officials said they saw further evidence of Hanoi's readiness to talk peace in Lau's acceptance of ground rules that both the Americans and the South Vietnamese feel bolster their view of the conference as "two-sided."

Good Evening . . . The News Today

World

A second attempt at suicide by fire presented Czech Communist leaders with their gravest crisis since the Soviet invasion. Another attempt at self-immolation was reported in Budapest, the Hungarian capital. A 25-year-old brewery worker in Pilsen poured inflammable liquid over himself in Dukla Square and set off the flames. Officials said his motive was undetermined, but Prague students assumed he was emulating Jan Palach, a student who protested by fire against the reversal of the reform movment and died. There was a veiled warning Soviet occupation forces might intervene in the student protests.

Using rockets, grenades and mortars, Viet Cong and North Vietnamese troops attacked U.S. land, river and air forces. Other attacks were thwarted by American troops who uncovered munitions caches and broke up a convoy of enemy sampans south of Saigon. A new wave of terrorism is being directed at the GIs in an atempt to increase antiwar sentiment in the states.

Nation

Jeering antiwar demonstrators were in jail after failing to interrupt the pageantry of inauguration day in Washington. Eighty were arrested — some nursing bloody heads—but the violence was far short of the pitched battles at the Chicago Democratic Convention. Army paratroopers formed a second line of defense for President Nixon's armored limousine after demonstrators rushed a line of policemen guarding the Pennsylvania Avenue parade route. Secret Service agents batted down several objects hurled at the car.

Selection of the Clay Shaw conspiracy trial jury started in New Orleans in a courtroom showdown on Dist. Atty. Jim Garrison's claim that President John F. Kenedy was killed by a band of conspirators—not just a lone sniper. One hundred sixty-nine citizens were summoned for jury duty examination; more are available. The courtroom was under extraordinary guard with deputies ordered to search all spectators.

State

California was without a lieutenant governor and a Democratic state senator held the governor's chair until Gov. Reagan returns tonight from Washington. Reagan has been gone since Saturday and Lt. Gov. Robert Finch resigned Monday to become secretary of Health, Education and Welfare in the Nixon Cabinet. By law, Democratic Senate President pro tem Hugh M. Burns was moved up to acting governor. Republican Rep. Ed Reinecke of Studio City will be sworn in Wednesday as Finch's replacement.

A Negro professor and a Mexican-American social worker are heading racially-troubled San Fernando Valley State College's new program to recruit and counsel minority group students. College officials hope the appointments will help curtail student tumult.

Sports

There'll be some familiar faces at different schols in the Grossmont League this spring and next fall. Among several coaches named in the league is Pat Carroll, former Grossmont mentor, who will be footbal coach at Monte Vista — Story, Page 1B.

Stan Musial and Roy Campanella have been named to baseball's Hall of Fame. The annual balloting was held this morning — Story, Page 2B.

School planning urged

By DEL HOOD
The Daily Californian

EL CAJON — The ninth high school hasn't even been built.

But already trustees of the Grossmont Union High School District are being urged to do some long-range planning for the 10th one.

"We've got some critical decisions to make," Supt. Austin R. Sellery told the board Monday night. "A master plan for the district is of chief importance."

The district administration unveiled a report on space needs which recommends a two-campus continuation school, a permanent adult school campus and enlarged facilities for special education and library services.

Sellery estimates the district will have to raise $500,000 in taxes during the next three years to get the extra space and shore up the $4 million fund for construction of the ninth high school.

The 10th high school came up in a discussion of future population pressures.

"We've got the potential for another new school in the west end of the district," Sellery said. Officials indicated this facility probably would not be needed until 1975 at the earliest.

The district is in the midst of a $2 million expansion program which involves major improvements at all eight high schools.

Some of these projects are costing more than anticipated, so money is being "borrowed" from the $4 million set aside for the new high school tentatively scheduled to open in the fall of 1972.

Both the new high school and the expansion projects are parts of a $6 million bond issue package approved by the voters in late 1967.

Trustees took the first step for getting the new high school plans off the ground by authorizing the superintendent to recommend for appointment a principal who will serve as chairman of the planning committee.

The site for the new school presumably will be the Jamacha Road-Hillsdale Road area southeast of El Cajon.

Once a principal for the school is named, he will be in charge of the group planning the structure. Teachers who will be working at the new school are to participate in planning it.

Until the new high school is completed, the district plans to accommodate some of the enrollment increase by purchasing portable classroom buildings. These structures would be used at continuation school and adult school campuses after the new high school opens.

Officials predict 33 portables will be needed during the next three years.

This September's enrollment is expected to exceed last year's total by 1,182 students. The figure is based on the actual number of eighth graders who will be moving into the high schools and does not take into account any growth factors.

Part of the money for developing continuation and adult school campuses would be derived by selling surplus land the district owns. Sale of the land is expected to yield more than $400,000.

The continuation school has been housed in old quonset huts on Mission Gorge Road in Santee since 1962. This was to have been a "temporary" facility in use no more than five years.

School administrators are recommending that two campuses be developed for continuation school, each having an enrollment capacity of 300 students.

The adult school campus would have 14 to 18 classroom units.

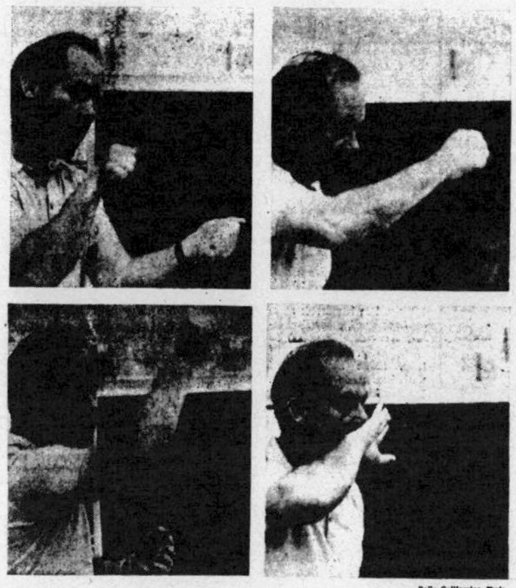

Daily Californian Photo

What's He Doing?—See Page 5A

More Rain Here May Mean Trouble

The sponge is full

When there is little that mortals can do, they frequently call upon Lady Luck and God.

Today those who must solve problems caused by heavy, persistent rain in sunny Southern California were stroking rabbit's feet, crossing their fingers and saying silent prayers.

While less than an inch of rain has pelted the Inland Empire in this current storm, conditions were ripe for heavy flooding, wind-felled trees, broken utility lines and the other numerous problems and inconveniences which beset a soaked, semi-arid region.

These conditions are two-fold: first, thus far this month 2.93 inches of rain have fallen at Gillespie Field. It has fallen close enough together to keep the ground from drying out. Right now the Inland Empire is deeply soaked.

The sponge is full.

Second, forecasters at the official weather station at Lindbergh Field predict that another 1½ to 2 inches will fall before the storm ends, hopefully on Wednesday.

When the sponge is full and there's more to come, this means flooding. Strong winds coupled with soggy ground means trees can be uprooted easily.

John Dainwood, assistant city engineer in El Cajon, said this morning "we have no reports yet of serious problems, but if this keeps up we're in trouble."

Carl Welti of San Diego Gas & Electric Co. and Cam Miller of Pacific Telephone both reported no problems in the Inland Empire. They also were concerned what the next 24 to 36 hours might bring.

La Mesa reported the same thing.

The precipitation had even been gentle enough to permit Via Zapador to remain open in Santee. But sheriff's deputies were keeping a close watch on the perennial trouble spot to erect barricades quickly.

As of 4 a.m. today Lemon Grove had reported the most rain during the preceding 24-hour period. That station measured .61 of an inch. Other points: La Mesa .57, Alpine .42, Campo .57, San Diego State College .48, Ramona .26, Spring Valley .55, Lakeside .49 and Grossmont College .21.

San Diego's Lindbergh Field station had reported a storm total of .49 by 4 a.m. today.

Even with the heavy rainfall of January, Lindbergh and Gillespie fields were still short of their seasonal norms. Gillespie Field is 3.63 inches deficient and Lindbergh Field, 1.28 inches.

Moderate to heavy rain is expected tonight and Wednesday in the Inland Empire and weathermen anticipate the mountain region will be hit hardest.

Gusty winds will accompany the rain, just as they did Monday night. Especially strong wind is forecast for the mountains.

(Details on weather elsewhere in California appear on Page 2A and the detailed weather report is on Page 5B).

Pueblo was short of arms

By RICHARD E. MEYER
Associated Press Writer

CORONADO, Calif. (AP) — The skipper of the USS Pueblo says the Navy didn't provide retaliatory help or adequate guns, communications or explosives to destroy secret equipment when North Koreans captured his intelligence ship.

Cmdr. Lloyd M. Bucher testified Monday at the opening of a court of inquiry into the loss of the ship last Jan. 23, the death of one crewman and imprisonment of the 32 others for 11 months.

Bucher, apparently still tense from his prison experience, was expected to testify for two or three days. The court of five admirals could recommend anything from medals to court-martial.

But Navy lawyers told Bucher that so far he was not suspected of violating any military laws.

The Navy said Bucher will be followed on the stand by his superior, Rear Adm. Frank L. Johnson, former commander of naval forces at Japan, and Cmdr. Charles R. Clark, skipper of a sister intelligence ship.

When he sailed the Pueblo on its mission to scout North Korean radar and North Korean and Soviet ships in the Sea of Japan, Bucher testified, he wanted twin 20 or 40 millimeter guns.

But instead, Bucher said, he got two .50-calibre machine guns, 3,000 to 5,000 rounds of ammunition, a spare barrel and a mount for a third .50-calibre machine-gun he never received.

The weapons were much smaller and lighter than those he said he had requested.

They were installed in Japan, Bucher said, a few weeks before the Pueblo was to begin her intelligence mission off North Korea.

Bucher said he was under orders from Adm. Johnson to "employ the guns as a last resort only in cases where threat to survival is obvious . . . and not to practice the use of those guns or uncover them in the presence of foreign ships."

Bucher said this was to keep the intelligence ship from appearing aggressive.

He said the guns were temperamental, difficult to keep adjusted and hard to prepare for firing.

Bucher said he picked what he thought were the best places to mount the weapons — one fore and one aft — but they still left portions of the side of the vessel uncovered.

Clasping and unclasping his hands at the witness table Bucher said he also asked for explosives to destroy secret equipment and codes in the event of capture.

The request was "deferred," Bucher said, because his commander told him "in order for the destruct system to be effective . . . it must be integral to secret equipment.

"Since the equipment had already been installed they said it was not possible to put in the explosives without a great deal of expense and time.

"I had as destruct equipment fire axes and sledge hammers capable of being swung by a standard size sailor to bash in the equipment." He said it would have taken 2½ hours to scuttle the ship.

Communications aboard ship were inadequate, he said, because the Pueblo was not equipped with a Navy telephone system — only an old Army system insufficient during emergencies.

Figure 18–19 This newspaper's make-up departs from the traditional eight columns and even the innovative six columns to use five wider columns—giving more readability but allowing space for fewer stories.

Los Angeles Times

CC R PART II †

FRIDAY, MARCH 10, 1972

Kathy the Waitress Turns Up--$100 Richer

$100 SERVICE—Kathy Collins demonstrates the smile and service that won her a $100 award.
Times photo by Vince Streano

BY BRYCE NELSON
Times Staff Writer

Kathy, the excellent Anaheim waitress, has been found and will receive her $100 "best waitress" award.

In fact, it's on the way, said William Simmons, a cement plant laborer from Mason City, Iowa, who conceived the contest while in Anaheim last January during a vacation in the West.

Simmons, a 31-year-old laborer who earns $170 a week, awarded first prize of $200 to Jewel Bradshaw, who works at the Noisy Water Cafe in Three Rivers, Calif. Kathy was awarded second prize, but Simmons later was unable to locate her because she had given him another name the night he was in the restaurant.

But Kathy Collins, 18, saw an article about Simmons' contest in The Times and sent him a photograph.

But although Kathy will get the $100, Simmons will come out way ahead in the long run. After reading about his best waitress award, the producers of Garry Moore's television program "To Tell the Truth" gave him an all-expense paid trip to New York to appear on the show.

He was paid $35 for appearing on the show and given $70 in spending money.

The money, naturally, will go to

Please Turn to Page 10, Col. 3

ART SEIDENBAUM

It's Black Humor

A black woman in whiteface and mammoth cotton mammaries stood on the Janss steps at UCLA, carrying a cardboard torch of liberty.

A black man in American bunting and white beard stood on a platform below, guarded by a creature in pig mask and Keystone cop costume.

They were doing a preview of Bodacious Buggerilla, which is street theater, to whet appetites for a larger performance tonight at UCLA's Royce Hall. "One of my jobs here," said Ed Bereal from beneath his Uncle Sam suit, "is that all of you come out of here undangerous." A college degree, he continued, is a proof "this person ain't gonna cause no problems."

The surreal Bereal was fierce and funny. He tried to auction off a black girl with a doctorate in science as the perfect domestic. He dipped into a white pillowcase to show the ways to "deorganize niggers" and he pulled out a bottle of cheap wine, a mock marijuana joint, a Bible and a fancy steering wheel.

Not Many Appear

But campuses are sort of surreal themselves these days. Only about 60 students showed up for the free preview performance at noon. Three years ago, suggested an NBC cameraman, there would have been hundreds crowding around, yelling encouragement, shoving their middle-class souls into the black experience.

Not now. The Grits and Guts and Grandpersons show that preceded Buggerilla into Royce attracted only half a house although the troupe had the double sponsorship of UCLA's Committee on Fine Arts Productions and the Center for Afro-American Studies.

When the mock cop tried to lure a larger crowd by crossing campus and giving a black man a bogus beating, most people hardly looked up from their lunches. Some smiled. A few giggled nervously. A couple of black students refused to react at all.

Maybe UCLA undergraduates figure they have seen and heard it all, in theater and in reality. Maybe the excitement about ethnicity in arts is fading as fast as the student movement.

Guess on Promotion

Phil Henderson, programmer for the Afro-American center, doesn't think so. He guesses UCLA's "Up from the Roots" series simply needed some promotion. When the mock cop came back with hardly any new audience, Henderson shrugged and said, "I guess it's not true that everyone loves a circus."

My guess is that the particular circus was too close to the campus truth of a few years ago to be funny. Somebody giggles nervously when somebody recognizes the pain in comedy as too close for comfort.

I almost would have said that black humor from the street is losing its legitimate shock value for audiences because blacks and whites have lived through so much outrage. But then another newsman said he found the Buggerilla material in bad taste. That means he still has to learn a few things.

Guerrilla art is about life, not taste. And since ghetto life has not improved much in the intervening years, the art becomes a surreal substitute for total anguish. Art is no more surreal than apathy. Just healthier.

PART II INDEX

L.A. Planning Unit OKs Guidelines for Elevated Walkway

The Los Angeles City Planning Commission Thursday approved guidelines for the first phase of an elevated pedestrian system that eventually could link 45 downtown blocks.

The first three-block-long section would extend south from the new Atlantic Richfield Plaza on 6th St. and would cost an estimated $1 million, according to city planners.

Under the plan, the elevated walkway would be located in mid-block and would enter some buildings at the second floor. It would include a series of open plazas and bridges over streets.

Voting 3 to 1, the commission overrode the objections of some property owners who claimed the walkway would be detrimental to their buildings by wiping out valuable floor space.

Aid to Traffic

However, another group of property owners, including developers of the Atlantic Richfield towers, described the plan as a "key in the development of a strong Central City."

Stuart Ketchum, spokesman for the group, said the walkway—designed primarily to separate pedestrians from vehicular traffic — would not solve downtown's traffic problems but would help.

Commission President David S. Moir voted against the pedestrian-way plan, arguing that once it is approved it would be "part of the law of the city."

The first-phase plan was developed by the City Planning Department as an element of the city's General Plan. It must be approved by Mayor Sam Yorty and the City Council before it is formally adopted.

State Seeks to Bow Out of El Pueblo Park Development

Officials Dissatisfied With Way 43-Acre Monument Is Being Operated, Would Like L.A. to Assume Control

BY RAY HEBERT
Times Urban Affairs Writer

California parks officials are dissatisfied with the way El Pueblo de Los Angeles State Historic Park has been operated and would like the city to take it over, it was learned Friday.

"State people in Sacramento are fed up and want to wash their hands of the whole project," an informed source said.

The troubled 43-acre state monument—an urban park—is on the edge of the Los Angeles Civic Center and includes Olvera Street, a prime tourist spot, the historic Pico-Garnier block and other attractions.

One of the park's focal points is the Old Plaza, site of the city's founding.

Talks Under Way

State officials confirmed that studies have been under way for about two months to determine what government jurisdiction would be best qualified to administer the historic area.

William Penn Mott Jr., director of the California Department of Parks and Recreation, is scheduled to make a report on the findings at a meeting of the California State Park and Recreation Commission today in Solvang.

Mott was not available for comment but, it was understood, he has been disturbed by the park's slow-moving historic preservation and development program and many aspects of its administration.

Primary control is in the hands of a quarrelsome joint powers commission. The 11-member body is composed of state, county and city appointees.

In Los Angeles, Robert Baker, assistant deputy state parks director in charge of the Southern California area, confirmed that the state has been trying to find a way out of the project's operational problems.

"The state is unhappy," he explained. "Everyone—the county and city included—is displeased. Turning the project over to the city seems to be the most feasible solution."

Baker said the major problems revolve around "the very difficult situation of trying to mix historical

Please Turn to Page 7, Col. 4

$10,000 BAIL SET FOR MAN ACCUSED IN FATAL STABBING

SANTA ANA—Bail for Robert J. Brooks, charged in an Anaheim slaying, was set at $10,000 Thursday.

Superior Judge William L. Murray denied a motion for $3,000 bail despite the fact that Dep. Dist. Atty. A. A. Wells agreed to it.

Dept. Public Defender Mike Pursell argued that Brooks was an "aider and abettor" and should be released on the lower bail.

"The court represents the citizens of the community," Murray observed. "And when they get the facts of this case from the press they would think I was an absolute idiot for releasing this man on $3,000 bail."

Brooks and Linda R. Shea have pleaded innocent in the Jan. 2 fatal stabbing of Stanley (Caveman) Joyce, 24, of Fullerton. Mrs. Shea is free on $10,000 bail.

Authorities Seize Film Barred From Being Shown at UCI

BY SCOTT MOORE
Times Staff Writer

IRVINE—An explicit homosexual film was seized by authorities, acting on a Superior Court warrant, during a meeting Thursday night of the Gay Students Union at UC Irvine.

Earlier in the day, the administration had ruled the 90-minute feature film could not be shown on campus on grounds it was hard core pornography with no educational value.

The film had not been shown when campus police chief Robert Heavey and two sheriff's deputies confiscated it from the floor of the 350-seat science lecture hall which was filled to capacity for the meeting.

Heavey presented a search warrant signed by Superior Court Judge Robert Rickles. The administration denied any knowledge of the warrant, and it was not immediately known who had requested the warrant.

No Interference

Immediately prior to the confiscation, there was considerable discussion of screening the film in spite of the administration's ban. However, there was no interference as Heavey seized the film canister.

After the administration had banned the film, it impaneled a nine-member committee to view the film behind closed doors Thursday afternoon and make a recommendation to Chancellor Daniel G. Aldrich Jr. on possible future showings.

Given the administration opposition, however, it was considered unlikely the film ever would be shown, no matter what the panel's opinion.

The panel included an attorney from the American Civil Liberties Union, the chairman of the school's department of psychiatry, and other faculty and students.

After the administration action, the homosexual club, which has about three dozen members, offered a second film it said was produced five years ago and does not contain explicit or simulated sexual acts.

The administration responded that the second film also would have to

Please Turn to Page 10, Col. 6

Cities League Rejects Ban on Fireworks Sale

Group Also Recommends Unincorporated Areas Be Free of Restrictions

BY DON SMITH
Times Staff Writer

ORANGE—Directors of the Orange County League of Cities voted overwhelmingly Thursday night to reject a proposal to ban the sale of fireworks countywide.

The recommendation, made by the Orange County Fire Chiefs Assn., was turned down by a vote of 21 to 2, with one abstention.

In a related action, League directors recommended that the County Board of Supervisors not adopt any restrictions on the sale of fireworks in unincorporated areas.

The proposal to outlaw so-called "safe and sane" fireworks had been forwarded to the League by county supervisors after adoption by the County Planning Commission. Last month, the county's fire chiefs unanimously recommended that the League go on record in favor of the ordinance.

3 Cities Ban Sales

Only three cities in the county now ban the sale of fireworks. They are La Habra, Laguna Beach and Newport Beach.

In a related action, League directors voted in favor of suggested county recommendations governing the sale of Christmas trees. However, the League said a proposed 14-day limit on such sales should be expanded to 35 days to coincide with scheduled shipments of the holiday decorations.

Both recommendations will be forwarded to the Board of Supervisors for its consideration within the next two weeks.

League president, Mayor Robert Finnell of Placentia, also announced that he had appointed Mayor Walter Evans of San Clemente and Councilman Don Fox of Brea to serve as League representatives on the County Harbors, Beaches and Parks Commission.

Two Places Created

Legislation adopted by the 1971 State Legislature created two city seats on the commission which also was expanded to include the administration of county regional parks.

Finnell also announced that he had appointed Councilman Jack Turk of Huntington Beach to serve on the County Human Relations Commission and had reappointed former Councilwoman Doreen Marshall of Newport Beach as the League's representative to the County Citizens Direction Finding Commission.

Yellow Cab Given Franchise Renewal

BY ROY HAYNES
Times Staff Writer

The Board of Public Utilities and Transportation voted unanimously Thursday to continue the Yellow Cab Co. franchise for the central Los Angeles area.

The vote was taken at a board meeting at City Hall after the transportation department staff recommended continuing the franchise and no one appeared to protest the arrangement.

A second staff recommendation that other taxicabs be allowed to pick up passengers at Los Angeles International Airport if they had carried passengers there was not acted on.

At Board President Jerome J. Mayo's suggestion, it was taken under submission for a week. Other taxi company representatives appeared at the hearing and asked that the airport franchise be ended.

Please Turn to Page 10, Col. 1

ECOLOGICAL EXERCISE—An unidentified girl rides her bicycle along a street in Westminster, aiding environment by not contributing to smog and at same time apparently walking her dogs.
Times photo by Ken Hochfeld

Dynamite Seized as Evidence Poses a Problem for Police

BY BILL HAZLETT
Times Staff Writer

COSTA MESA—A cache of deteriorating dynamite, seized by police following the arrest of an ex-convict, Thursday posed a major dilemma for officials.

The 64 one-pound sticks of 40% nitroglycerin-ammonium nitrate dynamite were found by officers in a storage shed at the rear of a rented home at 614 W. Bay St.

Det. Capt. Robert Green said the renter, James P. Marsh, 39, a self-employed trucker, was arrested on suspicion of illegally possessing explosives in violation of the state's health and safety code.

Marsh denied any knowledge of the explosive, claiming it had apparently been in the shed when he rented the house about six months ago.

Marsh was released on $12,000 bail pending a March 20 preliminary hearing.

The dynamite, which Capt. Green said was capable of causing widespread destruction and breaking every window in the area, was seized as evidence and turned over to Reserve Capt. Bill Savage, an explosives technician, for storage.

"That's the cause of our problems," Green explained. "The stuff was in such bad shape Savage didn't want to handle it, yet it's evidence in our case."

The detective captain said the dynamite, ordinarily a stable explosive used in quarry work, stump blasting and mudcapping, has deteriorated to a point where it is unstable and highly dangerous.

"We're trying to determine a legal means of destroying the stuff without destroying our case at the same time," Green said.

"We plan to ask the District Attorney's Office or the courts if photographs of the dynamite will serve as

Please Turn to Page 10, Col. 1

Figure 18–20 The myth that heads should not "bump" is exactly that to seasoned journalists. Type stretching across the top of the page is broken by a story "box." Below it, three heads are at the same level but are readable because of the variety in type, columns, style, and number of lines.

·····Pitcairn Is Talking About·····

The 'Dying' Island

By Glen Wright
Copley News Service

Pitcairn Island

HISTORY will repeat itself if the 83 inhabitants of this tiny isle accept the invitation to abandon it and resettle on Norfolk Island. Norfolk Islanders are urging that public land be made available by the British government for any Pitcairner who will live on it.

Young people — there are less than two dozen under 21 — drift away to New Zealand and Australia to get work when they are old enough and the oldsters, most of whom are more than 50 years old, are finding life increasingly difficult on Personnel.

The original settlers of the island were mutineers from the HMS Bounty. They sailed to the island with 12 Tahitian women in 1780. By 1856, they numbered 194. The British government then transferred them to Norfolk, about 400 miles northeast of New Zealand, some 3600 miles due west of Pitcairn.

* * *

BUT MANY of the expatriates were unhappy there and soon returned to their former home. Population on Norfolk is 1232 of whom 589 are descended from original Pitcairners.

However, Pitcairners are not reacting enthusiastically to the invitation to move. They like their island.

Nearly everyone has modern stoves, refrigerators, telephones and other appliances as the island is well supplied with electricity by its power generator. It has two telephone lines, one for government and one for the private sector.

A permanent record of happenings is printed in the monthly Pitcairn Miscellany.

THERE ARE ALSO a few cars and motorcycles, a movie theater, co-operative store and several well-equipped playgrounds. Of great interest is the new dome-shaped geodetic survey station that New Zealand is building.

Public parties are frequent. Frequently all 83 residents feast at outdoor tables laden with meat, fruits, vegetables and bread.

When cooking for everyone Pitcairn women prefer their traditional stone ovens to modern ranges. These cookers are about 4 feet deep, 2 feet wide and 20 inches high. A fire is laid inside and when the temperature is right the ashes are scooped away and the food put in.

My hostess used her arm for a thermometer. She ran it into the oven and when the skin got hot but didn't burn, the temperature was right and the loaves were popped in.

* * * *

IT WAS a tasty and filling banquet. The fish are wahu and tuna. The meat tasted like good New Zealand mutton, but it was goat. Six of the island's remaining 12 wild ones had been killed for this feast.

Nearly all families have at least one pet goat, however, so there is no danger of extinction. Nor does there seem to be any shortage of any necessity here. Coconut palms, banana, citrus and tropical fruits grow everywhere. Every family has a well-tended garden. Roseapple wood is used for fuel. It grows so fast that the supply always exceeds demand.

London Paper in Trouble--Secrecy Act

London

A Conservative newspaper, its editor and a noted young journalist-politician were charged yesterday with violating the Official Secrets Act in a story on the Nigerian war.

Summonses were served on the Sunday Telegraph; its editor, Brian Roberts, and Jonathan Aitken. Aitken, a great-nephew of the late Lord Beaverbrook, has been chosen as a Conservative candidate in the next general election.

The charges concerned from the lead article in the Sunday Telegraph last January 11. This gave details of what was said to be a confi-

dential report by Colonel R. E. Scott, a military expert in the British mission in Lagos.

The Scott report, as quoted in the story, was critical of "poor leadership" on the federal side. But it concluded that the federal army should defeat the rebel Biafrans if handled more efficiently.

The report gave what were said to be the precise dispositions of federal forces on the date it was written — Dec. 13, 1969. The Sunday Telegraph article said another copy of the report had been transmitted to the rebel leader, General Odemegwu Ojukwu.

The Telegraph story was known to have embarrassed the British government. Nigeria demanded the recall of Scott, and he quickly left Lagos.

The whole affair came too late to benefit the Biafran side. For on the very day of

the Sunday Telegraph story, Biafran resistance collapsed and the war effectively ended.

The decision to bring a security prosecution over the

story astounded political observers. The case seems certain to bring on the biggest clash between Fleet Street and a British government for many years. *New York Times*

CONSTIPATED?

DUE TO LACK OF FOOD BULK IN YOUR DIET

TRY Kellogg's BRAN BUDS'

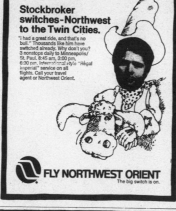

Stockbroker switches-Northwest to the Twin Cities.

"I had a great ride, and that's no bull." Thousands like him have switched already. Why don't you? 3 nonstops daily to Minneapolis/St. Paul. 6:45 am, 3:00 pm, 6:30 pm. International style "Regal Imperial" service on all flights. Call your travel agent or Northwest Orient.

FLY NORTHWEST ORIENT
The big switch is on.

Plant manager switches-Northwest to the Twin Cities.

"It's the growing thing." Thousands like him have switched already. Why don't you? 3 nonstops daily to Minneapolis/St. Paul. 8:45 am, 3:00 pm, 6:30 pm. International style "Regal Imperial" service on all flights. Call your travel agent or Northwest Orient.

FLY NORTHWEST ORIENT
The big switch is on.

3 Villages Shelled, Says Lebanon

Beirut

Israeli forces shelled three villages in southern Lebanon with mortars yesterday, killing two civilians and wounding five others, a Lebanese spokesman reported. Israel said Arab guerrillas shelled an Israeli village near the Lebanese border.

The Beirut military spokesman said the mortar attack lasted an hour and a half and was the second by Israel against Lebanon in 24 hours. An Israeli spokesman had "no comment" on the Lebanese reports.

(In the west, Israeli jets attacked Egyptian military installations and personnel along the Suez Canal for an hour.

A Lebanese military spokesman said a two-year-old boy was killed and three other civilians were injured in the village of Meiss El-Jabal by Israeli mortars. He said another civilian was killed and two injured in nearby Mitroun. Five houses were reported damaged in the two villages and light damage was reported in the third village, Bleida.

The villages are all about one mile from the border with Israel. The spokesman said the Israeli bombardment took place between 4 a.m. and 5:30 a.m. and Lebanese artillery returned the fire.

In Tel Aviv, an Israeli army spokesman said Arab guerrillas early yesterday attacked an Israeli border police station in Nebi Yosha village with bazookas. Neither casualties nor damage were reported in the village, a mile from the Lebanese frontier and traditionally known as the burial place of the prophet Joshua.

United Press

50 Arrested In Israel as Terrorists

Jerusalem

Israeli authorities announced last night the arrest of 50 members of two Arab terrorist rings suspected, among other things, of having planned to explode a carload of dynamite in this city.

The arrests brought to 85 the number of terrorist suspects arrested in Israel in the past several days, and attest to the continuing Arab opposition to the Israeli occupation of Arab lands captured in the 1967 Arab - Israeli war. At least 35 other terrorist suspects were arrested Monday and over the weekend in the Israeli - occupied Gaza Strip.

Last night's announcement said that the 50 arrested "recently" included 37 nabbed in Bethlehem "before they could carry out" some unspecified terrorist acts.

Times-Post Service

Nuclear Sub

Groton, Conn.

The Nautilus, first atomic-powered submarine, was launched Jan. 21, 1954, at Groton, Conn.

Associated Press

Italy Sex Class

Rome

The Angelo Monteverdi school will begin teaching sex education in April, marking the first time it has been offered in an Italian classroom.

United Press

Figure 18–21 Inside pages are important, too. This page, from the *San Francisco Chronicle*, provides interest with a large box. Heads "bump," but the effect is interesting because of variances in type.

LYNDON BAINES JOHNSON, 1908-1973

Story on page 2

Figure 18–22   Here is a front page from the tabloid *New York Daily News*, America's largest-circulation (2 million) daily. Note the big play given to headlines and photographs.

point of the story, the editor will return it to be redone. A good copy editor has the ability to make positive suggestions for improvement and will tell why he wants the head done over. These suggestions help the copyreader to do a better job.

Proficiency with Heads. The beginning copyreader will require a great deal of time with the first few headlines. Once he understands how to "exchange" words and work with phrases, he will gradually build speed so that he can do one in five minutes or less.

EXERCISES

1. Using local daily and weekly newspapers, check the headlines to determine how well copyreaders filled lines.

2. Note the "headlinese," or abbreviations and word selections, used in the heads of these newspapers.

3. Obtain a copy of the head schedule from your campus or community newspaper; note how the "counts" vary according to (*a*) type families and (*b*) type sizes.

4. To introduce yourself to head writing, compose heads for your own or classmates' stories; ask third parties to decide whether the heads give them an idea of what the stories contain.

5. Invite a copyreader from a local newspaper to attend a class question-and-answer session on writing heads.

19
Make-up

Make-up is the layout and designing of newspaper pages. It encompasses the choice of stories, size and style of headlines, illustrations and their sizes, and the relationship of these elements with each other. Make-up serves these purposes:

1. To identify the newspaper as different and apart from its competitors.
2. To attract the buyer so that he will be impelled to select one newspaper as more appealing over others.
3. To emphasize, through placement, the relative importance of stories and photographs in the newspaper.
4. To achieve variety and an artistic appearance for the newspaper, thereby relieving monotony.

MORNING VS. EVENING NEWSPAPERS

In general, morning newspapers have a greater depth of appeal than do afternoon newspapers. It should be emphasized that this is a *general* statement, and that there are many great afternoon newspapers that are higher in quality than their morning competitors'. As previously noted, however, the more favorable deadlines and delivery times, along with their more affluent readers, help make morning newspapers more penetrating.

Afternoon papers usually are designed to appeal to the newsstand customer; they emphasize stories expected to attract the casual or impulse buyer to a greater degree than do most morning newspapers. This emphasis is carried to the front-page make-up which is designed to "stop" the prospective buyer.

Whether morning or afternoon, most newspapers remake at least the front pages. The home-delivered edition has smaller front-page headlines than the one designed for street sales. The philosophy behind these differences is that the home-delivered newspapers have already been purchased through the subscription, while the street-sales edition must be sold daily through attractions such as large headlines beckoning for attention and stories which arouse curiosity or emotions.

More newspapers are sold from newsstands in the afternoons and evenings than during the mornings because commuters have more time to read, combining travel time with an evening at home. Afternoon newspapers, therefore, "build" or sensationalize headlines more than do their morning counterparts.

IMPORTANCE OF STREET SALES

Until the impact of television news in the late 1940s street sales of all newspapers were a much more important factor than today. Virtually every downtown street corner had news vendors personally selling papers and urging the public to buy their particular newspaper in preference to another. Television news gradually reduced the numbers of these vendors, who were both adults and youngsters. Big-city newspapers produced an edition for home delivery *plus* 6 to 10 editions designed to freshen street sales. With reduced street sales, newspapers cut the number of editions. Unmanned stands, most of them coin-operated, replaced the human news hawkers.

Despite television, street sales remain important—particularly in the larger cities. These sales help to increase the total volume, which is a factor in establishing advertising rates. The newsstands also serve as "billboards," advising the public that a particular newspaper exists. Even though stand sales may not be great, their presence may encourage the public to subscribe regularly to a certain newspaper. This is true particularly in areas where newspapers, even though produced in different cities, circulate and compete regionally.

In large cities, where there are proportionately more people on the streets, sales from stands or dealers are an even more important factor. New York City, Chicago, Boston, Philadelphia, and Los Angeles are typical places where street sales comprise a large percentage of total circulation. An attractive front page can make the buyer select a particular newspaper, while an unattractive one may do the opposite.

DIFFERENCES IN FORMAT

While morning and afternoon newspapers are generally more alike in their contents than they are different, two variations help distinguish them. These are the size and location of the flag, or newspaper name, on the front page, and the kind of type used for heads.

The Flag. Morning newspapers customarily have a flag that extends across the *entire* width of the newspaper, while the afternoon publication's flag "floats" at different points on a page and varies in size from two columns to the entire width.

The reason for this display is to help the afternoon newspaper accomplish more variety and use larger headlines to attract prospective readers. While most newspapers adhere to this pattern in the use of the flag, it should be emphasized that there is no "rule" requiring it. In fact, some morning newspapers "float" their flags to allow more spectacular make-up in street editions.

Head Type. Morning newspapers, depending less on street sales, generally use lighter-faced types and rely on simpler make-up. Afternoon newspapers are more inclined to use bolder and more spectacular type to attract readers. They also tend to use more type "boxes" and other techniques designed to attract attention.

DIMENSIONS OF NEWSPAPERS

There are two basic "sizes" of newspapers. The most popular is the "standard" format, which has a printed image approximately 14 to 15 inches wide and 20 to 22 inches high. The other is the "tabloid," which is produced by the press folding the standard format in half, producing a newspaper with a printed image approximately 10 inches wide and 14 to 16 inches high.

Typical standard format newspapers include the New York *Times*, Chicago *Tribune*, Dallas *News*, and Los Angeles *Times*. Tabloids include the New York *Daily News* and *Post*, Philadelphia *Daily News*, and *Chicago Today*.

Introduced in Great Britain during the early 1900s and in America in 1924 with the birth of the *Daily News*, tabloids were designed to serve commuters through appealing front page make-up and the convenience of smaller pages that could be handled easily on buses and subways.

The tabloid format has been used in small-town situations when publishers wished to give the impression of being "larger" newspapers because of the increased number of pages allowed by the same amount of actual space. One disadvantage of the tabloid format is the loss of advertising and news space that results from the margin between pages. This 1 inch by 16 inches means the loss of one full standard-sized page for every 20 tabloid pages.

Incidentally, newspapers must follow the standard or tabloid formats because national advertisements, comic strips, printing equipment, and newspaper puzzles and other features are geared to these measurements.

THE WIDTH OF COLUMNS

The "traditional" width of columns has been $11\frac{1}{2}$ or 12 picas, or approximately 2 inches. This means that a standard newspaper would have eight columns and a tabloid five. Each would be separated by a column rule or line. While many newspapers continue to follow these standards, there have been tendencies to break away from these traditions and develop more creative and innovative pages. With the conviction that there is nothing "permanent" in make-up, newspapers continue to experiment and make changes.

Removal of Column Rules. One method of adding "white" to pages and thereby increasing readability has been the removal of the column rules or lines on many newspapers. The one-pica (approximately $\frac{1}{8}$-inch) space between columns serves as sufficient break between columns to make stories readable.

Varying Column Widths. For improved readability, many standard-sized newspapers are using six-column formats at least on the front pages of sections. Some use the wider columns on inside pages, too. Financial, classified, and other specialized pages remain with the eight-column format because of the nature of the subject matter. The six-column format gives a column width of 13 picas, or $2\frac{1}{8}$ inches.

Instead of the usual five columns, modern tabloids often use three- or four-column for-

mats to accomplish more pleasing design and greater readability. The three-column formats produce columns of approximately 17 picas, or $2\frac{3}{4}$ inches, while the four-column formats give widths of approximately 14 picas, or $2\frac{3}{8}$ inches.

Computerized typesetting, requiring minimum mechanical adjustments over other methods, also allows increased use of variable column widths. With skillful designing, an editor can combine widths on one page to build interest and variety. For instance, two 17-pica columns can be combined with two $11\frac{1}{2}$-pica columns to fill 60 picas on a typical tabloid page.

TYPE SELECTION

Type is important because it attracts attention to a newspaper. Properly used, it also makes a publication more readable. The selection of particular kinds or styles of type also can give a newspaper character or personality. Readers may not consciously recognize it, but type styles identify or "trademark" a newspaper as well as its writing and reporting standards. Type can vary in several ways.

VARIANCE BY SIZE

Type is measured in "points," with each point being approximately $\frac{1}{72}$ inch. Nine-point type, in which the bulk of stories is set, would be $\frac{9}{72}$ (or $\frac{1}{8}$) inch high. Twenty-four point type, popular for medium-sized heads, is $\frac{24}{72}$ or $\frac{1}{3}$ inch. Here are typical type sizes:

This is 5 point type, used in classified ads.

This is 6 point type, for lengthy quotations.

This is 9 point type, for most news stories.

This is 11 point type, for stories which are set over two $11\frac{1}{2}$ pica columns (approximately four inches).

This is 12 point type, for stories set over three or four $11\frac{1}{2}$ pica columns (approximately six to eight inches).

This is 14 point type, suitable for one-line heads over short stories.

This is 18 point type, used for heads over two or three paragraph stories.

This is 24 point type, suitable for heads over medium-sized articles.

This is 36 point type, for heads on longer stories.

This 48 point type

is for even longer articles.

This 72-point type is for main

head-lines!

FAMILIES OF TYPE

There are literally hundreds of styles or families of type, each of which would be available in various sizes. The more ornate types are unsuitable for page-after-page of reading, but may have special meaning for layouts in magazines or in advertisements. Here are samples of type "families":

This is a sample of condensed type.

This is a sample of normal type.

This is a sample of extended type.

Other Variables. There are even more ways to vary type among families. Each distinct variation and size of type comes from a different *font*, or carrier, of type. For letter-press, the font is a metal case carrying mats that come in contact with lead; in phototype-setting for offset printing, the font is a film transparency used in connection with sensitized paper. Here are variables that one would expect to find within a family of type.

Density of type. A different emphasis or effect can be achieved by darkness or lightness:

This is lightface type, suitable for the body of stories.

This is boldface type, used for subheads or other matter to be emphasized.

"Straight" or "slanting." Although most people are unaware of it, at least consciously, type is designed with a directional "bent."

Roman is used for virtually all story matter and is popular in heads.

Italic achieves a contrast, and is used in heads.

Width of letters. Variety is also achieved by designing letters to be condensed or extended. The former are sometimes popular for heads because they allow inclusion of more words and letters. Extended type is more usable in advertisements. Examples:

P.T. Barnum is the name of a "pioneer" type for magazines or ads.

Old English, used for "flags," is difficult to read.

Vogue is readable and is used in heads.

Tempo also is suitable for headlines.

Selecting Type. Editors frown on mixing several families of type in one section of a newspaper because too much variety can confuse readers. In general, newspapers depending largely on home-delivered circulation will favor lighter-faced, Roman styles in as little as a single type family and seek variety with kicker and all-capitals heads. Those relying on street or newsstand "impulse" sales generally use bolder and darker type and will employ two or three type families to achieve emphasis and attract attention.

Because readers identify their favorite newspaper with its type and head styles, editors are reluctant to make frequent changes in major types unless surveys or studies indicate that good will be accomplished. Changing types, particularly when operating with letterpress, is also costly.

MAKING UP THE NEWSPAPER

While an architect produces blueprints for a builder to use in erecting a house, the

Raid alerts
greet POWs
loved ones

Indians
Will Get
Facilities

Watson Hits Committee
On Tax Shift Proposal

'SPECTRUM 73'
AT THE FORUM

*Pat Nixon warns
of 'overconfidence'*

WAR ENDS FOR 3 PW'S

Figure 19–1 Head styles can be capitals for the first letter of the first line and proper nouns (two upper left heads), or capitals for the first letter of each word (two upper right heads). They can also be all capitals (bottom).

journalist uses "dummies" to show the printer how the completed newspaper should look. Dummies are 25 to 50 per cent of the actual page size so they can be handled easily. If they were the actual dimensions of a page their size would make them difficult for people to handle while seated together around a copy desk. Dummies begin in the advertising department, where ads are dummied onto pages. The number of pages in a paper each day is determined by the business department on the basis of ad revenue and the "normal" ex-

pectancy for news volume. If a special event were scheduled or a catastrophe occurred, extra pages would go into the newspaper.

The formula or ratio between news and advertising varies from newspaper to newspaper. Obvious considerations include what ad ratio is required to make a profit and the amount of news offered by a competitor.

When the advertising department completes the dummies, one set goes to the printers, who begin placing the individual ads on the pages designated. Another set goes to the

Progress Is Hinted
in W. Berlin Talks

*Streisand to Appear
with Little Angels*

IRA Vows Attacks
Upon Big Hospital

**Drug-Dealing Nations
Get No Aid—Nixon**

Figure 19–2 Head and type styles help newspapers achieve individuality and variety. Top, both types have serifs but the one at the left is Roman (straight) and the other is italic (slanting). Bottom, these types are *sans* serif; the one at the left is Roman and the other is italic.

Taft Makes Favorite Son Bid for Nixon

Ogilvie Blames Appropriations Delay on Dems

Perry to Retire as Federal Judge

Boy, 2, Drowned Near His Home

Soviet-Egyptian Talks Continue

U. S. Center Will Assist State Courts

Concorde SST Flight Opens Paris Airshow

Final Package of Tough Crime Bills Passed by State Senate

Figure 19–3 Here are type sizes of one family, in Roman and italic, showing various column widths and point sizes.

news department, which inserts stories in the "open" or news spaces, then sends the dummies to the printers. Neither the news department nor the printers can move the advertisements, since many are on specific pages because of arrangements with the space buyers.

Members of the sports, society, opinion, and other specialized sections dummy their own sections or pages, since they are familiar with their own stories and pictures. Most inside pages often are assigned to individual copyreaders for dummying under direction of the chief copy editor. The city editor or assistants dummy the first page of the "city" or local news section.

Page one is held until the last for the latest and most important news. The news editor dummies this page after conferring with the wire, city, picture, and regional editors to determine which stories and photographs are the most relevant.

As quickly as dummies are filled with news and pictures, they are sent to the printers. The make-up editor, a member of the news department, coordinates operations by working with the printers in clarifying questions that arise over dummies and cutting stories that are too long for the allocated space. If a story is too short or one is missing, he obtains one to fill the "hole." On larger newspapers, the make-up editor may have several assistants.

Pages "move" to the printers throughout the day, so that all pages will not arrive at the same time. The news department operates with deadlines for specific pages, which are completed by printers and placed on the press hours before it is time for them to roll. Page one, with the most important news, frequently is held by the news department until minutes before press time.

DESIGNING A PAGE

Each page in a newspaper deserves consideration so that it will be artistic and pleasing to the reader. The ingredients for designing a page are basically photographs and

Puerto Rican
Exodus to U.S.
Turning Around

Rockefeller Acts to Stem
N.Y. Police Corruption

Names Special Prosecutor With Power
to Supersede Work of District Attorneys

Aerospace Workers
in L.A. Area May
Receive Pay Hike

'BAIL BY CHECK' PLAN
OK'D BY SUPERVISORS

9 More Groups Support
Challenge of Gag Rule

IN THE NEWS

President of
U.N. Suited
to New Job

Hopes for Better Life on
Mainland Prove Futile
for Many Immigrants

Council Overrides
Redistricting Veto

False Reports
Laid to Orders
by Gen. Lavelle

Figure 19–4 Typical heads from a single newspaper, showing how a general family or style of type is used. Variables so important for make-up are obtained by width, size of type, number of lines, and the use of all capitals.

type, all in varying sizes so that the make-up will create eye appeal.

The use of photographs today is a highly important factor, since readers are accustomed to visuals in picture magazines and on television. *A good photograph, therefore, should dominate a page*, particularly when the page contains no advertisements. To force a photograph between stories does little justice to the picture and in fact detracts from it. To assume punch and a forceful page, most editors dummy photographs *first* and build the stories around them.

The Choice Areas. Surveys indicate that right-hand pages attract higher readership than left-hand pages because the public almost automatically looks first at the former. The top of a page, whether it is on the right or left, commands more attention than the bottom. Editors regard the upper right-hand corner of the right page as the most choice, or the place where readers will look first.

Right vs. left pages. For artistic balance, and for maximum use of the areas where eyes look first, editors often "weight" or place the emphasis in the upper right-hand half of the right page or in the upper left-hand half of left-hand pages.

Bottom of the page. On pages without ads, editors regard the bottom area as a place

COUPLE FACES LONG TERMS
Producer's Kidnapers Guilty

VEGAS SCHOOLS OPEN
Philly Teacher Strike
Goes Into 3rd Week

Universe Used as Scales
No Weight Problem
For Elusive Neutrino

Need Help, Too
Many Unmarrieds
Go to Counselor

Says he'll resign
Head of monetary fund
seen rejected by U.S.

Figure 19—5 Different styles of "kicker" heads, with the overline in all capitals or capitals and lowercase, and with or without underlines. Varying ways of handling heads help create a newspaper's "personality."

where considerable interest can be created. An editor frequently will balance the bottom with a good photograph or a large head stretching over a story covering several columns. This picture is usually placed in different columns from the art at the top. This tends to prevent monotony for the casual reader, who subconsciously finds variety pleasing.

VARIETY IN MAKE-UP

Journalists usually are reporters and subsequently copyreaders before undertaking make-up duties, and they serve apprenticeship in page design by occasionally assisting an editor. After mastering the principles, one can learn make-up best by doing it under knowledgeable supervision and practicing techniques under the trial-and-error method.

The basic purposes of make-up are to create variety and interest, while at the same time advising the reader regarding the relative importance of stories. Heads, of course, help advise of the story contents.

After selecting pertinent stories and photographs, editors dummy them on pages according to their relative importance: major stories and the most newsworthy photos go on page one or the first pages of sections, while the least important material is placed on inside pages. As indicated, a photograph should be dummied first as the main point on a page; news articles follow. The longer stories, which logically would have larger heads, go at the top of the page. Progressively shorter stories go lower on a page, with the exception of long ones which can "anchor" a layout by stretching across the bottom.

Irregular vs. Square Make-up. The two basic schools of thought on make-up can be described best as the "irregular," using headlines one, two, three, four, or more columns wide, and the "square," composed primarily of rectangular or square shapes in stories with mostly multi-column heads. The "irregular" is more traditional and produces more variety, while the "square" offers more white space and therefore helps readability. More newspapers, both daily and weekly, use the "irregular" make-up than the "square."

While both types of make-up are acceptable, editors would frown on mixing them or even using them on alternate days in the same newspaper. Switching would interrupt reading habits and make it harder for the reader to find stories.

Pictures against Pictures. To create more interest, editors prefer not to use photos side-by-side on a page unless the pictures concern a related situation. The reasoning is that adjoining pictures suggest a relationship, and if it is not there, confusion will develop in the reader's mind as he seeks to find a link.

Use of Boxes. Editors create "boxes" with stories in several ways. One method is setting a two- or three-paragraph story *narrower* than the conventional column; the box is created by the white space of the indentation or by the printer's actually inserting a thin line (for instance, 2 points or $1/32$ inch) on all four sides. "Boxes" two, three, or more columns wide can be used for longer stories by setting the stories $1/4$ to $1/2$ inch *narrower* than conventional columns. In offset printing, editors often use a 20 per cent tone to shade a story and thus give it emphasis over the articles that appear without the tone.

"Boxes" are used extensively to emphasize stories and create variety in make-up. They are regarded as "art" in dummying a newspaper, and consequently would *not* be used against each other or alongside photographs or cartoons.

Heads against Heads? Some journalists argue that "bumping heads," or headlines that appear directly opposite each other, should *never* be used. Placing heads against each other is also called "tombstoning."

Editors on virtually all major metropolitan newspapers and many weeklies and small dailies reject this injunction as unrealistic and too restrictive. They use a variety of techniques to eliminate the possibility of adjacent heads being read as one headline, which is the fear of those concerned with the problem.

Those claiming that heads should not "bump" would in effect mandate that a three-column head *must* appear under a three-column photograph. Modern newspaper editors reject this rule on the basis that a worse crime is putting an overly large head on a relatively minor article to avoid side-by-side heads. The better technique, in the case of the three-column picture, would be to use a two-column head with two lines alongside a one-column head with three lines; one head would be in Roman type, and the other in italic—either larger or smaller—to create contrast. An alternate method would be using a one-column "box" story with one-column heads of varying lines and type styles on either side.

Despite the fact that these heads may bump, the contrasts in type and headline styles make it obvious to readers that they are separate. At the same time, the head sizes are in accordance with the importance of the story.

Frequently there are inside pages where an editor has a choice of running one large headline across the top or using a group of smaller heads. Assuming that there was no "major" story worthy of a large head, the preferred method would be to use the smaller ones rather than a large headline over an unworthy story. Variety can be achieved in these "bumping" heads through different head styles and type. A photograph or "box" story will also help to avoid the possibility that the heads would be read as one and thus be confusing.

The single large head may be a crutch that avoids the antiquated "no bumping heads" mandate, but it often makes a minor story appear more important than it really is.

OTHER PROBLEMS IN MAKE-UP

Some aspects of newspaper make-up call for specialized heads or type. The purpose of these heads is to assist the reader and create interest.

Use of Subheads. Large story areas unbroken by conventional headlines will produce gray areas and give the reader a feeling of monotony while he is pursuing lengthy stories. Subheads, inserted by copyreaders, break these areas to create variety and increase readability.

One method of producing these "breaks" is by putting the first two or three words of every third to fourth paragraph in boldface (or blacker) type. Unlike italic, boldface type can be set without mechanical problems. The disadvantage for this method is that if paragraphs are discarded from a story after it is set in type, those with the boldface may be omitted. Another method is inserting, in boldface type, two to four words between every three to four paragraphs. These words give some digest or thought regarding the material that is following. The type size is the same as in the text of the story. Two advantages for these subheads include their remaining if a paragraph is cut, or the fact that they can be discarded when it is necessary to shorten a story slightly so that it will fit in a designated spot. These points help make the "inserted" subheads more popular than those self-contained in a paragraph.

Both kinds of subheads can be all capitals or capitals and lowercase. The latter are more widely used because all capitals, regardless of how they are utilized, are more difficult to read.

Referral Lines. References to related stories or pictures are inserted at the beginning of a story or in the middle of it to guide a reader to another page. In the case of pictures, the photograph running on the front page may advise in its cutlines "See Story on Page 4," or the article may appear on page one with a referral line indicating that a photo is on a specific inside page.

"Jumping" a Story. When a story is too long for a front page, it may be continued to inside pages. Editors prefer never to jump less than 2 column inches of a story, with the reasoning that a short jump "cheats" the reader, who logically would expect to see more of an article. In the case of a jump regarding a story on an election, lines such as the following would guide the reader:

(Continued on Page 3, Col. 2)

(See ELECTION, Page 3)

For a story guided by page and column number, the jump head typically would repeat part of the article with a two- or three-line head over one or more columns. The jump guided by the page number alone would have a large head corresponding to the line at the end of the story on the first page; in this example, it would be "ELECTION."

The origin of the story would be indicated at the top of the jumped material. Example:

(Continued from Page 1)

"Trimming" the Pages. While the dummies serve as blueprints for the printers, there are variables that require newsroom attention as the pages are "locked up" or completed. Stories may be longer or shorter in type than estimated, and heads may run over their allocated length. The make-up editor, along with assistants, works with printers to trim stories and rewrite heads that do not fit. This editor also has a list of stories not dummied that (1) can fit in spaces left by articles that fall short of the expected length or (2) can be used if scheduled stories do not appear.

Qualifications for the position of make-up editor include being able to write and rewrite heads and to recognize where "trims" can be made quickly without hurting the thought of a story. The man or woman who succeeds best with these duties is usually one who has been a reporter and copyreader.

Necessity for "Shorts." Many story situations are told best in one or two paragraphs, which are called "shorts." Despite their brevity, some shorts are important enough for dummying on page one or another key page.

Many such articles, however, are not dummied but are sent to the printers as "wild," or stories that can be placed on any page where room develops.

Shorts are necessary to fill "holes" in the newspaper. Most editors prefer to dummy papers "loose," or without designating places for the shorts. This allows printers to put short articles where they wish when minor changes are needed because stories are longer or shorter than estimated.

EXERCISES

1. Contact the circulation managers of local newspapers and determine the percentage of street or stand sales as compared to home-delivered sales; compare these figures with the make-up appeal of newsstand editions.

2. Visit a local corner or other place where several newspapers are displayed in stands; note the varying appeal of make-up.

3. Invite the news editor of a local newspaper to attend a question-and-answer session to discuss make-up techniques as practiced by his staff.

4. Assemble samples of local newspapers, and note (a) contrasts in their head types and styles; (b) to what extent they use "bumping" heads and how they contrast type when doing so; (c) how they use "referral" lines; (d) the methods used for "jump" heads; (e) the similarities or differences in column widths; (f) the kinds of subheads used; and (g) whether they use "irregular" or "square" make-up.

20

Photographs and Picture Editing

Few people today could visualize a newspaper without photographs or other illustrations on virtually every page. Yet the substantial use of pictures began only in the late 1890s and early 1900s when technical know-how developed and newspaper czars Hearst and Pulitzer waged circulation battles. Photographs, increasingly important in recent years, help meet the visual competition of television and magazines. The average reader can logically understand a news situation better if pictures help develop it. As the Chinese proverb puts it, a single picture is often worth ten thousand words.

Two New York City newspapers, the *Post* and *Daily News*, are excellent examples of how appealingly displayed photographs will help impel people to buy from street stands. These publications almost daily display front pages dominated by large photographs that attract attention. Buyers are not disappointed, since inside pages also are generously adorned with pictures supplementing stories. While few newspapers in America depend on street sales as much as those in New York City, editors throughout the nation recognize the value of

photographs and use them to enhance their pages.

Several developments, some interlocked, helped make photographs as important as they are today. The invention of fast and efficient means of transforming photographs into zinc halftones permitting reproduction on high-speed printing presses was a major breakthrough that made pictures more widely used in the early 1900s. A second enabling factor was the development of printing inks and papers that allowed good reproduction on increasingly faster and more versatile presses.

The spectacular growth of photography as a hobby coincident with the founding and almost instant popularity of photography and picture magazines during the 1930s also served as a catalyst for increased emphasis on photos in newspapers. The perfection of means to make news pictures more available by transmitting them over wires and via satellites also increased the use of photos.

Television news gave additional impetus to the trend as journalists realized, more than ever, the importance of visuals.

PICTURE EDITING

Selection of photographs for a weekly or daily newspaper must be done by a person who can evaluate pictures with the eyes of both an artist and technician and who understands news values and page layout. The person who chooses pictures, whatever his title may be, realizes that the photographs published must be selected for the reader—*not* the photographer who took the picture or the person whose image might have been snapped.

The criterion of reader interest rules out, therefore, the use of photographs that might please only a small percentage of subscribers. Since a system of interest values similar to those for news stories applies to news photo-graphs, this rules out pictures of people passing gavels, presenting checks, shaking hands, or passing out presents.

News values and technical realities also rule out photographs of large groups of people posing for a camera. Few such situations contain news, and the faces in large-group pictures usually are so small as to be unrecognizable. Most editors instruct photographers not to place more than four people in a picture and to resist pressures seeking to overrule this injunction. After all, journalists would explain, the photographs are taken for and by the newspaper—not the group involved.

Photographers crave action pictures, and editors play up such materials. Many assignments, unfortunately, are routine, and the pho-

---

PHOTO ASSIGNMENT

Picture Situation/Comments:

Location:

Date:

Time:

Person to Contact:

Print Deadline:

Assigned by:

DISTRIBUTION: Top and second pages, PHOTO DEPARTMENT; 3rd Page, EDITOR

PHOTOGRAPHERS: Be sure to provide first and last names (and titles) of those in your pictures. Provide your name.

Assigned to: _____

Figure 20–1 A typical photo assignment form used by the news department to advise photographers of picture needs.

tographers must use their skill and ingenuity to produce pictures to tell the story.

PICTURE ASSIGNMENTS

Handling photographs for a newspaper follows a procedure that is challenging and fascinating. Weekly or daily, virtually all newspapers have their own darkrooms and equipment because photographs must be processed quickly to meet deadlines.

Photographic Staff Organization. On a medium to large newspaper, two staff members work together in photography. One is the picture editor, usually a writer who won the position after working as a reporter or copyreader. The other is the chief photographer, often starting as a photographer and obtaining the promotion after demonstrating ability with the technical and artistic requirements of the craft as well as showing that he can work with others. On smaller newspapers, the city editor may double as picture editor and the staff may include only one or two photographers, thus eliminating the need for a "chief."

Making Picture Assignments. Editors or reporters can originate photo assignments, but all usually clear through the picture editor so there will be coordination and no duplication. Most newspapers, large or small, have printed assignment sheets with blanks to provide the information necessary for the photographer.

The person who makes the assignment advises the photographer, via the form, whom to see, *exactly* where to go, when the picture is scheduled, and pertinent information regarding *why* it is being taken. There is also space to show who made the assignment, in the event that more information is needed. The assignment form also notes the print deadline, which like all deadlines is the *latest* time to provide a photograph so that it can appear in the paper.

Assigning the Photographers. The picture editor passes the assignments to the chief photographer, who allocates them to photographers according to a number of considerations. One, of course, would be the approxi-

mate amount of time an assignment might require. For example, one photographer could take several face or "mug" shots in the newspaper office while another is spending an entire day covering a political convention. Another consideration would be the "specialty" of the photographer, who, like the reporter, will develop adeptness at certain fields. Some photographers take their best pictures of social events, while others excel at sports, features, children, disasters, or police situations.

Except on the largest newspapers, specialization is not so refined that an assignment waits for a photographer. In this regard, the photographer is like the reporter who is ready to do any writing job when the need arises.

Duties of the Photographer. The photographer's duties include taking a picture with good composition and with news values that illustrate the story situation. He also must produce a photographic print of excellent technical quality. Pictures that are too "gray" or contain too much contrast are marks of the amateur and will not reproduce well. When a reporter and photographer are working together, the writer obtains the identification of the subjects according to their position in the picture. If a photographer is alone, *he* must obtain the identification. This includes not only the *first* and *last* names and where the individuals are in the prints, but also a brief explana-

Figure 20–2 News photography can be demanding in technical perfection. Note the sharpness in this picture of a shrimp-like creature placed on a pencil to show its size. (*Oakland Tribune* Photo by Lonnie Wilson)

Figure 20–3 The wide-angle or "fish-eye" lens can help add variety to what could be a routine photo. Caution: Overuse of camera "tricks" renders them ineffective by immunizing readers with too many gimmicks. (Orange Coast College Photo)

Figure 20–4 Photographers frequently must be at the front when trouble develops. This Associated Press photo shows an FBI agent aiming at a would-be hijacker at New York City's John F. Kennedy Airport. (Wide World Photos)

tion of *who* they are and *what* the story situation concerns. A picture without this vital information normally would be unusable, since deadlines prevent "back-tracking" for data.

Training for Photographers. Taking news pictures is a specialized field, like writing news stories. The techniques of exposure and developing are similar to those for other forms of photography. It should be noted that prints must be clear and sparkling, since newspaper reproduction is of a lower quality than that of

Figure 20–5 Photographers lucky enough to be on the scene at the right time get on-the-spot pictures. This assassination, by a foot-long dagger, of Japanese socialist chairman Inejiro Asanuma in 1960, won the Pulitzer Prize for photographer Yasuki Nagao of the Tokyo newspaper *Mainichi*. (United Press International Photo)

top-grade magazines where even shadows have considerable depth. Artistic techniques and composition are considerably different from those required in portrait, industrial, commercial, or studio photography. There are numerous books on news photography, and many colleges offer courses in this art.

Reporter-Photographers. An area of interest to journalism newcomers is the use of reporter-photographers, commonly called "combination men" (even when the dual jobs are performed by women). Being versed in both skills can be an asset in obtaining a job. Many smaller newspapers do not have the funds to warrant sending both a reporter and a photographer to cover some story situations, and even the larger ones frequently prefer combination men for events which are a considerable distance away and would require extra manpower for what is often a story of fringe interest.

An excellent example of the typical use for a combination man is the beat which covers an area some distance from the newspaper's main office. Many such situations need coverage, but it is uneconomical to keep both a reporter and a photographer on the beat. The combination man can fill the dual need, covering an area reportorially and photographically.

Combination men typically are staff members whose basic skill is reporting and who learn to handle a camera.

What Kind of Equipment? The heavy, bulky 4- by 5-inch view camera with flash powder or tin-foil-filled bulbs of forty or more years ago has gradually given way to lighter and more sophisticated equipment. Faster films and lenses permit vastly increased use of natural lighting without flash. Increasingly smaller and lighter cameras, using finer-grain films, are becoming popular as they are developed. The lighter equipment helps the photographer to achieve more mobility and to operate less obtrusively.

To meet deadlines with quality pictures, most newspaper photo laboratories are equipped with modern equipment to facilitate operations. As papers install more sophisticated presses capable of printing full-color pictures, labs are including color-processing facilities.

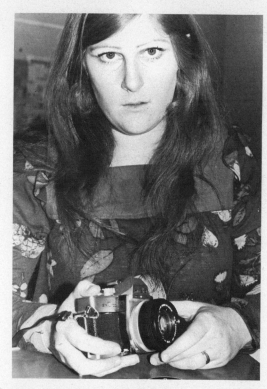

Figure 20–6 Some reporters learn to use cameras and double as "combination men" (or women). This is Susan Hanson working on the Orange Coast College campus newspaper.

Figure 20–7 Don Camp, photographer for the *Philadelphia Bulletin*, shows an example of the smaller type of camera preferred by most photo-journalists.

HANDLING PICTURES

A typical day at a weekly or daily newspaper can produce many picture situations, each usually offering different scenes from which to select. Editors make their selections based on how well a photo tells the story and on the availability of space.

SELECTING THE SCENE

Picture editors typically would have several methods of making the preliminary scene selection. The oldest way is for the photographer to provide finished prints from the negatives he believes are best. The disadvantages to this method include the fact that the photographer must spend time and materials making prints that will not be used and the possibility that the editor will miss seeing specific scenes which would be more desirable in overall planning.

A highly popular alternate is for the photographer to provide contact or "same-size" prints of all negatives. The editor marks the ones he wishes to consider, and carefully printed enlargements are provided.

Many picture editors can "read" negatives by holding them to the light and thus visualizing how important points would look in prints, thereby making a selection and bypassing the time for making contact prints. Looking at negatives and determining minute points such as facial expressions or other details is an art that one develops through practice.

Negative "readers" are a modern and efficient way of determining what a negative holds. Relatively expensive and therefore used at larger dailies, these machines project a positive image of the negative onto a viewer to assist editors in deciding on prints.

HANDLING THE PRINT

Photographers as a rule of thumb provide 8- by 10-inch glossy prints. These are standard for handling by editors, copy runners, artists, and printing craftsmen. Since most photographs are "blown" or enlarged from their print size to reproduction dimensions, smaller pictures would be likely to show grain after being increased substantially.

Exceptions to the 8- by 10-inch standard include pictorial or other special scenes to be reproduced in extremely large proportions. Such photos are often printed on 11- by 14-inch paper to give mechanical technicians a better opportunity for good reproduction. On the other hand, "mug" or face pictures are printed on 5- by 7-inch or smaller paper because the photos will not be blown up when reproduced.

"Sizing" the Print. Since variables in make-up remain, a good photographer would not provide a print cropped so closely that the picture editor would not have room to delete more of the picture. Prints for salon display must be cropped of extraneous material so that they will give the effect the photographer wants. In journalism, however, make-up considerations contribute greatly to the way a photo will be cropped. Each photo is competing with other pictures on the basis of news values as well as technical and artistic merit; in addition, minute-by-minute news develop-

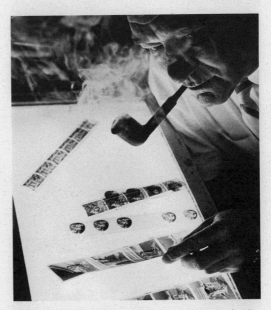

Figure 20–8 An editor uses a light table at the *San Diego* (Calif.) *Union-Tribune* as he examines negatives to make a preliminary selection for a photographer to print. Editors become accustomed to "reading" photo negatives to determine the best. (Copley Newspapers Photo)

Figure 20–9   A "contact sheet" showing what is available to the picture editor. He makes a selection by designating frame numbers or crossing out unwanted scenes as a preliminary to having enlargements made for use in the paper.

ments can alter the situation to make more or less room for photographs.

The editor, therefore, needs ample "air" in photographic prints so that the reproduction size can be wider, narrower, deeper, shallower, etc. If the photographer, in making the print, cropped it so close that nothing more could be taken off, *he* would be dictating the proportions. The "air," or area that is optional for use, lets the editor decide the proportions.

The photo wheel. To determine the dimensions for reproduction, the editor uses a proportion scale that is usually circular in shape and therefore is called the "photo wheel." It operates on the same principle as a slide rule. Although comparatively few people on the staff of most newspapers can operate the scale, simply because the majority have never taken the time to learn, one can master its use with two to five hours' tutelage under a picture editor.

The scale shows by what proportions a photograph will be reduced or enlarged into a halftone. Basically, it works like this: the inside circle (usually colored) contains numbers to indicate the *actual* size of the photo, and the outer circle (usually white) has calibrations to

Figure 20–11 Robert Pineda and Charlene Lopez Willey dummy a page for the campus newspaper at Orange Coast College.

show the *reproduction* size. All measurements go *up*—or *down*—proportionately, and the gauge gives exact dimensions in seconds. Inside the inner circle is a gauge which shows the percentage of increase or decrease from the size of the original.

A 50 per cent reduction, for example, means that the photograph will be only one-half its actual size when reproduced. For a large photo, such a reduction probably would present no problems. If the photograph—or part of a photograph—being reduced was small in the beginning, a 50 per cent reduction could mean that it would be so small in the newspaper as to be meaningless.

A 200 per cent blow-up would mean that the photograph would be twice as big in the newspaper. This increase in size would make little difference for a sharp photograph, but if the print were fuzzy or out of focus, these imperfections would be magnified in the reproduction.

Experience teaches the picture editor what to expect in the way of latitude for blow-ups or reductions for photos of different quality.

Importance of cropping. Two vital functions are associated with cropping photographs. One is eliminating unneeded or confusing parts of a picture. For example, a face

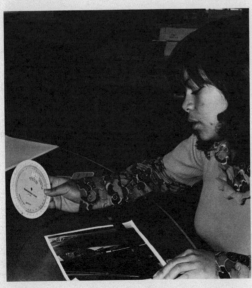

Figure 20–10 Orange Coast College journalism student Roberta Almerez demonstrates how a picture editor uses a proportional scale in reducing or enlarging a photograph to appear as a halftone in a newspaper. Instructions are passed to the newspaper's mechanical department.

or "mug" shot may include the subject's shoulders and a large blank area surrounding the head. The reproduction will be more effective if the photo is "blown" to show only the face, excluding the shoulders and unimportant background. Thus the face, the most important part of the photograph, is much larger.

The other important purpose of cropping is varying the proportions of the reproduction. By cutting in on the sides, the editor increases the relative height of the picture. Using the entire available width makes the height relatively shorter. A vital part of make-up is creating variety by using photographs in different column widths and heights. Skillful cropping accomplishes these effects.

Cropping is, in effect, one form of photographic composition. The basic purpose of cropping, or varying composition, is to achieve the best artistic presentation and maximum visual impact within the scope of available space.

Reproducing from Other Publications. Many people contact newspaper editors with requests to use pictures that have appeared in other publications. While some halftones can be reproduced the *same* size as originally used in offset newspapers, it is generally technically impossible to copy them for letterpress publications, which use engravings. Attempts to reproduce such pictures usually results in a displeasing effect similar to poor television reception overlaid by confusing patterns.

WRITING CUTLINES

The duty of writing cutlines, also known as "captions," to explain a photograph is vari-

Figure 20–12 Cropping can greatly vary a picture's message or effect. Without cropping, the subject is in a business or professional setting. Cropping to include the tie and arm is still formal but permits use of less space. The maximum cropping gives the effect of moving in closely for informality. The subject: Dr. Norman Watson, chancellor of Coast Community College District, Costa Mesa, Calif., and president of KOCE-TV, Huntington Beach.

ously assigned at different newspapers. Those responsible may be the photographer who took the picture, the reporter writing the story, an editor, or the copyreader handling the article. Often the latter will "boil" or condense cutlines written by another staff member.

Writing cutlines is an art. They must be brief and to the point, but not so short that they leave the reader wondering about the situation involved. Good cutlines supplement and even explain the pictures, but they do *not* repeat obvious information in the photograph.

While brevity is essential, cutlines should *not* be telegraphic and omit words that are important for smooth reading.

People in the pictures should be identified by their full names and, if necessary for understanding, with their titles or other explanation of *who* they are.

When a story accompanies the photo, the cutline writer must take care not to repeat lengthy facts from the article: the cutlines are *not* intended to be a condensation, but are expected to supplement. A good rule of thumb is that if the story can be told in the cutlines, it should be, and the article can be eliminated.

SENATE WITNESS—Air Force Maj. Gen. Alton Slay being wheeled from testimony before Senate committee probing unauthorized bombing of North Vietnamese targets.
(AP) Wirephoto

A policeman in riot gear stands ready with the stun gun.
UPI Telephoto.

LITTER AT CRASH SCENE
Football Shoe, Helmet

James S. White

Stanislaw Trepczynski
(AP) photo

G. GORDON LIDDY
Ex-FBI Agent

Figure 20–13 Typical ways that cutlines are handled for one-column photos.

SNOW ALREADY

A girl brushes snow off the family car as an early season snowfall left the Denver area under 3 inches.

Fraser, Colo., a mountain town, reported 10 inches of white stuff. (AP photo)

A New York City policeman pins a demonstrator to the hood of a car as she grabs him by the throat in melee outside of the Bachelors III restaurant Wednesday. (AP)

UPI Telephoto

TAIL SECTION OF WICHITA STATE PLANE SMOLDERS AFTER COLORADO CRASH
Twin-engine Craft Plummets Into Forested Area Near Rugged Loveland Pass

[TRIBUNE Staff Photo: By George Quinn]

'Rodeo' on the Expressway

Steer is tied to tree beside Dan Ryan Expressway at 43d Street after animal pushed open gate of truck on way to stockyards to escape.

Steer was captured by member of State Highway Department after hour's chase between 7 and 8 a. m. yesterday. Other photos on back page.

Historic site dedicated

Although the building at 1240 N. Lake Shore Dr. is a luxury high-rise apartment building, the place was dedicated Wednesday as an historic site. The land was once the home of Robert Todd Lincoln. Larry Belles of the Evanston Historical Society, Paul Angle of the Chicago Historical Society and John Mack, president of the realty company that constructed the building, were on hand for the dedication. (Daily News Photo/William De Luga)

CHICAGO TODAY Photo
Assistant State's Atty. Richard Jalovec holds club taken from a courtroom rioter and Detective James Nolan shows tooth marks on his arm. Brawl broke up trial of 11 in U. of I. disorder.

Figure 20–14a and b: Representative styles newspapers use to write cutlines for pictures of two or more columns.

Subjects should be identified as to their places in pictures, because most readers will not know them well enough to recognize them.

Techniques for Identification. There are numerous ways, all elastic, for identifying people in a photograph. The one to be preferred is the method which is the most understandable and readable according to the individual picture situation.

One person. The simplest cutlines are those involving only one person. "Name lines,"

(UPI Telephoto)

FLYING BLIND — Two-year-old Andy Losasso finds himself suddenly in the dark after donning his dad's too-big airline pilot's hat during an anti-hijacking demonstration at the United Nations Airline Pilots Association members Tuesday wound up their six-week vigil in protest against hijackings. Young Andy holds the symbol of the pilots' campaign for international ratification of the 1963 Tokyo Convention and all subsequent treaties dealing with air piracy.

READY FOR OPENER—Cypress College football coach Bill Price gathers team together following workout prior to opening of season Saturday night. Price is hoping Chargers will have their first winning season in the school's history.

Times photo by Hal Schulz

'RACQUETEER' PREVAILS

Dr. Bud Muehleisen (with racquet) ran handball champion Paul Haber ragged Sunday while winning racquetball-handball exhibition at Long Beach Athletic Club. Muehleisen, avenging an earlier loss, won 21-9, 18-21, 21-8.
—**Staff Photos by TOM SHAW**

LONG BEACH STATE UNIVERSITY'S TUBA PLAYERS TAKE A REST
Gary Horimoto, Chris Hansen, Gerry Gilmer, Doug Harris pause
—Staff Photo by KENT•HENDERSON

Going home

Israeli tanks head homeward from southern Lebanon Sunday after two-day incursion to destroy Palestinian guerrilla bases of operation.
—**AP Wirephoto**

Bay area workers strike . . .

Postal workers at Rincon Annex, San Francisco's main post office, walked off the job Friday. The walkout was spreading today and halting service to some Northern California areas.

(UPI Telephotos)

Herald Examiner Photo

Southern California Gas Co. vice presidents Bill Cole, left, and John Abram tell need for new natural gas sources at three-day symposium.

UPI Photo

HUMAN GRAPEVINE ON COLOMBIAN TRAINER
Sailors aboard Colombian Navy training ship 'The Gloria' man the spars during visit to Le Havre Harbor in France en route to Canary Islands.

---

or only the individual's name, are often enough if there is an accompanying article. An explanation would be needed if the person in the picture were doing something that might not be clear to the average reader.

Example:

Fred MacPherson demonstrates the way he tunes a bagpipe.

Two people. If a male and female are in a photograph, their names should be sufficient to tell the reader which is which (unless a beardless male has long hair, in which case the journalist must decide if a clarifying "right" or "left" is required).

Example:

John Jones and Mary Wilson exchange antique buttons during a session of the Hobby Convention.

When there are two men or two women in a picture, one should be identified as being "left." Readers will know that the other person is the one at the right, thus eliminating an unnecessary "right."

Example:

Mary Wilson (left) and Elizabeth Gregory prepare displays for the Hobby Convention.

Three people. When there are three people in a picture, identifying one as being "left" and another "center" leaves the understanding that the third person is the one at the right. This saves the use of an unnecessary and redundant "right" to clutter the cutlines.

Example:

Mary Wilson (left), Elizabeth Gregory (center) and Janet Young prepare displays for the Hobby Convention.

Several subjects. If there are a number of people in a photograph and they are roughly in a line, an understandable way to identify them is "from left," followed by their names.

Example:

Registering for the Hobby Convention are (from left) John Jones, Peter Smith, William Arnold, Mary Wilson and Ted Johnson.

When there are several rows, journalists continue the "from left" format but break the identification down by front, center, and back rows. The procedure usually is to begin at the front row since it is the one readers note first.

Example:

Registering for the Hobby Convention are (front row, from left) John Jones, Peter Smith, William Arnold and Mary Wilson, and (back row, from left) George McClure, Elizabeth Gregory and Janet Young.

Sometimes, thanks to imaginative photographers, the subjects of a picture are in the general shape of a circle. A method of identifying people helpfully under these circumstances is to make cutlines read "from left, clockwise beginning at . . ."; for the starting point, the writer selects an area where the reader's eye will fall logically.

Example:

Holding exhibits for the Hobby Convention are (from left, clockwise beginning at center) William Arnold, Mary Wilson, George McClure, John Jones, Elizabeth Gregory and Janet Young.

Groups of pictures. Journalists are divided on how to handle cutlines for picture layouts. One school advocates individual cutlines for each photograph. The other argues that one set of cutlines can serve several related photos and eliminate repetitious statements.

Example:

Exhibitors prepare for the Hobby Convention opening today. TOP LEFT: John Jones and Mary Wilson exchange antique buttons. TOP CENTER: Joan Williams (left) and Elizabeth Gregory erect displays. TOP RIGHT: Janet Young (left), John Jones and Phyllis Shannon register. LOWER RIGHT: Peter

Smith, convention chairman, arrives. LOWER LEFT: William Arnold (left) and Ted Johnson.

Since readers' eyes instinctively move from the left, "master" or single-set cutlines usually describe photos in a clockwise order. The point where the movement starts depends greatly on positioning the cutlines on the page.

Note: Readers are conditioned to identifications that are "from left." The term "from left to right" is redundant: in what other direction could the identification go when it *starts* from the left?

Indentions and Type Faces. Most cutlines are *not* indented for the simple reason that indentions denote new paragraphs, and each cutline *is* a paragraph by itself. Many newspapers vary their cutlines from the body or story type to achieve variety. Some use italic, while others use boldface or a larger size of their standard type. Cutlines usually are set separately from stories, thus permitting use of different type fonts.

Credits for Photographs. While by-lines are given to reporters, photographers receive "credit lines" for their pictures. Just as a reporter does *not* receive a by-line on every story he writes, so the photographer receives a credit line only on his above-average pictures. Newspapers vary in the method of giving this credit.

Examples:

Staff photo by Thomas Williams

Daily News photo by Thomas Williams

Photographs that do not carry individual credits usually are credited to the newspaper's staff. If a free-lance or nonstaff photographer takes a picture, he is often given credit.

Examples:

Daily News Photo
Photo by Paul Carson

The credit line is often set as part of the cutlines. An alternate and popular method is placing it in smaller boldface type between the cutlines and the photograph.

EXERCISES

1. Purchase a proportion scale from a store dealing in art or drafting supplies. Set the percentage scale for reductions of 25 and 75 per cent and increases of 125 and 175 per cent; note the sizes that would result when increasing or decreasing an 8- by 10-inch print.

2. Look at representative photographs in your local newspapers; determine whether they could be cropped closer or whether the picture editor "sized" them so that there was no excess space at the sides.

3. Analyze local newspapers to determine their styles of writing and setting cutlines.

4. Contact a local newspaper and invite the picture editor and chief photographer to attend question-and-answer sessions at different class meetings. Afterward, compare their viewpoints on news photography.

21

Sports, Women's, and Other Special Sections

Specialized sections provide a great many opportunities on newspapers. Two of the best known are the sports section, providing entry positions for young men, and the women's section, which enables young women to start in journalism. The latter sections have been changing greatly in recent years due to a number of factors, including the women's liberation movement and an increased awareness of the perspectives of democracy. Both sports and women's sections develop specialized writing and editing talents because of the audiences reached.

In addition, specialized sections include opportunities in producing the "general" magazines distributed with many Sunday magazines and the "special" supplements published in conjunction with events or occasions.

SPORTS SECTIONS

Sports *pages* have become so popular that on many newspapers they have developed into sports *sections*, offering a great depth of coverage. Many subscribers turn to the sports section before reading any other part of a newspaper. With the tendency toward more leisure time, sports undoubtedly will command a greater amount of newspaper space.

HISTORY OF SPORTS NEWS

Americans, traditionally competitive and fond of the outdoors, have shown a preoccupation with sports. Increased emphasis on sports coverage paralleled the industrialization of newspapers and the commercialization of sports in the era from 1890 to 1930. During this era, the average person enjoyed shorter work hours and higher pay, giving more time and money for sports. Coincidentally, more and more people moved to the cities—centers for sports events. Better news coverage itself also increased the interest in sports as it gave fans topics for discussions and betting.

"Name" sports reporters developed in the 1920s and 1930s. Associated Press increased emphasis in 1945 with its "sports wire," eventually refined to a service offering regional sports news exclusively. The growth of professional teams in many areas during the 1960s and 1970s called for even more space to be devoted to sports news.

THE WRITERS

Sports reporters are necessarily a similar breed to the writers of conventional news. They must know how to gather facts, type, write a correct sentence, spell, and follow a stylebook. They also must have a great interest in sports and must understand not only the rules of the games they cover but also their heritage and history. They must be curious about what is happening in the sporting world and interested in talking with coaches and players to obtain stories. Covering games is an important part of a sports reporter's job, but background stories also are vital. On larger newspapers, sports writers can develop specialties, while on smaller ones they serve as generalists in dealing with many phases of sports.

It should be emphasized that one does *not* need to have played a sport in order to write about it, and no longer are sports pages and sections dominated by males. Men *and* women serve on sports staffs and succeed according to their abilities as observers, writers, interviewers, and depth of interest in the particular sport.

The only barrier that women sports writers have not yet overcome is the "Do Not Enter" sign on the locker room door.

TYPES OF STORIES

A sports section is composed of basic stories. The "spot" news or game story is obviously the biggest played and most widely read. Other types of stories are the "advance," the "personality," the "feature," and the "round-up." Incidentally, both sexes read the sports section, but by far the biggest audience is composed of men. Sports writers know this, and so do the advertisers. The advertisements in sports sections deal with shaving products, auto tires and batteries, work clothing, and other items whose purchase ordinarily is decided by men.

Spot News Sports. The coverage of a game or a timely story involving a "name" personality provides the most widely read type of sports article. The game provides the conflict and culmination that the fans crave. "Objectivity" is a virtual impossibility in almost any story on sports, which in itself is subjec-

tive. There is a possibility of "fairness" in reporting what happened in a game, but even here there is more flexibility for expressiveness than would be permitted in a non-sports story.

In a great sense, a sports event may be likened to a dramatic production or play. The reporter who covers a sports event actually is writing a "review" of what happened, just as the drama critic reviews the presentation of a play. One group is on a field and the other occupies a stage, but both are playing for the pleasure of the audience. Both groups are craftsmen who have practiced, and aside from the score, the reporter comments on how well they perform.

Until recent years, the emphasis in sports stories was on the game's score. While the results obviously remain vital, more and more importance is placed on the interpretative approach, or "how" and "why" the game was won and what it means for the team's standing.

One reason for this changing emphasis is television, which by its very nature gives great insight into any event it covers. Spectators, or readers, therefore expect an interpretation or explanation of what they saw on television.

Despite these changes, scores are important and belong near the lead of a story. Other highly relevant facts, including the time and place of the next game, also are vital and should *not* go toward the end where they might be deleted by a make-up editor or printer trimming a story to fit a space.

Advance Stories. Articles telling about forthcoming games often discuss conditions that will help or hurt the competing teams. The professional betting odds also provide background of interest to fans.

Advance stories are by no means confined to a single article. The earlier stories may give information on practice sessions or coaches' forecasts. The reporter should have a background about his sports subject so that he can review the rivalry between the teams. The writer also can speculate on what will happen when the teams clash by comparing how each did when playing strong opponents. Shortly before the game, a story can deal with line-ups or the possible effect of weather.

DAVIS LEADS TROJAN OUTBURST

USC Swamps Cats, 48-6

By DWAIN ESPER
Staff Writer

The new look on the USC football team packed plenty of punch Saturday night, as a throng of 56,589, gladly will testify.

The Trojans thundered their way to a 48-6 victory over outclassed Northwestern in the Coliseum intersectional, and many went away wondering if John McKay's 1969 production might even be better than 1967 and 1968.

Clarence Davis, a transfer from East LA, dazzled the crowd with a touchdown the first time he touched the ball. In all, Davis carried 21 times for 165 yards and two scores — certainly qualifying as O.J. Simpson figures. Davis, of course, has replaced Simpson as tailback.

Quarterback Jimmy Jones zipped and flitted around the field making big gains on broken plays.

And a rock-ribbed defense cut the Wildcats to pieces, until McKay hauled out the reserves in the final period.

If that wasn't enough, the Wildcats were penalized eight times for 140 yards, making things even easier for the Trojans.

And McKay hinted of things to come with his own version of the triple option offense.

Impressive was the word for the Trojans.

The incredible Davis put the Trojans on the scoreboard the first time he handled the ball in the Coliseum. He took a pitchback from Jones and cruised around right end.

Following Jones and Evans, Davis broke loose along the north sidelines, and went all the way on a 73-yard dash. Although Ron Ayala missed the conversion, USC held a 6-0 lead after only 16 seconds of action.

Midway through the first period, the Trojans put together an 88 yard march, culminating in another Davis score. Actually the big gainer came on a penalty.

Pass Interference.

Jones lofted a long pass intended for Sam Dickerson. The ball fell incomplete, but officials ruled that Northwestern's Rick Telander was guilty of interference, giving the Trojans the ball on the Wildcat 10. It was a 38 yard penalty.

Three Davis runs, the final a short jaunt of two yards, got the score with less than a minute to go in the period. Then Jones passed to Bob Chandler for the two-point conversion.

David accumulated 116 yards on 10 carries for two touchdowns in the first quarter.

More penalties against Northwestern paved the way for the third USC score in the second quarter. One put the Wildcats back on their nine, bringing on a quick kick that went out to the 47.

Twice Jones completed passes to Evans and Mike Berry while the Wildcats were detected for infractions. With a third down on the Northwestern 11, Jones found Chandler in the end zone for the touchdown.

The Wildcats made one bid to get on the board before intermission on three consecutive completions by Dave Shelbourne to Mike Hudson and Ken Luxton (twice).

But the stiff Trojan defense, headed by ends Charlie Weaver and Jimmy Gunn, put a halt to the march, and USC took over on downs.

The Trojans padded their margin on the first series of the third quarter, a drive of 56 yards in nine plays, with Evans powering over from the one. Jones passed to Chandler for another two-point conversion to make it 28-0.

Jones gave way to Jim Fassel as the USC quarterback midway through a 79-yard drive later in the third quarter. Two unsportsmanlike conduct penalties on one play were assessed against the Northwestern bench, costing the Wildcats 30 yards.

Then Fassel stepped in to rifle a 27-yard pass to Dickerson for the touchdown. Ayala kicked goal.

Shortly after the fourth period opened, Fassel guided an 89-yard drive, highlighted once again by a 20-yard penalty. Lou Harris, a sophomore from Sacramento, scampered 25 yards for the score.

Cliff Culbreath, a substitute

USC: See Page A-2

PROUD MOMENT — Don Drysdale, wife Ginger and daughter Kelly share a proud moment surrounded by gifts at end of the pre-game ceremonies at Dodger Stadium which honored Big D for his achievements. Cocker spaniel was new addition, too.

—AP Wirephoto

ELEVATOR JOB—Wisconsin's Harry Alford (35) lifts UCLA's Bob Manning clear off his feet in Madison Saturday as teammates move in to add crusher. Bruins won, 34-23.

SPORTS

PAGE A-1 — PASADENA, CALIF., SUNDAY, SEPT. 28, 1969

Pancho, Richey Tangle

By DICK CHARNOCK
Special Correspondent

Ageless Pancho Gonzalez and youthful Cliff Richey cross raquets today in the titular round of the 43rd Pacific Southwest $30,000 tennis championships, being concluded at the Los Angeles Tennis Club.

They will split $6,000 between them, $4,000 to the winner and $2,000 to the loser, as final round prize money in the men's singles.

Gonzalez, king of the world tennis realm from 1950 to 1960 used all of his cunning and strategy to subdue Honolulu's James Osborne, 6-2, 7-9, 7-5. 41 year old Malibu tennis pro, Gonzalez grabbed the first set with a barrage of well earned aces and placements.

Double Faults

Osborne, despite his frequent double faults, broke Gonzalez' serve in the 16th game of the second set in that stanza's only service break. Serves were held in the third set until Osborne twice double faulted to allow a break through and Gonzalez was quick to grab the opportunity to run out the match with a 4-0 final game on serve.

In the Richey-Buchholz semi-final, the younger U.S. Davis Cup squad member from San Angelo, Texas, Richey, bounced around the court with dexterity personified, beating his pro opponent, Earl Buchholz of St. Louis, 6-4, 6-4.

Both semi-final round losers, Buchholz and Osborne took home checks for $1400 for their efforts in the men's singles.

In women's singles, Billie Jean King of Long Beach and Ann Haydon Jones of England, both touring pros in the George MacCall troupe, reached the title round for another of their many showdown matches. Mrs. King had to beat her perrenial nemesis, Nancy Richey of San Angelo, Tex., in her semi-final duel, Saturday. Mrs. King played a sparkling game in overcoming Miss Richey, 6-3, 6-3.

Earned Points

She pounded across 22 earned points to Miss Richey's 7, their errors were about even, 39 for Mrs. King and 36 for Miss Richey, with 3 double faults for Mrs. King and 4 for Miss Richey. Neither scored any service aces. Mrs. Jones gained the final round on Friday.

The men's doubles final will have Gonzalez on the center

PANCHO: See Page A-2

—Staff Photos by Herb Shoebridge

HAPPY EVENT—Star-News Sports Editor Joe Hendrickson (right) presents Don Drysdale with present from Baseball Writers' Association during pre-game ceremonies at Dodger Stadium Saturday afternoon. Drysdale retired during season and Dodgers and several organizations set up special event prior to game with Giants.

Wisconsin Second Best, 34-23

Greg Jones Gives Bruins Big Lift

Special to the Star-News

MADISON, Wis. — UCLA coach Tommy Prothro turned senior halfback Greg Jones loose for the first time in 1969 and the results proved to be extremely gratifying Saturday.

With Jones leading the way, the Bruins rolled to their third consecutive victory of the season, a 34-23 conquest of Wisconsin before 49,243 at Camp Randall Stadium.

Jones scored three touchdowns during a productive afternoon. He carried the ball 26 times, as compared to 24 in two previous victories over Oregon State and Pittsburgh.

With this opportunity to sparkle, Jones scampered for 145 yards, which compares to his 103 coming into the contest.

The effort gave Jones 1386 rushing yards in a Bruin uniform, tying him with Bill Kilmer at sixth place on the all time list with seven games to go. He has an excellent chance to overtake the UCLA recordholder, Kenny Washington, who compiled 1915 yards in 1937-9.

Prothro hinted Jones may operate in high gear when he employed Bob Manning at fullback in place of Mickey Cureton. Manning's blocking ability promotes Jones running skills whereas Cureton is more of a breakaway threat and has to have the ball.

In a way Prothro's use of Jones mirrored the tailback offense made famous by John McKay at USC with Mike Garrett and O. J. Simpson.

Joining Jones as a hero for the Bruins was quarterback Dennis Dummit, who completed 14 of 21 passes for 209 yards and one touchdown (to Jones). Dummit also scored twice himself on short keepers into the line.

The Bruins thought they scored a safety on the first play of the game when Greg (Grape Juice) Johnson fielded Bob Geddes' kickoff. Johnson was nailed by Bob Pifferini in the end zone. But the play was called back because UCLA was offside on the kickoff.

Johnson returned the next Geddes boot to the 42, from which point the Badgers moved downfield to the Bruin six. Key gain was a 23-yard bolt by tailgack Joe Dawkins.

The UCLA defense then stiffened, bringing on Roger Jaeger for a successful 24-yard field goal.

Dummit marshalled his forces for a 64-yard march in 15 plays to the Wisconsin one. But the fired-up Badgers held for downs as the crowd screamed encouragement.

As the second period opened, UCLA achieved possession on the Wisconsin 47. Dummit's pass to George Farmer picked up 27 yards, setting up Zenon Andrusyshyn for a 45-yard field goal. But it was short, leaving Wisconsin in front 3-0.

A fumble gave UCLA another chance at the Badger 33, and Dummit didn't waste any time getting on the scoreboard. He completed passes to Farmer and Jones and then took it in himself on a keeper from the one. Andrusyshyn kicked goal for the 7-3 Bruin lead after 2½ minutes of second quarter action.

A fumble by Jones on the UCLA 15 led to Yaeger's second field goal of the day, a 37-yarder. Thus the Badgers trailed 7-6.

Ron Carver, the sensational sophomore safety, got the Bruins out of their rut to initiate two touchdowns.

His 42-yard return of the Badger kickoff put the Bruins on the 48. After a completion to Gwen Cooper for 16 yards, Dummit let fly to Farmer on the Wisconsin 10. Although the pass fell incomplete, Wisconsin's Nat Butler was called for pass interference. Jones then slashed over for the touchdown, giving UCLA a 14-6 lead.

Carver's next contribution was an interception of a Neil Graff pass and 23-yard return to the Badger seven. A six-yard dash by Jones set up Dummit for another one-yard keeper.

The Badgers got in position for Yaeger to boot a 48-yard field, his third of the afternoon, to cut the Bruin lead to 21-9 at intermission.

In the third quarter a Dummit fumble on the Wisconsin 11 nullified the first Bruin scoring opportunity.

But Dummit made up for it

GREG: See Page A-8

Dodgers Win in 11th

Big D. Day Does In Giants, 2-1

By JOE HENDRICKSON
Sports Editor

Big D Day meant destruction and disaster for the San Francisco Giants.

For the Los Angeles Dodgers, it stood for delight.

The Dodgers defeated the Giants 2-1 in 11 innings to knock the bay area tormentors 2½ games behind the Atlanta Braves in the National League Western Division Saturday afternoon. With only four games to play, the Giants are nearly out of it as Atlanta's magic number reached two.

The 36,170 faithful Dodger fans, who came to the park to cheer Don Drysdale on his day of honor, enjoyed a most satisfying victory over the team that had knocked the Dodgers out of it a week ago and held a 12-4 edge over the Dodgers for the season.

Len Gabrielson, pinch hitter extraordinary for Los Angeles this year with 12 pinch hits in 35 appearances for a .343 average in that role, singled off reliefer Don McMahon with one out to score Manny Mota from second base with the winning run in the last of the 11th. Mota had singled to right off southpaw reliefer Ron Bryant and was advanced by Willie Davis who singled to left, forcing Giant manager Clyde King to call upon the veteran McMahon, a right hander, when Walter Alston had chosen John Miller to bat for winning pitcher Jim Brewer. Alston immediately switched to Gabrielson who delivered without any extra festivities. Gabe's hit was a line shot to right center that Willie Mays handled too deep for anything but a token underhand throw — a throw that pretty well demonstrated how little was left of the Giant pennant bid.

The Dodgers missed a great chance to win it in the 10th when they filled the bases with one out only to have Bryant get out of it when pinch hitter Billy Sudakis hit a shot to short for a double play after Bryant started with a 3-0 count on Billy.

And so an eight-game Dodger losing streak ended to set the stage for today's 1 p.m. duel between Bill Singer (19-11) who can pass Juan Marichal (20-11) if Singer can annex his 20th. Winning 20 games is tough business, as Claude Osteen found out when a fine nine-inning effort wasn't enough as he was

BIG D: See Page A-2

LA BACKED IN OLYMPIC GAMES BID

SEOUL (AP) — South Korea has assured two Los Angeles city representatives of its support for the American city's bid to host the 1976 Olympics.

A spokesman for the Korean Olympic Committee said Saturday the assurance was given when Deputy Mayor Joseph M. Quinn and Harbor Commissioner Fred Isamu Wada of Los Angeles met Korean sports leaders.

SAN FRANCISCO LOS ANGELES

—AP Wirephoto

SHORT GAIN—USC tailback Clarence Davis (28) is stopped for short gain by Northwestern's Joel Hall (66) during Trojans-Wildcats game Saturday night at Coliseum. Coming in are John Derning (83) and John Rodman.

SHOCKERS

California 17, Indiana 10
Tennessee 45, Auburn 19
Kentucky 10, Mississippi 9
Oklahoma State 24, Houston 18
Fresno 28, Montana State 20

Baseball Standings

NATIONAL LEAGUE

AMERICAN LEAGUE

Figure 21–1 This sports page from a medium-sized city daily newspaper combines local and national events to provide appeal to a broad readership.

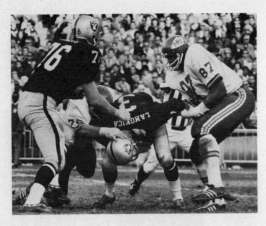

Figure 21–2 Despite action in an exciting game, the photographer produced a sharp, sparkling print of a moment of interest to sports readers. (*Oakland Tribune* Photo by Lonnie Wilson)

Figure 21–3 Moving in close for an unusual view added interest to this photo. Fans show great interest in stories regarding well-known or local players. (Panax Corporation Photo)

Feature Articles. The sports writer is fortunate in being able to deal with many facets of the field he is reporting. Here are typical areas open to him:

The personality sketch deals with a coach or player and is a favorite for readers. The story may delve into the subject's background, hobbies, his leisure hours, or his outlook on the sport. Reporters get their information simply by sitting down and chatting with the subject.

The team story is similar to the individual sketch except that it is more general. Other teams and players often are compared, with the reporter using a rich background of knowledge or extensive research to provide statistics on scores and information on players.

A particular sport also can make a story, with the reporter assembling information on developments in a particular area. New players, coaches, popularity, and techniques in a sport can be woven into stories to add considerable interest.

Training programs help advise the fans what they may expect when the teams clash. Recruitment programs, always fascinating because they introduce new names with expected potential, present stories closely related to those concerned with training.

Inter-team rivalry, while known best in the stadium or on the field, also develops when teams bid against each other for players. Reporters should recognize that, outside of the scholastic level, teams are businesses whose owners expect to make profits. Record payments for telecasts or arguments over stadium rentals also make stories.

The fans also can produce interesting feature articles. Every sport and team has its oldest and youngest followers. Fans often become angry, and stories telling about these conflicts are of interest to other fans.

Use of Names. Names rate high in importance in all news stories, since people like to see their own names in print and those of people they know; this is only human nature. Names are even more important in writing sports stories because the coaches and players are the personalities that fascinate the fans. Without names, sports stories would hold little interest to readers.

Sports writers usually have biographical information on team members, making pertinent material readily available for background in their stories. The public relations representatives who prepare this data also eagerly schedule interviews for the press. Reporters have access to locker rooms, where they can talk with the players. To emphasize: names are highly important in sports stories, and articles that lack names will not hold reader interest.

Scores Alone. Larger dailies cover such a great geographical area that they are unable to run stories of any length on anything but

Figure 21–4 The photographer captured an exciting moment at a baseball game, thus making the word-story more interesting. Surveys show that many male readers turn to the sports section before looking at other pages. (*Oakland Tribune* Photo by Lonnie Wilson)

major sports events. Their space problems force them, therefore, to use scores alone as their only coverage of many games. In doing so, their goal is to provide "spot news" with the scores, knowing that readers will consult community newspapers for details. Weeklies and small dailies fortunately can do a good job in covering most sports events in their circulation areas. This ability is a factor that makes these newspapers so important to their communities.

ETHICS IN SPORTS WRITING

Sports reporting, like other forms of writing, attracts people who want special favors. Sometimes this is especially true since sports events are heavily dependent on advance coverage to attract spectators. The ethical sports reporter, however, remembers that his loyalties belong to the newspaper and its readers and writers fairly.

The sports reporter, like other news writers, is paid to provide news for his newspaper, not to publicize events for commercial or noncommercial promoters. When events are worthy of publicity, the writer should give them the space they honestly deserve. To overpublicize an event because of a gift or other reward shows a lack of forthrightness.

Many reporters, in sports or other fields, are inclined to reject any gifts valued at more than $5 or that come at any other time than Christmas. The team or individual presenting gifts presumably acts out of gratitude and friendship. The thought behind the gift, rather

Figure 21–5 Routine games sometimes develop exciting moments. (*Oakland Tribune* Photo by Lonnie Wilson)

Figure 21–6 He missed! The photographer was ready at a critical moment in this race. (*Oakland Tribune* Photo by Lonnie Wilson)

than the monetary value, is the most important thing. Declining expensive presents gives the reporter integrity and keeps him independent.

Ethics in all kinds of reporting extends to confidences and the treatment of individuals.

Athletes and coaches often confide in reporters, giving information that they obviously do not expect to be published. The good writer, when advised he is being given a confidence, will not betray that trust. Reporters also should be forthright and honest in obtaining information and should not misrepresent a situation to make someone talk.

Fairness also extends to matters of race, religion, geographical origin, or national background. These factors have no bearing on the abilities of a player or coach.

WOMEN'S SECTIONS

Specialized sections for women's interests have changed immensely in the past half century, and they will continue to change as woman's role in society expands. The trend, more and more, is for these sections to provide feature news for the *entire* family.

HISTORY OF WOMEN'S SECTIONS

The rise of newspaper sections for women's interests parallels the development of the penny or popular press (1833–1880) in America. James Gordon Bennett, publisher of the New York Herald, surmised that the woman factory worker or retail clerk would be fascinated to know what the woman in high society wore, how she entertained, who her guests were, and the style in which her children made their debuts and were married.

Bennett guessed correctly, and "society" pages were copied throughout America. In New York City, society pages dealt primarily with the Social Register's "400." When newspapers throughout the nation copied society pages or sections, those who were considered to be the local elite dominated the coverage, and the rank-and-file reader presumably enjoyed this news. Minority and middle-class groups had little chance to win a mention on these snobbish pages.

Traditional society pages began to change during World War II, which produced a more mobile social structure and made people begin to question a "closed" society. Middle-class families found that newspapers would mention their parties and weddings, although a community's "exclusive" women's clubs—and their members—continued to dominate the pages. Most society sections were little more than a repetitive diet of fashions, food, brides, and bridge.

THE "NEW" SECTIONS

Major changes began in women's pages in the 1960s, a time marked by increased awareness of equality and readerships distinguished by better educational backgrounds and inclined to view artificial social structures as meaningless.

Spearheading the changes were metropolitan dailies, which found they no longer had space to cover society in large geographic areas and noted that interest in these events waned as subscribers moved to the suburban areas. First, many newspapers dropped the "society" designation and became "women's" sections, at the same time adding features of interest and value to the woman *not* interested in club or social life. This trend was followed in varying degrees by weekly or smaller daily newspapers.

The next step was more radical, with decreased use of conventional contents and an emphasis on material of interest to both sexes. Replacing "women's" news were reviews of books, motion pictures, and plays; articles on family planning and social welfare, for example; and serious discussions of national and international problems. These sparkling, challenging sections used weddings, engagements, club items, and teas only in abbreviated form.

Medium-sized and smaller daily and weekly newspapers have resisted changes in the traditional contents of women's sections. In doing so, they have made themselves valuable to subscribers in supplementing the coverage provided by metropolitan dailies.

TRADITIONAL CONTENTS

Newspapers in smaller communities where

Around the Island' Luncheons Scheduled April 15

AROUND THE ISLAND – Mrs. Robert Rebuschatis (left), president of the Republican Women's Club of Alameda, and Mrs. LaVerne Randall, general chairman of the "Around the Island" luncheons April 15, check map to see locations of the 11 homes open for the annual spring event.

11 Homes Open For GOP Women's Party

Eleven homes will be the setting for luncheons when the Republican women's Club of Alameda presents its annual "around the Island" luncheon on Tuesday, April 15.

The committee, headed by Mrs. LaVerne Randall as chairman, promises a delightful luncheon and funfilled afternoon for members and guests.

Following luncheon, there will be bridge for those wishing, while at the home of Mrs. William Tildesley on Northwood Drive there will be special games for those not wishing to play bridge, according to Mrs. Robert Rebuschatis, president of the club.

Reservations Still Available

Homes where reservations are still available include those of Mrs. S. Chesley Anderson on San Jose Avenue, Mrs. A. Hubbard Moffitt Jr. on Grand Street, Mrs. Sidney Traver on Eastshore Drive, where Mrs. O. M. Simmons will be co-hostess; Mrs. William Kirkland on Palmera Court, where Mrs. Donald Payne will be co-hostess; Mrs. M. G. Harvey on Marina Drive, with Mrs. Russell Federspiel and Mrs. Joseph Bianco as cohostesses; and Mrs. Tildesley on Northwood Drive.

Homes where reservations are already filled include those of Mrs. Fay Fletcher on Otis Drive, where Mrs. Jack Daniels and Mrs. Rich Birkholm are to co-hostesses; Mrs. Wallace Short on Fernside Boulevard; and Mrs. Sidney Dowling on Waterview Isle, with Mrs. Russell Franck and Mrs. Markham Happ as co-hostesses.

Plans And Arrangements

Assisting Mrs. Randall with plans and arrangements for the annual event are Mrs. Stewart Lindsey, Mrs. Lee Keilbar and Mrs. Eugene Shortt, who have charge of the food; Mrs. Norman Eierman, table decorations.

Mrs. Malcolm Kangas is chairman of hostesses, with Mrs. William Kittredge in charge of prizes, and Mrs. Al Wilson in charge of programs.

Tickets and reservations, at $3, may be secured by calling Mrs. Hugh Brenton, ticket chairman, LA 2-3439.

in the Times-Star Social Whirl

BARBARA STEVENSON
WOMEN'S EDITOR

Page 4 Saturday, March 29, 1969

Name Designers For 'Symphony House' Event April 13-27

Ten well-known Bay Area designers will produce a showplace of interior design at "Symphony House", 284 Indian Road, Piedmont, to be open for public showing from Sunday, April 13, through Sunday, April 27.

The project to benefit the Oakland Symphony Orchestra is the second annual joint venture of the Oakland Symphony Guild in cooperation with the California Northern District Chapter of the American Institute of Interior Designers.

Various rooms in the contemporary style home of G. William Jamieson will serve as showcases for the art of the interior designer. Of added interest will be a special display of landscaping for pool and deck areas.

East Bay A.I.D. members participating include Carl H. Braune, Melvin Collins, Martha Groves, Virginia Hussey, Barbara Maynard of Lafayette, Ruth Dibble and Elsie Semrau.

Mrs. Michael Rafton, show chairman, announced a list of Guild members serving as chairmen. Mrs. John L. Bonham, is designers liaison. Jim Aldrich serves in this capacity with the A.I.D. group. Mrs. George W. Shomas will coordinate fashion showings which will form part of the daily events scheduled throughout the two weeks.

Ticket co-chairmen are Mrs. Raymond J. Bergez, and Mrs. Herbert Severns. Tickets at $3 are available in advance by writing to Symphony House, Box 11179, Oakland.

Other committee appointments include Mrs. J. D. Howard, staffing; Mrs. Raymond S. Plock, souvenir program; Mrs. Colette Samuelsen, ways and means; Mrs. John Karsant, refreshments; Mrs. Cecil S. Riley, posters; Mrs. Ruth Oliver, transportation; Mrs. David S. Tucker, Jr., printing; Mrs. Charles G. Davis, donations; Mrs. James Schmerl, bill stuffers and flyers; Mrs. Robert B. Holroyd, staffing for season ticket sales desk; Mrs. Clinton W. Lee, preview party; Mrs. George Koregelos, clerical, Mrs. Thomas F. Kling, housekeeping; Mrs. William S. Weichert, boutique; Mrs. John A. Poulos, special events; and Mrs. Wanda Harkins, publicity.

Among special events planned are music under the direction of Oakland Symphony concertmaster, Nathan Rubin; "art in action" by California College of Arts and Crafts and Technical High School, Oakland; flower arrangement demonstration by Vi Martinson; a musical trio from the Oakland Symphony Youth Chamber Orchestra directed by Robert Hughes; oil paintings by Edith Gardner, also paintings by Swazo Hinds, Victor Abitol and Karen Rafton; and poetry reading by Barbara Westerfield.

A black-tie champagne reception from 6 to 8 p.m. at Symphony House on Saturday, April 12, will initiate the benefit.

Opera League To Meet

Program chairman, Mrs. Leslie Houdlette, announces that Pietro Marcagni's opera "Cavalleria Rusticana" will be presented at the April 15 meeting of the East Bay Opera League, to be held at the Claremont Hotel.

Luncheon parties before the performance, to be held in the Claremont's Garden Room, will include the President's table, headed by Mrs. Oliver J. Meigs.

The story of "Cavalleria Rusticana" opens in a Sicilian village on Easter Sunday, with quiet, prayer-like music. The role of Santuzza, the worried fiancee of the fickle Turiddu, will be sung by soprano, Corinne Christopherson. Turiddu, a recently returned soldier, is having an affair with Lola, wife of Alfio, the village teamster. This role will be played by tenor Victor Hubbard. Lola will be portrayed by mezzo soprano, Marjorie Pinto. The part of Mamma Lucia (mother of Turiddu) will be sung by contralto, Mildred Owen Simon.

The East Bay Opera League, through Mrs. Irvin C. Cotanch of Moraga, has invited a group of students from the Joaquin Moraga High School to attend this performance.

Ladies Home Society Installs Officers At 97th Annual Meeting

Mrs. John A. Barthrop has accepted the gavel for a third year as president of the Ladies Home Society, probably the "grandmother" of women's philanthropic groups, at the 97th annual meeting held earlier this month at the Matilda E. Brown Home for elderly women.

Mrs. Paul C. Skinner, a past president, was the center of attention at the gathering, as this business session and luncheon was the 47th annual meeting she has attended.

Elected to serve with Mrs. Barthrop were Mrs. J. Frederick Seulberger, first vice president; Mrs. E. C. Lipman, second vice president; Mrs. Herbert Shuey, third vice president and garden chairman; Mrs. Truman Mitchell, recording secretary; Mrs. J. Marcus Hardin, corresponding secretary; Mrs. William Blair Smith, treasurer, and Mrs. Frank H. Pierce, financial secretary.

Serving on the executive committee for the coming year will be Mesdames Frederick M. Dorward, Nils O. Eklund, Richard Lyman, James Hannan, Howard McLure, William Wolfenden.

Mrs. Steven D. Bechtel is chairman of the membership committee; Mrs. Hugo Methman is chairman of public relations and Mrs. Bestor Robinson, will have charge of activities in the home.

In 1872 a group of women formed a sewing club to aid those left destitute by the Chicago Fire, and the group was long known as the Ladies Relief Society. In its early years it supported an infant's home and a children's home, as well as the home for the elderly.

As other organizations became active (many with an assist from this pioneering society) responsibility was transferred and only the home for the elderly women remained under its wing. In 1956 the name of the group was changed to the Ladies Home Society.

Egg Hunt Scheduled Tomorrow

If you see Easter bunnies in Franklin Park tomorrow afternoon, they will be assisting with the annual Easter Egg Hunt sponsored by the Alameda Family Service League.

The annual egg hunt for children from two through seven years of age, will start promptly at 3 p.m. in Franklin Park. There will be special prize for lucky winners, and there also will be ice cream and balloons.

Tickets for the hunt must be obtained in advance and may be secured by calling Mrs. Frank Ghiglione, LA 2-6243, or Mrs. William Dodge, LA 3-7802, who are co-chairmen of the event.

Proceeds will go to the Alameda Family Service Agency for its counseling program.

Among mothers who will be assisting with the hunt are Mrs. Lloyd Hurwitz, Mrs. Robert McPeak, Mrs. Gene King and Mrs. Dan Rourke.

REPUBLICAN PARTY – Eleven homes will be open for the "Around the Island" luncheons of the Republican Women's Club of Alameda, and working on decorations for the tables for the luncheon are (center photo) Mrs. Norman Eierman, chairman of decorations, and Mrs. Hugh Brenton, who is handling tickets and reservations. Enjoying a cup of coffee while they plan the food for the luncheon are Mrs. Eugene Shortt, Mrs. Stewart Lindsey and Mrs. Lee Keilbar, who are serving on the food committee for the event. Homes are rapidly filling for the party, and reservations should be made as soon as possible.

(Bordanaro and Zarrone Photos)

Hadassah Program

An armchair trip to Cochin, India, the vanishing Jewish community (population 100) which recently commemorated the 400th anniversary of the founding of the synagogue there, will be featured at the next meeting of the Oakland and East Bay Chapter of Hadassah.

The meeting is scheduled for noon Tuesday in the William Stern Hall in Oakland.

The program will be presented by Seymour Fromer, who was in Cochin with a delegation of Indian leaders. He will present a resume of Jewish life in India.

Director of the Jewish Education Council of Alameda and Contra Costa Counties, he is also director of the Judah L. Magnes Memorial Museum in Berkeley.

World Premiere Of Play Slated

The world premiere of Moody Blanchard's "The Vindication of Richard III" wil open April 3 at the California State College, Hayward, Highlands Playhouse at 8 p.m.

The play is directed by James Cady, a graduate student at the college, and a former professional actor.

"The Vindication of Richard III" is the culmination of years of research into the life and history surrounding the notorious British monarch who is best known through Shakespeare's play.

Performances of the play will be given April 3, 4, 5 and 6 at 8 p.m. in the Highlands Playhouse on the Cal State, Hayward, campus. Ticket prices are $1 for students and $1.50 general admission. Reservations may be made by phoning the Auxiliary Foundation Office at 538-8000.

Program At CHN

Electronic music and "environmental" dance will fill the College of the Holy Names gymnasium tomorrow at 4 p.m. when the College Dance Group presents its program "Looking 4 Directions."

Mrs. Ruth Hatfield will direct the CHN Dance Group, dance students from Fremont High School and members of the Berkeley Teen Dance Workshop in the ultra-contemporary performance.

The dancers will use the full environment of the gymnasium for their program placing dances at the perimeter of the room and utilizing its furniture as well as its four walls as the title of the program suggests.

The program will be a varied one with dances done to poetry, to a Marshall McLuhan tape, and to music. Featured will be a dance expecially choreographed to "Spatial Sonorities: Electronic Tape No. 3X," an electronic composition by Sister Theresa Agnes Breier of the College Music Faculty. This will be performed on a set of varied levels by the entire college group. Also included will be a group dance choreographed by Mrs. Hatfield to Vivaldi's "Concerto for Guitar and Strings" and a number of solos choreographed by the dancers performing them.

Tickets for "Looking 4 Directions" are $1 to the general public and 75 cents for students and will be available at the door.

Figure 21–7 A well-planned women's page following the traditional approach, which emphasizes the social and club news. Relatively few women attend the meetings, but theoretically many are interested in the stories.

𝒲omen 𝒯oday

The REGISTER Tuesday (m) September 19, 1972 D1

Anchor Weighed In NB For Thursday Club Tea

The annual Friendship Tea of Thursday Morning Club of Newport Beach is set for 3:30 p.m. Friday, Sept. 22, in Balboa Bay Club. Special guests will be prospective members of the group and leaders of the community.

Mrs. Robert E. Anderson, special events chairman for the tea, is being assisted by the Mmes. John R. Eden, J. Thomas Callaway and Fordyce Boyd. Newest fall fashions, modeled by members of the Mannequin Section and commentated by Pat Harrison, will be provided by Lido Fashions, Newport Beach.

The receiving line will include past presidents, headed by Mrs. Robert W. Roper, founder, first president and honorary life member of the club. Others are the Mmes. John E. Williams, Jack W. Marshall, Robert W.

Goedhart, James A. Lee and Robert D. Smith.

Continuing their custom of previous years, Thursday Morning Club has extended special invitations to leading women in the area. Included are the Mmes. Dorothy Sheeley, Newport Beach city librarian; Howard Circle, Child Guidance Clinic; Wilhelm De-Nijs, Services for the Blind, Incorporated, and Daniel G. Aldrich Jr., wife of the Chancellor of University of California at Irvine.

Since 1960 Thursday Morning Club has made contributions to various organizations in the area. Among recipients last year were Services for the Blind, Inc.; Unicamp, Newport Beach City Library and United Cerebral Palsy Association of Orange County.

Mrs. James C. Stamper first vice president and program chairman, has

announced the entertainment schedule for the club's general meetings held on the second Thursday of each month in Balboa Bay Club. They include Robert L. Baltzer, newspaper wine columnist; Janette Farrell of the Lawrence Welk Show and in March, Kay St. Germain in the Airporter Inn.

Current officers serving with the president, Mrs. John Morris, are the Mmes. James Stamper, William McFarland, Robert E. Anderson, J. O'Hara Smith, vice presidents; John P. Wright, J. Wescott Loos, Mario C. Pacini, William F. Blocher, secretaries; and John D. Carson, treasurer.

Sections offered members this year will include art and crafts, bowling, bridge, globetrotters, golf, hi-timers, mannequins, singlesires, tennis and theater.

FRIENDSHIP TEA — Balboa Bay Bay Club will be the scene of the annual Friendship Tea of the Thursday Morning Club of Newport Beach slated for Friday, Sept. 22. Dropping anchor for the 3:30 p.m. event are (from left) the Mmes. John R. Eden, Herald Standefer and John Morris.

Erma Bombeck

Woman Years Behind In Ironing Is Housewife After Her Own Heart

An ad in a midwest newspaper read, WANTED: Woman to do ironing for housewife 10 years behind in everything. Must have strong courage and sense of humor.

Now there's a woman I could live next door to in perfect harmony. I iron "By appointment only." I learned long ago that if I ironed and hung three dresses in my daughter's closet, she would change three times during dinner.

The other day my son wanted me to iron his jeans for a class play. "Which leg faces the audience?" I asked with my iron poised in mid-air.

"Boy," he said, "you're sure not like Mrs. Breck."

I hadn't thought about Mrs. Breck in years. She was an antiseptic old broad who used to live two houses down from me. She had an annoying habit of putting her ironing board up on Tuesdays and putting it away again at the end of the day. (What can you expect from a woman who ironed belt buckles?)

One afternoon I dropped in on her as she was pressing the tongues in her son's tennis shoes.

"You know what you are, Mrs. Breck?" I asked. "A drudge."

"Oh, I enjoy ironing," she said.

"You keep talking like that and someone is going to put you in a home."

"What's so bad about ironing?" she grinned.

"No one does it," I snapped. "Did you ever see the women on soap operas iron? They're just normal, American housewives. But do you ever see them in front of an ironing board? No! They're out having abortions, committing murder, blackmailing their boss, undergoing surgery, having fun! If you weren't chained to this ironing board you, too, could be out doing all sorts of exciting things."

"Like what?" she chuckled, pressing the wrinkle out of a pair of sweat socks and folding them neatly.

"You could give Tupperware parties; learn to Scuba dive, learn hotel management while sitting under a hair dryer, have an affair with the Avon lady's unemployed brother-in-law, sing along with Jack La-Lanne, collect antique barbed wire, take a course in Hebrew Flower Arranging, start chain letters . . I don't know, woman, use your imagination!"

I read the newspaper ad again. It intrigued me so that I dialed the number and waited.

"Hello, Mrs. Breck speaking . . ."

Son of a gun. It sure makes you feel good when you had a part in someone's success, doesn't it.?

Copyright 1972 Field Enterprises, Inc.

Leaguers To Enjoy Oriental Cuisine

Anaheim Assistance League will hold an "Evening of the Moon Flower" Sunday, Sept. 24, at 5 p.m. in the home of the Ted Dinklers, Anaheim.

An oriental meal will be prepared by league members from special recipes. Assisteens will serve. Music for listening and dancing will be provided by Gene Galente and artist Roger Kuntz will display paintings and sculpture.

Mrs. Ralph Stokes, vice president of ways and means is chairman of the affair. On her committee are the Mmes. Jack Flammer, C. B. Miller, Alex Morales, Kenneth Keesee, Emmett A. Tompkins and C. J. Vandruff.

The evening will be the league's fund raising project for the year and money will go into ways and means projects.

ORIENTAL EVENING — The gardens of the Ted Dinkler home in Anaheim will be the setting for Anaheim Assistance's League's "Evening of the Moon Flower." Preparing for the evening are from left Mrs. Ralph Stokes, chairman for the event and Mrs. Albert Burton, Assistance League President.

Figure 21-8 Society pages primarily dealing with activities available to a relatively small segment of the population remain a part of many newspapers. The theory is that the general readership wishes to hear about these clubs.

Caution Can Discourage Attacker

By ALLISON DEERR
Of the Daily Pilot Staff

Like the burglar, he uses a cover of darkness and looks for targets behind unlocked doors an. in unguarded homes.

Like the obscene phone caller, he anticipates reactions of shock, fear and hurt.

But the rapist also is an immediate, frightening threat to his victim.

A rape victim seldom wants to talk about the experience. Many never report the crime, so their attackers go free to look for other victims.

Why do the victims react in this manner? Is there anything a woman can do to prevent rape? How should she react? Should she report it? What are the legal procedures? How does she cope with the psychological problems that may follow?

PREVENTIVE MEASURES

Police, attorneys, psychologists and the victims themselves agree that women should do everything possible to make it hard for the would-be attacker to find a victim.

Women who live alone, it was advised, should not list their names in the telephone book except by initials. Names on mailboxes should be avoided or kept to last name only.

A dog can be a warning device. Learning a little judo, karate or basic self-defense techniques might be helpful.

Keeping doors and windows locked as well as adding extra locks and a form of alarm system will discourage intruders looking for easy access. Don't admit casual male acquaintances who arrive for no apparent reason.

RUSE USED

Many rapists gain entry into the home of a potential victim by using a ruse such as asking to use the telephone to report an accident, to get directions or to sell something. The single woman, or single women living together should never let strange men know there is no man in the house.

"If someone asks to use the phone to call ambulance or police, don't let him in," a police officer advised, "tell him you'll call the police or better yet, your husband will. Go into another room and talk to your husband. This will discourage the intruder."

"Don't be afraid to call the police if you think someone is following you home or if someone suspicious is hanging around the neighborhood.

"Even if he has no ill intentions, police will then have a field identification card on him on file if he's reported again. It may help catch him later."

A police investigator, who deals primarily with the woman victims, said that "each woman reacts in her own way. Some try to fight the attacker. Sometimes this provokes him to be more violent. Other times he may just leave.

Other victims have decided just to submit."

NO REACTION

Pierce Ommaney, director of the Psychological Guidance Center, explained that the best reaction may be no reaction.

"All torture is an unconscious identification with the victim," he explained, adding that this is true of child-beating and obscene phone calls as well as rape.

"The torturer is feeling emotionally what he assumes his victim will feel. If the victim does not react the way he planned it, the victim defeats his purpose for the attack."

He likened this to the person who m..kes obscene phone calls. If he gets no reaction, he does not call back.

Ommaney added that the persons who commit these kinds of crime want to feel strong, be the aggressor. They cannot succeed in normal relationships, so they resort to abnormal ones. His colleague Ommaney said that he works with rape

said, however, that screaming will scare off many attackers.

A key, he said, is that the last thing these people want is to be caught. Making a lot of noise in most cases will scare the rapist away because he can always find a new victim.

DON'T REPORT IT

Most women do not report rape, he added, because they feel guilt or shame, are afraid of their spouse's actions, are frightened of the legal process and the treatment they may receive by callous officials.

In Washington, D.C. and in New York, clinics have been opened for rape victims, staffed by sympathetic lay people rather than police. Victims are much more willing to talk to someone other than police or immediate family, and many more cases have been reported. In some cases the contact is by telephone.

victims by getting them to talk to him. Talking it out, he added, relieves the mind of the victim.

Along with fear of husbands or relatives blaming the victim, many women are reluctant to report an assault because they know little or nothing about court proceedings.

NO ABUSE

According to Stewart Grant, deputy district attorney in the Orange County Harbor District Court, Newport Beach, the procedures are relatively simple.

After statements have been taken from all concerned, he explained, police investigate the case and present a report to the district attorney's office.

Then a date is set for a preliminary hearing where it is determined if there is enough evidence that a crime has been committed. Next step is a trial in superior court.

(See ATTACKER, Page 19)

Rape: Some Myths Debunked

Women
BEA ANDERSON, Editor
Thursday, September 2, 1972   Page 17

Victims may be surprised by their attackers but experts say chances are they have met before.

Rape is probably the most myth-ridden of all crimes.

In a two-year study of Philadelphia rape cases, reported in his book "Patterns of Forcible Rape," sociologist Menachem Amir debunked several.

Among his findings were:

— Rape is not typically the manic, impulsive affair portrayed in novels. Three quarters of the rapes he studied were planned in advance. One third of the victims knew the rapist prior to the attack.

— In two-thirds of the cases the rapist hadn't been drinking.

— There was no evidence that these men raped because they were deprived of other sexual outlets.

— Most rapes occurred on weekends. Peak hours were 8 p.m. to midnight on Friday nights.

— Most offenders were unmarried and ranged in age from 15 to 25. Peak ages for victims were 15 to 19, but ages of victims ranged above and below these figures.

He offered this composite picture of the victim:

"The typical victim will be young — age 10 to 19 — and unmarried. Her assailant (or assailants as she has an almost even chance of being attacked by more than one man) will be in his late teens.

"He will have met or seen her somewhere and planned to rape her. She will be raped on a weekend night and when she is alone. She will be raped in her home neighborhood and probably indoors.

"She will be threatened with words, gestures or a weapon and she will submit quickly and out of fear. She will be handled roughly and probably bruised but she will not be brutally beaten."

Tidiness Helps Burglars Clean Up

By CAROL MOORE
Of the Daily Pilot Staff

When it comes to burglary, harried housewives will be glad to know the "lived-in look" is a good deterrent and dusty fingerprints are good clues.

Investigator Walt Silver of the Costa Mesa Police Department advised Mesa-Harbor Club members to leave lights, radio or stereo on when going shopping or out for the evening.

Or a few toys scattered about will give the impression of occupancy during a vacation or prolonged absence.

"And after a burglary, don't bother to clean up the house before the police come," he said. "We appreciate the thoughtfulness but the evidence you wipe off or put away is important."

Silver admitted that a determined burglar can gain entry to a house no matter what.

HARDER JOB

"But 75 percent of residential

burglaries are done by juveniles, 12 to 18 years old. So yc1 can deter the crime by making it more difficult. Time, noise and light work against a burglar."

Some degree of meticulousness, however, does pay off.

—Join Operation Identification by borrowing an electric pencil from the police department, etching your driver's license or Social Security number on valuables and receiving a membership decal to be placed in a window.

—Take pictures of other valuables with serial numbers either showing or printed on the photograph.

—Make certain all windows and doors are secured before departure. An empty garage advertises your absence so close the doors.

—Don't leave notes saying you are gone or put keys in such obvious places as flower pots, doormats, mailboxes or over the doorway.

MORE CHECKS

The precautions are longer for longer absences:

—Discontinue milk, newspaper and other deliveries ahead of time.

—Arrange for lawn care and have someone remove advertising circulars and other debris regularly.

—Notify the post office to hold your mail or have a trustworthy person pick it up daily. This is particularly important for apartment house tenants where stuffed mail receptacles are a give-away when no one is home.

—Have the phone temporarily disconnected. Burglars may try calling to find out whether anyone is in.

—Don't publicize your plans when you leave. Some burglars specialize in reading newspaper accounts of vacation activities.

—Tell your local police or sheriff station how long you will be gone.

(See CLEANING UP, Page 19)

Tell-tale signs, such as notes, darkness and unchanged windows, show burglars when homes are empty.

Figure 21–9 This "women's page" from the *Orange Coast* (Calif.) *Daily Pilot* is typical of the new approaches that are replacing the traditional society news.

Witchcraft Made Her a 'Kind Person'

BY JEAN DOUGLAS MURPHY
Times Staff Writer

Dame Sybil Leek, English-born author, astrologer, entrepreneur, lecturer, publisher, radio and television producer and personality, mother, manufacturer of sailboats and jewelry, has no patience with the myriad uninformed Americans who want her to talk about, of all irrelevant things, her religion.

"I hate to talk about witchcraft. My religion is a very personal thing, a simple Druidic religion," she protested politely during a visit this week to Los Angeles. "I'm not the Billy Graham of witchcraft."

Nevertheless, Dame Sybil, stretching her patience and sipping her Scotch and water, graciously answered a few questions. (Too many questions might have proved risky; even though she is a good witch and has expunged black magic from her life, Dame Sybil is not one to antagonize. She is a formidable woman, intellectually and physically; a gutsy lady, apparently quite capable of righteous human wrath.)

A witch, she explained slowly but firmly, as if she were trying to describe a moonrise to a blind joint, is "a follower of the ancient occult pre-Christian religion called wicca, an Anglo-Saxon word meaning the craft of the wise . . . closely related to the ancient Druid religion, a nature religion in which life forces are respected."

A member and leader of the coven (congregation of witches) in England's New Forest since she was 18, Dame Sybil said that "we acknowledge a supreme being as a life force or stream of energy, energy being interchangeable with matter, and reincarnation."

Please Turn to Page 6, Col. 1

CALORIE CONFERENCE — Karen Owens, right, chief nutritionist at Orange County Medical Center, looks over diet manual with Mrs. Louis End, who has lost nearly 100 pounds under Mrs. Owens' nutritional program. Mrs. Owens will be opening speaker at UCI extension nutrition, health program.
Times photo by Maxine Reams

WHEN BANANAS WERE IN BLOOM—Carmen Miranda appears in "The Gang's All Here," a 1943 Busby Berkeley musical, playing at the Monica II and Granada.

MEDICAL CENTER NUTRITIONIST

Food for Thought From an Expert

BY SHEARLEAN DUKE
Times Staff Writer

IRVINE—"What's wrong with a burrito and an orange milk shake for breakfast?" asks Karen Owens.

And for that matter, as a snack, Mrs. Owens would recommend a bag of potato chips over an apple.

Before you get the idea that she is out to undermine the health of America, you should know that Mrs. Owens is a professional nutritionist with a long list of credentials.

She holds a master's degree in human nutrition and foods. She is working on her Ph.D. in nutrition and biochemistry. She was health nutritionist and senior dietitian at City of Hope Medical Center in Duarte and is currently chief nutritionist at Orange County Medical Center.

Mrs. Owens' basic aim is to help dispel some of the nutritional misconceptions of Americans in general—and Orange County residents in particular.

As opening speaker in the UC Irvine extension lectures series on nutrition and health which opens today, the outspoken young woman will introduce a 10-week course featuring guest lecturers who will discuss such topics as "Vitamins: Facts and Fallacies," "Obesity: Causes and Cures," and "Organic and Natural Foods: Fads or Facts," and "Supermarket Nutrition."

Please Turn to Page 9, Col. 1

OPERA REVIEW

'Figaro' Revived
in San Francisco

BY MARTIN BERNHEIMER
Times Music Critic

SAN FRANCISCO—Take out a second mortgage on your home. If need be, sell your sister. Do anything. But for the love of Mozart, don't miss the current version of "Le Nozze di Figaro" at the San Francisco Opera.

It is, in a word, wonderful.

Not the physical production. Leni Bauer-Ecsy's postwar Stuttgart sets and costumes are serviceable rather than distinguished, and they do not age particularly gracefully. Ghita Hager's handme-down staging, though perfectly fluent and responsive to both score and libretto, sheds no new ight on either Mozart or Da Ponte.

But, no matter. Under these special circumstances, the players are most emphatically the thing. The quality of the theatrical framework is, for a change, only of incidental importance.

For the second installment of San Francisco's Golden Anniversary season, Kurt Herbert Adler has managed to assemble what must be a dream cast. He has found five extraordinary singers for the central roles, all of whom happen to be blessed with just the right voices and faces and bodies and brains.

What's more, they happen to be performers who interrelate sensitively while they are acting persuasively and singing beautifully.

Primary Revelation

The revelatory evening's primary revelation, at least for one inveterate "Figaro" follower, turned out to be the Susanna of Judith Blegen—enchanting to behold and enchanting to hear.

Miss Blegen may not command a remarkably large or lustrous voice, but it is perfectly controlled, perfectly focused and manipulated with belllike purity right up to a child's-play high C. This young lady looks like a porcelain figurine, acts with gusto and personifies taste and charm. Unlike so many successful soubrettes, however, she never seems self-conscious about it.

And when it comes to the serene legato of "Deh vieni non tardar," she can compete with the most exacting mezzoes, even those of Bidu Sayao and the young Irmgard Seefried.

Please Turn to Page 11, Col. 1

MOVIE REVIEW

Berkeley's 'Gang's All Here' Again

BY CHARLES CHAMPLIN
Times Entertainment Editor

Busby Berkeley has been one of the major retrievals of these recent nostalgia-nutty years. The multitudinous, pulchritudinous dance numbers he engineered for Warner Bros. musicals 40 years ago have found a whole new generation of camp followers.

Berkeley's infinitely spiraling stairways, his acres of baby grands and forests of neon-edged violins, the sly suggestiveness of his massed lances peered at from overhead or underwater have a confident, extravagant foolishness which is still generally fun to watch.

Now, out of the vaults, comes "The Gang's All Here," a Technicolor musical which Berkeley made at Fox in wartime 1943. It opens today for two weeks at the Monica II in Santa Monica and the Granada on the Sunset Strip, along with the trailer for the movie and the Movietone news-reel (voice of doom narration by a young George Putnam, Lew Lehr at a high-diving meet).

What I think we have to consider is the possibility that there is good nostalgia and bad nostalgia, and that if there are forgotten treasures in the past there are also certain ruins that ought to be left to rest in peace.

"The Gang's All Here" is a garish curiosity, not so much a delight like the earlier Berkeley-enriched musicals as a reminder of the bloody awful things we sat through in our youth.

To judge by the whoops and chortles at the preview I attended, the principal appeal of "The Gang's All Here" is to the coterie of trivialists who embrace the movie past as a shelter from and evaPlease Turn to Page 12, Col. 1

Figure 21–10 The society section of the *Los Angeles Times* was renamed "View" and expanded to cover areas of much broader interest. Many other newspapers are making these changes in their "society" pages.

Figure 21-11 More and more women are becoming sports writers on commercial as well as campus newspapers. Here, Allene Danielson, elected sports editor of the campus newspaper at Orange Coast College, interviews football player Alvin White.

there is more cohesion and interaction than in large cities find that the traditional "society" news remains a big attraction for readers who want to know what neighbors are doing. Their effective coverage of social activities makes them invaluable to their subscribers who cannot get this news elsewhere.

Weddings and Engagements. An editor's interpretation of social values places—or excludes—a wedding or engagement announcement in a newspaper. One basic yardstick is the length of residence of the man or woman involved: if both are newcomers to the community, they are less likely to have a wedding or engagement story published than if one (or both) has been reared in the area. The reason for rationing the space is that many readers would recognize the names of the long-time residents, while the newcomers probably would not have had time to make friends.

Some engagement or wedding stories run alone, while others accompany a photograph of the woman. Only a few newspapers have enough space to use pictures of the bride and groom together, although exceptions are made in the case of those well-known locally. The

newspaper does *not* provide the photograph: the bride obtains it from a portrait studio.

The use of forms. To facilitate gathering of information, many newspapers provide forms for the family to give facts about an engagement or wedding ceremony. Some forms explain what information the newspaper will or will not use, giving the reasons, which usually involve the limited amount of space. Using forms saves the reporter the time involved in asking obvious questions and helps assure the correct spelling of names.

Club News. The amount of club news varies in newspapers according to the size of the community covered. The larger publications devote less space to individual organizations because they serve larger areas with many clubs, most of them seeking publicity. Some editors are forced to "ration" space and give organizations stories only on certain occasions: the election of new officers or a visit by a national or regional executive might be a club's selection for its "two" stories per year. Clubs with the most members logically win the most generous coverage, while those with only a handful on their rolls receive less. When "real" news develops, such as a talk by a nationally known celebrity, the general yardstick of news values is applied, and coverage may hit the front page.

Publicity representatives. Many clubs appoint publicity officers, whose duties include channeling news to journalists. Most newspapers recognize the value of this assistance and welcome the opportunity to cooperate. Publicity officers learn the preferences of individual newspapers for stories and pictures and can help steer the club toward programs that develop news, realizing that journalists cannot publicize activities that are not newsworthy.

SUNDAY MAGAZINES

Many medium-sized and large newspapers produce locally edited magazines for distribution with the Sunday editions. The writing and editing in these publications are of a high quality. These magazines usually operate with an editor and an assistant, who have their own

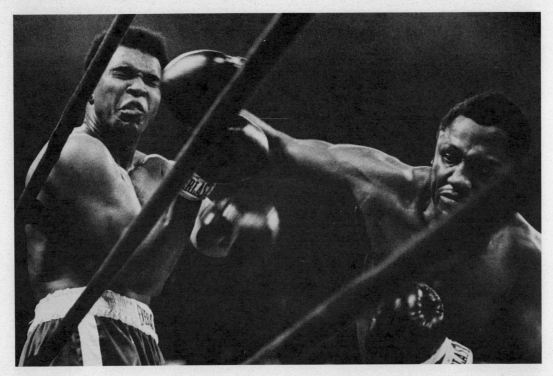

Figure 21–12   Pictures add a great dimension to sports stories. Here, Joe Frazier connects with a long right to the face of Muhammad Ali in their 1971 title bout. (United Press International Photo)

staff of writers or rely on articles produced on assignment by members of the general news department.

Since these magazines are produced at a more leisurely pace than daily editions, many staff members seek the assignment of working for them so that they can perform more research and take greater pains in producing articles.

OTHER "SPECIAL" SECTIONS

Weekly and daily newspapers of all sizes often produce "special" supplements for such occasions as the beginning of school, a community festival, the introduction of new-model automobiles, or the start of the vacation season. A staff member serving as editor for such a project coordinates the gathering of stories and photos and eventually the dummying of the edition.

These sections differ from regular magazines in that most are "one-time" productions. Many editors, writers, and photographers

Figure 21–13   Newspapers are including additional features to round out reader interest. Often one staff member is assigned to supervise this area. Here is Beverly Kees, editor of special sections for the *Minneapolis Star.*

prefer these assignments because their "single-deadline" nature allows time for more skillful handling of stories, pictures, and layouts than daily deadlines.

EXERCISES

1. Analyze the sports section of a local newspaper and determine the number of "spot news" or game results stories as compared to feature-type "advance" articles.

2. By analyzing the subject matter of "traditional" women's news as compared to general interest stories, determine whether your local newspaper is edited for the woman or for all members of a family.

3. Invite a member of the sports staff of a local newspaper to attend a question-and-answer session on how he does his work.

4. Determine the name of a local newspaper's "women's" section; invite a member of its staff to a classroom question-and-answer session to discuss duties.

22

Editorials, Columns, and Related Features

Many writers are anxious to express their own views and opinions, rather than report news or the statements of others. The avenues open to these people are editorials, columns, "think" contributions, and editorial cartoons.

EDITORIALS

Editorials are the considered opinions of a newspaper reflected by its owners, as represented by the publisher or editor. They usually appear on the editorial or opinion page to differentiate them from news stories. Editorials comment on material previously presented fairly or objectively in the news columns. Weighing and presenting various arguments, an editorial reaches a conclusion and makes a recommendation regarding an issue.

While "we" and "our" are not used in news stories because the first person indicates subjectivity, they *are* proper for editorials. "I" and "my" are *not* used, however, since editorials presumably speak collectively for a newspaper's owners and editors.

Individual reporters or other staff members do not necessarily need to agree with their newspapers and in most situations are expected to write their stories fairly.

Many would-be editorialists think of the legendary pioneer editor who in a TV western shows concern over a problem, sits down at a typesetting machine (or sets the type by hand), and proceeds to write a courageous editorial calling for the eradication of the town's evils. Readers obediently respond to his editorial edict, and justice is done.

Such a situation might have been true on a few frontier newspapers, but today editorial writing is a bigger project, except on tiny one-man publications. It is usually the joint concern of several people.

THE IMPORTANCE OF EDITORIALS

Vital for a newspaper and the community it serves, editorials reflect and influence decision making and can direct, positively or negatively, actions by readers. Surveys show that editorial pages do not have the proportionately high readership enjoyed by the comic or sports pages, but they do command the attention of an important part of the population: those who make decisions.

SAN JOSE NEWS

AN INDEPENDENT EVENING NEWSPAPER

J. B. RIDDER — Publisher

KENNETH S. CONN, Executive Editor — ANTON F. PETERSON, General Manager

MONDAY, APRIL 7, 1969

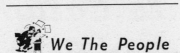

San Jose Needs More Than Cars

The "car explosion" in Santa Clara County is something. The mere fact that the population is growing would mean we were getting more automobiles. But there is more to it than that.

Paul Yarborough, who is supervising the elaborate countywide transportation survey now in progress, notes that ten years ago there were 2.4 people per car here. Five years ago that figure was 1.7. Today there are 1.2 persons for every car.

This means that the percentage of two-(and more)-car families has climbed sharply.

We are cheered by all signs of prosperity, including this one.

All these cars, however, do put a tremendous burden on the streets, expressways and highways. And on the air we breathe, too.

The problem here is that the public transportation system is so bad that the "extra" car is more than just a luxury.

Look at this imaginary but not untypical family. The husband uses a car to drive to work. A son goes to City College and contends he needs a car to get there. A daughter attends San Jose State College, and how is she to get to classes? And there is the wife with the shopping to do and perhaps a younger child to chauffeur.

County government, in cooperation with the cities, is working on a transit plan. The State Legislature and the voting public willing, it could have the first phases of a mass transit bus system functioning here by 1970-71. Yarborough believes the full system could be in operation a year later. We hope so.

Council Election

San Jose voters will elect four city councilmen Tuesday. That represents a majority on the city's governing body. Four councilmen can make decisions that affect everybody, for better or for worse.

They can decide what to do about taxes and streets; about police protection and mass transit; about zoning and housing; about parks and libraries; about youth programs and facilities for the elderly; about regulations that protect us and regulations that annoy us.

All this, and more, concerns us. Between elections we citizens spend a lot of time second-guessing the Council. We exhort City Hall and gripe about it—maybe even praise it now and then. Some, of course, just take it for granted. But a lot of us complain that it spends too much of our tax money for this and not enough for that.

That is fair enough. It is our Council, and we have a right to criticize it or praise it. Every two years we can do more than that. We can pick some of its members. This year we can select four from a list of 30 candidates.

It behooves all of us, who had enough foresight to register, to get to the polls Tuesday and pick the four best men we can find on that list.

Pop Art

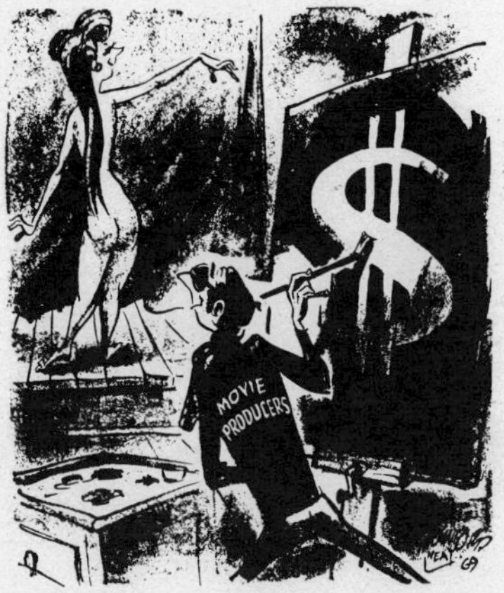

We The People

Supervisors Club

Editor: One day we read our PART TIME BOARD OF SUPERVISORS are getting a pay raise from THIRTEEN THOUSAND FIVE HUNDRED DOLLARS A YEAR to SIXTEEN THOUSAND DOLLARS A YEAR. NOT TO MENTION THEIR NON REPORTABLE EXPENSES OF TWO THOUSAND FIVE HUNDRED DOLLARS. Then a few days later we read PAY REQUEST POSTPONED to pay the salaries of two librarians for young adult libraries.

As I see it part time jobs at $13,500 per year is considered underpaid while full time jobs at $6,000 per year is enough for anyone — that is unless he is a member of the illustrious Supervisors Club.

JOSEP H. DONOHUE

Downtown Parking

Editor: I would estimate at least five hundred cars used to find free parking from 7 A.M. to 5 P.M. in the streets now cut off to the public, from W. Santa Clara to Park Ave., and Market to River St. These people work or study in technical schools downtown and many park in our private

(The San Jose News welcomes letters of interest on all topics, local, state, national and international. Please confine them to no more than two pages, preferably typewritten. The News will not print communications that bear on religion or favor particular candidates during a campaign. Comments on public issue are accepted. Please address letters to The Editor.)

parking lot because they can't afford the dollar or two it costs to park all day downtown.

There is no construction of any kind going on in these four square blocks of empty space and streets, why not leave it open to help desperate working people until the city gets round to building anything on it?

I wish the five hundred or more people who used to park there when shopping or working would join in this complaint. It's for them.

Also S. San Fernando from Vine to Spencer is marked no stopping even. Why? It's not even a thru street. Why not save the signs until it becomes a thoroughfare?

REV. MORGAN CURRAN
Holy Family Rectory

So They Say

Educated Catholics are not going to pay any attention to this statement. If they did, we'd be back in the Dark Ages.

—The Rev. Robert Johann, Jesuit philosopher, on Pope Paul's encyclical banning artificial birth control

OTHER VIEWS

Volunteer Army Plan

President Nixon's appointment of an advisory commission to study and recommend by November a program to eliminate selective service in peace-time and to move toward an all-volunteer armed force is the proper way to proceed.

There are many unanswered questions about a volunteer force to be answered besides the acknowledged inequities of conscription. It is extremely unlikely that selective service can be abolished before the end of or great diminishment of the Vietnam war. But Mr. Nixon has set no time-table other than that of the committee's report.

Public opinion polls for years have been balanced against selective service but in favor of requiring service by all young men for a short period either in military or civilian programs of the government as they chose. But the government does not need and cannot afford to put all young men on the payroll. The supposedly higher cost of a volunteer army — although this may be shown to be erroneous by the committee's study —would be lower in any event than universal service. — The Oregonian

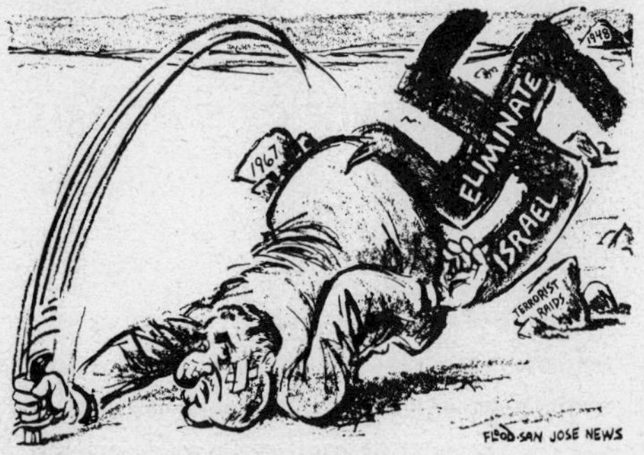

"I keep tripping over my own feet!"

25 Years Ago

Wendell Willkie withdrew from the presidential contest following his decisive defeat by Gov. Dewey in the Wisconsin primary.

• • •

Invading Japanese forces cut British supply lines in India.

• • •

San Jose Chamber of Commerce mailed booklets to inquiring easterners, explaining there would be no housing here until after the war.

15 Years Ago

Los Gatos approved plans for construction of Route 5 through that town.

• • •

The San Jose board of education was planning a junior college for 2,000 students.

• • •

Israeli and Egyptian troops clashed in a border incident.

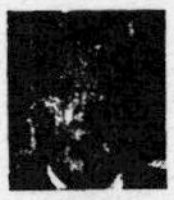

William S. White

Kennedy Pulls Away Early In Demo Race

The so-called contest for the 1972 Democratic Presidential nomination is like nothing ever before seen in American politics.

To begin with, Sen. Edward Kennedy of Massachusetts is so far out in front, nearly four years ahead of time, as to suggest that the 1972 Democratic convention is more likely to be only a rally to ratify a certainty than a meeting seriously to consider alternative choices.

Hardly any experienced observer now believes that Kennedy can be stopped. Many believe, indeed, that nobody will really try to stop him — unless, just possibly, Sen. Eugene McCarthy of Minnesota.

While former Vice-President Hubert H. Humphrey is occasionally making noises suggesting that he himself might have another go at the nomination, his genuine concern is far more simply that of seeking to return to the Senate from Minnesota in 1970. And while Sen. Edmund Muskie of Maine, the 1968 vice-presidential designee, is still hypothetically in the running, he is most gravely handicapped by lack of money, relative to what is easily available to Kennedy, and lack of access to national publicity, practically all of which is preempted by Kennedy.

Muskie is most unlikely in all these circumstances to make much of a fight of it.

Thus as a practical matter the potential anti-Kennedy field dwindles down to one — Sen. McCarthy himself. Even this possibility, however, is a fairly dim one.

First of all, McCarthy's Senate term expires at the beginning of 1970 and he has already announced that he will not seek reelection; not, at any rate, as a Democrat. This, to be sure, leaves him the option of running as an independent. But that is a hard course, indeed, and should McCarthy at length elect to take it, he would by definition pretty well simultaneously write himself off as a Democratic party force.

Should he decide to leave the Senate but not the party and to occupy himself in the meantime in speaking and writing, he would no doubt remain in position at least to challenge Kennedy in the 1970 primaries. Some who know him well believe that this in the end will be his decision. Even so, however, he could at maximum only arrest Kennedy's march toward the nomination in behalf of some third figure. McCarthy's own nomination would be a substantial impossibility in any event.

But — and here is the core of it — who would this hypothetical third figure be? The old expression is that you can't beat somebody with nobody, and the fact of the business here is that no somebody to take on Kennedy for the actual nomination is now in sight. If, to paraphrase the Goldwater slogan of long ago, there is to be a Democratic choice rather than a mere echo, where can the choice be found?

The reality is that Kennedy has been allowed to preempt the field of real issues, with such personages as Humphrey and Muskie, and basically McCarthy, too, simply trailing on behind and saying, "Me, too."

Kennedy is anti-Vietnam war; but so are the others. Kennedy is against the Nixon Administration's antiballistic missile system; but so are the others. Kennedy is vastly critical of the Nixon people on poverty and welfarism and so on; but so are the others.

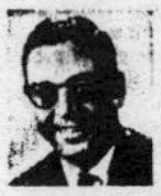

Joseph Kraft

Negro Leaders Turn To Localized Action

A year after the murder of Martin Luther King, racial unrest seems to be on the wane, with the ugliest features of protest behind us. And it is tempting to sit back and let tension wind down by itself.

Tempting but probably wrong. For the recent events in Detroit suggest that a new kind of confrontation may be shaping up unless deliberate efforts are made to humanize life in the great cities.

Vast changes, to be sure, have transformed the racial situation during the past year. Negro leadership has ceased to emphasize the universal theme of equality across the nation. Instead, the militants have turned to their own turf, and are directing their efforts to specific conditions in particular places. There has taken place an "implosion of black power."

One sign of this inward turning is that no national Negro leadership has emerged to replace Dr. King.

Instead, as the current issue of Time magazine points out in an excellent essay, there have emerged a series of regional leaders rooted in local communities. There is Jesse Jackson in Chicago, Leon Sullivan in Philadelphia, the Stokes brothers in Cleveland, Julian Bond in Atlanta, Channing Phillips in Washington, Donald McCullum in Oakland, and many others.

The stock-in-trade of all these leaders is the effort to use favorable local conditions for the building of black power structures. Thus in the Philadelphia ghetto Dr. Sullivan has set up a black shopping center and a black company for aerospace works. In Cleveland, the Stokes brothers are building on a large Negro electorate, a base for control of the local Democratic party.

Moreover, because the black militants are concentrating on their own thing, they have steered clear of the most radical whites. Just as the Chicago Negroes did not join the protests against the Democratic convention last summer, so black students have tended to stay away from the demonstrations organized against the major universities by the left-wing Students for a Democratic Society, or SDS.

In consequence of these developments, the racial situation seems to be shaping up not badly. The black movement is not connected with violence perceived by most whites, or with the most extreme troublemakers. And it looks as though the right thing to do is just to let matters cool off, in the fashion of the Nixon administration.

What the Detriot events suggest is that the winding down of race tension is not automatic. The implosion of black power can set the stage for confrontation between Negroes contending for their own turf and authorities trying to maintain order. And such confrontations can split communities among racial lines.

Thus it is not enough for the white community simply to stand aside and let blacks settle their own affairs. There is a continuing case for actions and programs by official and private authorities to engage the responsible participation of the Negro community in the totality of American life.

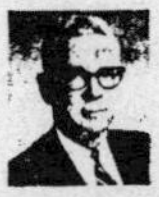

Bruce Biossat

Southerner Softening Segregationist Views

TUSCALOOSA, Ala. — Southerners, like everybody else, simply do not fit the easy labels many try to apply to others they see at some distance. A man in one of the poorer rural counties in the northern half of Alabama demonstrates the case.

He cannot be identified because it would be to his disadvantage. For the same reason, he cannot even be "placed" more precisely.

This man falls in the 35-45 age bracket from which the state is now taking some of its new leadership at various levels.

Unsurprisingly, he is by upbringing and basic emotional bent a racial segregationist. He was a supporter of George Wallace as governor, is still an admirer and presumably would back him again of he decides to run for that office in 1970.

If this anonymous rural southerner were to appear suddenly in a setting with northern doctrinaire liberals, they would quickly seize upon some of his utterances to brand him unacceptable according to their rigid moral judgments.

But the significant fact about this fellow is that he has moved away from the pole of total segregation where he once stood.

Indeed, he has changed sufficiently to adjust himself to the idea of a 50-50 ratio of whites and blacks in the public schools of his town and county. He seems also to accept some racial mixing of the faculty in formerly all-white schools.

Part of the reason for his change he would never confess publicly to his neighboring southerners. In a substantial period of military service, he decided on the basis of his actual experiences that desegregation is "not all that bad."

Beyond that, he is responding further to the inescapable pressures of federal court orders to desegregate. Says he:

"The courts have lifted a burden off our consciences. We know the law provides that they (Negroes) can go to our schools."

This man, like many another southerner, sees a sharp distinction between the edict of a court acting under the color of law, and federal guidelines which represent the discretionary judgments of HEW administrators. When the latter speak, it is the "government telling us what to do," and most southerners get their backs up.

Says the anonymous rural leader again:

"We are going to respect the law here. We intend to see that Negroes have the privilege of a better education."

There is one other factor in his change, a factor this reporter had mentioned to him often as he toured Alabama extensively. The average segregationist white southerner has lost some faith in those politicians who promised that desegregation would never happen.

There can be no great credibility granted such political figures on this score today. What they said would not occur has occurred.

The rural man's continuing admiration for Wallace is on grounds other than race. He sees him as a man who got things done, who built trade schools and roads, provided free textbooks, and persuaded Alabama citizens to bear the higher taxes to pay for all this.

Yet no make-over miracle has been performed with this man. He does not want to see white youngsters in his area going to present all-black schools.

Figure 22–1 A typical editorial page includes a "box" with names of major executives (upper left); editorials (left); editorial cartoons; letters to the editor (center); editorial view from another newspaper (center); and columnists (right column).

Who Writes The Editorials?

It's a fair question, probably one of the most frequently asked about the newspaper. And the answer at the DAILY PILOT is no one — no one person, that is.

Editorial writing is a team effort at the DAILY PILOT. It is the art of phrasing thoughts so that the finished editorial represents the newspaper's opinions on news events and problems of the day. The editorials do not express the opinions of any one man.

The newspaper speaks with one voice only after many have been heard.

The voices are heard — loudly and clearly — in the informal atmosphere which surrounds the weekly meetings of the editorial board. Out of these meetings come the foundations on which DAILY PILOT editorials are built.

At the head of the editorial board are Robert N. Weed, publisher; Thomas Keevil, editor; and Albert W. Bates, editorial page editor.

Other board members are Thomas Murphine, managing editor; Richard Nall, assistant managing editor; L. Peter Krieg, Newport Beach city editor; and Terry Coville, West Orange County city editor.

As they discuss news of the week or of weeks ahead, the talk ranges over topics affecting each of the Orange Coast communities the DAILY PILOT serves as well as the state, the nation and the world.

There is a three-way test of any topic proposed as the subject for an editorial:

1. Is it a topic which merits editorial comment?

2. Will the commentary serve the newspaper's readers in terms of their particular interests?

3. Does the newspaper know enough about the topic to make an intelligent, responsible comment?

Often the third question is the most difficult to answer. And sometimes the answer is "no."

Even after considerable research and further discussion at a later editorial board meeting, a topic can be dropped altogether because the newspaper still does not have sufficient knowledge to make a meaningful editorial comment.

Discussion in an editorial board meeting can modify the conclusion, shift the emphasis or even reverse the position of the board member who was the original proponent of a certain position and posture the newspaper should assume on a given topic.

But who actually writes the editorials for the DAILY PILOT?

The editorial board calls on any man or woman on the staff — the one most qualified to write on the specific topic selected for comment.

A reporter whose assignments have placed him closest to the facts surrounding the editorial topic may write the first draft.

Most often the original draft is written by one of the senior editors. And usually even a "first draft" represents several rewritings by whomever produces it.

It will be reviewed as many as three times — once by Editorial Page Editor Bates, again by Editor Keevil and, finally by Publisher Weed (where "the buck stops," as the saying goes) — before it finally reaches the publication stage. Each review usually brings some further editing and refining.

Any member of the news team with knowledge to contribute on the subject is invited to put forth his best effort.

Many voices blend into one. The editorial speaks in the single voice of the newspaper. Who wrote it? The DAILY PILOT did.

Though they call it "edit board" for short and it meets in a shirt-sleeve atmosphere of informality, the job of the editorial board is serious — and taken seriously by (left to right) Charles Loos, assistant managing editor; Thomas Keevil, editor; Thomas Murphine, managing editor; Albert W. Bates, editorial page editor; Robert N. Weed, publisher; Richard P. Nall, assistant managing editor; L. Peter Krieg, Newport Beach city editor; and Terry Coville, West Orange County city editor.

And Other Good Questions

What is an editorial?

An editorial is a statement of the newspaper's opinion on a topic it feels is of interest or concern to its readers. "The fire destroyed the building and three adjacent structures." That's a news story. "The fire could have been prevented if the city council had condemned the ancient building . . ." that's an editorial.

Why do you endorse candidates for public office?

Many people go to the polls without knowing the candidates well enough to vote on them — or don't go to the polls at all, for the same reason. We feel these readers are open to reasoned suggestions. We know the candidates both personally and from their records because we think this is part of our job. We share our special knowledge with our readers when we carefully exercise our privilege to suggest that a given candidate is best qualified for the job he seeks. We also are careful to see that our editorial opinions, expressed on the editorial page, do not influence our reporting of the campaign — or any other news — in our news columns.

Do your editorial writers have full freedom of their convictions or does somebody tell them what to write?

No staff member is obliged to write an opinion he does not share. He is respected for his dissent. And dissent is frequent, though not bitter, among the writers and editors who produce the DAILY PILOT editorials.

Why do you publish "editorials" which disagree with your stated position?

Often the comments of columnists whose work appears on the editorial page are considered "editorials" by readers. The top of the editorial page containing the editorials is where the DAILY PILOT states its position. The rest of the page is turned over to readers' comments (letters and Gloomy Gus) and to writers and cartoonists with whose views this newspaper may or may not agree. These range from the satirical political comment of Art Hoppe to the hard-nosed investigation of Washington bureaucracy by Robert S. Allen and John A. Goldsmith. Their comments are not editorials. But they often counter-balance ideas expressed in DAILY PILOT editorials and, thus, give our readers a more balanced diet of opinions on a given subject.

Gloomy Gus . . . Is He One of Us?

Without letter-writing readers I'd lose my voice.

G.G.
(Himself)

Gloomy Gus literally is the voice of the people. No staff member "writes" the Gloomy Gus feature. All of Gus's quotes are contributed by readers — many more than can be printed, in fact. That is not to say that none of the DAILY PILOT'S some 200 employes may not occasionally contribute a Gus quote. After all, they're subscribers too.

Page proof is checked in composing room by Albert Bates (left), editorial page editor, and Thomas Keevil, editor. It's last chance to correct typographical errors.

Final review of intent and content of an important editorial likely will find Publisher Robert N. Weed and Editorial Page Editor Bates meeting under plaque on Bates' wall which keeps reminding them the DAILY PILOT editorial page has high standards to maintain. Plaque is first place award in California Newspaper Publishers Association competition for 1968.

Figure 22–2 This page in a daily newspaper told readers how an editorial board formulated topics for handling on the editorial page.

Who Writes Editorials? The early-day newspaper found the editor—who probably also was the owner—performing almost every job. He would write and edit the news, compose the editorials, solicit advertising, set type, run the press, and even help circulate the newspapers. Except at the smallest of newspapers, publishers today would not have time to perform all these tasks. Instead, the publisher oversees the many jobs connected with producing a newspaper.

This is true even in writing editorials.

Editorials are produced, therefore, in several ways. The "personal" publisher, who has strong views he wishes to emphasize, hires an editorial page editor who shares his basic viewpoints. This editor and his assistants, understanding the publisher's views or receiving direct assignments, produce editorials tailored for his tastes. They may submit each to him for approval.

This personal journalism helped bring fame to many early press barons, including Joseph Pulitzer, Horace Greeley, James Gordon Bennett, and William Randolph Hearst. The latter typified personal editorial control, maintaining telephonic contact with his newspaper empire stretching from New York City to San Francisco while at his isolated castle at San Simeon on the California coast. Hearst personally wrote many editorials which appeared in identical form the same day in each newspaper.

A Problem for the Idealist. Publishers who continue to practice personal journalism still set rigid standards regarding what their newspapers will oppose or endorse. The idealist who may have different ideas for editorials would find little pleasure in writing material with which he disagrees, and obviously he should not accept such a position.

The Editorial Board. The modern trend for newspapers is more enlightened in the eyes of the idealist and also serves to develop editorials which are more meaningful and effective for a reading public that is growing in intelligence.

This trend is to set up an editorial board composed of representative staff members, for instance the editorial page editor, the publisher or his representative, the executive editor, and one or more reporters representing contrasting viewpoints. Membership often is rotated to assure fresh and changing opinions. Board members reach decisions on editorial policies by voting.

In these situations, the publisher frequently reserves the right to "veto" proposed policies even though the majority approve them. The reasoning is that the publisher represents the publication's owners, who by this virtue are entitled to overrule employees. The publisher who frequently used the veto option, however, would undermine the effectiveness of the editorial board system and probably would find few staff members willing to participate in deliberations.

Once a topic for an editorial is approved, a board member writes the first draft. After all members have an opportunity to read and comment on it, a final draft is written.

The inclusion of representative staff members on the board helps make such a system effective. Reporters handling special assignments or key beats bring fresh viewpoints to the editorial page.

The Editorial-page Editor. Another method of producing editorials is through the system of an editorial-page editor who develops ideas under guidelines set down by the editor or publisher. Under this method, the editorial-page editor will meet occasionally with one of the former to discuss *general* policies. The editor then has the freedom to run editorials under these policies.

The position of editorial writer is one of prestige and increased pay on most dailies. A newspaper of 100,000 circulation normally would have two to four people (out of a staff of approximately 100) to perform editorial page chores. The editorial writers would have ample reference material and time to conduct research on pros and cons to be considered in editorials.

Qualifications for editorial writers. Since writing editorials is a pleasant yet challenging position, there often are more qualified applicants than there are jobs. Individuals would win their jobs on the basis of aptitude, educa-

Figure 22–3 Publisher Robert Weed (center) presides over a meeting of the *Orange Coast* (Calif.) *Daily Pilot's* editorial board, which is typical of the modern trend for staff participation in policy matters.

tion, seniority with the newspaper, and agreement generally with its policies—not to mention the luck of such a position being open. Since many newspapers dictate subjects for editorials, importance also would be placed on an individual's ability to write *for* or *against*—as the occasion dictated—an editorial position.

LETTERS TO THE EDITOR

Readers have the opportunity to reply to editorials or comment on news situations in the "letters to the editor" column, usually found on the editorial or opinion page. Unlike editorials, letters frequently comment on issues that have *not* been presented in news columns.

Most newspapers receive more letters than they have room to print, and the editorial-page editor makes selections based on how pertinent they are, their conciseness, their organization, or the cleverness or originality of their approach. Sometimes a letter is worth using because of its source: a city official making a point or the subject of a story providing material he felt should have been in the original article.

Space limitations force newspapers to set a word limit on letters, and most editors refuse to use anonymous letters—although they often will delete the name on request if there is a reasonable chance that the writer may face recriminations. Editors will *not* run letters they believe are libelous, since the newspaper as well as the writer could face a damage suit.

COLUMNS

Individual opinions and expressions, so important in the world, can be presented effectively in columns. Columns run at regular intervals—daily, weekly, or monthly—and can cover a wide range of issues ranging from politics to hobbies. They represent the opinions of the author, whose by-line appears at the top of each installment. While many writers use the third person in columns, most prefer the more personal first person singular: "I" or "my." Some writers use the collective "we" or "our" in a figurative sense to create variety even though the column has only one writer.

Most newspaper staffs have several members who crave to become a columnist, a position that brings prestige and often lets the writer select his own hours and subjects. To achieve the goal, a writer first must persuade an editor that the newspaper has the space for another columnist. Then the writer must produce a column idea designed to fill reader needs and convince the editor that he is clever and energetic enough to provide enough material to keep the column alive.

"THINK" CONTRIBUTIONS

Many newspapers reserve space for reporters to rotate as columnists and thus produce "think" pieces reflecting the background of some of their stories. By doing this, editors make it possible for readers to gain invaluable insight and opinions not given in "objective" stories.

EDITORIAL CARTOONS

Cartoons are an important part of the editorial or opinion page. They can graphically and humorously give new dimensions and perspectives to the news. Large newspapers often have one or more cartoonists on their staffs. Small ones must depend on talented staff members who are skilled as cartoonists as well as in other areas or must purchase cartoons from a syndicate.

EXERCISES

1. Compare editorial or opinion pages in several local newspapers; note the balance of editorials, columns, letters, cartoons, and other features.

2. Write an editorial opposing or supporting a controversial issue that has been considered in a news story at your college; write in the third person or use the editorial "we."

3. Write a sample column dealing with campus issues, and outline the contents for four additional columns.

4. Invite an editorial writer from a local newspaper to attend a question-and-answer session; ask him to describe how he decides to support or oppose various issues.

23

Starting Your Own Newspaper: Campus or Off-Campus

There are no foolproof rules for starting a newspaper, but there are standards for organizing one and obtaining production costs. Most colleges find such a publication can serve the dual purposes of being a workshop for prospective journalists and providing the campus with news. The production suggestions in this chapter also can be adapted for starting an off-campus or private newspaper.

PROBLEMS OF A NEWSPAPER

All newspapers, whether supported privately or by a campus, face common problems. These factors include choosing printing methods, financing costs, setting editorial goals, obtaining a staff, and evaluating and improving the product with the passing of time. There are various solutions to these problems.

THE METHOD OF PRINTING

While publications can be "dittoed" or mimeographed, they must be reproduced by commercial printing equipment if they are to look professional and serve journalists as a workshop and an audience as a readable product. Most colleges or beginning newspaper entrepreneurs can't afford printing plants, so the logical move is to contract with a commercial firm for production services.

Letterpress vs. Offset. The most reasonably priced printing method usually is offset, the process using photography and light-sensitive plates. Offset plants are more liable to have computerized typesetting and other automation that can reduce costs. Another important advantage of offset is that black-and-white line cartoons and advertisements as well as photographs can be reproduced at a comparatively low cost. Letterpress requires the more expensive and time-consuming photoengraving.

The exception to offset printing being lower in cost would be the modern letterpress plant which is highly automated and therefore in a position to compete.

In essence, there is little difference between good offset and good letterpress printing as concerns quality. There can be great differences in quality if the work is done on second-rate equipment or by poorly trained craftsmen.

The wise shopper therefore will seek prices from offset and letterpress plants and will inspect printing samples to determine quality.

Obtaining Bids. Even when dealing *only* with quality printers, there can be great differences in prices because of variables in the use —or lack of use—of automated equipment and volume profit margins. To be sure that the newspaper backers get the most and best for their money, bids should be obtained from a number of printers. Bid forms can be developed best by conferring with available printers to determine reasonable standards. Factors to be considered include the newspaper's dimensions, pictures, typesetting, make-up schedule, and delivery requirements. All possible information should be made clear to avoid costly misunderstandings.

Paper dimensions and quantity. Prime decisions cover the dimensions of the newspaper and the number of pages for an average issue. The paper may be a tabloid (printing area: approximately 10 x 15 inches) or standard (printing area: approximately 15 x 18 inches). Pages usually increase in multiples of four, so that a newspaper can be four, eight, twelve, or sixteen pages.

How many copies to print raises an excellent question that will have different answers in different situations. Ordinarily, the biggest cost of producing a relatively small newspaper is that involving the typesetting, halftones, make-up, and plates, along with the production of the *first* copy. After these preliminary costs, copies can be printed at a comparatively low price. Even so, a judicious newspaper management does not want to waste copies. A good rule of thumb is to print enough copies for one-fourth of the college's enrollment or other expected circulation, and have a provision in the bidding specifications for increasing the press run in multiples of 250 and 500.

The cost of illustrations. The bidding specifications also should request a statement of costs for using various sizes of halftones and line shots. These items usually will be more expensive for letterpress than for offset print-

ing. When dealing with offset, it is the custom for the printer to make *no* charge for black and white matter such as cartoons or advertisements when they are to be reproduced the *same* size, since they will be photographed with the pages. If this material must be enlarged or reduced, a charge is assessed.

The use of color. The charge for using a color, if available, should be specified. There are multicolor presses which can add this paper brightener at relatively low costs.

Standards for typesetting. Preliminary discussions with prospective printers should verify the availability of adequate type styles and sizes. Editors would need to know that the body type, in which all stories are set, complies with accepted newspaper standards and is not an unusual face that would be difficult to read. There also should be adequate large type for headlines. The specifications should state whether the printers or editors are responsible for checking proofs for typographical (i.e. printer's) errors. If the editors check such errors, the printer should make an allowance for this time-consuming chore.

A schedule for make-up. Mechanically preparing the pages from dummies supplied by the editors is the work of the printer, particularly when dealing with letterpress. Some news staffs prefer to paste their own pages when using offset. The bidding specifications should state the deadline day *and* hour for proofs. This permits the staff to check pages at a designated hour without waiting for type to be set. *Note:* If a staff elects to do its own "paste-up" for offset, the printer should make a reduction in price for this substantial work. One way to measure possible savings is to have alternate bids, one with the printer doing the "paste-up" and one with the newspaper staff performing the work.

Delivering the newspapers. The bid specifications also should designate a day and "deadline" hour for delivery of the newspapers. Some staffs arrange to pick up newspapers at the printing plant to save money, while others require delivery to a specific place. The contract should designate a reduction in the charge for the papers if they are not delivered by a given hour: newspapers are worthless if delivered too late to be distributed to prospective readers.

Screening of bids. In the case of a college newspaper, the staff can receive valuable assistance and advice from the campus purchasing agent. Those starting an off-campus publication will wish to consult an attorney for advice before signing a contract. The newspaper's managers should not be hesitant to ask prospective printers to show samples of their work and provide references.

FINANCING

Privately financed off-campus newspapers face the problems of any business enterprise: finding the money not only to begin operations but to continue them until a profit develops. There is no capsule advice or sure formula for financing a newspaper. Publications started on a shoestring have flourished, while others with considerable funds have failed.

One method is to talk with printers, prospective advertisers, businessmen, and publishers of all types of newspapers to gain more insight. Their views can help guide the prospective publishers in or out of the field.

Campus newspapers are an entirely different type of situation. Most finance operations through one or a combination of three ways. These methods and the rationale for the funding are as follows:

Student-body Appropriations. Most colleges have student governments with funds to budget for campus activities. Use of a portion of this money to print a college newspaper can be justified on the basis that a publication edited for and by students is an ideal way to communicate opinions and news.

College Educational Funds. The use of tax or other educational funds to support a student newspaper is justified in that the publication is an instructional vehicle that also serves the function of publicizing the college's academic and vocational programs.

Sales of Advertising. Making advertising space available to commercial or other organizations wishing to reach students can be an excellent means of providing operating rev-

enue. The advertising rate can be decided by ascertaining the cost per column inch of printing the newspaper, and then setting a reasonable profit. Many college newspapers fix their rate at three to four times the per column inch cost.

If the college is large enough, it may have an advertising class which can undertake ad solicitation as part of its course work. The college which has no such course may arrange for a business-oriented student to undertake advertising responsibilities on a commission basis.

ESTABLISHING THE NEWSPAPER'S POLICIES

The college newspaper must fill the campus need just as a community newspaper attempts to meet the needs of its readers. Good campus newspapers vary in contents according to the nature of the college and its students. What is good for one college is not necessarily important for another one. Campus newspapers should individually set guidelines in regard to written statements of policy, editorial boards, staff members, and selection of editors.

Written Statements of Policy. The policy that governs the least is the best in keeping with the principles of the First Amendment to the Bill of Rights and its guarantee of press freedom. Written rules for editing a newspaper often are used as clubs to interfere with editorial prerogatives and privileges through debates over interpretations.

The few rules adopted by a student government or college administration should be positive statements of ethics affirming the freedom of the press without retaliation and stating the newspaper's duty of trying to publish various sides—including antiadministration and anti-student government viewpoints even when these units provide financial support.

Formation of an Editorial Board. While most newspapers have a publisher clearly representing the owners, the position is difficult to formulate for a campus newspaper because of the diverse interests and groups that may support the publication. One excellent way to achieve balance when there may be differ-

VALLEY STAR

LOS ANGELES VALLEY COLLEGE

Vol. XXI, No. 6 — Van Nuys, California — Thursday, October 23, 1969

Increase Shown on Spring Dean's List

Star Achieves High Honors In Judging

THE MAKING of a president, 1949-1969. Pictured from left to right are Robert Cole, dean of educational services; Vierling Kersey, Valley's first president; Walter Coultas, past president; William McNelis, past president, and Robert G. Horton, current president.

Alumni Highlight 20th Anniversary

By DALE SPINA
Managing Editor

HOLDING SON who is six months old is Mrs. Chris Probst, who stated that in 18 years she will not want her son to enter the Armed Forces. She was speaking before a large assembly of people at the Vietnam war moratorium.

FIRST PRESIDENT Vierling Kersey came back to Valley to celebrate the school's 20th birthday. Kersey served as president in 1949-1955.

Protesters' Rallies Back 'Mobilization'

College News Briefs

Smog Control Co-Sponsored

AWS Presents Karate

Queen Applications Available

Tutoring Service Offered

Honor Societies Give Pot Luck

BSU Rally

Business Class Takes Tour, Sees L.A. Superior Court

Court Subpoenas Another Witness

USSF Projects Spirited Equality In Current Policy

TALKING FROM EXPERIENCE is Donald Duncan, former green beret and current military editor of Ramparts Magazine, who resigned. Duncan was a featured speaker at rally protesting Vietnam war.

"Who Pays What?" Committee To Investigate

WEEKLY **College of Marin Times** Est. 1960

SERVING CAMPUS AND COMMUNITY

VOLUME 9, NO. 3 | COLLEGE OF MARIN, KENTFIELD, CALIFORNIA | FRIDAY, OCTOBER 4, 1968

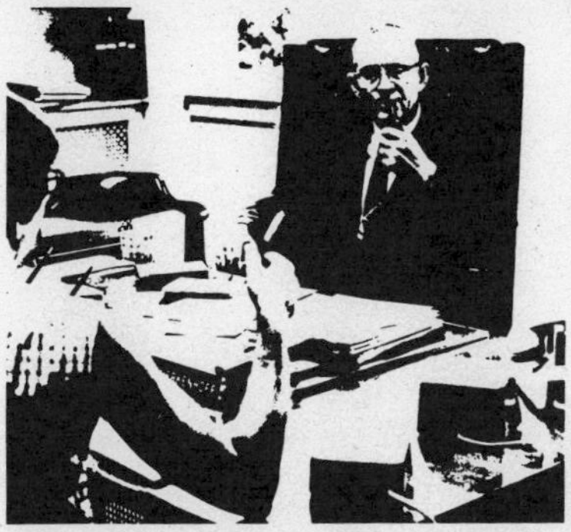

SAF Appoints Budget Committee

The Students for Academic Freedom met last Tuesday to organize a sub-committee to go through the present student budget and determine areas that could be the Board of Trustees' responsibility. The committee will be concerned with nine areas with six separate budgets. Each will make recommendations to the Board (areas covered: ICC, dances, replacement college center upkeep, etc.).

Members of sub-committee are Dean of Students Irwin Diamond, David Garber, an advisor to ASCOM, Mike McGinn, David Bersin, Ranald Bruce, (all SAF members) and two other students.

EXECUTIVE COUNCIL

At the last Tuesday meeting the Executive Council, appointed Ranald Bruce to form a committee to revue the budget and to make recommendations to the Executive Council. To avoid duplication of effort, Bruce appointed members of the sub-committee as members of his own committee. Bruce's committee met for the first time on Tuesday to start the analysis of the present budget. Mike McGinn said the committee will meet again next Tuesday.

Tuesday evening the Executive Council met again to approve the budget as it stands with provisions that no action or changes would be made until the committee returns its findings to the Executive Council. There were eight members present.

PETITION

A petition by SAF vas proposed to activate the rewriting of the present constitution.

SAF presented their initiative petition to a chaotic Executive Council meeting on Wednesday, and President Dave Long empowered the secretary to check the validity of all 431 signatures. As soon as the validity is checked, there will be an election within ten days.

The Executive Council also set up a workshop to review the new constitution and work out any hassles in wording which may arise.

A question was also raised on the validity of the initiative petition, and Parliamentarian Dave Brown is expected to have a ruling by the next Executive Council meeting.

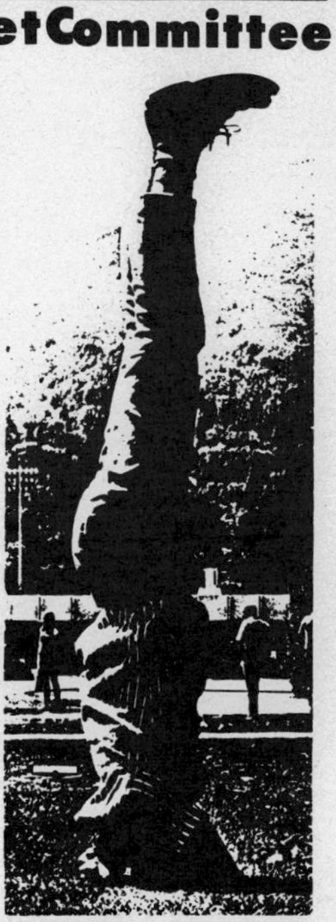

FEED YOUR HEAD?-No, this is Times reporter Ken Mueller demonstrating the hatha yoga (the physical aspect of the art of yoga). Classes in hatha yoga began last Tuesday at COM.

North Campus In View

Editor's Note:

Last year the Times ran a series of articles concerning the planning of the proposed College of Marin campus in Novato. Much controversy had arisen on campus and in the community concerning this issue. At this time it seems appropriate to run an article to inform all new students and faculty members, as more concerning this issue is sure to arise this semester.

The site for a Northern Campus of the Marin Junior College District has been approved by a seven member Board of Trustees. The Board has purchased five of the six parcelled sites for a total of 292 acrea. The remaining parcel of 41 acres will be purchased in the near future. The initial campus should be completed by the fall of 1972.

The site for the new campus lies a few miles southwest of Novato, accessible from Ignacio and San Jose Boulevards. Dale Fleming, Director of Planning and Research at COM describes the site as "beautiful", with rolling hills, many trees and a stream. The site, once part of the Pacheco Ranch, abounds with deer and other wildlife.

The Board of Trustees plan the northern campus to be similar to the Kentfield campus with a beginning student capacity of 1500 to 1600 students. This capacity will later be extended to 3500 as the community grows.

The first increment of the campus cost will be around $14,000,000 with initial facilities. During the coming months the Board will work on a basic concept of organization for the college; its relationship to the community and to other colleges. From this will evolve facilities needed for the basic campus foundation.

The committee working on the college includes students as well as faculty and administration from COM. The Board is trying to find a constructive way in which the community and the students and faculty of COM may become more involved in the planning of the coming campus.

Neptune and Thomas, an architectural firm of Pasadena, has been contracted for the master planning. They will design the initial buildings based on the educational specifications of Marin County. It is hoped that the master plan for the college will be drawn up by early winter.

Fleming will want a group of COM students to help with the planning of the student center. However, at this time he does not know whether or not a center will be included in the immediate plans for the college.

Herkenhoff Answers Critical Questions

By Bob Hallatt

There was some dispute last semester between the faculty and students of College of Marin and the Board of Trustees headed by former president of COM, Dr. William K. Ramstad.

The dispute, based on many problems that still plague this campus and community, may be boiled down to a lack of communication between faculty and students of COM and Ramstad.

This lack of communication finally resulted in Ramstad's resignation. Ramstad was replaced by acting president, Dr. Lewis H. Herkenhoff, who was appointed president of COM for a one year period starting last June.

I interviewed Herkenhoff and left with the following opinions:

Herkenhoff was asked by this reporter if Ramstad's resignation was a voluntary one on his part, or if he was forced to resign. "There was pressure from faculty and students for his resignation," said Herkenhoff.

He went on to explain that the faculty and students last semester were disconcerted because of their involuntary lack of involvement in the Board of Trustees. When both Mrs. Elizabeth Deedy, President of the Board (now V.P.) and Vice President (now President) Theodore Wellman submitted their resignations, Ramstad felt he had lost the majority support of the board and submitted his resignation also.

The new Board never asked for Ramstad's resignation, reminded Herkenhoff.

NORTH CAMPUS

Herkenhoff is in favor of the proposed Northern Campus. He maintains that it would not only be more convenient for the students living at the northern section of the district to have another campus, but that the problem of housing the growing student population would also be solved.

When asked about how he felt COM students were reacting to the construction of another campus, he stated frankly that ". . .I would have no way of assessing."

Upon being asked if he thought the students of COM held too much power, Herkenhoff replied, "No. . I think the interest that has been shown. . .(at COM) . . .is healthy and important."

He continued that actions shown are "an indication that students are accepting increasing responsibility for their education and their own lives."

THE BIG SHIFT

I asked Herkenhoff to clarify the Board's decision for the remaking of an athletic field behind the P. E. department.

He reported that the reclaiming of the land for the new athletic field has been okayed by the Board of Trustees. A proposal for the construction of bleachers, lights, snackbars, and restrooms has been made but no money has been allotted.

The old science building will be torn down and replaced by a new library. A new science building will be constructed on the old football field.

The old library, when vacated, will be refurnished and made into the Student Services center. It will "house" COM counselors, health service, nurse, attendance department, admissions department, records, and the registration department.

Ultimately, Herkenhoff explained, all final building decisions lie with the Trustees.

He hopes that any decisions made by the board will reflect the interest of the total community. " added also that the COM student body is certainly an important part of the community.

This Weeks' Happenings

The first dance-concert of the Fall Semester, featuring the Steve Miller Band and the Transatlantic Railroad, was an "unqualified success" according to ASCOM Vice President Pat Blake.

Even though there was a $250 ddeficitt, and a few shaky moments before it got under way, response of the student body was enthusiastic enough to warrant "continuing the dance-concert series on the same scale."

The next dance-concert, scheduled for Friday night, Oct. 11, at 9:00, will headline the Santana Blues Band and feature Together and Annie's Little Gang. There will also be a 20 piece light show, which, according to. Blake will surpass the Fillmore and the Avalon. The proceeds, if any, will go to the Business Club to finance their activities.

Tickets are $1.50 with a student body card and $2.50 without. Tickets at the door will be $2.50 for all.

Dialogue

SAF, FACOM, and AFT are sponsoring **Dialogue,** described as "an ongoing, open conversation on education," every Tuesday at 1 p.m. in FA112. All interested students are invited to attend.

A G.I. March for Peace is scheduled to be held in San Francisco on October 12. The march will begin at 11:00 a.m. at the Golden Gate Park Panhandle, and end at the Civic Center.

A rally will be held following the March, and speeches will include G.I.'s (active and reserve), veterans, and well known civilian critics of the war.

Active support of dissident G. I.'s is desperately needed. Any contributions, financial or organizational will be deeply appreciated.

Further information can be obtained by calling: Sacred Heart Church; 552-2939 or the Glide Memorial Methodist Church: 771-5650.

Shorts

"The world is going on outside and we've got to find out what's happening." Rick Beban is trying to do this in his position as Chairman of Controversy '68 is the ASCOM sponsored series of lectures and debates about the issues of the day. The ASCOM budget has appropriated $1300 for both this semester and next for this purpose.

Charles Garry, Huey Newton's defense lawyer, will speak on October 3rd. Terrance "Kayo" Hallinan will speak on October 24th. In addition tentative arrangements have been made for American Independent Party's Presidential candidate George Wallace on October 17th and Peace and Freedom Party's Presidential candidate Eldridge Cleaver on October 31st.

Dr. Don Edright will lecture on his recent survey from Korea to Afganistan on Oct. 10 in Olney Hall. In addition, he will discuss the concern of the surrounding nations towards red China's territorial aims.

Dr. Edright received his Ph. D. from the University of Chicago. He has recently returned from Asia after living there for 22 years. He now directs a representative party between 40 foreign countries.

Elections

In a typically poor College of Marin poll turnout, four students running together as "Students for Unification" swept all four class representative positions in this week's election.

Winners of the elections, which polled about 500 students or slightly less than 10 per cent of the total number of students, were Marti Musgrave and Dave Hyams for freshman class representatives and Lynne Anderson and Christopher Musser for sophomore representatives.

The results: (top two)

Freshmen Women
Susie Davidson 132
Marti Musgrave 289

Freshmen Men's
Dave Hyams 214
Paul Thomson 121

Sophomore Women
Lynne Anderson 280
Eileen Ann O'Connell . 110

Sophomore Men
Christopher J. Musser . 182
Mike Fusiliera 87

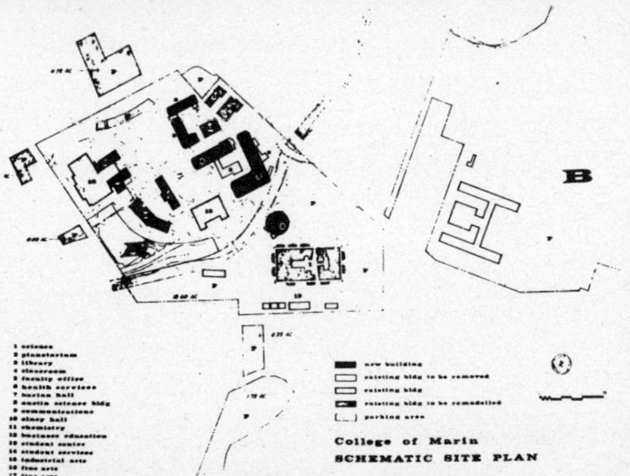

MAP OF CAMPUS-A. designates the area of the football field where it now stands. B. location of new football field in the gym complex. Other buildings as they stand now and where they will be relocated (such as the library) are also shown on the map provided by the office of Planning and Research.

Drama Play Cast Picked

Next month the College of Marin drama department will stage its first play of the year "Mother Courage".

"Mother Courage", written by Bertolt Brecht, is a satirical play based on the campaign in Poland during the early 1600 s. "Although Mother Courage is spoken of as a war play, it is actually a business play, in the sense that the incidents in it, one and all, are business transactions."

The production of "Mother Courage" is headed by Jim Dunn, of the Drama Department, with a cast of fourteen. The leading players include Elizabeth Huddle as Mother Courage, Mark Rasmussen as Eilif, Bruce Webster as Swiss Cheese, Corinne Atkinson as Kattrin, Don Carrol as Chaplain, Robert Deckelman as Cook, and Ann Early as Yvette.

This year for the first time a theater professional will be cast Miss Elizabeth Huddle, the leading lady, has been hired by the Committee of Social Projects for COM. She was with the Actors Work Shop in San Francisco and Lincoln Center in New York. She has been with the California Shakespearian Festival for the past two years.

The opening weekend will be the 18th and 19th of October, with following performances from the 23rd to the 26th. Reserved seats went on sale October 1st. Seats will be $.75 for students and $1.25 for general admission.

Draft Counselor Here Next Week

Starting next week for 3 hours each Thursday, there will be a draft counselor available for men students. The counselor, who is from the San Francisco State Draft Counseling service, will answer questions regarding draft and military service, deferments, class and grade requirements, and will also instruct students about draft laws. Location of this counseling service will be posted in the College Center by Monday.

Freshman student Gary Gunn has taken charge of the On Campus Housing project. A questionnaire wil be sent to all COM students to aid in determining the housing needs of students, and what they can afford. If it is felt that such a project will be economically feasible and of service to the students, a proposal will be made by Student Government to the Board of Trustees. Possible locations of a 100 to 300 student dormitory are being investigated as well as estimated costs of construction.

Student Government representatives are contacting San Mateo Junior College regarding their highly successful tutoring program. It was instituted to aid students who were having various scholastic and financial difficulties. It has also proved helpful to individuals who originally had been unable to attend college for both scholastic and financial reasons and who with the assistance of this service are in attendance at SMJC. If possible a similar program will be started on the COM campus.

Inadequate college parking is an item of concern to most COM students. ASCOM is taking immediate action to alleviate the problem by applying pressure on the appropriate people to increase parking facilities.

Starting next week there will be a 5¢ litter charge on food service for some items. This was passed by the College Center Commission. It is planned to decrease the charge as the amount of litter decreases.

Figure 23–2 This community college newspaper, printed by offset in standard format, deals with varied campus activities.

Figure 23–3 A college editor presides at a horseshoe-shaped copyreading desk similar to those on dailies as students produce a campus newspaper. (Orange Coast College Photo)

ences of opinion among editors or pressure on the newspaper from nonstaff forces is to form an editorial board.

Such a board can be composed of representatives of student government, the faculty senate, the administration, clubs, athletes, women's organizations, and other viewpoints or special interests. Such a board ideally would function only to mediate disputes; it would not dictate or even suggest newspaper policies.

Selecting Staff Members. The association of the student newspaper with journalism classes is desirable to achieve a quality publication. Some colleges permit students to serve as reporters only after completing an introductory course in journalism, while others allow students to be on the staff concurrent with enrollment in such a class. Newspaper staff members should have class training not only in reporting but also in make-up and copyreading.

Producing the newspaper as a workshop class project is an excellent way for staff members to receive technical assistance and evaluation of their efforts. There is little direction or continuity to newspapers operated as an activity, as opposed to a course. Staff members are inclined to cover only the stories they wish to, instead of those assigned by editors, and to drop the activity when they have written about the subjects which are their particular interest.

Choosing the Editors. Even though a class produces the newspaper, there is still a need for an editor to direct the operation. The instructor can make the appointment, or the staff can elect the editor.

Arguments for selection by the instructor. Those favoring the selection by a journalism

Figure 23–4 College editors use big-newspaper techniques to produce their campus publication. (Orange Coast College Photo by Joan Milcarek)

Figure 23–5 College newspaper reporters work in their newsroom, modeled after those at dailies. (Orange Coast College Photo)

instructor assume that this person knows the quality of work which a student can produce and will appoint an editor who displays the qualities of journalistic skill, leadership, independence, and fairness. The main argument against this method of selection is that the instructor will select a student who would echo his own prejudices in editing the newspaper.

Arguments for selection by staff members. Journalism students would name an editor who has demonstrated talent and perseverance as a reporter and has shown leadership ability. The argument against this way of selecting an editor is that a popularity contest could develop, with the winner having little talent.

EVALUATING THE NEWSPAPER'S SUCCESS

A commercial newspaper is evaluated each time its readers choose to renew—or not to renew—their subscriptions. A campus newspaper usually is circulated without cost, and

its success or failure must be measured by polls, discussions, local contests, and national competitions.

Polls. Questionnaires asking readers what type of stories they like can be indicators of the directions in which reporters should move, but they should not govern the editing of a newspaper. Readers are inclined to report that they dislike stories dealing with a subject that is treated contrary to their own views. Actually, they read the articles but disagree with what is being said. Polls are good as barometers, but not as editors.

Discussions. Daily newspaper editors are so pressed for time that they seldom have an opportunity to meet with readers. Campus editors are more fortunate because they are in the midst of activities. In give-and-take discussions with readers, they can understand where stories are reaching—or missing—the audience.

Local Contests. Regional college press associations and area commercial newspaper groups frequently have contests. These competitions serve as excellent means to assess how the campus newspaper compares in writing, make-up, editing, and photographic achievements with other publications. *Regional* contests provide good yardsticks for quality and recognition because they are based on local considerations.

Moratorium — A Day Of Mourning

Funeral Procession and Speakers Protest War

By SHEILA BOOTH
Barnacle Staff Writer

"Acting in the best tradition of American democracy" as noted Dr. John L. Jensen, professor of history, students rallied at OCC last Wednesday to protest the Vietnam war as part of the nation-wide moratorium—the largest single anti-war demonstration in the history of the United States.

OCC's observance of the moratorium was attended not only by its own students, but also by a number of students from Costa Mesa High School, non-students, several young Christian evangelists who passed out literature, and many faculty members.

At 11 a.m. approximately 400 participants, most wearing black mourning bands, followed a flag-draped coffin in a march around the main campus area while two buglers echoed a mournful taps—a symbolic funeral procession for those who have died in the Vietnam war.

Bradley Offers Eulogy

This moving state of solemnity was continued as the pall-bearers placed the black box in front of the auditorium, which was to be the stage for the moratorium, as a dirge-like national anthem was played and the flag was folded and laid on the coffin, several students raised their hands in a clenched fist salute.

Still in the funeral mode, Lee Bradley, associate professor of psychology, was called upon to offer a eulogy. Bradley asked everyone to hold hands and observe a few moments of silence, contemplating that "many of you here could be in that coffin and how senseless a death that is."

Don Sizemore, student government director of convocations and forums, then introduced the first speaker-a representative of SDS who spoke of his personal experiences and observations in Vietnam, citing many of 'the United States'

Expelled And Back!

Barry Weinberg and Jack Vaughn, OCC's SDS leaders who received suspension notices from Joseph Kroll, dean of student activities, were reinstated last Thursday.

Kroll suspended the pair Oct. 10 for the continued advertising of an appearance by Angela Davis, a Communist UCLA instructor, even though it was uncertain she would show up. He said that the advertising disrupted the campus.

The action reinstating Weinberg and Vaughn followed a motion Oct. 14, by Tony Turner, senator-at-large, and passed by the Student Council.

The motion declared:

"We do not support Dean Kroll's suspension on the grounds that there has been a lack of communication in that the chain of events were in too close a conjunction, and that on these slim grounds action on such a matter would be detrimental (to us) the student government if

outrages "against humanity and against man."

Wert First to Speak

Several OCC faculty members then addressed the crowd which was seated on the grass at the foot of the steps. Thomas C. Wert, assistant professor of political science, was the first speaker.

Explaining that he was "not speaking for the administration of the college, nor for the faculty, or even for my department," he added "I wish I were." Wert first acknowledged that the constitutional right of free speech

provides protection for the individual who expresses ideas that differ, not just the majority.

"Heartfelt Revulsion And Contempt"

He then reacted to President Nixon's remark that the president would not allow himself to be affected by the moratorium, saying that "the presidency is not intended to work within a cone of silence." Nixon, he continued, is failing to acknowledge those who want to change policy peacefully, democratically, those who want to express "heartfelt revulsion and

contempt...for a policy which we consider wrong."

Dr. Jensen spoke next and read the resolution passed by the OCC Faculty Senate which "urged to support the move for worldwide peace." Jensen was cheered as he emphasized that "anyone who would call you Communists or Communist dupes is showing that he is ignorant of history."

Jenson Gets Ovation

Jensen quoted Assembly Speaker Jesse Unruh saying "you have every right to protest. Why? Because your lives are at stake,

that's why!" As he closed, stressing that "your protest will have an effect" and urging action" against this immoral war," he received a thunderous standing ovation.

Jon S. Brand, instructor in geography, stated "I'm here because I'm an American...and protest is the American way of life." In his protest, he urged Nixon "to end this senseless war."

Credibility Gap Beyond Control

Michael G. Crow, assistant professor of history, after introducing some relevant statistics (38,000 dead, approximately 400,000 maimed or injured in Vietnam over the last nine years) explained control by China to the present day.

Although the longest address, (speakers were limited to five minutes), the audience was attentive and respectful and applause resounded as Crow ended with "the credibility gap is beyond control."

Michael Finnegan, assistant professor of English, pointed out that two years ago similar peace demonstrations forced "our warrior king, Lyndon Johnson, out of office," but added that "more has to be done."

Finnegan urged each person present to write to the president protesting the war. He also called on the faculty to support and attend the teachers' peace march in Los Angeles on Nov. 6.

Open Immigration From Vietnam

John Buckley, political science instructor, suggested that since "the only valid reason for war is to save lives," there be established an "open immigration policy from Vietnam to the U.S." Edward A. Burke, assistant professor of history, spoke on the economic aspects of the war.

Following the faculty speakers, Don Sizemore offered the microphone to anyone who wished to express an opinion. Among

(Continued on Page 9)

Putnam Art In Gallery

The works of Don Putnam, a Hermosa Beach artist, are on exhibit in the OCC Art Center Gallery until Nov. 5. His oil paintings reflect the people and atmosphere of the circus he spent many years with.

Putnam's paintings show people of the circus in their everyday lives: playing cards in the dressing room, applying make-up, or waiting to perform. In the Gallery are also some western scenes, such as Indians during the hunt and Old West character studies.

Now Putnam divides his time between painting and teaching at the Art Center College of Design in Los Angeles. He has had shows in the Grand Central Station in New York, the Jones Gallery in La Jolla, Perry House on the Monterey Wharf and at the Saddleback Inn in Santa Ana and Phoenix.

The Art Center Gallery will be open daily from 9 a.m. to 4 p.m. and from 7 to 10 p.m. on Wednesday.

orange coast college BARNACLE

VOL. 11 — No. 6   Costa Mesa, California   Wed., Oct. 22, 1969

If the pursuit of Peace is both old and new, it is also both complicated and simple. It is complicated, for it has to do with people, and nothing in this universe baffles man as much as himself. -- Adlai Stevenson

taken place."

The motion was passed by 14 to 1, with one abstaining.

After this motion, Willie Collings, director of publicity, requested that "the decision of Dean Kroll come back to be passed by student government" if Kroll wished to continue with the suspensions.

On Oct. 13, the Student Council met and heard the cases of the two suspended students. Jack Vaughn and other SDS proponents were

(Continued on Page 9)

ON THE INSIDE . . .

Figure 23–6 This tabloid community college newspaper played major campus news on the front page, and an index showed the way to lesser matters.

National Contests. College newspapers can compete nationally in contests that produce trophies to be proudly exhibited. These contests, however, do not prove that the publications are meeting the needs of their college readers. There are many local variations in newspapers which these contests cannot measure. While winning a high place in such a competition can be an honor, a paper that is accorded fewer points may well be serving its audience better. Some contests, for example, make awards on the basis of space allocated specific sports, without considering regional differences in student preferences. One competition penalizes a newspaper for certain techniques in making up ads, when these in fact have been designed to please the buyer of the advertisement. Few editors would want to produce a newspaper worthy of a once-a-year honor certificate but disappointing to its weekly reading audience.

The Final Judges. The ultimate judge of the good campus newspaper is the student. If students pick up copies regularly, the paper contains news that interests them.

EXERCISES

1. Prepare a list of specifications suitable for a printing plant to use in making a bid for producing a newspaper; detail page dimensions, number of pages, paper type, delivery days, and other information.

2. Compare the bids of three or four printers for producing this newspaper.

3. If your college has a student newspaper, determine how it is financed.

4. Prepare a simple statement of editorial policy under which staff members of a campus newspaper could work independently and at the same time serve the college with news.

24

How to Apply for a Job

Many people completing journalism or communications courses do so to develop a better understanding of the ways to gather and present news. Others want to prepare themselves for careers in one of the media. Most professionals urge those interested in a career to get a journalism position, even though part-time, as soon as possible. Practical experience helps to round out class studies.

Job opportunities in journalism vary from time to time and according to areas. A person with an above average aptitude for the field may get a position after completing only one journalism course, but this fortunate individual must be in the right place at the right time.

OPPORTUNITIES

Weekly and daily newspapers offer the greatest number of employment opportunities for journalists. *Editor & Publisher*, a weekly magazine for the newspaper trade, features a classified advertising section listing many news department jobs. Numerous ads state that beginners will be considered. While many of the positions are in small towns or rural areas, they offer an excellent opportunity to get started in journalism.

Many beginners aspire to work at metropolitan newspapers, with their relatively higher pay and specialized positions. Much-sought-after openings on leading newspapers often go to journalists who have refined their skills by serving apprenticeships on smaller publications. While positions on larger newspapers are not beyond the reach of beginners, the successful candidates must have well-developed skills.

OTHER FIELDS OF OPPORTUNITY

Journalistic skills also are keys to other fields. Radio and television stations require news writers. Many journalists prefer careers on regional magazines, on company publications produced for employees or stockholders, or with public relations agencies. Some journalists adapt their skills for writing advertising copy.

STARTING POSITIONS

Gaining experience is the way to finding

Figure 24-1 Work experience or intern programs conducted by newspapers or TV-radio stations in cooperation with colleges help beginning journalists get started. Harold S. (Hal) Heffron, assistant city editor of the Denver (Colo.) *Rocky Mountain News*, talks with (from left) interns Anne Beaton, Keith Mitchell, Shirley Simon, and Frank Estill Moya. (*Rocky Mountain News* Photo by Mel Schieltz)

a better job. One way to gain this experience is by being willing to work part-time in a relatively low position. There are several work areas which can lead to more challenging positions as the prospective journalist demonstrates reliability and talent.

Copy Boy. This person (who may be a male or female) does errands for the news department. Duties may include cutting stories from the wire machine, taking copy to the printers, going out for coffee, or even lending a hand occasionally by doing stories or copyreading. This position is available at newspapers, radio and TV stations, public relations and advertising agencies, and magazines. Those involved prefer to hire someone who is interested in entering journalism instead of an individual who only wants a job.

Stringer. This individual covers a geographical or subject area not assigned to a staff reporter. Examples include covering a city government meeting once or twice monthly in a distant city, or covering high school sports events. The reporter is paid by the inch of copy published. The "stringer" title comes from the old-time custom of measuring a correspondent's total inches of stories with a string of a given length to determine his pay.

Part-timer. Working a few hours weekly is an excellent way to get started, because the journalist can combine classroom studies with on-the-job experience. While some employers are unwilling to risk beginners on a full-time basis, they will give part-time jobs so the journalist can adapt to the job. When the part-timer becomes experienced and valuable, he often becomes a full-time staff member.

Free-lancer. Some newspapers buy and use stories on a "piece" or free-lance basis.

This is particularly true of those with Sunday magazine sections. Selling these articles helps the journalist to show his talents to editors. Clippings of these stories also are valuable in seeking jobs.

Work Experience Programs. There is a tendency for the media to have "intern" or work experience programs in cooperation with colleges. Under such a plan, journalists spend a specified number of hours working under the direction of professional journalists. Interns, while not paid for their work, gain invaluable experience and may eventually become members of the staff if they demonstrate aptitude.

APPLYING FOR A JOB

While a work application by mail may be necessary because of distance, a personal contact is the best way to achieve recognition from a prospective employer. An editor likes to know how a candidate talks, dresses, listens, and reacts.

Making an Appointment. Editors are busy, and applicants should show courtesy by making an appointment by telephone or with the editorial department receptionist. Editors would be annoyed if an applicant appeared at a busy time. In any contacts with newspapers, applicants should remember that afternoon dailies are busiest from 10 a.m. to 2 p.m., and weeklies usually are on deadlines the day before the date of publication. Job seekers should check radio and TV broadcasting schedules to be sure they do not attempt to make a contact immediately before or during a broadcast.

How to Dress. Employers respect college life, but few seek to import campus styles to their offices. Wear clothing that complements the garb worn by the people with whom you would like to work.

Samples of Stories. Samples of an applicant's work help an editor to have a better insight. Journalists can begin accumulating samples by clipping their stories from college newspapers or showing copies of articles written for journalism classes. *Note:* If clippings will be mailed or left with an editor, it is wise to retain photocopies as a protection against their loss.

Persistence. Even though an applicant is once refused a job, this does not mean that the employer will not have an opening in the future. Renewing a contact with a prospective employer, particularly one who is friendly and shows an interest, helps to notify him that you *are* interested and have the persistence and energy to follow through on stories. Situations change daily, and the fourth or fifth time you apply may be the time when there is a job opening.

EXERCISES

1. Make a list of the newspapers, magazines, radio and TV stations, and public relations agencies locally that might hire beginning journalists.

2. List companies in your area with employee or stockholder publications on which beginning journalists might work.

3. Look at a copy of *Editor & Publisher* in your local library or at the office of a newspaper and examine the classified advertisements seeking news department employees.

4. On separate occasions, invite representatives from local newspapers, magazines, radio and TV stations, and public relations agencies to discuss the methods and standards they use in hiring journalists.

Glossary of Journalistic Terms

Ad abbreviation for advertisement.

Add (a) copy added to a story that has been written; (b) the second (or other additional) page of a story.

Advance (a) copy to be held until a specific release date; (b) a preliminary story about a coming event.

Afghanistanism avoiding treatment of local controversies but dealing with those in distant places.

Agate type 5½ points high (often used in classified ads).

Agate line the unit of measurement for advertising; 14 agate lines equal one inch.

American Newspaper Guild a labor union for newspaper, magazine, and wire service employees in other than mechanical departments.

American Newspaper Publishers Association the organization of newspaper publishers in the United States.

American Society of Newspaper Editors a prestigious organization that considers the ethical and technical aspects of newspaper editing.

Ampersand abbreviation (&) for "and."

Angle the aspect (women's, "local," regional, etc.) emphasized in a story. *Note:* this term is not to be confused with "slant," which indicates bias.

Art any newspaper illustration (drawing, map, or photograph).

Banner the main headline on page one.

Beat (a) a timely news story acquired ahead of the competition; (b) a regular place or subject assigned to a reporter for gathering stories.

Body type the smaller type (usually 8- or 9-point) in which most stories are printed.

Boil down condense the story.

B.F. or **b.f.** the abbreviations for boldface (dark) type.

Box a story enclosed by lines, borders, or white space.

By-line the reporter's name at the start of a story. In some situations, the author's name appears at the end.

C & LC or **clc** capital and lowercase letters.

Canned copy (a) publicity material; (b) material from a syndicate.

Caps capital letters.

Caption a headline over a photograph.

Note: this term often is misused to indicate a *cutline.*

City editor the person who directs reporters gathering local news.

Cold type photographic or art type, used for offset printing.

Copy a story or article.

Copy boy a person (male or female) who does errands in the news department.

Copyreader or **copy editor** the person who edits stories and writes headlines.

Credit line the name of the photographer who took a picture as it appears with or near the cutlines.

Crop to edit or delete portions of a photograph to increase interest or change proportions (i.e., vary the composition).

Cutlines the explanatory material beneath a photograph.

Dateline the first words of a story telling the city where the story originated. *Note:* the actual date was included at this point years ago, but it now is not given because of the speed at which news is published.

Deadline the latest time at which a story can be accepted.

Desk (a) where the city editor sits or (b) where the copyreaders work.

Dummy the diagram used for advising a printer how to make up a page.

Ear small box in the upper corner of page one used for the weather forecast or other information.

Editorialize to include the opinions of the writer in a news story.

Electronic media radio, television, and other means of communicating through electronics.

Flag the name of the newspaper appearing on the front page.

Folio a page or page number.

Follow, follow-up, or folo a story giving new developments after one article has appeared.

Follow copy instructions for the printer to set a story exactly as written, even though words may be misspelled.

Font an assortment of type of one size and style.

Fotog short for photographer.

FYI "for your information," indicating material to be read but not necessarily used in a story.

Head short for headline.

HTK or **HTC** abbreviations for "head to come," advising printers that a head will come later (with the story to be set in type first).

Hot type type set with lead and used in letterpress printing.

Kill (a) delete or exclude a story or part of a story; (b) destroy type that has been used or will not be used.

Letterpress printing a method of printing which uses metal type that contacts or "presses" the paper directly.

Localize emphasize the local angle in a story.

Log (a) the city editor's assignment book; (b) a record of stories that have been sent to the printer.

Logotype or **logo** The newspaper's nameplate or flag.

Managing editor the news executive who coordinates operations in the news department and usually hires news staff members.

Masthead the statement, usually on the editorial page, listing the newspaper's name, publisher, principal officers, editorial executives, and related information. *Note:* The term often is misused in referring to the *flag* on the front page.

Media plural of medium, referring to means of communicating: newspapers, magazines, radio and TV stations, books, films, cassettes, etc.

Mill slang for a typewriter which "grinds out" copy.

Morgue journalistic slang for "library," where clippings and pictures are filed for reference.

Must designating copy that must appear in a specific edition of a newspaper or broadcast.

Nameplate the newspaper's name or *flag* on the front page.

News hole the amount of space in a specific edition for news after deducting advertising.

Offset printing a photographic-oriented method of printing in which a thin metal plate transfers the image to a rubber-covered roller which in turn transfers the image to paper.

Overset copy set in type but not used because of space limitations.

Paste-up a layout of proofs and art to be photographed for offset printing.

Pica 12-point type; approximately 1/6 inch; a unit of measurement used instead of inches by printers.

Point a measurement of type: 1/72 inch.

Proof an impression of type taken for comparison with the original copy to determine whether there are typographical (i.e. printer's) mistakes.

Proofreader a person (usually a printer) who reads proof to correct typographical errors.

Public Relations Society of America an organization for people in public relations.

Publisher the principal owner or representative of the owners of a newspaper.

Railroad rush copy to the printers; often implies that copy is not carefully edited because of the rush.

Release date the time when a story issued in advance can be published or broadcast; the media operate under a "gentlemen's agreement" not to jump dates set by story sources.

Reverse white on a black background; this technique helps create emphasis.

Rewrite (a) to write a new version of a story which has appeared in another newspaper; (b) to redo a story to make improvements; (c) to write a story from facts given (often by phone) by another reporter; (d) to produce a story based on a publicity release.

Rim the outside edge of the copy desk where copyreaders work.

ROP short for "run of press," meaning a story or ad runs in all editions.

Rule a metal strip that separates columns or makes borders.

Running story (a) a story sent to the printers in sections so that it can be set in type faster; (b) a story situation that continues for several days with new developments.

Schedule (a) the list of reporter's assignments; (b) the editor's log of completed stories.

Sigma Delta Chi a professional journalism society (for men and women) to which newspaper editors, publishers, and reporters belong. The organization seeks to improve journalistic standards and promote freedom of information.

Skyline the headline at the very top of page one.

Slant to make a story biased toward a particular viewpoint.

Slot the inside of the horseshoe-shaped copyreading desk where the chief copyeditor sits.

Slug (a) the one or two words that a reporter uses to identify a specific story; (b) a line of lead type used in letterpress printing.

Soc abbreviation for "society."

Stet retain the text of copy that has been crossed out (used by copyreaders and proofreaders).

Streamer a large headline covering a newspaper's entire width; also called a *banner.*

Stylebook a booklet or list of rules stating a newspaper's preference, when there are choices, of spelling, punctuation, capitalization, abbreviations, and use of numerals.

Syndicate (a) a company that distributes editorial material (columns, cartoons, puzzles, features, etc.) to newspapers; (b) ordinarily competing journalists who pool information gathered from their beats.

Take one part of a running story being sent in sections to the printers.

Thirty end of the story, used as a numeral, "30."

Time copy stories that can be held and used when needed.

Typo short for typographical error.

U.C. & L.C. uppercase and lowercase type.

Women in Communications, Inc. an organization for women in journalism; originally Theta Sigma Phi.

Wrong font or **W.F.** wrong font or size of type; used on proofs to indicate printer's errors.

Zone a section of a publication that is changed (in regard to ads or news) to meet the interests of various geographical areas.

The Stylebook

Stylebooks seek to achieve standards for capitals or lowercase letters, abbreviations, punctuation, the form of titles, whether numbers will be figures or spelled, and other matters that contribute to a reader's "comfort." Failure to follow reasonable uniformity would distract the reader.

The following style guide is based generally on the Associated Press and United Press International *Joint Wire Services Stylebook*, which is used by many newspapers and forms a basis for numerous stylebooks produced by individual newspapers. The person familiar with these style points should be able to adapt easily to using most stylebooks.

I. CAPITALS AND LOWERCASE

High school and college composition classes usually produce writers who *overcapitalize*. Journalism tends to use more lowercase letters *when there is a choice*. (Proper names, days of the week, months, and the names of nations always begin with capital letters.)

1.1 *Capitalize* titles preceding a name; *lowercase* titles standing alone or following a name. *Exception*: always capitalize President when referring to an incumbent President of the United States. Do *not* capitalize references to a candidate for president.

Examples:

Secretary of State John Smith will be guest speaker. Thomas Jones, also a former secretary of state, is now chief adviser to the President. William Daniels, candidate for president, will be a guest.

Queen Elizabeth II and Prime Minister Ronald Young were aboard. The queen and the prime minister will arrive tomorrow.

1.2 Long titles should follow a name to avoid confusion and because readers *identify* with people's names.

Example:

Fred Morgan, executive director of financial and auxiliary services, will speak at 1 p.m.

1.3 *Lowercase* occupational or "false" titles, even though they come before a name.

Example:

The group included day laborer John Hanson, rookie left-handed pitcher Bill Wills, defense attorney Henry Woods and writer Betty Feldstein.

1.4 *Capitalize* Union, Republic, or Colonies when referring to the United States or any other nation.

Example:

The British sometimes jokingly refer to America as the Colonies. The President spoke on matters pertaining to the Union. He said the Republic will long endure. The question developed regarding exchanging missions with the People's Republic of China.

1.5 *Capitalize* the proper names of organizations when used in their entirety; lowercase portions of the names used alone; capitalize references to the U.S. Senate and House of Representatives.

Examples:

Members of the Senate and House will meet jointly to hear a Security Council report. The council will consider several matters.

The City Council and Student Judicial Board will stage a program. Four council members and two board representatives will speak.

1.6 *Capitalize* committees and commissions when their names are used in their entirety; lowercase portions of the names used alone.

Examples:

The Senate Judiciary Committee and House Ways and Means Committee will hold a joint meeting to consider legislation pertaining to the Interstate Commerce Commission and the Federal Communications Commission. The committee members will study each commission.

The Student Inter-club Council will meet Tuesday. The council was formed last year.

1.7 *Capitalize* the names of specific courts when used in their entirety; lowercase portions of the names.

Example:

Judge John Jones of the 10th U.S. Circuit Court of Appeals will preside at the meeting. The judge recently was appointed to the court.

1.8 *Capitalize* the complete name of an act; lowercase parts of it used alone or references to the law in a general sense.

Example:

The Social Security Act covers most retail clerks, but government employees receive social security through other legislation.

1.9 *Capitalize* U.S. armed forces; lowercase references to the armed forces of foreign nations except the Royal Air Force and the Royal Canadian Air Force.

Examples:

The Air Force announced that it is ordering fewer planes during the coming fiscal year.

The Army is tightening its budget for the coming year. The Spanish army announced promotions. Members of the Royal Canadian Air Force will be guests.

1.10 *Capitalize* holidays, historic events, ecclesiastical feasts, special events, hurricanes, and typhoons.

Examples:

Mother's Day will be celebrated Sunday. Hurricane Helen is sweeping the East Coast. The Battle of the Bulge was a World War II turning point. National Safety Week is in the planning stage. Most stores will close Christmas Day.

1.11 *Capitalize* Antarctica, Arctic Circle; lowercase antarctic or arctic.

Example:

The expedition reached Antarctica today. The antarctic weather was expectedly cold.

1.12 *Capitalize* specific regions; *lower-case* points of the compass.

Examples:

The delegates came from the Middle West, Texas Panhandle, Chicago's Loop and New York's East Side.

The group's first tour was to the west, after which trips were scheduled to the north.

1.13 *Capitalize* political parties but not "party" when used alone; *lowercase* forms of government.

Examples:

The Republicans and Democrats announced their candidates. All endorsed the democratic way of life and republican form of government.

The Democrats elected George Young chairman of the party.

1.14 *Capitalize* the names of fraternal organizations, sororities, and clubs when used in their entirety; *lowercase* the *general* portion of the name when used alone.

Examples:

The Kiwanis Club will meet at noon. This is the first meeting of the year for the club.

The Independent Order of Odd Fellows will meet at 7 p.m. The order will elect officers.

1.15 *Capitalize* references to the Deity, and "He," "His," and "Him" when denoting the Deity or Jesus. *Capitalize* Bible (and its books), Talmud, Koran, and other scriptures.

Examples:

Moses led God's children from the wilderness. The Book of Mark tells how Jesus and His disciples taught the people. Followers of Islam believe that Mohammed is Allah's prophet. The Book of Matthew is in the New Testament.

1.16 *Capitalize* the names of specific wars and revolutions when used in their entirety; *lowercase* portions when used alone. (See Numerals **4.4** regarding sequence.)

Examples:

The speaker will discuss the American Revolution, Civil War, World War I and the Korean War. He is regarded as an expert on the history of the Revolution. He also wrote a book on World War II. The program will include photos taken during the war.

1.17 *Capitalize* names of races: Caucasian, Chinese, Negro, Black, Indian, etc.

Note: Identification of an individual by race should be made *only* when it is pertinent to a story.

1.18 *Capitalize* a common noun when it is part of a formal name; *lowercase* the common noun when it is used alone.

Examples:

The group inspected Hoover Dam and the Missouri River. Ten officials saw the dam and four visited the river.

Tours are conducted of the Empire State Building. Many out-of-towners want to see the building.

The trial is scheduled for the Orange County Court House. Several notable trials have been held in the court house.

The regatta began in Newport Harbor. The sail boats left the harbor on Tuesday.

1.19 *Capitalize* trade names and trademarks, but when possible use the generic or broad name for a product.

Examples:

Coke is a trademark of Coca-Cola, but there are many cola drinks.

A Realtor is a member of the local unit of the National Association of Real Estate Boards, but numerous people are licensed real estate brokers.

Thermos is a trademark of a particular brand of vacuum bottle.

A Band-Aid is a trade name for a particular manufacturer, but other companies produce adhesive bandages.

1.20 *Capitalize* titles of books, plays, hymns, poems, songs, motion pictures, and television productions, and place them in quotation marks; capitalize "a," "an," "in," "of," and "and" only at the start *or* end of a title.

Examples:

"Of Thee I Sing," "All Returns Are In," "Gone with the Wind," "Bonanza," "What Price Glory?"

Note: Underlining a word or phrase on a typewriter advises the typesetter that *italics* are to be used. Italics present a mechanical problem at most newspapers and therefore are *not* used.

1.21 *Capitalize* the names of newspapers and magazines, but do *not* place them in quotation marks (or italics).

Examples:

The New York Times and The Los Angeles Times rate among the nation's top newspapers but are owned by different interests.

Among the leaders in the news magazine field are Time and Newsweek.

1.22 *Capitalize* the first word of a quotation making a complete sentence after a comma or colon; *lowercase* all other words except proper nouns. *Lowercase* portions using excerpts from quotations and not preceded by a comma.

Examples:

Benjamin Franklin said, "A penny saved is a penny earned."

Franklin said that a penny saved is a penny earned.

1.23 *Capitalize* the names of organizations, expositions, clubs, and groups when used in their entirety; *lowercase* minor portions of the names when used alone.

Examples:

The Boy Scouts, Iowa State Fair, Community Chest and Rotary Club, but the scouts, fair, chest and club.

1.24 *Capitalization* of names should follow the person's preferred use. In general,

foreign particles are lowercase when used with a forename, initials, or title; in Anglicized versions, the article usually is capitalized.

Examples:

Charles de Gaulle and Gen. de Gaulle, but De Gaulle; Fiorello La Guardia.

1.25 *Capitalize* fanciful appellations.

Examples:

Buckeye State, Leatherneck, Project Mercury, Golden State, Lone Star State, Operation Deep Freeze.

1.26 *Capitalize* decorations and awards when used in their entirety; *lowercase* portions used alone.

Examples:

He won the Medal of Honor. She received the Nobel Peace Prize. He placed the medal on display. She addressed the banquet after winning the prize.

1.27 *Capitalize* the letters of academic degrees such as bachelor of arts and doctor of philosophy when *abbreviated*. (See Abbreviations **2.13**.)

Examples:

He received his B.A. and M.A. in history. She earned her A.A. degree and transferred to the university where she received her Ph.D.

1.28 *Capitalize* "street," "avenue," or other street designations when used as part of a formal name; lowercase when used alone. (See Abbreviations **2.4**.)

Examples:

He formerly resided on Sunset Boulevard and worked on Figueroa Street. He parked his car on the street.

1.29 *Lowercase* "p.m." and "a.m." (and use periods) in time designations. (See Abbreviations **2.5**.)

Note: The average person has more difficulty reading *all capitals* than capitals and lowercase combined. To create emphasis, re-structure sentences to emphasize the important words or thoughts rather than using the "crutch" of all capitals.

II. ABBREVIATIONS

Do not use arbitrary or "manufactured" abbreviations, but utilize those which are widely accepted and easily understood by the average person expected to read a story. Abbreviations which are not readily understandable require a "code" book to decipher. *Note:* These recommendations are intended for stories; abbreviations for headlines vary because they are handled by copyreaders rather than reporters.

2.1 The first mention of organizations, firms, agencies, clubs, and other groups should be spelled out; thereafter, initialed abbreviations may be used *without* periods. *Exception:* Initials may be used for the first mention of organizations that are highly familiar to readers; the decision as to these groups must be decided at the point of publication and obviously will vary geographically.

Examples:

The American Tree Association (ATA) will meet tomorrow in the AFL-CIO Auditorium. The ATA convention is being held here for the first time.

UCLA will play the University of Oregon today. The speakers will discuss the North Atlantic Treaty Organization (NATO). Several guests served with NATO.

2.2 *Abbreviate* time zones, airplane designations, ships, distress calls, and military terms.

Examples:

EDT, MIG17, B60, Military Police (MP), absent without official leave (AWOL), SOS (but use "May Day" without abbreviating), USS Iowa, SS Brasil.

2.3 *Abbreviate* the names of business firms; spell portions.

Examples:

Warner Bros., Brown Implement Co., Amalgamated Leather Ltd., Smith & Co., Inc., U.S. Steel Corp.

The company issued a report. The corporation elected directors.

2.4 *Abbreviate* "St.," "Ave.," "Blvd.," and "Terr." when used with numbers, but not "Point," "Port," "Circle," "Plaza," "Place," "Court," "Drive," "Oval," "Road," or "Lane"; spell out when not used with a number. *Abbreviate* points of the compass when included with a street and number, using periods.

Examples:

16 E. 72nd St., 2840 Sunset Blvd., 5604 N.E. Gregory Ave., 15 Grand Terr.

They resided on East 72nd Street. The home was on Sunset Boulevard. The home was at 494 Grand Circle. They resided in the eastern part of the city.

2.5 Lowercase abbreviations usually take periods, particularly if the letters without periods spell words. Periods are not used in 35 mm (film), 105 mm (armament), or ips (tape recording speed). *Abbreviate* versus as "vs."

Examples:

The company's shipments were f.o.b. New York City. The department store shipped the merchandise c.o.d.

The cameraman used 16-mm film. The soldiers practiced with 32-mm ammunition. She recorded the sound at 10 ips. It was a matter of brains vs. brawn. The meeting was scheduled for 11 a.m., but did not start until 1 p.m.

2.6 *Abbreviate* states which follow cities, towns, villages, air bases, Indian agencies, and national parks. *Exceptions:* The state should *not* be used following cities within the state of publication or with cities which are widely known.

Examples:

They came from Edwards AFB, Calif.; Ely,

Nev.; Salem, Ore.; Arlington, Tex.; and Long Beach, Wash.

They also arrived from New York City, Chicago, Las Vegas, Philadelphia, Seattle and Miami.

2.7 These are the standard abbreviations for states. The rule of thumb is to abbreviate none of six letters or less standing alone. Do *not* abbreviate Alaska, Hawaii, Idaho, Iowa, Ohio, Maine, or Utah. Spell out states standing alone.

Ala.	Ill.	Miss.	N.M.	Tenn.
Ariz.	Ind.	Mo.	N.Y.	Tex.
Ark.	Kan.	Mont.	Okla.	Vt.
Calif.	Ky.	Neb.	Ore.	Va.
Colo.	La.	Nev.	Pa.	Wash.
Conn.	Md.	N.C.	R.I.	Wis.
Del.	Mass.	N.D.	S.C.	W.Va.
Fla.	Mich.	N.H.	S.D.	Wyo.
Ga.	Minn.	N.J.		

Examples:

He attended school in Athens, Ga., and Dubuque, Iowa, before working in Prescott, Ariz., Houston and New York City.

She was born in Georgia and educated in California.

2.8 *Abbreviate* Canadian provinces and well-known American possessions as follows:

C.Z.	P.R.	Alta.	B.C.	Man.
N.S.	Que.	Ont.	Sask.	Nfld.
N.B.				

2.9 B.C. as the abbreviation of the Canadian province must be preceded by a city or town; B.C., the era, must be preceded by a date.

2.10 *Abbreviate* U.S.S.R. and U.A.R. with periods.

2.11 *Abbreviate* United Nations and United States in titles with letters (using periods).

Examples:

The U.S. Tennis Championship, the U.N. General Assembly.

2.12 Spell United States and United Nations when used as a noun. U.S.A. and U.N. as nouns may be used in texts or direct quotations.

2.13 *Abbreviate* and capitalize religious, fraternal, scholastic, or honorary degrees; *lowercase* when spelled out. (See Capitals and Lowercase **1.27**.)

Examples:

They earned A.A., B.A., M.S. and Th.D degrees. Others held associate of science, bachelor of science, master of arts or doctor of philosophy degrees.

2.14 Abbreviate titles and capitalize before, but not after, names: Mr., Mrs., Ms., M., Mlle., Dr., Prof., Sen., Rep., Asst., Gov., Lt. Gov., Gen. Supt., Atty. Gen., Dist. Atty. (See Abbreviations **2.6** and **2.21** for military abbreviations.)

Examples:

Dr. and Mrs. William Hart will attend. The doctor recently completed postgraduate studies. Prof. Joan York will speak. The professor recently joined the college staff.

2.15 Mr. is used only with Mrs., in clerical titles, texts, or direct quotations; Miss, Mrs., or Ms. are used with women's names.

Examples:

John Jones, Bill Young, Ms. Mary Smith, Joan Arnold, Joseph Cohen and Mrs. Sara Thomas attended the meeting. Jones and Miss Arnold arrived early.

2.16 Do *not* abbreviate port, point, association, detective, department, deputy, commandant, commodore, field marshal, general manager, secretary-general, secretary, treasurer, fleet admiral or general of the armies. Do *not* abbreviate Christmas.

2.17 *Abbreviate* months when used with dates, but spell out if standing alone or only with a year. Abbreviations for months are Jan., Feb., Aug., Sept., Oct., Nov. and Dec. Do *not* abbreviate March, April, May, June or July except in tabular or financial matter when the abbreviations are Mar., Apr., Jun. and Jly. Always spell May.

Examples:

The election will be Jan. 12. The remainder of January will be devoted to routine business.

2.18 *Abbreviate* days *only* in tabular or financial matter, where they are Mon., Tue., Wed., Thu., Fri., Sat. and Sun.

2.19 *Abbreviate* St. and Ste. as in Sault Ste. Marie, St. Louis and St. Lawrence; *abbreviate* the mountain but spell the city: Mt. Everest, Mount Vernon; *abbreviate* the army post but spell the city: Ft. Sill, Fort Meyer.

2.20 Do *not* abbreviate first names unless you are following the person's preference.

Example:

Robert Smith and Benjamin Jones, unless they are generally known as Bob Smith and Ben Jones.

2.21 Military abbreviations when used *before* a name; spell out if used alone or after a name.

ARMY

General	Gen.
Lieutenant General	Lt. Gen.
Major General	Maj. Gen.
Brigadier General	Brig. Gen.
Colonel	Col.
Lieutenant Colonel	Lt. Col.
Major	Maj.
Captain	Capt.
Lieutenant	Lt.
Chief Warrant Officer	CWO
Warrant Officer	WO
Sergeant Major	Sgt. Maj.
Specialist Nine	Spec. 9
Master Sergeant	M. Sgt.
First Sergeant	1st Sgt.
Specialist Eight	Spec. 8
Platoon Sergeant	Platoon Sgt.
Sergeant First Class	Sgt. I.C.
Specialist Seven	Spec. 7
Staff Sergeant	S. Sgt.
Specialist Six	Spec. 6

Sergeant	Sgt.
Specialist Five	Spec. 5
Corporal	Cpl.
Specialist Four	Spec. 4
Private First Class	Pfc.
Private	Pvt.
Recruit	Rct.

NAVY AND COAST GUARD

Admiral	Adm.
Vice Admiral	Vice Adm.
Rear Admiral	Rear Adm.
Commodore	Commodore
Captain	Capt.
Commander	Cmdr.
Lieutenant Commander	Lt. Cmdr.
Lieutenant	Lt.
Lieutenant Junior Grade	Lt. (j.g.)
Ensign	Ens.
Commissioned Warrant Officer	CWO
Warrant Officer	WO
Master Chief Petty Officer	M.CPO
Senior Chief Petty Officer	S.CPO
Chief Petty Officer	CPO
Petty Officer First Class	PO I.C.
Petty Officer 2nd Class	PO 2.C.
Petty Officer Third Class	PO 3.C.
Seaman	Seaman
Seaman Apprentice	Seaman Appren.
Seaman Recruit	Seaman Rct.

MARINE CORPS

Commissioned officers are abbreviated the same as Army officers; warrant officers are abbreviated the same as Navy officers. Noncommissioned designations are the same as Army, except specialist and:

Master Gunnery Sergeant	Mgy. Sgt.
Lance Corporal	Lance Cpl.
Gunnery Sergeant	Gunnery Sgt.

AIR FORCE

Air Force commissioned officers are abbreviated the same as the Army. Noncommissioned designations include:

Chief Master Sergeant	CM. Sgt.
Senior Master Sergeant	SM. Sgt.
Master Sergeant	M. Sgt.
Technical Sergeant	T. Sgt.
Staff Sergeant	S. Sgt.
Airman First Class	Airman 1.C.
Airman Second Class	Airman 2.C.
Airman Third Class	Airman 3.C.
Airman Basic	Airman

The Air Force uses descriptions such as radarman, navigator, etc., but these designations are not abbreviated.

The Navy has ratings such as machinist, torpedoman, etc., and they are not abbreviated.

The Army, Coast Guard, and Marine Corps also describe personnel by duty in addition to rank; these designations are not abbreviated.

2.22 Do *not* use the abbreviation % (use per cent); do not use the ampersand (&) as a substitute for "and" except in company titles. (Abbreviations **2.3.**)

III. PUNCTUATION

Punctuation in journalistic writing follows the same rules as conventional English.

Exception: Newspaper usage has, in most cases, eliminated the comma before "and" and "or," but this practice does not lessen the need for correct use of the comma in other applications.

Examples:

The audience came walking, running or riding.

Red, white and blue decorations covered the platform, and the seats were painted green.

IV. NUMERALS

In general, spell below 10 and use figures (Arabic numerals) for 10 and above. Major exceptions are noted below.

4.1a Use figures for ages pertaining to man and animals; spell under 10 for inanimates; spell numbers in nicknames.

Examples:

John Smith, 32, took a four-mile trip; the girl is 3; a 4-year-old boy.

The Big Ten games; the USC eleven will meet Notre Dame.

4.1b Use figures, even though under 10, for tabular and statistical matter, records, election returns, speeds, latitude and longitude, temperatures, dimensions, heights, ratios, proportions, divisions, handicaps, and betting odds.

Examples:

Washington won, 6–3; the vote was 1,345 for and 1,300 against; the 5-mile-an-hour traffic; the 90-degree heat; the 5-foot-2 trench; she is 5 feet 2; the ratio was 6 to 4, but the 6–4 ratio; the 6th Fleet; a 6–5 favorite; the 2–1 odds.

4.1c Use figures, even though under 10, for times of day; do *not* use "00," but state minutes when involved. Use "noon" or "midnight" to avoid confusion regarding 12 a.m. or 12 p.m.

Examples:

The meeting will start at 1 p.m.; it is 1:15 p.m.; the show begins at 7 p.m.; the plane arrives at noon; the first session is at 8:30 a.m.; it concludes at 9 o'clock tonight; it begins at 10:15 this morning.

Note: Avoid using "morning" *and* "a.m." or "night" *and* "p.m.," because they are redundant.

4.1d Use figures, even though under 10, for dates. (See Abbreviations **2.17.**) Fourth of July or July Fourth, however, are acceptable but *not* required.

Examples:

School starts Sept. 9; the next program will be May 15; she was born Feb. 3, 1940; the first was on March 28.

Note: It is incorrect to use "1st," "22nd," "4th," or "23rd"; the figures *only* are used with the months.

4.1e Use figures, even though under 10, for amounts of money; use $ instead of spelling "dollar," and *spell* "cents" instead of using the abbreviation ¢; do *not* use "00" with $, but do use *specific* amounts of cents.

Examples:

Tickets cost $1; admission is 50 cents for children; there is a tax increase of 2 cents; the rate is $2.15; the fee is $10; this type costs 9 cents; the fare is $12.50.

4.1f In a series of numbers, avoid confusion by using the simplest related forms.

Example:

There are 3 cars, 5 tractors and 25 trucks.

4.1g When two numbers come together, use figures for one and spell the other to avoid confusion.

Example:

There are ten 15-room buildings and twelve 10-room buildings.

4.1h Spell *any* number that *starts* a sentence, but to avoid confusion with involved amounts *avoid* beginning with a number by rephrasing the sentence.

Example:

Ten candidates spoke at the meeting. Twelve dollars was the cost. A total of 1,015 members cast votes. A cost of $12.50 was announced.

4.2 Use figures for military, political, and other divisional units involving numbers.

Examples:

The 6th Fleet, 1st Army, 2nd Division, 10th Ward, 22nd District, 8th U.S. Circuit Court of Appeals.

4.3 Casual numbers are spelled.

Examples:

A thousand times no! He said he wouldn't touch it with a ten-foot pole (but the flag hung from a 10-foot pole—an exact measurement).

4.4 Roman numerals are used for sequence in identifying Popes, wars, royalty, theater acts, yachts, horses, and individuals unless the person has a preferred use (see Capitals and Lowercase **1.24**).

Examples:

Pope John XXIII, World War I, King George V, Act II, Shamrock IX, John Jones III (some may prefer and use 3rd).

4.5 Use figures, even though under 10, for highway designations.

Examples:

U.S. 301, Interstate 90, Illinois 34, County 305.

4.6 Use a comma in amounts with four digits or more.

Examples:

$500; $2,500; $10,000; $650,000.

4.7 In amounts of a million or more, round numbers take the dollar sign, and million, billion, etc. are spelled; decimalization is carried to two places. The same decimalization form is used for figures other than money. When exact amounts are used, figures are expressed in the conventional manner.

Examples:

The estimated cost will be $4.35 million to $5 million; the debt will rise $1.2 billion; there are 5.25 million cars registered in the state; population reached 10.75 million people.

The project cost $4,305,715; there are 5,217,000 cars registered in the state.

4.8 The English pound sign is not used; spell "pounds" after figures, and, to help reader understanding, convert to dollars with the latest available information; handle other foreign currency similarly.

Example:

The shipment cost 10 pounds ($25) in London.

4.9 Time sequences are given in figures: 2:30:21.6 (hours, minutes, seconds, tenths).

4.10 Serial numbers are printed solid: A1234567.

4.11 Use figures, even though under 10, for numeral designations.

Example:

She was the No. 1 choice; he was the No. 2 candidate.

V. SPELLING

The first preference in spelling is the *short* version in Webster's New International Dictionary, with exceptions given in this section, and the U.S. Postal Guide, the U.S. Board of Geographic Names, and the National Geographic Society, with exceptions given in this section. The news wire services have agreed on some spellings where authorities do not agree.

5.1 This list includes agreed spellings.

Algiers	Florence
Antioch	Formosa Strait
Antwerp	Frankfurt
Archangel	Genoa
Athens	Goteberg
Baghdad	Gulf of Riga
Bangkok	The Hague
Basel	Hamelin
Bayreuth	Hannover
Beirut	Hong Kong
Belgrade	Jakarta
Bern	Katmandu
Brunswick	Kingstown
Bucharest	Kurile
Cameroon	Leghorn
Cape Town	Lisbon
Coblenz	Macao
Cologne	Madagascar
Copenhagen	Marseille
Corfu	Mt. Sinai
Corinth	Mukden
Dunkerque	Munich

Naples	Sofia
North Cape	Taipei
Nuernberg	Tehran
Peking	Thailand
Pescadores I.	Tiflis
Prague	Valetta
Rhodes	Mt. Vesuvius
Romania	Vietnam
Rome	Warsaw
Saint John, N.B.	Wiesbaden
St. John's Nfld.	Zuider Zee
Salonika	

5.2 Where old and new names are used, or where quoted material uses a different form, one is bracketed.

Examples:

Formosa (Taiwan); Gdansk (Danzig).

5.3 In Chinese names, the name after the hyphen is lowercase.

Examples:

Chiang Kai-shek; Mao Tse-tung.

5.4 Often used and frequently misspelled (* indicates preferred spelling):

accommodate	consul
adviser	copilot
anyone	copter
Asian flu	disc
ax	drought
baby-sit	drunken
baby sitter	embarrass
baby-sitting	employe*
baritone	eyewitness
blond (male)	fallout
blonde (female)	fire fighter
box office	fulfill
box-office sales	goodby*
cannot	good will (noun)
cave-in	goodwill (adj.)
chauffeur	hanged
cigarette*	harass
clue	hitchhiker
consensus	homemade

home town	machine gun	restaurant	teen-age (adj.)
impostor	missile	rock 'n' roll	teenager (noun)
ionosphere	occur	schoolteacher	theater*
isotope	occurred	sit-down (noun)	under way
judgment	old-timer	skillful	wash 'n' wear
jukebox	per cent*	strait jacket	weird
kidnaping	percentage	subpoena	wiretapping
likable	permissible	swastika	X ray (noun)
			X-ray (adj.)

Index

DATE DUE

OC 27'81			